ART AS A
SOCIAL SYSTEM

MERIDIAN

Crossing Aesthetics

Werner Hamacher

& David E. Wellbery

Editors

Translated by
Eva M. Knodt

*Stanford
University
Press*

---

*Stanford
California*

2000

ART AS A
SOCIAL SYSTEM

Niklas Luhmann

Stanford University Press
Stanford, California

© 2000 by the Board of Trustees of the
Leland Stanford Junior University

Art as a Social System was originally published in German in 1995 under the title
Die Kunst der Gesellschaft, © Suhrkamp Verlag Frankfurt am Main.

Assistance for the translation was provided by Inter Nationes, Bonn.

Printed in the United States of America on acid-free, archival-quality paper.

Library of Congress Cataloging-in-Publication Data

Luhmann, Niklas.
[Kunst der Gesellschaft. English]
Art as a social system / Niklas Luhmann ; [translated by Eva M. Knodt].
     p.   cm. — (Meridian, crossing aesthetics)
Includes bibliographical references and index.
ISBN 0-8047-3906-4 (alk. paper) — ISBN 0-8047-3907-2 (paper : alk. paper)
1. Aesthetics.   2. Art and society.   I. Title.   II. Meridian (Stanford, Calif.)
BH39 .L8313   2000
306.4'7—dc21   00-041050

Original printing 2000

Last figure below indicates year of this printing:
09 08 07 06 05 04 03 02 01 00

Typeset by James P. Brommer
in 10.9/13 Garamond with Lithos display

Contents

ART AS A
SOCIAL SYSTEM

Preface

Art as a Social System continues a series that aims to elaborate a theory of society. Since the overall project focuses on theories that deal with individual functional systems, I have considered the elaboration of these systems a priority. The theory of society itself requires two different approaches, assuming (1) that the system as a whole is operatively closed on the basis of communication, and (2) that the functional systems emerging within society conform to, and embody, the principle of operative closure and, therefore, *will exhibit comparable structures despite factual differences between them.* Comparisons derive force when we recognize that the compared realms differ in all other respects; we can then highlight what is comparable and charge it with special significance. However, to illustrate this point requires an analysis of individual functional systems. The introduction to this series appeared as *Soziale Systeme* in 1984.[1] Since then, the following studies have appeared: *Die Wirtschaft der Gesellschaft* (1988; The Economy as a Social System); *Die Wissenschaft der Gesellschaft* (1990; Science as a Social System); and *Das Recht der Gesellschaft* (1993; Law as a Social System). The volume presented here is the fourth in this series. Further studies are planned.

This project seeks to distance itself from prevailing social theories that attempt to describe their object in terms of normative, integrative, and unifying concepts. Such theories envision society as a system determined by stratification, that is, by a principle of unequal distribution. In the eighteenth century, a counterdiscourse insisted on the possibility that mankind could nonetheless attain happiness. This promise was replaced in the nineteenth century by the demand for solidarity. In the twentieth century, pol-

itics was put in charge of establishing equal living conditions throughout
the world—a demand frequently made upon democratization or developmental and political modernization. As this century draws to a close, we
are far from realizing universal happiness and satisfaction. Nor have we
reached the goals of achieving solidarity and creating equal living conditions. One can continue to insist on these demands and call them "ethics,"
but it becomes difficult to ignore their increasingly apparent utopian component. This is why we recommend rewriting the theory of society. To do
so requires a shift, at the structural level, from stratification to functional
differentiation. The unity of society is not to be sought in ethico-political
demands, but rather in *the emergence of comparable conditions* in systems as
diverse as religion or the monetary economy, science or art, intimate relationships or politics—despite extreme differences between the functions
and the operational modes of these systems. Our theoretical proposition
offers the following: a clear demarcation of external system boundaries of
different domains and comparability between different systems. Talcott
Parsons launched a similar experiment, taking the comparability of all
subsystems of the general action system for granted. He believed that each
action system, even in the position of subsystem or subsubsystem, needed
to fulfill four functions to be complete, that is, if it were to exist as a system capable of maintaining its boundaries and orienting itself in relation
to temporal differences. This is not the place to argue with Parsons's position. What matters is that with Parsons, the comparability of subsystems
began to occupy a pivotal theoretical position in sociology. In what follows, we do not propose a theory as rigorously derived as Parsons's from an
analysis of the concept of action. Instead, what interests us is another one
of Parsons's ideas: that each evolutionary differentiation process must reconstruct the unity of the differentiated system. This does not presuppose
central norms, no matter how generalized. In our modern (some would
say postmodern) society, such norms are difficult to detect. It suffices that
all subsystems employ the operational mode of the system as a whole, in
this case communication, and that they are capable of fulfilling the conditions of system formation—namely, autopoiesis and operative closure—
no matter how complex the emerging structures turn out to be.

Carrying out this program in the realm of art requires theoretical models that cannot be extracted from observing works of art and can be demonstrated in the communicative employment of these works. Here we use
distinctions such as system/environment, medium/form, first- and second-

order observation, self-reference and external reference, and above all the distinction between psychic systems (systems of consciousness) and social systems (systems of communication); none is meant to assist in judging or creating works of art. We are not offering a helpful theory of art. This does not exclude the possibility that the art system, in its own operations, may profit from a theoretical endeavor intended to clarify the context and contingency of art from a sociotheoretical perspective. Whether such a transposition of insights can be accomplished and what kind of misunderstandings may contribute to its success must be decided within the art system itself, for "to succeed" can mean only "to succeed as a work of art." The issue is not to propose a theory that, if properly understood and applied, would guarantee success or assist the art system in coping with its worries about the future. It follows from the general theory of functional social differentiation that functional systems are incapable of directly influencing one another. At the same time, their coexistence increases their mutual irritability.

Science [*Wissenschaft*], here specifically sociological theory, must open itself to irritation through art. Science must be able to observe what is presented as art. In this basic sense, sociological theory is an empirical science (according to its own self-description, at any rate). But the labor of transforming irritation into information that can be used within science is an entirely internal affair. The proof must be delivered within science. Art becomes a topic in the first place, not because of a peculiar inclination of the author, but because of the assumption that a social theory claiming universality cannot ignore the existence of art.

In view of how these intentions have been realized in this book, we acknowledge that it turned out to be difficult, if not impossible, to distinguish the systematics of the system from the bare facts while bracketing historical analyses (as it would have been feasible with the economic system, the system of science, and the legal system). Aesthetic endeavors involving art have always separated themselves from a historical discourse oriented toward facts. This was the case in the *poesia/historia* discussion of the sixteenth century with its emphasis on "beautiful appearance," and it holds for twentieth-century hermeneutics, which distinguishes historical documentation that may be useful in the sciences from an understanding of the expression and significance of individual artworks. From a sociological standpoint, this separation is untenable and breaks down to the extent that art orients itself historically. This is the case in Renaissance art, for example. Art permits no simple repetition—except as the perpetual repetition of its own history. Even for a theory of society, there is ultimately no history independent of the continual reactualization of that history.

This is why the text presented here can offer neither a structuralist description of the system of modern art, nor a structured evolutionary history of the differentiation of the art system. The reader will find both perspectives interwoven. Each chapter is conceived in terms of its factual theme. We draw on historical retrospectives as we need them, especially in Chapter 4, in which we discuss the differentiation and self-description of the art system. Repetitions are inevitable. One should not expect a linear order, progressing from important to less important issues or from prior to subsequent events. I hope that the reader's understanding will benefit from the recognition that conceptual or historical materials reappear in different contexts. An extensive index should facilitate such a nonlinear reading.

N. L.

Bielefeld, March 1995

§ 1 Perception and Communication: The Reproduction of Forms

I

We are still spellbound by a tradition that arranged psychological faculties hierarchically, relegating "sensuousness"—that is, perception—to a lower position in comparison to higher, reflective functions of reason and understanding. The most advanced versions of "conceptual art" still follow this tradition. By refusing to base themselves in sensuously perceptible distinctions between works of art and other objects, these works seek to avoid reducing art to the realm of sense perception.

In the old European tradition, this hierarchical valuation rested on the idea that humans are distinct from animals,[1] which suggests a devaluation of the faculties humans share with animals, most notably sense perception. Furthermore, perception provides only factual/temporal distinctions, rather than units that persist across time (ideas). The mode of contact unique to humans was accordingly believed to reside in (rational) thought.[2] Conversely, one could argue that a comparison between humans and animals demonstrates the evolutionary, genetic, and functional priority of perception over thought. A creature endowed with a central nervous system must succeed in externalizing and constructing an outside world before it can begin to articulate self-reference on the basis of its own bodily perceptions as a result of its problems with this world. How this happens—perhaps by a sort of transcribing of the brain's "double closure"[3] into an inside/outside distinction within consciousness—has yet to be investigated in greater detail. Such clarification is beyond our present scope. It suffices to remain astonished that we see anything "outside" at all, even if our seeing happens only "inside." Granted this, self-perception becomes a copy of the form of external perception[4] and is processed analogously, as observation of an object. All communication consequently depends on perception; whether and in what ways perception is accompanied by thought is a question that, depending on the circumstances, permits a number of different and rather uncertain answers.

Whatever may have been written or thought about perception in literate cultures, it remains a special competency of consciousness, its essential faculty.[5] Day by day, minute by minute, consciousness is preoccupied with perception. Through perception it is captivated by an external world. Without perception it would have to terminate its autopoiesis, and even dreams can occur only by suggesting perceptions. Today we know that the external world is the brain's own construction, treated by consciousness as if it were a reality "out there." The extent to which perception is prestructured by language is equally well known. The perceived world is nothing but the sum total of the "eigenvalues" of neurophysiological operations.[6] But information attesting to this state of affairs does not pass from the brain to consciousness. It is filtered out, systematically and without leaving a trace. The brain represses, if you will, its own work in order to make the world appear as a world. Only by virtue of this repression is it possible to establish the difference between world and observing consciousness in the world.

We assume further that all psychic operations are conscious. Consciousness is the operative mode of psychic systems. But only a tiny fraction of conscious productions—and here we concur with Freud—can be controlled introspectively. In disposing over awareness, consciousness is not usually aware of itself. This applies particularly to what becomes conscious in the form of perceptions. It means also that only within certain bounds is consciousness available to answer questions, and that it can be drawn upon by social communication only in very limited ways.

In the course of (mutually inaccessible) neurophysiological and conscious operations, an operative certainty about the world is created (constructed), which leaves room for self-generated uncertainties, peculiarities, and surprises. That perception continually goes on by no means precludes consciousness from fitting itself out with thoughts and employing them to observe what it perceives. The tradition ontologized the objects generated by perception, in addition to what consciousness can be said to accomplish. The world was assumed (errors excepted) to be as it reveals itself in perception, so that it could then be prepared for communicative and technical purposes through language and conceptual analysis. The phenomenology of the world included an aesthetic conception of art that permitted art to represent the world, to make it perceptible in its ideal forms, and to furnish it with novel qualities of information that do not appear spontaneously. But suppose we venture from a phenomenon-centered to an operative doctrine of perception, and from a representational to a constructivist epistemology—the scientific system seems to force such a move. Would not the theory of art have to follow this paradigm shift and be based on radically different foundations? If perception and, even more so, conceptual thought are already constructed by the brain, then shouldn't art fulfill entirely different functions in shaping and utilizing the realm of free play generated in the process? The functional concepts of imitation and representation, now obsolete, would have to be rejected a second time—not because they unduly restrict the freedom of art, but because they indulge in, rather than unmask, the illusionism of the world. It is conceivable that art, though it cannot undo the "externalization" of the world through consciousness (consciousness would be unable to follow such a move), offers forms for precisely this externalization, forms that demonstrate the possibility of order and the impossibility of arbitrariness in the face of unforeseen information, even under the factual conditions of operative closure that define neurophysiological, conscious, and eventually communicative systems.

To the extent that it concerns humans, the thesis of the primacy of perception in consciousness includes imagined perception, that is, the self-induced simulation of perception. In the following, we shall call this type of perception *intuition* [Anschauung]. Intuition is commonly defined by its utilization of such media as space and time. It implies a double move—and this distinguishes perception from intuition—a transcending of what is immediately given in perception toward the *constitution of spatial and temporal horizons* and an *erasure of information concerning its own spatial/temporal location.*[7] Only in the form of intuition does art acquire the possibility of constructing imaginary worlds within the life-world while remaining dependent on triggering perceptions (not least, the reading of texts).

What is at stake in actual perception, as well as in reactualized intuitive representation [*Vorstellung*], results from simultaneously processing a manifold of impressions that allows a focus for awareness to be selected without letting the surroundings slip from view. This holds primarily for visual perception, but also for acoustic perception within a visual field that is presented simultaneously (or has been artificially neutralized by closing one's eyes). The same is true when tactile impressions are accompanied by the visualization of what is being touched. We need not go into more detail here; what interests us is the limiting effect of the proposition that perception is a special, if not the most crucial, competency of consciousness.

This proposition precludes the view that nervous systems can perceive. These systems must live and function if consciousness is to perceive at all, and the existence of structural couplings between the nervous system and consciousness can hardly be denied. To do so would be absurd and of no theoretical interest whatever. But any systems-theoretical analysis must account for differences in the respective modes of operation pertaining to both kinds of systems and must consequently assume two distinct systems.

This is why consciousness processes perceptions under the impression of their *immediacy*, while the brain is actually executing operations that are highly selective, quantitatively calculating, recursively operative, and hence always mediated. "Immediacy" is nothing primordial, but an impression resulting from the differentiation of the autopoietic systems of the brain and consciousness. In the experiential mode of immediacy, any explicit distinction (for example, between signifier and signified, or between mediated and immediate experience) becomes an exceptional case, selected and varied by consciousness according to specific reasons. The discursive sequentiality of conscious operations is based on an immediate relationship to the world that is always retained and carried along, neither depending on nor allowing for the possibility of designating the world as a unity. This is true for perception in general and thus holds for the perception of artworks as well.

In order to demarcate the nervous system from consciousness, we should keep in mind that nervous systems are capable only of self-observation and cannot establish any contact with the environment from within the recursive realm of their own operations. Needless to say, they cannot operate outside of their own boundaries. They serve, one could argue, the organism's self-observation with regard to its varying conditions, that is, with regard to a temporal modus that could perhaps already be called information. Most importantly, and in contradistinction to consciousness, nervous systems are incapable of combining self-reference and hetero-reference in their ongoing operations.[8] The neuro-magic that would accomplish such a thing is unknown. The ongoing activity, characteristic of the conscious system's operational mode, of distinguishing between self-reference and het-ero-reference in *all* of its operations presupposes, if not "meaning" [*Sinn*], at least a signifying structure that enforces the simultaneous processing of signifier (*signifiant*) and signified (*signifié*) in Saussure's sense. This activity rests on a capacity for "externalization," available even to animals but in-sufficiently accounted for in neurophysiological terms,[9] which may be re-lated to inconsistencies in the neurophysiological data processing that can be resolved via the regulation of awareness through consciousness. But only language forces consciousness to keep signifier and signified—and, in this sense, self-reference and hetero-reference—permanently separate while nonetheless processing these distinctions simultaneously. Consciousness corrects, as it were, the operative closure of the nervous system by means of a distinction between inside and outside, or self-reference and hetero-ref-erence, which remains internal. The specificity of consciousness thus re-sides, to borrow a formulation of George Spencer Brown, in a "reentry" of the distinction into the distinguished, or of the form into the form.[10]

Nor can communication systems—that is to say, social systems—per-ceive. This proposition is hard for consciousness to accept, since con-sciousness takes for granted, literally and without thinking, a world of per-ception and makes whatever happens to it occur in this world. Of course, communication occurs in this world, too. But when theoretical reflection shifts from "what" questions to "how" questions, no longer concerning it-self with the object of communication but asking instead how communi-cation works, then complications abound. Communication can no longer be understood as a "transmission" of information from an (operatively closed) living being or conscious system to any other such system.[11] Com-munication is an independent type of formation in the medium of mean-ing [*Sinn*], an emergent reality that presupposes living beings capable of consciousness but is irreducible to any one of these beings, not even to all of them taken together. Compared to consciousness, communication exe-cutes an extremely slow, time-consuming sequence of sign transformations (which means, among other things, that the participating consciousness gains time for its own perceptions, imaginations, and trains of thought). Communication recursively recalls and anticipates further communica-tions, and solely within the network of self-created communications can it produce communications as the operative elements of its own system. In so doing, communication generates a distinct autopoietic system in the strict (not just "metaphorical") sense of the term. And, given the form in which it organizes its own autopoiesis, communication cannot receive or produce perceptions. But it can certainly communicate about perceptions—for example, when someone says, "I have seen that . . . "

When thought to its conclusions, such a concept of communication precludes the assumption, unquestioned throughout the entire tradition, that communication can express perceptions, thus rendering the perceptions of others accessible. To be sure, communication can indicate perceptions, but what it indicates remains as operatively inaccessible to communication as does the entire physical world. If "indication" is possible and functions as a kind of ersatz for access, then this means only that indications can be processed internally. In linguistics and literary theory, this is by now a well-known thesis.[12] If it holds for verbal communication, then it does so even more for nonverbal communication. In other words, there is no reality continuum that would allow states of affairs pertaining to the environment to be transferred more or less adequately into the system.

Aesthetics has always claimed that the mere perception of the "material" of art does not yet make for aesthetic pleasure. An additional, selective reworking of the material must endow it with significance and, in simultaneously devalorizing and revalorizing it, transform it into the elements of an artwork. The "understanding" of this process was commonly interpreted in terms of a "mental" [*geistige*] process, whereby the psychic system was left to participate, or not, in Spirit (for example, qua *Bildung*). Apart from communication, final concepts such as "Spirit" or "mind" appear to be indispensable even today.[13] But what is "Spirit" if not a metaphorical circumlocution for the mystery of communication? And if so, shouldn't we take the selective arrangement of the artwork to be a condition for perceptible objects to become available to communication?

All of this follows from the insight that the feature of operative closure, already actualized in the nervous system and the conscious system, is present in social systems as well. Consciousness compensates for the operative closure of the nervous system, just as the social system compensates for the closure of consciousness. The world in which the system's unique reality is reproduced in the form of recursive connections between its operations is—as Husserl has demonstrated with regard to consciousness—a meaning correlate of the system's own operations.[14] Ascertaining a "reality" is based on the experience of a resistance in the system against itself—for example, in perception against perception, or in language against language —and not on a comprehensive impression of the world. The being-in-the-world of the communication system emerges from a continual coupling of self-reference and hetero-reference. As a result, the world becomes a medium for the successive formation of specific forms (including their generation, forgetting, and remembering), an elusive "horizon" of changing constructions which, as medium, outlives these constructions.[15]

The way in which the process of communication combines self-reference and hetero-reference can be described more accurately. In contradistinction to consciousness, communication accomplishes this combination by continually reproducing the distinction between utterance (self-reference) and information (hetero-reference) under conditions that generate the possibility of understanding (that is, of further employing this distinction in the communication process). The concepts of "information," "utterance," and "understanding" should be taken without direct psychic reference.[16] They refer exclusively to the components that constitute a communicative event as a unity. This unity cannot be decomposed infinitely, since it must provide a meaning that can still be negated in the course of further communication (for example, it cannot be the "c" in the word *communication*). It follows that information always expresses a hetero-reference within communication, even if it indicates the state of one of the participating conscious systems—for example, when someone says, "I'd like to be able to write such nice poetry, too."

Communication is a self-determining process and, in this sense, an autopoietic system. Whatever is established as communication is established by communication. Factually, this takes place within the frame of the distinction between self-reference and hetero-reference, temporally by means of recursively recalling and anticipating further communications,[17] and socially by exposing communicated meaning to acceptance or rejection. This is sufficient. There is no need for external determination via perceptions or other conscious events. Such determination is effectively excluded by the fact that communication consolidates itself within the framework of its own distinctions. This is why the selectional value of any particular determination cannot derive directly from the environment, although hetero-reference may help stabilize this value. Even the decision concerning the type of determination and the extent to which it is necessary is made within (and not outside of) communication. Communication can tolerate and even produce vagueness, incompletion, ambiguity, irony, and so forth, and it can place indeterminacies in ways that secure a certain usage. Such deliberate indeterminacies play a significant role, particularly in artistically mediated communication, to the point where we find ourselves confronted with the hopelessly unending interpretability of "finished" works.[18] The distinction between determinacy and indeterminacy is an internal variable of the communication system and not a quality of the external world.

If one takes the internal dynamics of communication into account, then a number of uncomfortable questions regarding consciousness are bound to arise. A theory of communication must be developed in the realm of abstraction. Given that physics has taken this step in the theory of relativity and quantum mechanics, abstraction should not in itself be an objection. Physics, too, suggests that perception, imagination, and intuition are special qualities of consciousness, presenting a world that can be processed exclusively by consciousness. The point of this argument is to counter objections of the type to be expected especially from sociology. It implies nothing about the correctness of certain abstract theories.

II

Conscious systems are mutually inaccessible because of their operative closure: this explains why communication is necessary but does not say how communication is possible, given such an infrastructure. Human beings appear to live alongside one another as isolated monads. The desire to "communicate," in the sense of establishing a common ground, is certainly there, but at the same time, we find ourselves in the position of individuals who can neither perceive or think in the other, nor produce operations that could be recognized as those of another rather than our own.

The classical appeal to the idea of inference by analogy merely displaces the problem to the question of how to trust the reality of one's own constructions. Belief in such externalizations comes easily because, like those of space and time, they resolve internal inconsistencies and because the task of clarifying remaining inconsistencies—whether successful or not—can be left to communication. At least since romanticism, one no longer seems to trust the purifying power of communication, because communication permits no access to the other's interiority, no possibility of intermingling his or her operations with one's own. Besides, how is the other recognized as another to begin with, and how does one get from simple contingency (in the sense of environmental dependency) to double contingency?[19]

A reconstruction of this problem compatible with the idea of autopoiesis assumes that the operative closure of autopoietic systems produces a *difference*, namely, the difference between system and environment. *This difference can be seen.* One can observe the surface of another organism, and the form of the inside/outside distinction motivates the inference of an unobservable interiority.[20] While it is impossible to verify the "truth" of such inferences, their consistency can be checked within the system, and they can activate a memory that employs the bifurcation of remembering and forgetting in order to establish connections between the past and the future. Because operative closure locks the door to the inner life, imagination, and thoughts of others, the other holds us captive as an eternal riddle. This is why the experience of other human beings is richer than any experience of nature, why one feels tempted to test one's own assumptions in communication. And it explains why lovers are capable of talking endlessly about themselves with no interest whatever in anything else.

These basic considerations concerning the familiar topic of subjectivity and intersubjectivity are phrased in such general terms that their ramifications for a discussion of art are difficult to foresee. One thing is certain: if it is generally true that psychic operations, not to speak of those of the living system, can never be executed in another consciousness, which because of its complexity and historically self-referential mode of operation remains opaque, then this holds also for the artist distanced by his work and for his admirers as well—no more and no less, for inaccessibility does not allow for augmentation. And yet, communication happens anyway, working with causal attributes and reproducing itself inevitably. This is why no general anthropological principles speak against the assumption that art is a kind of communication, which, in ways yet to be clarified, makes use of perception. There is, after all, a relationship of mutual enhancement in the nexus between operatively closed organic, psychic, and social systems, which suggests that we should explore the ways in which art in particular contributes to this relationship.

III

Thanks to its neurophysiological infrastructure, perception is intrinsically restless. Whenever there is any conscious activity, perception goes along with it. This parallelism results in a unique combination of redundancy and information. We are always dealing with recognizable objects, but always with different ones. Images succeed one another. Only momentarily and with great effort can we fix on a distinct object; if we close our eyes and concentrate, we see darkness, interrupted by an irritating play of colors. Perception (in contrast to thought and communication) can decide *quickly*, whereas art aims to *retard* perception and render it *reflexive*—lingering upon the object in visual art (in striking contrast to everyday perception) and slowing down reading in literature, particularly in lyric poetry.[21] Perception is ready to scan a familiar world for information without requiring a special decision on our part to do so. It enables consciousness to adapt temporarily to passing situations. All subsequent information processing is prestructured by the distinction between self-reference and hetero-reference. Works of art, by contrast, employ perceptions exclusively for the purpose of letting the observer participate in the communication of invented forms.

From the viewpoint of consciousness, all communication takes place in a perceptible world. Processing and cognitively focusing perceptions is the primary task of consciousness. Only when this is taken for granted can consciousness participate in communicative events (and in communication as such). The ability to locate one's own body (and other bodies) presumes the work of perception. In thought, one can be anywhere, but one can perceive only from the location where one's body is actually situated. Our own body *must* be perceived alongside other objects if consciousness is to distinguish between self-reference and hetero-reference. The body must experience itself in a kind of sensuously perceptible self-awareness in order to make this distinction or to determine, as Novalis puts it, "the seat of the soul."[22]

Because it includes our own body, the world is given to perception as a complete, compact, and impenetrable entity. Variations abound, whether self-induced or triggered by external events. But variations are always perceived within the world, as a form in relation to what is momentarily motionless or stable.[23] The world itself remains unalterable (in theological terms, the unmoved mover). The freedom perception imparts to consciousness is always restricted by the necessity of referring to something-in-the-perceptible-world. Consciousness can never entirely overcome this limitation, neither imaginatively—when intuition simulates perception in one way or another—nor when one actually participates in communication or imagines oneself doing so.

From the perspective of consciousness, perception frames all communication. Without eyes one cannot read, without ears one cannot hear. Communication must be highly conspicuous in the perceptional field if it is to be perceived at all. It must captivate perception—by means of some striking noise, through bodily postures explicable only as expressive behavior, or by employing special conventional signs in writing.

The distinction between perception and communication charts new territory for aesthetics as an academic discipline. To be sure, even before "aesthetics" was introduced as a technical term, some authors considered art to be a special kind of communication, designed to supplement and extend verbal (oral and written) communication through more expeditious and complex forms of transmission.[24] What mattered at the time, however, was communicating ideas that would represent the natural world more accurately. A special kind of Enlightenment was at stake when the notion of a distinct, albeit inferior, sensuous knowledge burst onto the scene, a notion Baumgarten sought to elaborate in the form of an aesthetics.

After all, aesthetics was founded upon another distinction, one more closely related to the idea of the subject: the distinction between *aistheta* and *noeta*, sensuous and rational cognition, or aesthetics and logic. Cognition (not communication) served as the master concept, and a great deal of cognitive activity was believed to be going on in the realm of sensuous cognition.[25] So long as the doctrine of the beautiful was called aesthetics, the distinction between perception and communication could not come into view. The term *aesthetics* fails to do justice to either side of this distinction. We are not accustomed to the idea that communication is unable to perceive. Nor are we inclined to ponder the sight of a mouse baked in bread as primarily an aesthetic problem. Once we switch over to the distinction between perception and communication, both cases present themselves as cognitive operations that develop distinct structures to process their information. The concept of observation designates what these cases have in common (or what is distinguished by the distinction between perception and communication).

This suggests many different ways of comparing perception and communication. In each of the above-mentioned instances, we are dealing with distinctions (or "forms") actualized by an observer. In both cases, this form could be called an observer (= can be distinguished as an observer). In both cases, the recursive mode of operation acquires its *own* determination only by referring to objects (= by calculating objects as "eigenvalues" of the system's operations). Interdependencies are readily apparent.

Communication relies on the perception of signs, whereas perception exposes its distinctions to the influence of language. Finally, in both cases, cognition is a variable dependent on operations, which presupposes that each system continues its autopoiesis at the operative level of metabolism or the material reproduction of signs. It follows that in neither case is cognition capable of controlling the system's adaptation to the environment or its own evolution.[26]

Belaboring this point leads nowhere. Suffice it to say that we must distinguish between perception and communication without grounding one in the other (as was common in the tradition via the idea of thought). The distinction must be presupposed when dealing with the psychic system's participation in the communicative process—when, in other words, one of the conditions of possibility of society is at stake.[27] In what follows, we shall restrict our focus to the question of how perceptible objects are tailored to a process of communication that operates independently. We presuppose language as given.[28] Verbal communication is always already established in the world of perception. Within the communication system of society, verbal communication manages its own operations together with the structures created by these operations, as well as its own standards of precision and criteria for tolerating errors—all of which are oriented toward what can be understood, that is, toward what secures the autopoiesis of communication. As indicated earlier, verbal communication operates in a very slow-moving and time-consuming manner. Whatever it communicates must be converted into a temporal sequence of information that amounts to a series of alternating system states. At any time, verbal communication may be arrested or reflexively turned back upon itself. When one doesn't understand, one follows up with a question. A piece of information is rejected, and one asks, "Why?" Communicated meaning must be specific, that is, highly selective, in order for communication to continue, and only communication (not the external world) can satisfy this precondition. Like any other form, language assumes the form of a difference that is foregrounded in consciousness against the background of simultaneous perceptions and that differentiates within communication between what is said and what is not said. In the meantime, the world is the way it is—whether it remains what it is or tolerates that things happen, move, and change. Whatever takes place in consciousness or communication is possible only on the condition that other things occur simultaneously.

One of the historically most important innovations in the realm of communicative possibilities entails the evolution of writing and the invention of the printing press. The resulting evolutionary leaps have been dealt with extensively in the literature and will not be treated here. The relationship between writing and art, however, warrants some attention. Prior to the invention of the printing press, and before the public became accustomed to its products, writing and art were much closer together than they are today.[29] The common distinction between linguistics (whose dependence upon writing is widely recognized today) and the study of art [*Kunstwissenschaft*] is not universally valid. If it were, then the literary culture of the Middle Ages would be incomprehensible. In those days, the distinction between the production of texts and of pictorial representations was much less pronounced.[30] Both types of representations were replete with ornamental and tactile components—and both showed them off. Like painting, scribal writing required both competency and form. Medieval perception was engaged differently in the production and contemplation—in the "reading"—of texts and images. Paintings such as the mural mosaics in Monreale or the tessellated pavements in Oranto served as encyclopedias for the people, but their intelligibility depended on the viewer's prior familiarity with stories based on written narratives. In the late Middle Ages, poetry continued to be composed—written—for oral presentation in a setting charged with social immediacy, rather than for solitary reading.[31] Cultural tradition relied heavily on oral communication and thus on individual intellectual achievements that engage all the senses, especially hearing in conjunction with seeing. Accordingly, the concept of art (*ars*) was far more comprehensive than it is today, and it had to bridge fewer internal differentiations.

Once art differentiates itself along the lines of a systems-specific play with forms, the situation changes. While still working from within the framework established by the principle of imitation, early modern art moves away from merely copying what might as well be just perceived and toward imitating foundational (Platonic) ideas. Art renders accessible what is invisible without it. In the wake of this transformation, the social relationship between the artist and his audience becomes more problematic, provoking debates on the social status of an expert culture of connoisseurs and art critics in the eighteenth century and eventually leading not only to the realization that conversing *about* art is different from conversing about other objects, but also to the possibility of communicating *through* art.[32] Is it conceivable that art, as a kind of "writing," builds a bridge between perception and communication, that it compensates for the communication system's inability to perceive? Or could it be that art discovers in this very lack a yet unoccupied field of possibilities in which it can unfold?

These incidental observations illustrate that the relationship between perception and communication is not a prior natural (or "anthropological") constant divorced from all social and historical reality. Whatever counts as art is marked by an inevitable historical relativity, even at the most elemental level of operation. Historical reflection upon the difference between the achievements of consciousness and those of communication fluctuates accordingly. A certain kind of anthropological reductionism continues to attribute both types of operation to human capacities, although the structural conditions of society have changed significantly since the invention of print.

In modern times, the interdependency between communication and consciousness was radicalized in the experience of a painful split between the two that prevents the communicative realization of imaginative possibilities. "Many things," writes Novalis, "are much too delicate to be expressed in thought, let alone, to be put into words."[33] In Jean Paul's novel *Siebenkäs*, the failure of communication destroys a marriage, and in his *Flegeljahre*, the relationship between two twin brothers breaks apart for similar reasons, despite their best intentions. One can talk about the victims. This topic, discovered in the seventeenth century when writers began to thematize the difficulties of communication, was later exploited by the romantics in a familiar, almost triumphant, sometimes profound, sometimes garrulous manner.[34] But this sort of talk is still talk, bound by linguistic forms and subject to their restrictions. Or is it?

The potential failure of communication raises the question of possible alternatives to verbal communication. After what has been said, such alternatives cannot be found in the products of consciousness, perceptions, imaginations, and so forth. These are autopoietic operations of a type other than communications. Instead, we must focus on types of nonverbal communication that realize the same autopoietic structure as verbal communication—namely, a synthesis of information, utterance, and understanding—but are not bound by the specific features of language and thus extend the realm of communication beyond what can be put into words (whatever consciousness may experience in the process).

Such alternatives are evident in forms of communication we tend to qualify as "indirect." Standardized gestures, whether or not embedded in conversation, belong to this type of communication—such as shrugging one's shoulders while speaking with someone or honking one's horn in traffic to warn others or express anger. In any of these cases, communication can distinguish between information and utterance; hence, it can understand—that is, connect to—further communications. If understanding fails, then communication breaks down, which in turn can be clarified or simply glossed over in further communication. Communicating by means of standardized gestures is no different, in principle, from communicating through words; it merely expands a given repertoire of signs.

Other types of indirect communication concern cases in which a communicative intent cannot be inferred unambiguously from a given behavior. Such cases indicate border zones of communication that are sensitive to behavior devoid of communicative intent. Someone has violated the dress code—because of ignorance or lack of appropriate clothing, or merely out of a desire to provoke. Bourdieu has dealt with such phenomena by analyzing the signal effect of difference in the realm of cultural artifacts and verbal styles.[35] When called upon to account for one's behavior, one can insist that it was unintentional, and being aware of this option largely blocks communication about it, except in the form of provocation. It takes a Bourdieu enthusiast to speak, or perhaps only to write about such matters.[36]

Indirect communications of this sort are highly context bound and make sense only situationally. Within given classifications, they can signal alliances. Within oral communication, they can serve a controlling function—as threats or warnings—so long as communication is working well otherwise. It is difficult, however, to think of indirect communication as differentiating itself in the manner in which, for example, the use of money differentiates an economic system. The meaning of a price tag is immediately apparent, whereas an indirect communication could hardly be addressed in the same manner to an anonymous audience.

None of the types of indirect communication discussed above, however, exhausts our search for communicative alternatives to language. Art, in the modern sense of the word, belongs to this category as well. In fact, art presents one such alternative, a functional equivalent to language even if, tentatively speaking, it employs texts as an artistic medium. Art functions as communication although—or precisely because—it cannot be adequately rendered through words (let alone through concepts).

Like indirect communication but in different ways, art escapes the strict application of the yes/no code. Art cannot, nor does it mean to, preclude the possibility of conversing about it, of declaring a work of art a failure or success and thus exposing oneself to rejection or acceptance. But this is communication about art, not through. The artwork itself engages the observer via the products of perceptions, and these are elusive enough to avoid the bifurcation of "yes" or "no." We see what we see and hear what we hear, and when others observe us engaged in perception it would be silly to deny that we perceive. In this way, a type of sociability is generated that cannot be negated. In avoiding and circumventing language, art nonetheless establishes a structural coupling between the systems of consciousness and communication. Once established, the question is how, and to what purpose, this coupling is put to use.

IV

Before we continue, we need to remind ourselves that both the perceiving consciousness and the communicating social system require time in order to establish themselves in a differential relationship to the environment. Both systems consist of events—events that cannot occur in isolation because their coming into being and vanishing depend on the system. As an event, each actualized present articulates a self-relation, but it can do so only if the present is established simultaneously as a difference between past and future, that is to say, if the present determines itself by reaching out recursively toward the temporal horizons of a past and a future that are momentarily not actualized.[37] This is what we mean by autopoiesis, and it should be clear from the above considerations that the reproductive modes of conscious and social systems differ radically from the (equally autopoietic) biochemical reproduction of life. We need to remind ourselves of this crucial insight, because it implies that communication through art, too, must take time into account.[38]

Not only must the artist produce the work before it can be perceived, but any observing participation in artistic activity is a temporal process, a systematically ordered succession of events. The actions that produce the work must succeed one another in time and orient themselves recursively in relation to what has already been decided and to the possibilities opened up or eliminated by these decisions. Moreover, the perception of art gains access to its object in temporal terms as well by actualizing step by step the work's references within a context of distinctions that shift from moment to moment. The work does not reveal itself "at a glance"; at most, it effects some kind of stimulation or irritation that might trigger a deeper, more penetrating concern with the work. One needs indicators to recognize a work of art as an object, but these indicators offer no clue to understanding the artistic communication. Some experiences and habits may help identify works of art, but there is no such thing as an instantaneous, intuitive comprehension of harmony.[39] We shall return to this problem in conjunction with the concept of form (Section VI below).

These observations apply to art in general, not only to the obvious cases of music, dance, or stage productions, in which the artwork exists only as a pure sequence of events. On the contrary, such cases are special in that they synchronize the sequence of performance and experience, thus creating a heightened sense of simultaneity, as has often been described. Reading texts is also a process that takes time—whether in narrative one reads the sequence that unfolds in the succession of sentences, or whether, as in poetry, one misses what matters if one thinks reading must begin at the beginning and end at the ending, and one will then have understood it all. When reading, and even more so when looking at paintings or sculptures, the observer is relatively free to choose the sequence of observations, so long as observational operations are arranged sequentially.

When supplemented by writing, verbal communication opens up a corresponding spectrum of disparate and yet coordinated ways of using time. Communication through art further extends these possibilities. Music, for example, intensifies the experience of simultaneity by blocking any meaningful hetero-reference, any kind of representation. At the other extreme, artistic communication leaves the observer of paintings or sculptures completely free to choose a sequence of observation without relinquishing its objective control via the artwork's play of forms. Thanks to composition, simultaneity is intensified or communication occurs even under conditions of complete de-synchronization. In both cases, communication controls the connectivity of observational events—increasingly so, the more improbable and exceptional the conditions under which this process takes place. Art is thus capable of intensifying the awareness of communication: consciousness becomes aware of being directed and captivated by communication, experiencing the discrepancy between an external control and its own, unrestricted operative possibilities. The self-awareness induced by art is always the experience of a difference. It would never happen if we were dealing only with a random coincidence of self-reference and hetero-reference in a singular event.

V

Art can exist only when there is language—this is less trivial than it sounds. Art is unique in that it makes possible a type of communication that, in the strict sense of the word, avoids language along with the routines involved in language use. The forms of art are understood as communications, but without language, without argumentation. Instead of using words and grammatical rules, people employ works of art to communicate information in ways that can be understood. Art permits a circumvention of language—of language as the form of structural coupling between consciousness and communication. Even when employing linguistic means, art engenders different effects. Language must be old; works of art must be new. These are significant differences that can be played off against each other. But how can a work of art, created for perception or imaginary intuition, be the bearer of communication?

A work of art can be the object of writing, printing, or radio transmission—but this is obviously not what we have in mind here. Secondary communications—those operating at the level of art criticism and commentary, through announcements, recommendations, or rejections—have their own purpose, especially at a time when works of art are in need of commentary (Gehlen). We are not thinking of this type of communication here.[40] Nor do we follow Kant's view (which nevertheless comes close to our own): aesthetic judgments (judgments of taste) are produced within consciousness, though their transcendental control presupposes the possibility of generalization.[41] We are not concerned with communicative reasoning as a supplement to judgment. Rather, we claim that the work of art is produced *exclusively* for the purpose of communication and that it accomplishes this goal or fails to do so by facing the usual, and perhaps even increased, risks involved in all communication. Art communicates by *using perceptions contrary to their primary purpose.*

Perception is at once a vital and an acquired operation. Consciousness usually relies upon itself and its habits. More accurately, it relies on its currently operating memory, on fast, unconsciously performed consistency checks, and above all on its ability to use its capacity for awareness economically by omitting things from view. Seeing is overlooking. Communication captivates perception and thereby directs awareness. Once we are warned, we start paying attention. But we can react fast enough only if consciousness remains within acquired habits of perception. Wandering through the museum, catalogue in hand, we are reminded where the Raphael is hanging and then walk over to take a closer look.[42] Control of awareness by communication, however, is not exactly what we expect from a work of art. But then, what do we expect?

Art seeks a different kind of relationship between perception and communication—one that is irritating and defies normality—*and just this is communicated.* Whether a work of art belongs to communication in our understanding of the term depends on whether a difference between information and utterance must be assumed, and whether understanding the work turns on this difference. More accurately, the evolution of art realizes this criterion to the extent that it emancipates itself from externally imposed or outwardly directed purposes (for example, of a religious, political, or pedagogical nature). Whatever is produced "artificially" provokes the question: "What's the point?" Nature, in the old European sense, emerges and vanishes spontaneously, whereas art or *technē* is made for a purpose. At first, the opposition *physis/technē*, or *natura/ars*, governs the semantics of the discourse on art. Religious timidity alternates with worldly admiration for what can be produced by deviating from nature while imitating nature or obeying its "laws." After these models dissolved in the eighteenth century, their semantics prevailed, though art and the beautiful were now declared purposeful without purpose.[43] A theory of art that negates traditional patterns of differentiation without ridding itself of these models runs straight into paradox.

We shall postpone the question of the art system's semantic reflection or self-description to a later chapter. For the time being, it is important to understand how such descriptions obscure the special communicative role of art. The question of what the intent of an artwork "without purpose" might be *enforces the distinction between information and utterance.* But so long as one is mainly concerned with dissolving the distinction between nature and art in the paradox of an "end in itself," this particular function of art does not come into view. One could point out that understanding a work of art requires understanding its artistic means. Even this objection remains within the ends/means schema, and ends always point to external effects, that is, to the cosmologically or socially grounded service functions of a given activity. Perhaps the vexing question "What's the point?" really aims at the information embedded in the work of art, and the finalizing formula an "end in itself" only obscures the communicative function of an understanding that must assume the difference between information and utterance and make it available for further communication—otherwise, communication fails. The same problem manifests itself from a different angle. Most of the time, artists are in no position to provide a satisfactory account of their intentions. A primary intention is necessary to pass from the unmarked to the marked space; but the activity of traversing this boundary—an operation that *produces* a distinction (delimits a form)— cannot itself *be* a distinction,[44] except for an observer who observes (creates, delimits) this distinction The first impulse is never the artist's "own" intention—in the sense of self-observed mental states—but something one attributes to the artist as intention when observing the work. One cannot reverbalize intention, at least not apart from the information one gathers from observing works of art. What presents itself to observation in the form of art is an independent contribution to communication that cannot be translated into any other medium. Even the artist can see what he wanted to do only upon realizing what he has done.[45] He is involved in the creation of the work primarily as observer or, physically, as a skilled handyman.[46] (We must keep in mind that, as far as causality is concerned, the work of art would not come about without the artist's involvement, which, however, is true for any communication.)

How one explains the emergence of a particular work of art—by attributing it to the signals and limitations it displays in the process of emergence, to the artist who creates it, or to the social system of art with its history of styles, its determination of judgments, and an art criticism always ready to make history—is ultimately of secondary importance. Moreover, the situation looks different depending on whether one adopts a sociological or an aesthetic viewpoint. What matters is that in art, just as in all other types of communication, the difference between information and utterance serves both as a starting point and as a link for further artistic or verbal communications. "What's the point?"—that is the question. There may be no straightforward answer to this question, or answers may have changed in the course of history. This is no objection; rather, it is typical of powerful and significant art. What is at stake in art is not a problem to be solved once and for all but a provocation—the provocation of a search for meaning that is constrained by the work of art without necessarily being determined in its results. In the beginning, there is a difference, the cut made by a form that begins to regulate the following steps, a form that structures what can be perceived and, as an "artificial" cut, establishes in the world the difference between information and utterance. Even if this form is introduced as random, indistinguishable from everyday life, or nonsensical,[47] the question remains why just this form is produced as art.

Once intended and recognized as art, the difference cannot disappear again. It is productive within the art system, or else it fails; it contributes to the autopoiesis of art, or else it ends up in the garbage. It distinguishes itself from verbal communication in that it operates in the medium of perception or intuition without drawing on the specific potential of language to produce meaning. Art may well take advantage of linguistic means—for example, in lyric poetry—but only to strike us in ways that do not solely depend on our understanding of what is said.

Since we began our discussion with perception, the reader might assume that all this holds exclusively for the so-called visual arts. On the contrary, it holds—much more dramatically because less evidently—for the verbal arts as well, including lyric poetry.[48] A poem's "message" does not allow for paraphrase, nor can it be summarized in a proposition that can be true or false.[49] Rather, connotations, not denotations, mediate its meaning. It communicates not through the propositional content of its utterances, but (as we shall see) by virtue of the ornamental structure of mutually limiting references that appear in the form of words. Text-art distinguishes itself from more common forms of writing that aim at what in postmodern jargon would be called a "readerly text" and condemn the reader to the passive role of understanding. It distinguishes itself by demanding a "rewriting," a new construction of the text. Text-art, in other words, does not seek automatically to repeat familiar meanings; although it must draw on such meanings, it instead aims at disrupting automatization and delaying understanding.[50] No matter how we conceive of conscious participation in this process, subsuming it under the concept of reading would be misleading.[51] Instead, we should investigate what kinds of verbal sounds and references to meanings mutually illuminate one another. We mean nothing else by suggesting that words are used as a *medium*, rather than for the purpose of expressing an unambiguous denotative meaning.[52]

The specificity of text-art does not depend on communicating propositional meaning—if it did, then such meaning would have to be formulated in an easily accessible manner. This is why, toward the end of the

eighteenth century, the author withdraws from his texts, or at least refrains from clarifying his communicative intentions.[53] The point is to
avoid the impression that the author wants to provide information or ad-
monish the reader to align his conduct with morality. Instead, the choice
of words as a medium creates a compelling and unusually dense combination of self-reference and hetero-reference running through the entire
text. Words carry and "signify" their ordinary meanings, and this is why
they refer to something other, not just to themselves. At the same time,
however, they also carry and "signify" a special textual meaning, within
which they execute and propel the text's recursions.[54] Text-art organizes itself by means of self-referential references that combine elements of
sound, rhythm, and meaning. The unity of self-reference and hetero-reference lies in the sensuous perceptibility of words. The difference between
these two types of reference can be pushed to the point of utter discrepancy—for example, when words in a poem come to mean the exact opposite of what they mean in ordinary language. The articulation of difference and unity is not, as one would think, mediated thematically (by such
topics as love, betrayal, hope, age, and so forth). Occasionally they are,
but the artistic quality of a text lies in the choice of words, not thematic
choice. Lyric poetry unites the work of art with its own self-description.[55]

All of this needs further elaboration. At this point, we only wish to emphasize the triggering effect of a specific difference. When it succeeds as
form, this difference sets in motion a special kind of communication that
draws on the capacity to perceive or on the imagination and yet cannot be
mistaken for the world we normally perceive. Because the work of art is
made, it is unpredictable and hence fulfills an indispensable precondition
for information. What strikes us in an art form—as, in a different way,
does the conspicuous character of acoustic and optic signals—engenders
a fascination that turns into information by changing the state of the system—as a "difference that makes a difference" (Bateson). And this is already communication. What else?

VI

Though at present its consequences are visible only in broad outline,
the shift toward difference-theoretical analyses will affect and radically alter the concept of world. This alteration can perhaps best be demonstrated in conjunction with the concept of form. Until recently, form was

conceptualized (without much effort, for there were practically no alternatives) in terms of an ordered nexus between elements. From the perspective of a certain immanence, it was defined by the distinction between the finite and the infinite. Form, in this sense, is synonymous with *Gestalt.*[56] Psychologically, it corresponds to the possibility of perceiving form as a unity directly and without analysis. Chance is its counterconcept in the sense that the simultaneous appearance of elements not bound by form was believed to be random. Earlier versions of information theory and cybernetics were still working from within this traditional understanding of form when searching for ways to quantitatively compute improbability in terms of a link between redundancy and information.[57] Such theories thematized form in relation to a recipient of information—that is, to an observer—but the only determining counterconcept available was the idea of chance.

A difference-theoretical reconstruction of the concept of form shifts the emphasis from the (ordered) content of form to the difference it makes. It extends and places on the "other side" of form the realm of what used to be considered chance and thereby subsumes under the concept of form any difference that marks a unity. This step was already taken by Kandinsky: "Form, in the narrow sense, is nothing more than the boundary against another form. This is its external indication. But since everything external contains something absolutely internal (which manifests itself more or less strongly), *each form also has an inner content. Form is the externalization of this inner content.*"[58] Despite the somewhat awkward formulation, the explosive effects of such a concept of form or, more accurately, the novelty of the artistic intent it attempts to capture in words, are readily apparent. But we must push Kandinsky's point even further by asking what precisely he means by "externalization." Is it the crossing of a boundary? An operation? Something that takes time? Today, the concept of form as limit, along with its operative understanding, is no longer shocking to artists and poets: "Form, in essence, is the way one part of the poem (one movement) *thrusts against another across a silence.*"[59]

Understanding difference as form (or, vice versa, form as a two-sided distinction) implies that the distinction is completely self-contained. "Distinction is perfect continence."[60] Nothing external supports it. Form is meaning, the reproducible result of the operation that introduces form into the world. In search of something that could be called "meaning" (*sens*), Deleuze arrives at the same conclusion. Meaning presupposes a "series" on either of two sides and (without implying "existence") "articulates difference,"[61] that is, a paradox. Distinctions participate in the world by cutting it up, leaving visible only what is marked by these distinctions. This notion of form is at odds with an ontology that conceived of everything in the world as being supported and sustained by a comprehensive whole. It is equally incompatible with a semiotic theory that thinks of form as a sign referring to something other. We need to give up not only the ontological unity of the visible world, which excluded only nonbeing, but also a semiotic theory that locates the significance of signs solely in their reference to something capable of validating their signifying function. As in ontology, a reference to "nothing" would deprive the sign of its meaning. A difference-theoretical theory of form, by contrast, treats forms as pure self-reference, made possible by the marking of the form as a boundary that separates two sides—made possible, in other words, by the fact that form is essentially a boundary. Form opens up the possibility of transgression. The *forma formans* is the *forma formata*.[62]

When distinctions are marked as forms, they can be distinguished and reproduced. Whereas perception can make do with unformed distinctions, communication requires articulated forms in a twofold sense: they serve as a condition for the cooperation of disparate psychic systems that perceive words or signs as differences, and they ensure the connectivity of communication. Communication must have recourse to past and future communications, that is, it must be able to identify something as repeatable. This is not merely a matter of producing a temporal series of "fitting" successions. Recursivity must be present in each and every moment that generates another operation. This fact must be apprehended precisely: already when dealing with language, but even more so when communication leaves the realm of linguistic articulation and begins to rely on other, self-produced forms in the sensuously perceptible realm.

Forms must be articulated *asymmetrically*, since only one of their sides (the internal side) but not the other (the external side) is needed for further operations (elaborations, increases in complexity, and so on). Forms are generated by a *rupture of symmetry*, which must be presupposed or posited as something that simply happened. This rupture exhibits a simple positivity beyond affirmation or negation—concepts that already mark a distinction. Here we are dealing with a prelogical conceptuality for which logic supplies specific applications. In retrospect, and from the midst of actualized distinctions, symmetry may appear, as it does in

Schelling, as indifference, a religious (but certainly not artistic) symbol of the world which must be relinquished if one is to create forms.

A difference-theoretical concept of form therefore presupposes the world as an "unmarked state." The unity of the world is unattainable; it is not a summation or aggregate, nor is it Spirit. When a new series of operations starts from a self-created difference, it begins with a blind spot. It steps out of the "unmarked state"—where nothing is visible and we cannot speak of a "space" to begin with—into the "marked state," and it draws a boundary in transgressing that boundary.[63] The mark creates the space of the distinction, the difference between "marked" and "unmarked" space. It (somehow) selects one of an infinite number of possible distinctions in order to constrain the work's further construction. The first difference separates two sides so that the next operation can be executed in the marked space. Distinctions serve to control connecting operations. These might subsequently yield further distinctions. For example, one needs to decide whether an object belongs to nature or art. One cannot perceive an object simultaneously as nature and as art, unless one enlists yet another distinction—for example, by adding that both are beautiful rather than ugly, or interesting rather than boring. In other words, using a distinction to illustrate the lack of differentiation in the distinguished defies the distinction's functional purpose as difference. One could, of course, point out that both sides belong to a particular (and not another) distinction, but this distinction would have to be distinguished in turn. Whatever distinction is used at any given time cannot be indicated as a unity—this condition reproduces itself with every distinction. It merely displaces the blind spot, thus frustrating once and for all the Hegelian expectation that eventually, after passing through a series of dialectical mediations, the opposition marked by distinction will become transparent to itself—in Hegelian terms, become "Spirit."

An arrangement of forms that claims to be art tends to strive toward "double closure." A work of art must distinguish itself externally from other objects or events, or it will lose itself in the world. Internally, the work closes itself off by limiting further possibilities with each of its formal decisions. Ultimately, external and internal closure amount to the same thing; both are supported by the frame that is produced along with the work and cannot be transgressed.

This is not to say that the artwork cannot integrate forms that point beyond it. A landscape painting presupposes that the represented space exceeds the frame. In a poem from his collection *The Underwoods*, Ben Jonson hopes to present the "morning kiss" in such a way that his verse should earn him another kiss.[64] Such a deliberate "confusion" of frames, however, is always produced within the artwork—for example, by self-quotation, as in the text just mentioned. The external frame reenters the work without—and this accounts for the appeal of the maneuver—being obstructed in its function of demarcating the work against the unmarked space of the world.

Regarding its external side, the distinction generated by an arrangement (of any sort) entails a twofold possibility. One can leave this side undetermined as an "unmarked space." One might still reach the unmarked side by crossing a boundary, but one would get nowhere, and upon return everything would be the same as before. If, however, one looks for another form at the undetermined side and marks this form, then one can return to the beginning and *find it changed*. It is now on the other side of the other side. Its meaning has become more complex, and perception encounters a contingency that was invisible in the first operation. The result is a redescription,[65] and perhaps a critical one likely to initiate a change. Any form, however, whether it is situated inside or outside of a given distinction, generates *eo ipso* another unmarked space and can therefore never fully comprehend or represent the world. Every distinction reproduces the difference between marked and unmarked space.

An arrangement of forms creates an open flank. Despite its closure, a work of art can be observed adequately only in its relationship to time—a topic much discussed since Lessing's *Laocoön*.[66] Thinking of the work as an arrested movement to be supplemented imaginatively does not suffice. Rather, the work's built-in temporality must be experienced as a reconstruction of its incompletion. One must observe forms as if the adjacent space were undetermined; then one recognizes how, and by what kinds of other forms, this space has been utilized. In other words, one needs to reconstruct the work's contingencies and the way in which they limit one another. A temporal scheme suggests that everything could be done differently—if not as convincingly as the actual work. A determined form always promises something else without defining it. It dissolves the homogeneity of the unmarked space—everything that is not form—into a space replete with suggestions, and it bifurcates this space in terms of the success or failure of further determinations.

George Spencer Brown's formal calculus provides a model for this phenomenon.[67] On the surface, the *Laws of Form* appear to reconstruct Boolean algebra under the condition that only a single operator may be used for arithmetic and algebra. This operator is introduced by the injunction: "Draw a distinction!" Without distinction, one would encounter the world only as unmarked state. Each operation creates a difference, and each operation discriminates. This does or does not happen—there is no other possibility. This is why the injunction requires a "motive," which becomes irrelevant as the operation continues. Once a distinction is drawn, a sequence of operations is set in motion, as it were, spontaneously. The initial motive remains accidental—the theory of evolution confirms this point—and is of no relevance to the construction of order. Any random event would do.

The passage from the unmarked to the marked state is particularly striking when the artist selects a *new* form.[68] Disregarding the preference for novelty that defined the historical differentiation of art in modernity, there is a *symbolic function* of novelty that needs no comparative dimension to be recognized. The impression of novelty immediately signals the passing over from the unmarked to the marked state, as well as the simultaneous creation of a marked space in which the work of art can unfold. But the work's context must be familiar enough to support and highlight the marking of novelty. A novel and striking work thus always has a double function: one of its sides is always overdetermined by the opposition marked/unmarked, the other by a combination of forms that incorporate familiar experiences (redundancies).

But how to begin without having begun, since one needs a distinction in order to begin?[69] And must not the distinction itself be distinguished from its indication so that the first distinction reenters itself?[70] In the older literature, this problem was treated in quasi-objectivist terms: by appealing to divine inspiration, to the inscrutability of sudden insights, or to the fortune of chance[71]—all of which obscured the issue. In the calculus of form, by contrast, object and creative process coincide (in this respect we are dealing with a kind of "constructivism"), since both emerge—simultaneously—from the imperative "Draw a distinction." An observer can once again distinguish between object and process when selecting this distinction as the form of observation. This is why it takes an observer to raise questions about objects; a system simply starts operating. It takes an observer to see the paradox of a beginning that presupposes itself, to recognize the self-implicative structure of the distinguishing act, and to plunge himself, at least logically, into confusion. Only an observer can run into paradox and be forced to admit that paradox is always presupposed—in mathematical and even more so in logical operations—as the blind spot that makes distinction, and thus observation, possible in the first place.[72] Operations, on the other hand, including observing operations, simply happen. A distinction discriminates; its mere occurrence creates a difference. To become relevant as form, the occurrence must be observed (retrospectively by the same system, simultaneously or later by another system); only then does the unity of the distinction become apparent as the blind spot that enables observation.[73] This unity remains invisible while the distinction is used—this holds for all distinctions. It is as indisputable as our certainty about the world, a certainty based on inaccessibility.

The first distinction posits everything it discriminates and indicates against the unmarked space of the world. "Everything else" is left on the other side of the distinction and remains necessarily undetermined. A narration opens with the phrase "once upon a time . . . ," which demarcates an imaginary space for the unfolding narration at the exclusion of everything else.[74] In the same way, an enclosed field is prepared for a painting, which can emerge only within the boundaries of this primary form. Or a stage is prepared for a yet undetermined performance. The rising and falling of the curtain draws a boundary around the performance, allowing the actors to step out of their roles and in front of the curtain to receive the ovations.[75] The purpose of writing—as one can read (!) in Derrida— is to mark absences for absent readers, that is, to permit the withdrawal of the author.[76] The unmarked space outside the text remains inaccessible (as the negative formulation indicates), but effectively bounded. Of course, once the painter has projected the plane for his painting, he can lean back and have breakfast, but doing so requires other distinctions that exclude an "unmarked space" on their part. The operative activity, in other words, goes on inside the form, but in the course of its execution, it can link forms to forms, distinctions to distinctions—for example, by drawing a line and observing its effects on a drawing in process, namely, the line itself and what is to be expected if the drawing tolerates the line. The emerging forms have a two-sided connectivity; an operation on one side affects and changes the other. But the unmarked space in which the operative sequence takes place remains an inaccessible precondition. *Every* use of form, *every* crossing of a boundary in a certain direction, regenerates the unmarked space of the world in the sense that further operative possibilities remain open—that is, in the sense of a future. The world remains the world, sustaining itself behind the forms that establish themselves, naturally or artificially, in it. The world remains invisible even when, and precisely when, it is laced with forms. (When one draws a circle, the world is not just outside but also inside the circle; it is what is severed by the circle.) The world enters into the play of forms only as the paradox of the indistinguishability of the distinguished, and it tolerates this paradox as a kind of placeholder that represents the world as unobservable. This is why artistic praxis (production and apprehension) can only be comprehended as a modification of this paradox, as an activity of creating and deleting forms, rather than as a matter of applying principles or rules, which would presuppose an initial situation without paradox.

One can translate this insight into a systems-theoretical formulation by saying that the sequence of operations closes itself off and in so doing excludes other things. Or one might say that it draws a boundary, which implies that only internal operations are henceforth possible—operations that are capable of observing this boundary, that can, in other words, distinguish system from environment and make indications that refer either to themselves or the outside world. To the unattainability of the world corresponds the closure of the work of art—and, ultimately, the closure of the art system.[77]

The same insight has been formulated in similar ways in quite different theoretical contexts. Following Gotthard Günther, Eva Meyer speaks of a choice of "contexture" when a distinction is selected that indicates something by excluding a third. The excluded third is evacuated into the contexture's "surroundings." Every choice of contexture generates a surrounding space, the unmarked space of Spencer Brown's formal calculus.[78] Bernard Willms illustrates what he calls the presence of the excluded in politics in conjunction with the problem of freedom and the sovereign's obligation to master the state of emergency.[79] Yves Barel shows how rejection "potentializes" by reproducing the rejected as a possibility and by incorporating it into the recursive network of the system.[80] Interpretations of the Talmud routinely transmit dissenting opinions to keep the future open; after all, the text has been revealed for all times, for written as well as oral tradition.[81] For Jacques Derrida, in his reading of Husserl's transcendental phenomenology, form indicates an absence—"form in itself already would be the *trace (ikhnos)* of a certain nonpresence, the vestige of the un-formed, which announces-recalls its other."[82] Focusing on works of art, Danto speaks of interpretations, but it is evident from his analysis that he is talking about the discovery of (visible or invisible) difference; what matters is not what a thing is in itself but what it makes visible.[83] We can summarize these and similar statements as follows: the world of meaning [*Sinn*] is a closed world (meaning, in other words, is a universal medium that cannot be negated), so that exclusion can happen only in the world and—just like any indication—only by virtue of a distinction. But if this is true, the act of exclusion is also constitutive of determination as such, and this is why we need to scrutinize ideas—especially those expressing a maximum or ultimate constitutive principle—with an eye to what they exclude and render invisible. Their foundational effort serves above all to make namable as antiform (or antimatter) what can be present only in its absence. At this point, we may be broaching the topic of religion.

A work of art that holds its own as a work of art in a differential relation to everything else initially excludes everything else and divides the world into itself and the remaining unmarked space.[84] To observe a work of art as a (produced) object endowed with certain attributes makes sense only when focusing on the work itself. It is of no particular artistic interest to cross the work's boundary for the sake of indicating something else; doing so and then returning to the work amounts to never having crossed or recrossed the boundary.[85] Situated within this distinction, the work of art is nothing but an object. Subsequently, one can ask how an art object distinguishes itself from other natural or artificial objects, for example, from a urinal or a snow shovel. Marcel Duchamp used *the form of a work of art* to impress this question on his audience and, in a laudable effort, eliminated all sensuously recognizable differences between the two. But can a work of art *at once pose and answer this question*?

This object-oriented perspective led to endless debates on the nature of such objects and how they can be distinguished and judged, until it was finally realized that the question itself is incompatible with the universalistic claims of the art system (*everything* can be art). Today, the work of art as communication appears to collapse under the weight of questions and answers, provoking nothing more than "so what?" Tracing this question, we return to art as if from the outside. What matters when an object is produced as a work of art is that the internally employed forms constrain the possibilities of their respective other sides. These constraints result neither exclusively from the material qualities of the medium (for instance, the density or weight of the material, the minimal duration of audible tones) nor solely from the purpose for which the object is used. The emphasis here is on "neither exclusively"—that these kinds of constraints do play a role, as in architecture, for example, should not prevent the work of art from coming into being. However, a work qualifies as art only when *it employs constraints for the sake of increasing the work's freedom in disposing over further constraints.* As an object, considered within the boundaries of a thing or process, the work of art opens up the possibility of a compact communication. In calling it a work of art, one arrives at a clear-cut distinction from which to proceed. Communication may come to an end here or begin to concern itself with the network of distinctions that constitute the work and identify it as art. As for the inner side of the form "work of art," this compact communication communicates its readiness for further analysis. It is a kind of communication on credit, it authorizes further elaborations, its predominant message is: "One could show that . . ."[86]

The external side of the form "work of art" remains unmarked space. Disposing over this side—by making decisions that affect what now functions as the other side (our initial starting point)—becomes possible only when the forms to be realized internally are observed. The chances of discovering something fitting are dwindling; going on becomes increasingly difficult. The beginning loses its momentum in an effort to salvage what has already begun. But the determination that indicates one rather than the other side of its form always constitutes that other side along with it. As a result, further determinations are needed until the forms close themselves off in a circle, where they comment on one another and reaffirm the beginning.

In the tradition, the circle that returns into itself was considered the perfect form. There is no need to reject this idea, but one can certainly raise further questions: What becomes of the outside? What does the circle make invisible by virtue of its self-perfection? Or further, how complex is that which the circle includes? How abundant are the forms it contains? And yet further, how complex must a circular structure be to include the possibility of a reentry of the form into the form—the possibility of a play within the play or of the "comme si" episode in Mallarmé's "Un coup de dès"?

Under the condition of sufficient structural complexity, which presupposes the law of crossing, the law of crossing no longer holds. Like any circular structure, such complexity presupposes both familiar and unexpected elements. If, upon performing operations on the other side, one returns to the side from which one started, then one finds it altered. But this does not change the underlying proposition that a distinction can be applied only to specific sides, never as a unity. The unity of the distinction is not a unit capable of operation. One can, however, use a distinction to observe other distinctions. The result is a work that becomes a (distinguishable) form by virtue of consisting internally of forms (distinctions) capable of specifying one another on either side: "The form within the form frames the enclosing form."[87]

The distinction between cases in which the law of crossing applies and those in which it does not apply, along with the insight that the law's authority is the precondition for its suspension in the work of art, defines in a theoretically rigorous sense the differentiation of the art system in a world that remains operatively beyond its reach.

These considerations set us apart from two other possible approaches to theoretical aesthetics: dialectics and semiotics. Taking differently constructed theories into account might nonetheless be fruitful, so long as we remain aware of the differences. The concepts of distinction and form do not imply negation. The other side remains presupposed when something determined by that side is indicated. We are dealing with mathematics, if you will, not with logic. Hence, our goal is not an aesthetics of negativity in Adorno's sense.[88] Such a project places too much of a burden on the concept of negativity, particularly when it is held accountable for the difference between the aesthetic and the nonaesthetic. In our view, the positive/negative distinction is a specific form that must be introduced with caution.

Nor do we think of the work of art as an arrangement of "signifiers" that refer to corresponding "signifieds." This distinction too—which generally defines the concept of the sign—is only one form among others.[89] When using the distinctions of semiotics, we need to remind ourselves that the signifiers of an artwork refer solely to signifieds within the work itself. Each time a determination specifies certain aspects of an artwork, it creates an open flank that requires further decisions—determination means nothing else. But if this is true, we might as well use the language of the formal calculus to begin with. The conceptual repertoire of distinction/form/ observer thematizes a precondition for the introduction of indications into a world that is and remains undetermined. This is where a theory of art must begin, if it wants to do justice to art's claim that it has something to do with the world.

VII

Theoretical figures as abstract and suggestive of paradox as these should help us conceptualize in sufficiently precise terms what happens when a work of art is made and observed. The notions of making and observing substitute for the traditional role-oriented distinction between the production and reception of a work of art. The conceptual pair "operation and observation" is meant to relativize this distinction.[90] We trace the distinction to what both concepts have in common—namely, the operative use of a distinction for the purpose of indicating one (and not the other) side—in other words, we trace the distinction to its use as form. We shall call such a use of form "observing."

Observing is a real, albeit prelogical mode of operation. It is prelogical because it does not distinguish between affirmation and negation; in this regard, observing (like the world) cannot be qualified. Observing presupposes a distinction, which it affirms through what it selects and indicates. At the same time, observing de-actualizes the other side of the distinction, including the distinction itself as what it does not indicate. The logical ambivalence of observing and the fact that it allows for no further qualification correspond to the impossibility of negating the medium of meaning [*Sinn*], the medium in which observation creates its forms by virtue of an operation that includes as well as excludes. Only what is indicated as included in the form's internal side can serve as a starting point for further operations. Only from this point—assuming one appends predicates of existence, of validity, modalizations, and so on—can positive or negative propositions follow. Any coding in terms of negative/positive is therefore secondary, which means it can attain only the status of an *interchangeable distinction*.

To be sure, every observation is an operation, or it could not happen. But not every operation implies that the other side is perceived as well; not every operation is an observation. The production of forms generates observational possibilities. The observer is not the form; he cannot observe himself while executing the operation. But his observing is bound by the form (when it is used), and, according to the formal calculus, it is bound tightly, that is, without alternative. In this sense, one might say with Spencer Brown that the observer, in the act of observing, is identical to the form he uses.[91] A work of art, too, determines, or at least strives to determine, the form to be used by an observer in such a way that the observing operation—in a self-forgetting (or, as the tradition believed, purposeless) manner—is nothing but this form. This argument disregards the fact that only *systems* can observe. The theory of forms is not yet a theory of systems.

At any rate, the activity of operating and observing (of indicating something on the basis of a distinction) is going on not only when a work of art is made but also when it is perceived.[92] An artist can control his production only through observation; he must, so to speak, let the emerging work show him what has been done and what can be done further. The theory of sketches has been a locus classicus for discussing this problem.[93] A painter needs to draw several sketches to record his ideas and determine the ones best suited for his purposes. This process can be contracted into an accelerated sequence of painting, stepping back, and observing. The same holds for the writer; he is always also a reader—how else could he write?[94] The making of an artwork cannot be understood—or can be understood only in a manner that remains insufficiently formalized—as a means to an external end that is apparent from the start. It escapes planning and programming; this may explain why, since early modern times, it has been necessary to separate artistic activity from craftsmanship. Artistic production amounts to observing distinctions whose empty sides need to be filled, or, to use Henri Focillon's beautiful formulation, it is a "poetry of action."[95] Observing an artwork is an operation as well—in perception as in understanding (or misunderstanding)—since observing amounts to operating in a special manner that does not just generate differences but also reproduces itself from moment to moment with the help of indications that are bound by distinctions.

What sense does it make to differentiate the roles of maker and beholder when both sides are conceived (observed) as observers? The conventional presentation of these roles in terms of the active/passive distinction misses the point; observing is always active. In most cases (even the art of writing is not completely exempt), the producer must deploy his body as a primary observer. He must rely on bodily intuition, teasing out the distinctions that matter, and in so doing, he must differentiate unconsciously. Eyes and ears can dispose over only what has already occurred and perhaps motivate corrections. The artist's genius is primarily his body. The observing activity that guides production distinguishes itself from the one that views the product in yet another respect: the former happens *only once*, whereas the latter *repeats*. Repetition always means repetition under different circumstances and, strictly speaking, repetition as *another*. An incalculable number of observers, among them the artist, can participate in observing the work, each of them as a "nontrivial machine" that assumes a different state or reconstructs itself as a different machine in each operation. It is the ultimate test for the quality of artworks that, despite our awareness of their "uniqueness," we can perceive them again and again, each time with different eyes.

This point becomes even clearer when the form of participation is considered primarily from the viewpoint of perception and only secondarily in terms of thinking judgment—that is, against the Baumgarten/Kant tradition and generally against the neglect of perception in the description of consciousness (of what, traditionally, sets humans apart from animals). While thought is highly aware of its obligation toward intersubjective agreement and deviations from this principle are considered mistakes, perceptions are "equivalent" only "in a weak sense."[96] But this simply means that perceptions are intersubjectively different and always new.

Of course, operations (and observations considered as operations) are always unique. They always take place for the first and for the last time. Only observations, when based on the same schema of differentiation, can be repeated and recognized as repetitions. We take the distinction between operation and observation to be fundamental, which is evident from its self-implicative structure. On the one hand, the distinction is the instrument of an observer; on the other hand, it indicates an operation—a mere operation, one could say—on one side of the distinction and an observing operation on the other. An analysis of these intricate conceptual relationships is beyond our present scope. What interests us here is merely that they help clarify *how art functions as communication*.

Observing works of art as art, rather than as worldly objects of some other type, succeeds only if the beholder decodes the work's structure of distinctions and infers *from* this structure that the object could not have emerged spontaneously but owes its existence instead to the intent of conveying information. The information is externalized in the work; the communicated content results from the artificiality of the information, which reveals the information to be contrived. Perception in this case no longer results from our worldly familiarity with objects (which does not mean that one cannot be content with registering the mere fact that a picture is hanging on the wall). In order to succeed as an understanding of communication, that is, in terms of understanding the *difference* between information and utterance, perception requires the perception of perception. Psychologically, this means that the normal externalization of consciousness takes place. Rather than being suspended, it is modified by the questions "What do I see? Am I seeing correctly what I see?"[97] This means that social communication is dealing with a self-generated difficulty of understanding to which open expectations concerning its meaning can attach themselves: "The . . . life of a poem is the way it performs itself through the difficulties it imposes upon itself."[98] The artist must therefore observe his emerging work in anticipation of its observation by others. There is no way of knowing how others (which others?[99]) will receive the work through their consciousness. But he will incorporate into the work ways of directing the expectations of others, and he will make an effort to surprise them. This is how, to borrow a phrase from antiquity, the work of art is created for the sake of astonishment. This is how it surprises with information about itself. This is how it unfolds the self-generated paradox of creating and disrupting illusion. And this is how it incorporates the blind spot—its own unity as unfolded paradox—that renders the work incomprehensible to whoever focuses on this spot.[100]

The artist might go astray in the process, projecting more into his work—or less—than others might be getting out of it. This is not the point, since it holds for every communication. Nor are we dealing with a teleological process that strives toward consensus or adequate understanding. This goal, too, may or may not be reached in any communication. What matters instead is the autopoietic organization of an activity that processes distinctions within the frame of self-generated uncertainties, independently of the desires, impressions, and feelings of those who participate in it. In other words, for communication to come about, it is irrelevant whether or not systems of consciousness are capable of figuring each other out. Communication occurs whenever the utterance of an information is understood—which may result in acceptance or rejection, consensus or dissent. Moreover, communication through art is not concerned with automating understanding. Rather, it is inherently ambiguous (semiologists speak of *polysémie*) independently of whether or not the divergence of observational possibilities was planned in the sense of an "open work." The fact that observers cannot agree on a single interpretation of a given artwork may even count as evidence of its artistic quality. This is an inevitable and often deliberately cultivated aspect of "differentiation."

VIII

We can recapitulate and deepen our analysis by returning to the paradoxical structure of the distinguishing indication or—which amounts to the same thing—to the arbitrariness of all beginnings. This is a general law of observation: whoever wants to observe must observe *something* and distinguish it from other objects. He must indicate and distinguish, hence be able to distinguish between distinction and indication. But how can he execute this distinguishing indication as an act? How can he operate if operating presupposes a built-in difference that needs to be distinguished prior to the operation, namely, the distinction between the indication and the distinction that is presupposed in the execution of this indication? The question leads to an infinite regress in search of the first distinction and therefore cannot be answered—one would have to start distinguishing in order to do so. This is why one needs to begin. This is why Spencer Brown's formal calculus—unlike the older cosmology—does not start from the assumption of a chaos waiting for love in order to assume a form or, in the manner of Hegel, from an immediate relationship to the world that requires determination.[101] Nor does it begin with an authoritative distinction or a code. Instead, it starts with an injunction—"Draw a distinction!"—that requires no justification, since it generates all further operations. Even chaos is created by a distinguishing operation. But the imperative conceals the fact that a prior distinction has already been made, namely, the distinction between distinction and indication.

One might ask how a distinction can be employed as distinction, if only one of its sides and not the other functions as indication—if, to speak with Spencer Brown, the distinction is to be used as form, or, as semiologists might say, if we are always moving within the realm of signifying signs (of language, for example) without ever arriving at the signifieds presupposed in language use. There is always a prior asymmetry—a break of symmetry that is put to operative use—while the original symmetry remains unobservable. Indicating both sides simultaneously neutralizes both the asymmetry and its difference, canceling the very distinction required in order to indicate one thing rather than another.

Such formal problems point to the original paradox of the unity of the distinguished—they can be indicated but not employed as such. Paradox arrests the observation that wants to refer to or indicate it in the form of an instantaneous oscillation.[102] Paradox lacks connectivity; it revolves within itself. Since observation depends on distinction, it must dissolve and make invisible the underlying paradox of the unity of the distinguishing activity, it must replace this unity with operatively useful distinctions, it must unfold the paradox—there is no other way of arriving at identities capable of operation.

Whatever can be observed in art is thus the unfolding of a paradox that, for its part, escapes observation. But even if the unobservable remains unobservable, it is important to keep in mind that this is so. The unobservability of paradox legitimates the arbitrariness of beginning. The first caesura, the first cut into the unmarked state of the world, must be executed, and not just to generate two sides. Rather, the cut must yield an asymmetrical use of these sides, which allows for connecting operations on one side but not on the other. This is how sequences are set in motion that reproduce the problem in the realm of already executed distinctions in such a way that further observations can follow. What emerges and becomes visible as a work of art is the unfolding of its own paradox, the substitution of interrelated forms for what cannot be observed. The work of art is unobservable as a unity—unless it is distinguished from something else (or everything else). The point, in other words, is not to make visible what cannot be observed (the world), nor is it a matter of symbolizing, representing, or revealing its hidden order, as the traditional doctrine of signs would have it. The problem is similar, but the solution is different. The only option is to observe forms *instead* of the unobservable, while knowing that this happens by unfolding a paradox.

Consequently, the unity of the work of art is beyond description. Description requires decomposition. To put it differently, the *nexus* of distinctions that articulate one another *cannot be generalized.* This is what makes each work of art unique and creates the impression that the network of interconnected details has come about ad hoc. This is, of course, no objection against the rationality of these interconnections or their deliberate nature—they can certainly be justified and understood—but we need to adjust our criteria of judgment as well as our concept of rationality to a situation that precludes generalization. Despite the built-in, local, and context-specific rationality of its decisions, the work of art itself, being neither the sum nor the aggregate of individual features, is not rational—in this respect it resembles the world.

The proposition that the work of art unfolds a paradox corresponds to the historical fact that the art system has become autonomous. Within the traditional framework of imitation, concepts such as distinction or difference played a limited role. They accomplished the task of imitation, of replicating natural differences within the work of art. There was an awareness of the unobservability of unity, but it was expressed in enigmatic forms, in terms that explicitly or implicitly referred to something external—such as religious inspiration, the natural talent (genius) of the artist, or the necessity of representing nature on a smaller scale.[103] If, by contrast, one begins with the paradox of distinguishing—understood as an operation—art appears as an articulation of its own self-reference. Accordingly, it can do whatever it wants so long as it produces self-referential connectivity.

Our exposition acknowledges that the artist and the observer of art are equally dependent on forms. To observe the work as a work of art, they must be able to perceive the forms that direct their observations. To both, forms appear as asymmetrical and two-sided, as forms that mark one side by indication and thus constrain what can be specified on the other side. This is not to say that both will arrive at the same judgment, nor that they bring to bear the same orientation of taste or the same aesthetic preferences. But their dependence on form and on the determination of the formal nexus that makes up the work provides—just as in the case of language—enough of a common ground to speak of communication between artist and viewer. Even under normal circumstances, the conditions of possibility of communication keep open the question of whether or not our judgments agree.

Focusing on the observing *operation*, one recognizes that artist and viewer are both engaged in judgment, albeit in different ways, at different times, in different operational sequences, and perhaps with different criteria. We are always dealing with a historical process that consists of operations, that is, with an eventlike process which can realize itself only in time. The observation accompanying the creation of a work differs from the observation of the beholder in that the former can occur only once, whereas the latter can be repeated (and is thus subject to variation). With respect to the operativity of its observation, the artwork must therefore be a *temporally abstracted* structure. It is a program for repeated usage which—like today's complex computer programs—blocks access to what is actually going on during the execution of the operation. To put it differently, the artwork itself offers no clue as to what happens in the process of understanding the work. It leaves open how artist and beholder are coupled by the work, while at the same time it guarantees that this coupling is not entirely ar-bitrary—this is what makes art a medium of communication. Physicists would perhaps speak of nonlinear structures of coupling; at any rate, they would exclude tight coupling and noncoupling.

Finally, we should emphasize that our difference-theoretical approach —the idea of tracing art to the unfolding of a paradox of form—implies a radically historical mode of observation: "If words and concepts receive meaning only in sequences of differences, one can justify one's language, and one's choice of terms, only within a topic [an orientation in space] and an historical strategy."[104] This does not simply mean that art has its time like everything else, that it comes into being and vanishes. Rather, it ex-plains why works of art must be constructed with an orientation toward time, why they must be *new*, following the requirement, in place since early modernity, that they distinguish themselves from everything that has been done before. The demand for novelty means not only that no two things are the same but also that the difference between them motivates both the work's production and the interest of the beholder. Only novel works can please. This is how art exposes itself to the effects of a self-consummation of forms. It positions itself historically. And this is why the future of art be-comes increasingly problematic—to the point where the claim is made and refuted daily that art has no future in the *posthistoire*.

IX

To determine how art defines itself, one needs to rely on what can be known about works of art. What is it that characterizes art in relation to everything else (to *its* unmarked space)? The tradition offers a number of specific distinctions. Works of art are *made*, in contrast to *natural* objects. Once artificiality as such no longer defines what counts as art, a second distinction is added: works of art serve *no external purpose*; having such a purpose is precisely what disqualifies a work as art. This raises the ques-tion what else could qualify works of art as art. With this question, the theory of art receives its admission ticket to the art system—until the the-ory of the avant-garde will proclaim that art is whatever we call art, thereby accomplishing the dual purpose of making works of art exemplify theory while at the same time relieving itself from the burden of further reflection.

For lack of a convincing alternative, we shall draw repeatedly on this historically exhausted theoretical framework. However, our considerations concerning perception and communication may yield a somewhat more complex treatment of the topic, particularly via the concept of form.

To say that artistic forms call attention to themselves as being made and without purpose circumscribes the reentry of the form into the form. Any artwork displays talent, no matter whether its figures are beautiful or ugly, distinguished or ordinary, benevolent or malicious, profound or nonsensical. The work displays, one might say, itself and its own self-description. It executes the paradox of "reentry" and shows that this is possible, whatever mathematics or logic may think.

The work of art draws on sensuously perceptible media for its own self-explication, no matter what is subsequently presented as an internal play of forms. It exploits evidence based on such media. Even if one knows that this happens only for the sake of communication, the fact that art draws on perception is not irrelevant to understanding *how* it happens. The question, then, is the following: How does an individual work of art present itself to perception in such a way as to be recognizable as art and to provide, by virtue of precisely *this* recognition, an opportunity and a motive for participating in communication?

The concept of form suggests that two requirements must be fulfilled and inscribed into perception: the form must have a *boundary*, and there must be an "unmarked space" *excluded by this boundary*. How both of these requirements coincide and how they are fulfilled in one stroke may vary considerably in different artistic genres. Whenever we think of "marked space" / boundary / "unmarked space" in combination, the constitution of an imaginary space is at stake. However, since every artwork constitutes its own imaginary space, the question is how this space is constituted *differently* in each case.

The typical case is a work of art enclosed within a beginning and end, within a frame or a stage, a work that ignores and does not interfere with its surroundings. In this case, the imaginary space is construed from the inside out, as if breaking through the frame or creating its own world behind the frame. The imagination is driven beyond the work.[105] One must at once see and think away the frame in order to gain access to the work's imaginary space. The guaranteed repeatability of observations might be of help in performing this operation.

Sculpture or architecture presents an entirely different case. Here, the boundary does not draw the viewer's attention inward but instead directs it outward. The work permits no view into its depths, no penetration of its surface (whatever the surface may betray of the work's mass, volume, or material). The imaginary space is projected outward in the form of distinctions suggested by the work itself. Here, too, space is work-specific space, visible so long as the focus is on the work and disappearing from view when the focus shifts to surrounding objects—to the weeds in the castle garden.

The boundary cannot be perceived,[106] unless we know whether it directs our attention inward or outward. The boundary itself can be shaped as a form—as a portal, an ornament, or a movement on the sculpture's surface, as the gorgeous frame of a painting or merely as a well-chosen one. Once we recognize this, however, we no longer see the boundary as boundary but observe differences between forms, which—one thing leading to another—we attribute to the work itself.

Classical aesthetics, which presupposed a creative or receptive subject in all of this, had no difficulties with these problems. Everything could be explained with reference to the enigmatic nature of the subject. The strict distinction between perception and communication, which dissolves the subject, changes this situation. Now it becomes important that, and in what ways, the boundaries of the individual work of art mark the structural coupling between perception and communication. Boundaries, however, cannot be observed in their capacity as structural couplings, since neither the perceiving consciousness nor communication can explode their operative closure and reach beyond their own systems into the environment.

Giving up the notion of the subject requires reconstructing the object, which loses its opposite.[107] If one starts out from the counterconcept of the "unmarked space," objects appear as repeated indications, which, rather than having a *specific* opposite, are demarcated against "everything else." Objects are forms whose other side remains undetermined. The unattainability of its other side accounts for the object's concreteness in the sense that determining its unity "as something" becomes impossible. Every analysis remains partial, depending on further specification of the other side—for example, with regard to color, magnitude, purpose, consistency.

George Herbert Mead (following Whitehead) assigned a function to identifiable and recognizable objects, whose primary purpose is to bind time. This function is needed because the reality of experience and actions consists in mere event sequences, that is, in an ongoing self-dissolution. Since the experience of others must be assumed to occur simultaneously if communication (Mead: interaction) is to take place, the reality of the other's operations remains in principle inaccessible; it can, however, be symbolized via the identification of objects.[108]

Michel Serres suggests that the stabilization of objects (identification, recognizability, and so on) is more likely to contribute to stabilizing social relationships than the famous social contract.[109] Via a different route, Heinz von Foerster arrives at the notion of objects as eigen-behaviors of recursive calculations.[110] Presumably, the objects that emerge from the recursive self-application of communication contribute more than any other kinds of norms and sanctions to supplying the social system with necessary redundancies. This may be even more true of objects that have been invented for the sake of this specific function, such as kings or soccer balls.[111] Such "quasi objects"[112] can be comprehended only in relation to this function. They assume a sufficient amount of variance, of recognizability in different situations, to keep up with changing social constellations. In contrast to concepts that are determined by specified antonyms, such quasi objects maintain their concreteness as objects—in the sense of excluding the unmarked space of all other events and conditions —throughout changing situations.

Works of art are quasi objects in this sense. They individualize themselves by excluding the sum total of everything else; not because they are construed as given but because their significance as objects implies a realm of social regulation. One must scrutinize works of art as intensely and with as close attention to the object as one does when watching kings and soccer balls; in this way—and in the more complex case where one observes other observers by focusing on the same object—the socially regulative reveals itself. The object relation thus helps differentiate recursive connections between observations—the court, the soccer game, the art scene—which subsequently construct their own guiding objects.

This is how the exclusion of the unmarked space is carried along—and forgotten. It might as well be left to religion.

X

Consciousness cannot communicate, communication cannot perceive —this is where we began. Correspondences between modes of operation as disparate as these must be formulated in a highly abstract manner. After all, we are dealing with two entirely different, operatively closed systems that do not interfere with each other. With concepts such as the self-referential event, distinction, form, and paradox, we have gained the necessary level of abstraction. This conceptual background, as we suggested earlier, permits conclusions concerning the specificity of art. Art makes perception available for communication, and it does so outside the standardized forms of a language (that, for its part, is perceptible). Art cannot overcome the separation between psychic and social systems. Both types of system remain operatively inaccessible to each other. *And this accounts for the significance of art.* Art integrates perception and communication without merging or confusing their respective operations. Integration means nothing more than that disparate systems operate simultaneously (are synchronized) and constrain one another's freedom. By participating in communication via perception, the psychic system might generate intensities of experience that remain incommunicable as such. In order to produce such experiences, it must be able to perceive differences between the forms created in the social system of art for the purpose of communication. Communication through art must present sensuously perceptible objects without being able to reproduce itself within individually encapsulated psychic systems. The need for structural coupling and the opportunity to establish such coupling impose rigorous demands upon the forms that specify and determine a work of art at the boundary between psychic and social systems.

A kind of quantum mechanical solution to the problem of integration is conceivable if one thinks of forms in terms of a distinction between two sides. One can always count on the other, operatively inaccessible system to operate in a binary manner, as a system that indicates one side of an actualized form and excludes (for the time being) the other. That much one can expect from communication with regard to perception, and from perception with regard to communication, *although the rich, reference-filled inner horizons of these systems remain mutually inaccessible.* Forms, in other words, ensure identity and difference at once: identity through their fixed outlines, and difference through the recursive system reference of the operations that actualize these outlines—in the form of a contrasting perception or intuition, or of a place where communication can continue by understanding and reconstructing its connective possibilities.

Since works of art are objects that bind time, such an integration can be

synchronized. It outlives the sheer eventfulness of system operations for as
long as a consciousness is occupied with the work of art. Since the focus
is on an object, this can happen recursively, that is, by recapitulating and
anticipating other perceptions of forms. Recursions of this type generate
so-called "aha" experiences, sudden flashes of insight that reveal the ordered nexus of the artwork. In this case, the coupling is unique in that it
does not require a merging of psychic and social systems. *Consciousness
remains entirely within itself.*

Our analysis has reached a point where it becomes apparent that, and
in what ways, communication through art tends toward system formation
and eventually differentiates a social system of art. In the following chapters, we shall deal both with the historicity of this inner-social process and
with its consequences. For the time being, our concern is to show, on the
basis of our analysis of artistic communication, that, and in what ways,
system formation is possible—much as the spectacular individual existence of artworks and the diffuse heterogeneity of observer perspectives
may speak against such an approach.

The problem of system formation is connectivity, the recursive reusability of events. Operations (conscious perceptions as well as communications) are nothing more than events. They cannot persist, nor can they be
altered. They emerge and vanish in the same instant, taking no more time
than is needed to fulfill the function of an element that cannot be decomposed any further. The art system has no reality except at the level of elemental events. It rests, one might say, on the ongoing dissolution of its elements, on the transitory nature of its communications, on an all-pervasive
entropy against which anything that persists must organize itself. Concepts
such as connectivity or recursive reusability indicate this process, but they
do not explain it. They only show that the stability of a system based on
time-sensitive events must be a dynamic stability, a stability that depends
on the continual change of the system's resources.

We shall call this state of affairs an "autopoietic system." This means
that the elements of the system are produced within the network of the
system's elements, that is, through recursions. A communication cannot
occur as an isolated phenomenon, as a singular event brought about by a
combination of physical, chemical, living, and psychic causes. Nor can it
proceed through simple replication, merely by substituting disappearing
elements for one another. It is not enough—and it wouldn't work, anyway—to repeat what has been said (shown, perceived, or thought) once it

dies away. Something else, something new must follow, for the informational component of communication presupposes surprise and gets lost in repetition.[113] Consequently, as we should note in view of what follows, art—once it is differentiated as an autopoietic system—must always present something new, something artistically new; otherwise its communication breaks down or turns into general social communication about artistic quality, prices, the private life of artists, their successes and failures. Operative closure, in other words, requires information in order to move from operation to operation. This is why artworks must convey information not only in themselves but also in relation to other works—by their novelty or by virtue of the fact that the viewer's observations are not determined unambiguously and can vary with each observation.[114] It is the ultimate reward for the complexity of formal arrangements that they provide an opportunity to discover something new, something that strikes us as more astonishing every time we look at them. Conversely, a work that lacks complexity is compelled to offer more conspicuous or, to put it bluntly, more scandalous forms of novelty. Another feature of autopoietic systems is that they are limited to one type of operation, which they must employ for the dual purpose of producing further operations and of creating structures that serve as programs for this production and allow the system to distinguish between system-immanent / system-external events. An autopoietic system reproduces both its reproduction and the conditions for its reproduction. The environment cannot participate in the reproduction of systems; the manner in which it affects the system's reproduction is never instructive, only destructive. Of course, structural couplings between system and environment are presupposed.[115] Without such couplings, the system could not exist. Works of arts need a material existence. Artists must breathe if communication through art is to be possible. But the effects of dissolving these structural couplings can only be obstructive or destructive. The persistence of such couplings does nothing more than prevent these effects from obstructing the continuation of autopoietic reproduction. The evolution of complex systems of this sort displays the complicated structure of a surplus production, of a structure that inhibits and de-inhibits possibilities.[116] We shall take up this point subsequently, speaking of medium and form.

Taken by itself, the concept of autopoiesis explains very little. It implies that any specification of structures (here, any determination of artistic form) is produced by the system itself; it cannot be imported from the outside. Moreover, the explanation of certain structural developments demands further analyses that must take into account structural couplings between autopoietic systems. One cannot derive the existence of worms, birds, and human beings from the singular invention of the autopoiesis of life. The autopoiesis of communication does not tell what kinds of social formations will emerge in the course of evolution. Nor can one infer from the autopoiesis of art which works will be created. The concept's lack of explanatory power stands in disproportional relation to its revolutionizing effect. (This insight could have avoided much controversy.) Instead of pursuing an ontology or a theory of essences, we follow the injunction: "Indicate the system from which you want to observe the world, draw a distinction, and distinguish yourself from what you observe while acknowledging the autological implication that the same holds when you observe yourself (rather than the external world)."

Needless to say, the autopoiesis of life and the autopoiesis of consciousness come about without art, although they may be influenced by art (the brain, for example, or the fingers of a piano player). Neither life nor consciousness depends on art in the sense of being unable to reproduce itself without art. The same is true for the communication system of society. We can certainly consider the structural consequences of a society without art. The regeneration of art is autopoietically necessary only for art itself. This is a matter of general agreement, even in aesthetic theories of quite different orientation.[117] Of course, artistic communication could never come about without society, without consciousness, without life or material. But in order to determine how the autopoiesis of art is possible, one must observe the art system and treat everything else as environment.

In the following, we adopt the communication system of art as our system reference. When using compact concepts such as "observer," "beholder," "artist," "artwork," and so forth, we are always referring to *condensations of the communication system of art*—to the sediments, so to speak, of an ongoing communication that moves from one condensation to the next by means of circumscribed recursions. Artists, artworks, and so on serve a structuring function within the autopoiesis of art. They bundle expectations. This is why they are less ephemeral than the basal events of artistic communication.[118] They make sure that communications—which operate as events—can reach back and forth while remaining focused on the same thing—on the same work, the same artist, or on the educational qualities of an informed observer. This is not to say that com-

munication reaches down to the physical substratum, to life or consciousness, or to the sum total of structural couplings that make such a construction of order possible. One can certainly speak of artists as human
beings or of artworks as material artifacts; indeed, one would need to thematize such matters if one's ambition were a complete description of the
object. Such a description, however, would have to deploy another system
reference or switch back and forth between different system references.

Against this theoretical background, the question of how art communicates is no longer trivial. The answer is obvious: by means of artworks.[119]
Artistic communication distinguishes itself both from communication that
relies exclusively on language and from indirect communications that are
either analogous to language or unable to secure the autopoiesis of communication, because the communicative intent of conveying information
can always be denied. Artistic communication, by contrast, employs perceptions that it prepares exclusively for its own use. In so doing, artistic
communication realizes specific forms of structural coupling between consciousness and society. It communicates by means of distinctions located
within the work or by means of forms, for the concept of form, in the
sense we use it here, implies a two-sided form, a distinction that can be distinguished. The work of art, then, is anything but an "end in itself." Nor
does it serve external purposes—for example, as ornament. It determines
forms which yield the dual insight that (1) distinctions make possible indications that enter into a play of nonarbitrary combination with other distinctions and indications, and that (2) along with this recognition, it becomes apparent that this order contains information that is meant to be
communicated and understood. Without the fixation of forms in the work
and without the opportunity of further actualizations by different observers, a communication of this kind would never occur. It is important
that communication can be preserved, just as language is preserved in writing. This does not mean that artistic communication aims at an identical
reproduction of the work (consensus and the like!). The mere fact that the
observational sequences that accompany the work's production necessarily
differ from those that occur in the perception of the finished work ensures
that there can never be a genuine agreement between the two—and yet
communication does take place! The artwork makes sure that the observation of observations—a second-order observation—continues, on the side
of the producer as well as on the side of the observer of art.

Until now we have focused on how a work of art mediates communication. An isolated work of art, however, is not yet a communication *system* of art. We therefore need to ask how and what the individual artwork contributes to the social system of art.[120] The question we raised in conjunction with the basal elements of artistic communication thus poses itself again: How do we get beyond the compact communication condensed in the individual artwork? And how are individual works of art possible within the reproductive network of art? To be sure, the artwork, in contrast to a communicative event negatable in the moment of its occurrence, is not a basal element of the system; nevertheless, it only comes into being by virtue of recursive networking with other works of art, with widely distributed verbal communications about art, with technically reproducible copies, exhibitions, museums, theaters, buildings, and so forth. This appears to be beyond dispute. A work of art without other works is as impossible as an isolated communication without further communications. The same holds for different types and genres of art—for sonatas and sonnets, for statues and still lifes, for novellas as much as for comedies and tragedies.[121]

Works of art, broadly speaking, lead the autopoiesis of art in two directions and, in so doing, expand and secure its continuation. On the one hand, one can learn from works of art how to observe and subsequently reintegrate what one has learned into the work's form. One can realize new variants of certain ideas—perhaps in better, more convincing ways and with less of an investment—or one can derive suggestions for new beginnings from works that are exhausted. An observer might then confront the task of understanding all of this as being communicated along with the artwork—Manet's black, for example, as a color. On the other hand, these and other issues can become a topic for art-related conversation and writing. One turns to the medium of language while retaining art and its works as a topic. It is well known that the romantics celebrated art criticism as the perfection of art, as the production of its history, even as its "medium of reflection" (Benjamin). Whatever one might think of this today, the fact that people write and speak about art contributes significantly to the stabilization and destabilization of its autopoiesis up to the remarkable point where the search for a concept of art and the probing of its limits begins to influence the avant-garde and their exploration of forms at the level of the artworks themselves.

§ 2 Observation of the First and of the Second Order

I

The activity of observing establishes a distinction in a space that re-mains unmarked, the space from which the observer executes the distinc-tion. The observer must employ a distinction in order to generate the dif-ference between unmarked and marked space, and between himself and what he indicates. The whole point of this distinction (its intention) is to mark something as distinct from something else. At the same time, the observer—in drawing a distinction—makes himself visible to others. He betrays his presence—even if a further distinction is required to distin-guish him.[1] Once a distinction is established as a form, it points back to the observer, thus generating both the form's self-reference and its hetero-reference. The self-referential closure of the form includes the question of the observer as the excluded third.

The forms of possible distinctions are innumerable. But when several observers select a certain distinction, their operations are attuned to one another. What they have in common is generated outside of the form in a manner that remains unspecified. (To call this shared space "consensus" as opposed to "dissent" would require another observer who employs just this distinction.) This common ground entails the prospect of a formal calculus that leads all participating observers to the same result. We can therefore say that the form is the observer. This notion presupposes the reduplication of the unobservable world in the imaginary space of math-ematical forms. The same procedure—which makes communication pos-sible by creating a shared space—is used in art. Here, too, there is no pressure to select a certain distinction and to transform the unobservable world into an imaginary space—now a space of art—by cutting up the world. But when this selection occurs by means of certain artistically determined forms, then the observers employing these forms all observe in the same vein. This is how the artist manages to bind the free-floating awareness of other observers.[2] As we indicated earlier,[3] a distinct "object" is thus secured as an "eigenvalue" of communication. Judgments might still diverge on the basis of different standards of artistic quality, but to deal with such differences one must focus on observing how different observers observe—which is certainly possible.

Each observation immediately observes something that can be distinguished—objects or events, movements or signs.[4] We cannot get rid of the immediately given world, although the philosopher may doubt whether it exists at all or whether it exists as it appears and may express his doubt by withholding judgment (Husserl's *epochē*). Nor can we completely divorce ourselves from the intuitively apprehended world, not even in our imagination; we can only simulate what we might observe under different circumstances. When reading novels, we need to have the text in front of our eyes, even though our "inner eye" can furnish the text with lively details and recall its fictional world once the text is no longer at hand. We know perfectly well that no real world corresponds to our imagination, just as we "know away," so to speak, an optical illusion while seeing it nonetheless. Yet, we still follow an experience that accepts the world just the way it could be. Nothing can change that.

We remind the reader of this basic situation in order to introduce the—not quite simple—distinction between first- and second-order observation. Every observation—this holds for second-order observations as well—uses a distinction to mark one side (but not the other). No procedure can get around that. Even negations presuppose the prior distinction and indication of what one wants to negate.[5] One cannot start from an immediately given nondetermination—an unmarked space, a primordial entropy or chaos, an empty canvas or a white sheet of paper—without distinguishing this state from what is being done to it. Even when moving toward fictionality, away from the real world in which we exist, we need this distinction in order to indicate the "whence?" and "where?" This is how we construct reality as reality.

We shall call observations of observations *second-order observations*. Considered as an operation, the second-order observation is also a first-order observation. It observes something that can be distinguished as observation. Accordingly, there must be *structural couplings* between first- and second-order observations, which guarantee that something is observed at all in the mode of second-order observation. As usual, there are two sides to the concept of structural coupling: the second-order observer is *more irritable* as a result of his first-order observations (of textual features, for example, or of the characteristics of another observer's observations), while at the same time, he is equipped with a *higher degree of indifference* against all other conceivable influences.

As first-order observer, the second-order observer remains anchored in the world (and, accordingly, observable). And he sees only what he can distinguish. If he wants to observe from a second-order perspective, then he must be able to distinguish observations from other things (objects, for example).

According to a certain tradition, which, however, we shall not be bound by here, one might say that he must be able to distinguish subjects from objects. But this linguistic usage itself needs explanation and unduly restricts the topics we seek to approach. Hence our attempt to use a more formal terminology and to speak of second-order observations only in terms of observations that observe observations. In so doing, we remain at the level of operations. Whether we are dealing with an observation of other observers is a different question. It certainly facilitates the observation of observations when we can hold on to an observer to whom we can attribute these observations. In the case of art, however, this is true only with certain reservations. We may decide to observe a work of art solely in view of its intrinsic observations without observing the artist; it is enough to know or to recognize that we are dealing with an artificial, rather than a natural, object.

The proposition that a second-order observer is always also a first-order observer rephrases the familiar insight that the world cannot be observed from the outside. There is no "extramundane subject." Whoever employs this figure of thought or wonders how a transcendental subject becomes an empirical subject[6] is thinking in the long shadow of theology or is led astray by a philosophical theory. As we know from operative epistemology—which is widely accepted today—the activity of observing occurs in the world and can be observed in turn. It presupposes the drawing of a boundary across which the observer can observe something (or himself as an other), and it accounts for the incompleteness of observations by virtue of the fact that the act of observing, along with the difference of the observation that constitutes it, escapes observation. Observation therefore relies on a blind spot that enables it to see something (but not everything). A world equipped to observe itself withdraws into unobservability.[7] Or, to use a more traditional formulation, the unobservability of the observing operation is the transcendental condition of its possibility. The condition of possibility for observation is not a subject (let alone a subject endowed with reason), but rather a paradox that condemns to failure those who want the world to be transparent. Many an artist may have dreamed of making it in another world, while being bound to reproduce the unobservability of this one.

In order to observe the world as an object, one would have to *indicate* the world as distinguished from something else; one would have to presuppose a metaworld containing the world and its other. What functions as world in each case resists observation—as does the observing operation. The retreat into unobservability leaves nothing behind in the world; it erases, to speak with Jacques Derrida, its own traces. At best metaphysics (or theology? or the rhetorical theory of how to use rhetorical forms?[8] or a second-order observer?) may just barely catch a glimpse of "the trace of the erasure of the trace."[9]

These considerations are meant to irritate philosophers. What matters to us is deriving foundations (which are no foundations) for an operative concept of observation, so that we can describe more accurately what is going on and what we have to expect when society encourages observers to observe observations or even demands that the conditions of social rationality be met at the level of second-order observation.

II

Once the conditions for second-order observation are established, sociocultural evolution embarks on a detour that—like the detour of capital according to Böhm-Bawerk—proves to be extraordinarily productive. One restricts one's observation to observing other observers, which opens up possibilities (social psychologists would speak of "vicarious learning") that are unavailable when the world is observed directly and on the basis of the belief that it is as it appears. Second-order observing maintains a distance from the world until it dismisses the world as unity (wholeness, totality) altogether, henceforth relying entirely on the "eigenvalues" that emerge from the dynamic-recursive process of ongoing observations of observations.

This is both true in general terms and a typical trend of all modern functional systems (and of their self-reflection as well). If one looks for further specifications within the larger framework of an operative episte-mology, one discovers a variety of starting points. This is due partly to the multitude of participating disciplines or research fields, partly to the con-cept of observation itself, which refers to a number of quite disparate em-pirical facts. The operative execution of observations can be described in physical, biological, or sociological terms, whereby in each case potentially disruptive realities come into view as well. As a physicist and mathemati-cian, Heinz von Foerster employs the notion of computing a reality. Humberto Maturana proceeds from a very general, biologically grounded concept of cognition. George Spencer Brown develops a formal calculus that builds on the concept of "indication." Indication presupposes a dis-tinction, but it can use only one side of this distinction as the starting point of further operations. In semiotics, one would describe the basal op-eration in terms of a sign use that makes the difference between signifier (*signifiant*) and signified (*signifié*) available for operations (primarily, but not only, linguistic ones). Gotthard Günther investigates logical structures that can describe in adequately complex terms what happens when a sub-ject observes another subject, not as an object but as another subject, that is, as an observer. For others, the problem is how to attribute observations to observers, and they tend to think of psychological processes that are in-vestigated in attribution research. In the social sciences, too, one typically thinks of psychological manifestations when methodological problems arise. This is because an observer who is doing research is observed in turn and can absorb only what is presented to him as a consequence of the ob-servation of his being observed. Cybernetics, which must be mentioned here, concerns itself with operations of regulation and control, whatever the apparatus might be that carries out these operations.[10]

All of these starting points remain capable of dialogue and mutually ac-cessible—although mainly because of an extreme formalization of the con-cept of observation, which is beginning to announce itself in the literature without yet assuming the form of an integrated interdisciplinary theory. By formalization, we mean the coinage of an operative concept with em-pirical reference, which leaves open at what level of reality a given opera-tion occurs and what kinds of realities must be presumed in order to guarantee that the operation proceeds smoothly and without destructive interference from the outside.

For our purposes, it suffices to define observation with Spencer Brown as the use of a distinction for the purpose of indicating one side and not the other. We disregard any reference, in the concept of observation, to the material conditions that make observation possible.[11] Considering such conditions would explode the concept's unity and lead us into quite disparate fields of reality. Moreover, the concept embraces—this distinguishes it from standard usage—experience and action,[12] both of which depend on distinguishing and indication (as opposed to mere behavior). As noted earlier, this conceptual disposition helps describe how artists and observers participate in communication. We further assume that observation does not merely happen (in the manner in which an avalanche tears down one portion of a snow field and leaves the other half intact); if it did, any operation that yields an effect would be an observation. Instead, the concept entails that the other side of the distinction is co-presented along with it, so that the indication of one side is decoded by the system as information according to the general pattern of "this-and-not-something-else," "this-and-not-that." That is to say, one can also observe operations that are not observations.[13] In the act of observing (as distinguished from simply operating), distinction and indication are executed *simultaneously* (rather than consecutively, that is, in the sense that a distinction is selected first and then followed by an indication). The observing operation—this is its distinctive feature—realizes the unity of the distinction between distinction and indication. The motivation for this unity resides in observation itself; it does not depend on the prior existence of corresponding objects in a world that exists separately from this unity. Finally, we shall speak of observations only when the indication of one side of a distinction is motivated by recursive interconnections—partly by prior observations, hence memory, and partly through connectivity, that is, by anticipating what one can do with the distinction, where one can go with it, what kinds of possibilities the observation discloses or forecloses. In this sense, observation is always the operation of an observing system (even if this fact remains unobserved). Observation cannot happen as a singular event; more precisely, when singular events occur, they cannot be observed as observations.

We shall apply this concept consistently whenever its features are given (to an observer), especially when dealing with second-order observation. Perhaps (we leave the question open) a capacity for observation can be attributed even to chemical processes in living systems, if the necessary "simultaneity" of distinction and indication can be represented in chemical terms. At the level of nervous systems or immune systems, one might consider the capacity for discrimination—which such systems undoubtedly possess—to be a form of observation. Animals certainly observe, and the same is true for systems of human consciousness that process meaning psychologically. One may equally well attribute a capacity for observation to communication systems on the grounds that such systems, in using language, simultaneously handle distinctions and indications. This raises the question as to whether the shaping of material by an artist's hand represents an instance of observation, in that it creates a difference not just for its own sake but in view of a two-sided form, in view of a difference that produces meaning. We shall return to this question below.

What interests us here are the consequences for the notion of second-order observation. We shall speak of second-order observation when two observations are coupled in such a way that both fully realize the features of first-order observation while the second-order observer, in indicating his object, refers to an observer of the first order and, in so doing, distinguishes and indicates an observation as observation. This raises the following question: What needs to be observed from a first-order perspective so that second-order observation becomes possible and can, so to speak, unfold what first-order observation observes directly? Or, what tells us that the activity of observing and indication is going on somewhere? Does it suffice to say that an "observer" must be observed? Or should we prefer formulations that, rather than aiming at compact, self-organizing realities, speak of the materialities involved in the process of observation? Wouldn't this lure us onto dangerous ground in the vain attempt to distinguish matter from "Spirit"?

In the face of such thorny questions, we retreat to a constructivist starting point: an observation of the second order is present whenever the focus is on distinctions or, to use a more pointed formulation, when one's own activity of distinguishing and indicating refers to further distinctions and indications. To observe in the mode of second-order observation is to distinguish distinctions—however, not simply by placing distinctions side by side in the manner of "there are large and small objects, pleasant and unpleasant things, theologians and other academics" and so forth ad infinitum. Rather, what is observed as a distinction—a distinction that both distinguishes and observes—must be observed in operation so that the features we identified above as constitutive of the concept of observation come into view: the simultaneity of distinction and indication (keeping an eye on the other side) and their recursive networking with prior and subsequent observations, which, for their part, must also be distinguishing indications.

First-order observation is an indication of something in opposition to everything that is not indicated. In this kind of observation, the distinction between distinction and indication is not thematized. The gaze remains fixed on the object. The observer and his observing activity remain unobserved. With the occurrence of second-order observation, the situation changes—whether or not the observer is the same. Now the observation indicates that the observation occurs as observation, that it must use a distinction, and perhaps even what kind of distinction it must use. The second-order observer encounters the distinction between distinction and indication. He treats the instrument of observation as the form of observation, which implies that there might be other forms (and observers). The form of observation (there is no need to elaborate this point) also implies a reentry of the form into the form, since the distinction employed in the observation presupposes a distinction between distinction and indication. This distinction is always already copied into itself as a distinction that distinguishes itself from the indication that it makes possible.[14] The second-order observer does not need to be as complex as to be able to observe this reentry, but he presupposes it as implied in the form he observes as the form of an observation.

The unobservability of first-order observation thus becomes observable in an observation of the second order—on the condition that the second-order observer, considered as first-order observer, can now observe neither his own observing nor himself as observer. A third-order observer can point this out and draw the autological conclusion that all this applies to himself as well. Focusing one's observation on the means of observation—on artistic means (such as the twelve-tone technique)—excludes a total view of the world. No further reflection can get around that. Nor is there a dialectical *Aufhebung* that would elevate the blindness of distinguishing into a form of "Spirit" for which the world, including Spirit, becomes fully transparent. Rather, second- and third-order observations explicate the world's unobservability as an unmarked space carried along in all observations. Transparency is paid for with opacity, and this is what ensures the (autopoietic) continuation of the operations, the displacement, the *différance* (Derrida) of the difference between what is observed and what remains unobserved.

Second-order observation observes only *how* others observe. Once the question "How?" is posed, a characteristic difference between first- and second-order observations comes into view. The first-order observer concentrates on what he observes, experiences, and acts out within a horizon of relatively sparse information. He may be puzzled by some things and look for explanations when his expectations go unfulfilled; this, however, is the exception rather than the rule and happens in accordance with his capacity to process information. The first-order observer lives in a world that seems both probable and true [*wahr-scheinlich*]. By contrast, the second-order observer notices the improbability [*Unwahrscheinlichkeit*] of first-order observation. A movement of the hand, a sentence spoken— every such act is extremely improbable when considered as a selection among all other possibilities. But since this improbability characterizes *every* operation, it is also quite normal and unproblematic. It remains latent in the operation itself, even the operation of first-order observing. There is no need to thematize this improbability, nor can it be thematized. One could never begin if one were to consider all possible beginnings. This holds for second-order observation as well, to the extent that it is an operation. It cannot think through all possible ways of observing an observer before settling on observing a certain observer. Second-order observation recognizes (and experiences in observing itself) that the total information contained in the world cannot be concentrated in one point—unless one assumes a God. But as second-order observation, it can at least thematize the improbability of first-order observation (including its own). It can comprehend more extended realms of selectivity and identify contingencies where the first-order observer believes he is following a necessary path or is acting entirely naturally.[15] Simplifying matters somewhat, one might say that only the second-order observer notices that the first-order observer "reduces complexity"; it makes no sense to ask a first-order observer to reduce complexity. Or to put it in yet another way, the world of possibility is an invention of the second-order observer which, for the first-order observer, remains necessarily latent.

From the viewpoint of an observer whose reality is guaranteed by his own observations, there are two ways of engaging in second-order observation: self-observation and hetero-observation. Such abstract terminology has certain advantages. It permits both types of observation to be considered as parallel possibilities, as two instances of the same principle, and it calls attention to the necessity of a system reference for the self/hetero distinction. Above all, we begin to sense that there may be a link between the possibility for self-observation, on the one hand, and of second-order observation of others, on the other. If one can see others as observers, then why not oneself, too?

But can observation turn reflexive in this manner? How does such a hyper-formation emerge on top of first-order observation?

It is important to preserve our astonishment in view of this phenomenon, because our goal is to combine second-order observation with a theory of modern society which claims that second-order observation is at once a highly improbable evolutionary fact and an entirely normal occurrence.

III

There is nothing extraordinary in the assertion that the functional systems of modern society should establish themselves at the level of second-order observation. Take the system of science [*Wissenschaft*], for example. Recent investigations of scientific laboratories amply demonstrate that first-order observation plays a role in science and that the behavior of scientists can hardly be explained in terms of a "striving for Truth."[16] Contrary to what such research suggests, however, scientific practice does not preclude second-order observation. The instrument that mediates between first- and second-order observation and ensures their structural coupling is the publication of articles. From a first-order perspective, these are produced and read as texts, but they acquire genuine scientific significance by providing a window onto the observational mode of other scientists.[17]

Publishing a text (including summarizing the current state of research and quoting other publications) becomes the basis of scientific production, the operation of the autopoiesis of science.[18] The semantics of the theory of science, the code true/untrue along with its own supplementary semantics, the special programs containing theoretical and methodological directives that rule over the code values true/untrue—all of these become meaningful only in relation to texts that are published for the sake of communication. This is how publications secure the continuity of the differentiated system of science at the level of second-order observation.

We can identify similar features in the economic system. Assisted by the market, the economy, too, has shifted toward second-order observation.[19]

This shift requires a focus on a medium of first-order observation. One observes payments in the context of transactions: How much for what? This requires and makes possible variable prices that indicate someone's readiness to sell or buy.[20] The transactions assume (and simultaneously bring about) a temporary stability of prices. This makes second-order observation possible. A player in the market watches others (and himself), asking whether they will buy/sell at a certain price; whether or not it may be worthwhile to produce and invest in view of expectations concerning future market prices. At the same time, the markets for products, raw materials, labor, and money generate situations at the level of second-order observation that are subject to change and need to be monitored constantly. Without market-dependent prices, there can be no second-order observation and thus (as socialist state planning learned the hard way) no specific economic rationality. This is why economic theory must distinguish values and prices, depending on whether it observes an observer of the first or of the second order. And it makes sense to transform values (ecological harmlessness, for example) into prices—not to make sure that such values are implemented, but for the sake of observing how an observation of observations establishes itself under these structural conditions.

Our third example is taken from the political system. Not surprisingly, the same structure is realized in this system as well, albeit in an entirely different context. Politics employs power to enable collectively binding decisions. At the level where power is exercised, this can be observed directly in institutions specifically designed for this purpose. Classical political theory insisted that the ruler ought not to be indifferent to public opinion; speaking with Machiavelli, he must have his fortress in the hearts of his people.[21] In Hegel's dialectic of master and slave, on the other hand,[22] the slaves must observe (whether and) how the master observes them, whereas the master is master only to the extent that he can be content with first-order observation—to the master, the slaves are merely objects who carry out orders or fail to do so.[23] According to the political concept of government, an asymmetry must be preserved wherever second-order observation occurs—whether it looks down from above or up from below.

In the wake of the so-called democratization of politics and its dependence on the media of public opinion, this situation has changed. Today, hierarchy plays a role only at the organizational level. Those participating in politics—politicians and voters alike—observe one another in the mirror of public opinion, and behavior is "political" when participants react to how they are being observed. The level of first-order observation is guaranteed by the continuous reports of the mass media. Initially, the effects of such media are information and entertainment. Second-order observation occurs via the inferences one can draw about oneself or others, if one assumes that those who wish to participate politically encounter one another in the judgment of public opinion, *and that this is sufficient.* Public opinion is not an aggregate of psychic system-states, but rather a product of a specific communication that provides the starting point for further communications.[24]

We could supply further examples. In the system of religion God has always been conceived as an observer, and this is why observing this observer became a problem that surfaced in the Devil's fate or the theologian's own, and for some courageous theologians even in the very notion of God. Under the logic of intimacy, modern families (for which there was no concept in the Old World) are hot cells of observation, burdened with a pressure to observe that makes spontaneous behavior difficult and generates either communication routines or pathologies.[25] In today's legal system, the relationship between legislation and jurisdiction is considered in terms of mutual observation, and in the so-called realistic legal doctrine, the law boils down to a mechanism for predicting the decisions of judges (instead of securing the implementation of norms that are recognized as correct). These analyses, evoked for the sake of comparison, cannot be pursued any further here. Our question is, rather, whether art—at least since it differentiated itself as the fine arts against the *artes* in general—unfolds its own dynamic at the level of second-order observation and distinguishes itself at this level as a social system from other social systems.

In order to pursue this question, we return to the concept of form introduced above, a concept that indicates a two-sided distinction.[26] One must get used to this concept. Being two-sided, a form presupposes the simultaneous presence of both sides. One side, taken by itself, is not a side. A form without another side dissolves into the unmarked state; hence it cannot be observed. Yet, the two sides are not equivalent. The "mark" indicates this. That asymmetry is difficult to interpret, particularly if one wants to give it a very general meaning. But this much is clear: only one side of a distinction can be indicated at any given time; indicating both sides at once dissolves the distinction. We assume further that an operative system must execute subsequent operations always on its marked side, and that this is the meaning of the indication. We leave the question open whether a system can cross the form's boundary, whether, in other words, it is capable of operating in the form of negation and can continue working on the other side. It goes without saying that no system can operatively step out of itself and continue operating in the environment. There are, however, form-coded systems—systems capable of employing a code of binary distinctions, such as true/untrue, having / not having property, being / not being an official, in ways that permit them to operate on both sides of the distinction without leaving the system. Someone who doesn't own a certain thing can buy it (only such a person), just as one cannot sell a thing unless one owns it. In the legal system, this rule—once it is codified in the institution of the contract—distinguishes between right and wrong depending on whether the rule is followed or not. This enables the legal system to operate legally (!) by declaring that something is legal or against the law.

The theory of art has always been concerned with form. This is an obvious starting point. The identity of the word *form* should not deceive us, however, when the concept undergoes a fundamental change. We are not referring to the controversial distinction between form and content;[27] hence, it is not our goal to overcome this distinction—whether in radically subjectivist terms or in a reductionist attempt at "pure forms." Nor are we thinking of the concept of the symbol. These efforts merely sought to eliminate the distinction as distinction. The opposition against the form/content distinction was meant to emphasize the autonomy of art and to reject any preestablished models, anything that could not be assimilated into art. In this regard, the discussion belongs to a history of the semantics that accompanies modern art. But why return to a root distinction that was never fully clarified? In view of what follows, we suggest that the distinction between form and content was meant to articulate the distinction between self-reference and hetero-reference. But we have not yet reached the point where this insight can be put to work.

Instead, we shall exploit the formal similarity, indeed coincidence, between the concepts of form, distinction, and observation. The observer uses a distinction to indicate what he observes. This happens when it happens. But if one wants to observe whether and how this happens, employing a distinction is not enough—one must also indicate the distinction. The concept of form serves this purpose. We call the instrument of observation—the distinction—a form, for example, in view of the possibility that there may be other forms that yield different observations.

Whoever observes forms observes other observers in the rigorous sense that he is not interested in the materiality, the motives, expectations, or utterances of these observers, but strictly and exclusively in their use of distinctions.

Once again, we encounter the extreme improbability of a second-order observation that has become established, institutionally supported, and habitual. At the same time, however, an analysis of other functional systems suggests that this is not an obstacle to evolution. (The noises we make in order to speak intelligibly are every bit as improbable in the world of noises, and yet we produce them routinely and without much effort.) Moreover, our previous investigations have shown that an observation of the second order—one that utilizes forms—does not exclude first-order observation. On the contrary, it presupposes and builds on the latter. Without seeing or hearing, without reading or drawing intuitions from works of art, no second-order observation could get off the ground. We need to know where to find artworks and artists, which buildings to identify as art, and which texts make artistic claims. Second-order observation, by contrast, requires a rigorous selection of its material regarding the "how" of first-order observation; it must penetrate to the observational forms that are fixated in these observations. Second-order observation transforms everything, including what it observes at the level of first-order observation. Second-order observation affects the modality of whatever appears to be given and endows it with the form of contingency, the possibility for being different.[28] And, for the sake of including the excluded, it must constitute a world that, for its part, remains unobservable.

Accordingly, the question is how to observe, from a first-order perspective, works of art as objects in such a way as to gain access to an observation of observers. We already know the answer: by paying attention to forms.

IV

The invitation to observe in such an unusual manner comes from the works of art themselves. (If in doubt, try it.) The *man-made* nature of the work, its artificiality, offers a first clue. In the course of a long history, this recognizable signal has become ever more prominent, gradually developing the specialized function of orchestrating second-order observations.

The necessity of affecting the modality of utterances by mentioning the observer provides a starting point. It is the only way of signaling that the

entire communication is to be carried out at the level of second-order observations. In early modern times, works began to be signed, thereby introducing the figure of the author. This subsequently gave rise to anonymous authors or "unknown masters." Mentioning the observer is not just
an option but a necessary signal by which one communicates that the ad-
dressee of the communication is being engaged as a second-order observer.

This function, however, remains latent. As is always the case in communicative systems, the topics of communication must be distinguished
from their function in guiding further communication and, ultimately, in
maintaining the system's autopoiesis. At the thematic level, artificiality is
introduced as characteristic of the concept of art and established as distinct
from nature. In explaining a work of art, one frequently draws on the
artist's *intention* in producing the work, but this is trivial, a tautological
explanation, because the intent must be feigned, while its psychological
correlates remain inaccessible.[29] Since the production of the artwork can
only be comprehended as intentional, this raises the issue of how to dissolve the tautological construct of productive intent and unfold this tautology in ways that yield intelligible representations. The perception or
communication of the work's artificiality provokes the question of purpose. The work of art does not emerge in the course of being perceived, it
deliberately calls attention to itself. It displays something unexpected,
something inexplicable, or, as it is often put, something new.[30] At the same
time, the work's artificiality signals that it cannot be the result of chance.
The question remains: "What's the point?"

With this question in mind, one initially sought to establish a connection to what is already known. To this desire corresponded, at the level of
reflection, the (Aristotelian) premise of a natural teleology of nature and
human action. Art could serve the purpose of glorifying both otherworldly
and secular powers, which starting in the seventeenth century were characterized with increasingly negative connotations as "pompous." Art symbolized what was otherwise invisible. Or it served as an illustrated Bible to
educate illiterate subjects. Another way of circumventing the dangers of
arbitrariness and randomness was by committing art to imitating nature
and by restricting one's astonishment to the skill capable of creating a resemblance between the two. Can art avoid such models? Can it forgo an
external relation to meaning and appear, as it was phrased around 1800, as
an "end in itself"? If so, then how?

Starting in the nineteenth century, connoisseurs and, above all, competent critics increasingly paid attention to the means by which a work elicits certain effects rather than to subject matter as such. This tendency announced itself as early as antiquity in the concept of the still life—which presented objects that were considered unworthy by the ancient imagination and that could acquire meaning only by presenting the art of presentation itself. With the expansion of the domain of the still life in Italian and Dutch painting, the same idea was suggested by the blatant discrepancy between the banality of the subject matter and its artful presentation.[31] But what is meant by the word *means* when there is no purpose or when a purpose is evident solely in the empty formula of an "end in itself"?

The formula "disinterested pleasure" is equally problematic. Apparently it was supposed to exclude certain interests in the use of art. It promises the possibility for demarcating phenomena that can claim artistic value. But the formula fails to clarify just how one goes about observing without interests, or how an observer can make sure that he or any other is in a position to bracket interested perspectives while retaining the motivation to deal with art. Is there perhaps a special interest in being disinterested, and can we assume that such an interest also motivates the artist who produces the work, and who can neither preclude nor deny an interest in the interest of others?

The theory of second-order observation offers a more appropriate answer to these questions. It proposes general correlations between the functional differentiation of the social system, the differentiation of individual functional systems that exhibit the features of autopoietic reproduction and operative closure, and their self-organization at the level of second-order observation. These correlations are not specific to art but are of a general kind initiated by the structure of society. They are realized in the art system and imprint on this system the specific signature of modernity.

To create a work of art under these sociohistorical conditions amounts to creating specific forms for an observation of observations. This is the sole purpose for which the work is "produced." From this perspective, the artwork accomplishes the structural coupling between first- and second-order observations in the realm of art. As usual, structural coupling means that irritability is increased, canalized, specified, and rendered indifferent to everything else. The unique meaning of the forms embedded in the work of art—always two-sided forms!—becomes intelligible only when one takes into account that they are produced for the sake of observation. They fixate a certain manner of observation. The artist accomplishes this by clarifying—via his own observations of the emerging work—how he and others will observe the work. He does not need to anticipate every possibility, and he can try to push the limit of what can still be observed, deciphered, or perceived as form. But it is always assumed that the point is to observe observations, even if the effort is directed at producing unobservability, for then we would be dealing with an unobservability of the second order. The same holds for the observer. He can participate in art only when he engages himself as observer in the forms that have been created for his observation, that is, when he reconstructs the observational directives embedded in the work. Produced without apparent external purpose, the artwork immediately conveys that this is the task. Subsequently, the work takes control and defines the conditions of inclusion, and it does so by leaving open the possibility for discovering something that no one, not even the artist, has seen before.

In the language of the seventeenth and eighteenth centuries, one can call what is thereby accomplished *pleasure* [*Genuß*]. This notion rests on a complex conceptual environment whose history has never been fully clarified.[32] At any rate, the notion of pleasure emancipates itself from the cold opposition *uti/frui* toward a juxtaposition between work and pleasure under conditions that revalorize work and accordingly problematize pleasure. Work is externalization [*Entäußerung*] or expenditure, whereas pleasure is appropriation, now above all appropriation from within. The distinction no longer refers to a hierarchical world architecture or a social hierarchy. It replaces this schema by the distinction between the "outside" and the "inside." For the pleasurable consumption of art, it becomes important, indeed indispensable, that the work of art contains information. Or, in contemporary terms, only what is new can please.

The positive value of pleasure appears to reside in an *artful concentration of observational relationships*—whether in social interaction or in the consumption of art. In the seventeenth and early eighteenth centuries, morality and aesthetics were generally not yet fully differentiated—both were concerned with the production and pleasurable consumption of "beautiful appearance." But at least a concept close to experience had become available. It implied the social reflection of pleasure in the pleasure of others (and, simultaneously, the possibility for reflexively enjoying one's own pleasure). Rather than indicating the activation of a certain kind of emotive psychological faculty, the concept of pleasure signaled a heightened experience that results from a reciprocity of observation created precisely for that purpose. As a semantic indicator, the concept suggests that social interaction searches for its specific rationality in this domain and that the arts and literature both serve this function. So long as these two aspects were joined, it made sense to call the critical judgment of artworks *taste.* Once the nexus between art and sociability was lost and no longer served as an orientation for art, it was impossible to recapture a concept for the unity of a second-order observation guided by art. The reflection on the unity of the art system that followed the differentiation of an "aesthetics" had difficulties going beyond simply naming the diverging perspectives of artist and viewer, that is, beyond the mere complementarity of roles. Correspondingly, positional theories, following the model of "production versus reception aesthetics," entered into controversy. But the problem resides in the *operational unity* that allows for the reproduction of the system and the system boundaries of art.[33]

The concept of form yields a more precise formulation of the increasing demands placed upon artist and observer as a result of the recursivity of observation. To the extent that we are concerned with first-order observation, the concept of form must be applied twice, whereas at the level of second-order observation, both applications merge and condition one another.

A first-order observer must first identify a work of art as an object in contradistinction to all other objects or processes. He succeeds when he produces the work himself and observes it as a work of art in progress. For those who do not work but instead consume the work, the situation is different. For them, the identification of artworks as special objects (from the first-order observer's viewpoint) may present a problem, especially if they are asked, in addition, to distinguish between art and *kitsch* or between original and copy. The work of art can be marked as such; it can be recognized by its presence in the museum, in galleries, in studios, in the concert hall, in the theater, in publisher's announcements, or by the names of well-known artists. This, too, has become a considerable problem ever since artists such as Marcel Duchamp and John Cage have specialized in eradicating any sensuously perceptible difference between art and nonart (with the exception of their names!), in order to confront the observer with the question of how he goes about identifying a work of art as a work of art. The only possible answer is: by observing observations, by observing the disposition[34] of the artist, which calls attention to itself by dismissing all other distinctions as irrelevant.[35]

Once we identify an object as a work of art, we can observe it as such and use it as a topic of communication. For a second-order observer, this is not enough. He searches the work for clues to guide further observations, and only when these observations succeed will he be ready to identify the work as art. In order to do so, he must follow the forms embedded in the work. All of these are forms of difference; they fixate something on one side, which eliminates, or at least constrains, the arbitrariness of the other side. A second-order observer will notice that multiple distinctions work together in such a way that the other side of the distinction (for example, what remains of a canvas when a line is drawn) is treated as the side of another side. By retracing the corresponding decisions, he is able to reconstruct the composition and observe what the observer of his observations expects from him. The point is to recognize what kinds of choices are still available on the other side of a determined form and what degree of certainty is involved in their execution.[36] The observer's hope of ever seeing a "harmonious whole" along this path is illusory. As the futile attempts to explain this concept illustrate, "harmony" is an embarrassing formula.[37] The metaphor of the organism ("organic unity" according to Kant and Coleridge) has failed. A judgment of unity comes about only when, after working through the play of differences, after reconstructing the work's inner circularity, one distinguishes the work from something else (above all, of course, from other artworks).[38] Unity requires other distinctions, distinctions external to the work. But then everything depends on *how* one distinguishes the work as a work of art (and not just as an object) from other things. This calls for second-order observation, more specifically, for the reconstruction of the referential nexus of forms that are open toward one side. Undifferentiated unity, unity "as such," is encountered and lost in distinctions, and whether or not these distinctions "fit" can be experienced only by crossing the boundary of each one of the work's fixed distinctions. Disregarding this necessity leaves one with a disjointed collection of static details.[39] What is at stake, operatively speaking, in the production and observation of a work of art is always a temporal unity that is either no longer or not yet observed. In this sense, the artwork is the *result* of intrinsic form decisions and, at the same time, the *metaform* determined by these decisions, which, by virtue of its inner forms, can be distinguished from the unmarked space of everything else—the work as fully elaborated "object."

There are some distinctions whose other side is what remains when something is selected and indicated—for example, when we are speaking of a specifically marked object. Spencer Brown's calculus accounts for such a case. In our daily lives, however, an indication we use is more likely to constrain its other side as well. Suppose we ask ourselves, "Where did I put my keys?" This question turns the world into the totality of possible key locations marked by different probabilities.

What used to be called "nature," too, is constructed in such a way that it is altered by the interaction of different composites—just as the chemical combination of elements into molecules alters the electronics of the participating atoms, or living in communities changes the interior life of animals. Whatever can be described as an "emergent order" rests on the fact that the qualities of components require composition, and composition cannot come about without changes in the qualities of the components.[40] The same is true for semantic concepts. The meaning of nature changes once it is distinguished not from technology but from grace, and it shifts again when it is distinguished from civilization. Art counts on the mutability of concepts—and in this sense one can once again speak of an imitation of nature.

Every operative intervention into an emergent work of art alters far more than what the intervention indicates. Adding an accent calls for corrections in other places. These corrections are not automatic or determined in advance—they create complications because they occur in the context of distinctions that cannot be specified without generating a corresponding demand with regard to their other side. Operatively speaking, one intervention follows another. However, the consciousness that accompanies and controls the operation always perceives (no matter how incompletely and tentatively) both sides simultaneously—that is, it perceives the form. The operational mode is always concerned with unfolding a temporal paradox: it must either realize simultaneity sequentially or control a sequence of operations through an observation that exists only as an operation, that is, in the instantaneous simultaneity of the two sides of its distinction. Observing art amounts to observing an emergent order that evolves or has evolved like nature—albeit not as nature—but with different forms and under different conditions of connectivity. For the artist (as observer), observation unfolds the temporal paradox that the simultaneity of the distinguished and the consecutive nature of the operation occur simultaneously. For the beholder (as observer), observation unfolds the factual paradox of a unity that can be apprehended only as a multiplicity (which cannot / can be apprehended). Both observers coincide in the mode of second-order observation. Both are called upon to get down to work.

The possibility for creating the possibility of being observed enables the artist to separate himself from his work. *In himself, the artist cannot be observed (or can be only at the cost of intolerable simplifications).* If, despite this limitation, he manages to represent himself in his work—as an author who mentions himself, or as an actor, singer, or dancer concerned to display his talents—he copies himself into the work. This creates a problem of authenticity—the temporal problem that the artist can be observed repeatedly although he is always already another. Traditional rules banned the ostentatious presentation of the artist's talent in the work.[41] (This is why the signature was invented.) This might have been good advice. At any rate, the reentry of the creative operation into the work gives rise to the paradox that the authentic (that is, immediate) action is observed as inauthentic—both by the observer *and by the artist, who counts on this effect.*

Summarizing, we can say that the work of art presents itself to observation as a series of intertwined distinctions, whereby the other side of each of these distinctions demands further distinctions. The work becomes observable as a series of deferrals (*différance* in Derrida's sense) that objectify the perpetually deferred difference in the "unmarked space" of the world, thus rendering it unobservable as difference. And all this shows (to whom?) that a work of art emerges only on condition that the world's invisibility is respected.

V

What distinguishes the art system from other functional systems is that second-order observation occurs in the realm of perception. Objects or quasi objects are always at stake in art, whether we are dealing with real or imagined objects, with static objects or with sequences of events. To cover all of these distinctions, we shall speak of forms in terms of their object-like determination. The formal decisions embedded in objects permit us to observe observations by observing the same object.

This proposition has considerable consequences. It *liberates art, to a large extent, from the demands of consensus.* The sameness of the object substitutes for the conformity of opinion. Without losing contact with the artist's formal decisions, the beholder can arrive at judgments, valuations, or experiences that radically diverge from the artist's. One stays with the forms created by the artist while perceiving things other than what he intended to express. Likewise, when producing for other observers, the artist need not surrender to their gaze or become dependent on them. The artist knows that his decisions remain his own; he can go about his work authentically and leave it to the observer to form his own judgment.

In this way, judgment is released from the constraints of consensus, while its relation to the object is preserved. This is worth emphasizing because it flies in the face of widely held notions concerning the conditions of social communication. Once the old European idea of a natural correspondence between art and nature became obsolete, one began to count on consensus. This shift is evident in the social contract doctrines of the seventeenth and eighteenth centuries, and even more so in Enlightenment premises of a public circulation of ideas and rationally disciplined control of opinions.[42] The one-sided understanding of society as a kind of substantial consensus (of opinions) leads to complications that surface in certain aberrations in Enlightenment thematizations of art. On the one hand, the debate about good and bad taste failed to come up with the desired criteria. Instead, it drove home the point that all so-called objective criteria have the effect of social discrimination; that is to say, those who experience differently find themselves in bad company. On the other hand, the entire realm of art is degraded because it is contaminated with sensory experience and compromised by its dependence on inferior types of cognition. In a state of turmoil, society decides to search for consensus, generalizing as transcendental a prioris or as new mythologies to be expected from the future only those symbols capable of binding each and every subject. In the meantime, one puts up with ideologies.

Today the realization that communication is coordinated by objects rather than justifications is gaining ground.[43] Dissent in the realm of justifications is tolerable so long as adjustments mediated by objects are at work. This situation implies that bodies can be treated like phenomena, without understanding the biochemistry of their lives, the neurophysiology of their brain processes, or the conscious states actualized at any given moment.[44] Limited resources prevent society from overestimating its need for consensus and ensure that object orientation will have its proper place. This has at least one significant advantage. It releases further communication from its fixation on any given topic and leaves it to communication to decide whether or not opinions are at stake, and if so, how serious and binding they are meant to be.

All of this considerably affects our understanding of art as a form for second-order observations. Art permits a kind of playful relationship to questions of reasonable consensus or dissent. It avoids degrading or excluding those who think differently. And it does so in such a way that doubts about whether or not one communicates about the same thing never arise. This is not to say that art does not place high (and exclusive) demands on an observation that seeks to be adequate. The measure for adequacy is not a consensus determined by a "shared symbolic system" (Parsons), but resides instead in the question of whether the viewer can follow the directives for adequate observation embedded in the work's own formal decisions.

VI

Traditionally, the theory of art and literature did not describe the relationship between artist and observer (author and reader) in terms of an observational relation. Instead, it assumed a causal relation, an effectuation of effects. Accordingly, the artist was believed to be interested in eliciting a certain *impression* in the beholder, an endeavor at which he could be more or less successful. The modern critique of this theoretical constellation led to the discovery of the observer of art and, in literary theory, to the demand that the texts be understood from the perspective of the reader.[45] While this shift is a plausible reaction to the causal theory of art, it fails to provide a sufficiently adequate theory of art (of the artwork, the text). We must assume that the author of an artwork adapts to the beholder in the same way as an observer anticipates another observer, and that the artwork must not only mediate between diverging observational modes as they arise but also needs to generate such diverging perspectives to begin with. This is why the demise of the causal theory of art calls for a theory of second-order observation.

Many endeavors point in this direction. The widely popular "symbolism" in twentieth-century literature, for example, can be taken to imply that *every* interpretation, including the author's own, imposes limitations.[46] This may be a calculated effect aimed at the author's own incompetence. In a series of significant phenomenological investigations, Roman Ingarden has called attention to the "blanks" embedded in literary works. Such blanks both assume and require an independent "concretization" on the part of the reader.[47] An observer can perceive only schematically; he cannot simultaneously see the front and the back of the same object. But he can check his speculations against reality and find out if the rear of a red sphere is as round, smooth, and red, and so forth as its front. In art, this kind of reality check is not possible. The viewer needs to conjure up the necessary completion (and which one would that be?). The creator of the work or the author of the text can know that. But is he also in a position to control, direct, mislead (as in the mystery novel), deliberately obstruct, or confuse the observations generated by his work? Ingarden notes—without pursuing the question—that the author may have a stake in inviting the reader to a "grotesque dance of impossibilities,"[48] but then focuses only on the limits of what is aesthetically acceptable.

Umberto Eco's *Opera aperta*[49] takes a step further in this direction. Eco considers an intentional and deliberate need for supplementation built into the work itself. The observer is called upon to participate in the artistic process. The performers not only supplement the work but engage in its composition (a feature already present in the structure of the commedia dell'arte and its *lazzi* [jests]). Finally, the spectators step onto the stage, or the actors into the audience, to give the play a deliberately spontaneous twist. Literary works, too, increasingly expect the reader to engage on his own in the production of meaning (in a manner that differs from case to case). Eco's prime example is *Finnegan's Wake*. We still find the most daring experiments of this sort in literature or in works that require performance. But the visual arts follow closely with works whose meaning or even their status as artworks reveal themselves, if at all, only at a second look. And this seems to be just what the artist has in mind. He revels in saying farewell to the idea of a passive consumption of art and takes delight in the prospect that the beholder will have to do some work on his own.

Calculating this effect amounts to observing observers, which was unnecessary when observing an artwork simply meant supplementing indeterminacies. Today, this is no longer a matter of supplying accidentals but of cooperating at the level of second-order observation. And the observer too must know, must be able to recognize the choices conceded to him as well as the boundaries he cannot overstep without rejecting the work as a work of art.

We leave our presentation on so abstract a level because it must account for every artistic genre. We could supply concrete examples from painting or lyric poetry, from ballet or drama. For the time being, however, we only wish to show that, and in what ways, art participates in a specifically modern type of operation, how it constitutes itself at the level of second-order observation as an autopoietic, operatively closed subsystem of society that decides what does and what does not concern art.

VII

The time has come to explicate the nexus between "second-order observation" and "operative closure" with reference to our example, the functional system of art. To do so, we shall draw on the concept of communication.

As noted earlier, what is at stake in this system is not the mere fact that one can speak and write about art. Works of art, just like everything else, are potential topics for communication, but this does not qualify them as something out of the ordinary. Nor does it follow that the functional system of art can differentiate itself as a social system that consists entirely of communications. Rather, works of art themselves are the medium of communication, insofar as they contain directives that different observers follow more or less closely. They are *designed exclusively for that purpose*. Both the artists and their audiences participate in communication only as observers, and the abstract concept of observation, related to distinction and indication and encompassing action and experience, permits us to formulate what they have in common when they participate in communication. Following Gotthard Günther,[50] we presume that the distinction between action and experience resides in the application of the distinction between self-reference and hetero-reference, or, from the viewpoint of the system, in the distinction between system and environment. From the cognitive perspective of the observer, experience appears to be determined by the environment. Against this determination, one posits one's own distinctions—true/false, pleasure/pain, agreeable/disagreeable—as if one could thereby cancel its effects. If, on the other hand, we are dealing with participation through action, then the system determines the environment. The system establishes a difference, and assuming the unity of the will, this difference exists in the environment (which does not preclude judging this operation from a cognitive viewpoint as a success or failure). *Both* perspectives (which may appear in complex combinations), presuppose an observer who draws distinctions and can distinguish their locations.[51] In *both* cases, a distinction is posited against what would otherwise be experienced as determined in order to ensure the continuation of the system's autopoiesis and the perpetual oscillation between the perspective of cognition and the perspective of the will. Since both positions mark observer

standpoints, one might say that art observes itself from alternating perspectives. The forms that constitute the work's structure are initially fixated by an observer for other observers. Like texts, forms abstract from the
physical and mental aspects of whoever produces or observes them. Like
writing, they assume a material expression that overcomes the temporal
distance between subsequent observations. Today, we can find art forms
that deliberately focus on a singular event or are performed in front of a
random group of spectators—so as to reduce the work's social and temporal components to a minimum. But even if the performers staged the
work entirely for their own sake, it would still be an art that experiments
with its own boundaries, and it would still be communication addressed
to an audience, albeit an audience tending toward zero. To produce observability is to communicate order within a formal arrangement that
doesn't come about spontaneously. The harlequin may dance in the
dark—but his dance is still communication, a communication that sabo-
tages its own perfection only to convince itself that it owes its existence to
itself alone, not to the gaze of an observer. To top this triumph, one would
have to observe what others would observe if they were not excluded from
observation.

The other is always anticipated as observer. The audience, too, is bound
by communication. They attribute the work of art to an artist. They don't
confuse the work with nature. They are aware of themselves as (anonymous) addressees of a communication and take the artwork as a minimal
guarantee for the sameness of their experience. They assume that this is
intentional, that something was to be shown to them. And this suffices for
communication to realize itself in the observation of a difference between
information and utterance.[52]

Understanding system formation via communication requires excluding the material embodiment of artworks from the system. Bodies belong
to the system's environment—although they are connected to communication through structural couplings. What counts is their objecthood.[53]
The system knows only one operator: communication. Communication
is reproduced by communications and not by operations consisting of
marble, colors, dancing bodies, or sounds. One can speak of autopoietic,
operatively closed systems only when the system's elements are produced
and reproduced by the network of the system's elements and no prefabricated, heterogeneous parts are used within the system.[54] Like any other social system, the art system is closed on the operative basis of communica-

tion—otherwise it would not be a system but something randomly selected and "thrown together" by an observer. Materials of any kind are
merely resources that are used by communication according to its own
measure of meaning, even when they display their idiosyncratic materiality (for example, as raw materials). The social autonomy of the art system
rests on its ability to define and use resources in ways that differ from
those of society at large.[55]

Communication by means of art, like communication about art, was
customary long before the art system organized itself on the basis of communication. Several attempts were necessary to gain autonomy. The first
efforts to systematize second-order observation might conceivably be
traced to ancient Greece, where they were facilitated by writing, by a high
degree of diversity within structures and semantics, and by the privatiza-
tion of religion.[56] The role of the chorus in Greek drama highlights this
development. It would be difficult to account for the evolutionary emergence of autopoietic closure in art—or in any other domain—if there had
been no prior experience with suitable components of meaning, here
works of art. For autopoietic systems to emerge, the ground must be
ready. But the stratified societies of the Old World were far from realizing
a fully differentiated art system. Art had to please, and whom it should
please was no matter of indifference. Not until modernity—we can date
its beginning in the Renaissance—did the art system begin to set its own
standards for recruiting observers, and the heyday of the arts in the Middle Ages most likely facilitated this change. For an artist who worked in
the service of God, it was only a small step to present himself as directly
inspired by God. We will elaborate these issues in the following chapters.

VIII

Looking at a painting, listening to a piece of music, or simply identifying a work of art (as opposed to another object) from a first-order observer
position does not yet imply a capacity for judging the work. The naked
eye does not recognize artistic quality. But if this is true, how do we account for the possibility for qualitative judgment?

The standard answer to this question invokes the role of experience, education, or socialization in dealing with art. In the seventeenth and eighteenth centuries, the problem was solved via the idea of (cultivated) taste.
Taste, while not innate, can be acquired in the course of a class-specific so-

cialization and then judges intuitively. The notion of good/bad taste was a first attempt to introduce the recipient or consumer into the theory of art and to problematize, on this basis, the criteria according to which the fine arts ought to be judged. This gave rise to the trend (which did not yield results until the mid-eighteenth century) of subsuming all the arts under a unified concept. This solution may have worked at first, but it begged the question of how taste is acquired to begin with, and how one can recognize its lack when it is not yet fully developed. Staring at the work of art for a prolonged period of time is of no help in this matter. Rather, the observer must assume the presence of qualitative differences that can be mastered in principle, even if they are now beyond his reach. A temporal horizon of further observations is projected into the work— the possibility for observing with more precision, for using further distinctions, for dissolving identities in dissimilarities—in short, the possibility for learning. Since the future is unknown, the evidence for such prospects relies on observing observers; one must observe that, and in what ways, others arrive at cultivated judgments. This temporal dimension refers to the social dimension, not necessarily to the artist but to a generalized observational competence that can be activated in the en counter with art.

These considerations suggest that a differentiating awareness of quality emerges, along with a fully differentiated art system, at the level of second-order observation. (This can be verified historically.) Prior to the emergence of this system, art depended on catching the beholder's eye (no matter by what means). By the seventeenth century at the latest, works that all too deliberately called attention to themselves became suspect. It might be necessary to impress the crowd, but the connoisseur preferred simpler and less pompous means. According to French classicism, the artist had to avoid baroque overkill, strive for natural expression, and reduce the work to clear and essential forms. In the early eighteenth century, the upper classes were still expected to distinguish themselves by acquiring good judgment.[57] One still thought of the relationship between artist and admirer in terms of direct interaction, which meant that the artist had a right to be judged competently and critically. As the system evolved, the demands upon the experts kept growing. Professional art criticism turned into a business and became the target of criticism. The growing dissatisfaction with arrogant "connoisseurs" and experts reflected changes in the relationship between artist and audience, which was increasingly mediated

by the art market and generated a need for certain kinds of expert knowledge that were no longer considered as appurtenances of the privileged
classes.[58] Whether or not there were explicable qualitative criteria that
could be employed in the manner of cognitive rules became more and
more questionable.[59] But the ability to differentiate between qualities undoubtedly emerged and was subject to variation within the context of
second-order observation.

Once even the experts no longer provide security, the problem of criteria resurfaces in a more radical form. Since the seventeenth century, the
originality or authenticity of an artwork has generally been considered the
condition of its aesthetic value. But when impostors become experts, surpassing even the true experts, one can no longer trust one's trained eyes.
Nelson Goodman has raised the question of how to preserve authenticity
as a criterion for art when the experts (in our sense, *all* second-order observers) have failed and recourse to extra-aesthetic (for example, chemical)
criteria becomes inevitable.[60] His answer is not entirely satisfying, however. Goodman begins with the content of the criterion and then points
to the future: one cannot claim that one will never be in a position to distinguish the authentic work from a copy (no matter how perfect a copy).
In contrast, we draw again on the concept of second-order observation. If
it is true that there cannot be two authentic instances of the same object,
then one assumes that a criterion capable of distinguishing the two can be
found—even if one has no idea who will discover it and when. One pos-
tulates an unidentified observer, whom one would have to observe in order to arrive at an answer to the question. The problem does not pose itself unless art shifts to the mode of second-order self-observation.

The restoration of art belongs to the same context. If the aging of artworks, to the point of decay, is considered part of their authenticity, any
restoration (even if based on credible theories about the work's original
appearance) becomes problematic. Several potentially contradictory criteria are at work in such attempts, but one thing is certain: restoration becomes a problem that can no longer be disposed of once the primary form
of observation in art shifts to the level of second-order observation.

IX

In what follows, we will address a special problem that belongs to the
realm of second-order observation but displays different logical structures.

This problem concerns the observation of what other observers can *not* observe.[61] In operative terms, there is nothing extraordinary about this. Negative versions of, say, neurophysiological processes, thought, or communication are no different from the general form of such processes. Executing a negative version does not require a specialized brain, consciousness, or language. But to an observer, it makes a difference whether another observer affirms or negates a proposition. We are led into regions of improbable observations when second-order observation *deliberately* chooses a negative version and distinguishes itself from the observing observation *by this very negativity*; in other words, when it wants to observe what another observation does *not* observe, or, to radicalize the issue, when an observation specializes in observing what another observer *is incapable of observing*. In this case, it is not enough to observe observations as particular phenomena. Rather, the second-order observer must focus on the instruments of observation, must observe the distinctions used in the other's observations in order to determine what these distinctions, considered as conditions of possibility for observations, *exclude*. In this case, the other's mode of observation is observed as a unity, as a form that *enables* the observation of something by the *exclusion* of something else. What is excluded from observation is, first of all, the unity of the distinction that underlies the observation in the form of "this and nothing else." This is not merely a matter of positional advantages/disadvantages that could be altered by a certain shift of perspective or temporal progression. What is at stake here is rather the exclusion implied in the necessity of basing one's observation on a (any!) distinction.

The abstractness of these introductory remarks is meant to call attention to the extreme improbability of observational forms that focus on latencies. When thought was still based on the idea of perfecting one's nature, not being able to see was simply registered as an imperfection, as *stēresis*, or *corruptio*, as the loss of a basic faculty. After all, we always already find ourselves in the position of an observer and can take this fact for granted. Gradually, the negative version of habitually performed operations turns into a figure of reflection. Blindness—not seeing—becomes the condition of possibility for seeing (and replaces other transcendental categories).

One and a half centuries of "ideology critique" and a hundred years of "psychoanalysis" have failed to incorporate this possibility into our common epistemology or even to consider it as a potential expansion of that

epistemology.[62] The debate about truth claims in the "sociology of knowledge" shows that the ambition to do so ruptures the cosmos of truth in
ways that can no longer be bridged—neither by "Spirit" in the Hegelian
sense nor through the construction of "metalevels" common in logic and
linguistics.[63] Any attempt in this direction must rely on distinctions and
meet observational requirements that replicate the problem. This is why we
need to think of this form of latency observation (as we shall abbreviate it
here) in terms of a technique of distancing by a second-order observer that
explodes the unity of the world or displaces it into unobservability. The
question is: What kind of social order can afford and tolerate such a move?

Against this evolutionary theoretical background, we can see that society apparently used art to play with the possibility of second-order observation before art was adapted to the realms of religion and knowledge,
where it would have more serious consequences. The traditionally antago-
nistic relationship between art and philosophy can help us understand this
process. Philosophy is concerned with the nature and essence of things,
whereas art is content with appearances. So long as it remains focused on
imitation, there is no need for art to penetrate to the essence of things; it
can gain (from the philosopher's viewpoint, superficial) access to nature
simply by observing and replicating observations. Second-order observation is at first tested in the fictional realm, and only when this practice
yields sufficient evidence so that analogies to everyday experience and actions suggest themselves can one begin to dissolve the unity of the Great
Being, of the visible universe, of the cosmos resting securely in its forms,
and reduce this unity to relative conditions of observation. This has not
yet been done in an appropriately radical manner. Kant's version of transcendental theory still assumes that consciousness (that is, every single
consciousness) has access through reflection to the conditions of possibility for knowledge. Einstein's relativity theory still assumes the calculability
of observational differences that can be traced to differences in speed/
accelerations between observers. It takes a radical constructivism to dissolve these last residues of certainty. But how could one know that this is
a possible, indeed, an inevitable, condition of knowing the conditions of
possibility for knowledge?

In the realms of architecture and sculpture, the study of observational
perspective began as early as antiquity. Art objects were designed to elicit a
certain impression. Occasionally, forms required deformation for the sake
of a certain optical impression, that is, they had to deviate from nature.

The pathbreaking discovery, however, remained dependent upon individual objects.[64] In the early Renaissance, painting adopted second-order observation along with new requirements that demanded the integration of an aggregate of objects via a vanishing point or unified perspective without giving up the freedom of shaping individual objects.[65] The painter was now in a position to organize space (with the help of a mathematical grid) in such a way that the viewer got to see the world like God, as if from the outside. By reducing the canvas to a single space, he created an enormously intensified combination of variety and redundancy.[66]

The reconstruction of perspective captured an imperceptible condition of habitual seeing but did not yet position itself against the presupposed visibility of the world. One had always been able to see, even before the discovery of perspective. Perspective renders the observer visible, precisely at the point where he cannot see himself. But it assigns him a single, correct position—which makes observing him unnecessary. Other than that, the introduction of perspective remains restricted to the realm of painting, which necessitates the exclusion of many previously possible choices—such as the depiction of situations belonging to different temporal frames or of multiple appearances of a figure in one and the same painting. People began to wonder *how* they perceived the world, thus questioning perception in the mode of second-order observation, but only to create paintings that imitate nature not only with regard to its "what" but to its "how." One began to inquire into the latent conditions of seeing, only to let them vanish again in the painting, only to accommodate the vision made possible by art to the nature of seeing. The procedure still rested on the old European, quasi-normative understanding of nature. Reconstructing a unified perspective was meant to realize what nature wants the human eye to see so that the failure of imitation, imperfection, and corruption could be avoided or so that they could be made visible and corrected with reference to the intended perspective. In this sense, unified perspective was and remained a technical (artistic) invention, a scaffold for mounting experiences of seeing and painting.

Observing observations was not the genuine aim; it was merely a precondition for acquiring appropriate artistic tools. To study these tools and work with them was to confront in full the contingency of appearances. The mastery of perspective permitted experimentation with the difference between reality and appearance, to the point where it became acceptable to present distorted objects, so long as the deviation from standard expectations called attention to something specific.[67] The art of perspective borders on the rhetorical, literary, or poetic technique of creating paradoxes. One exploits the malleability of impressions and the corresponding contingency of the object world for the sake of new artistic liberties and representational goals, which the artist must now determine all by himself. Once this happens, the accent can shift to the side of a constructed appearance. "Perspective no longer appears as a science of reality. It is a technique of hallucinations."[68] The world of natural and artificial objects continues to be the theme of art—not the observation of the act of observing as such. The main concern is with technical instruction and schematic reproduction (for example, by means of a pyramid whose top serves as the vanishing point), rather than with observation, let alone with the observational mode of other observers.[69]

In addition, perspective allows observational relations to be integrated into the unity of the pictorial space; it displays what the depicted figures, due to their spatial position in the painting, can see and what they cannot see. The unity of space guaranteed by perspective renders the represented figures observable as observers. The painting's unity is thus no longer guaranteed solely by the composition but also by the observational relationships displayed within the painting. The frame does not cease to function as the boundary of the composition, but the painting's internal observational relationships, together with its vanishing-point perspective, reveal the world as transcending the frame and as the true object of representation. In this way, even the invisible can be drawn into the painting and rendered visible. To be sure, relationships of observation and nonobservation were represented prior to the invention of unified perspective, but exclusively in context-bound forms that were intelligible only with reference to a shared body of knowledge (for example, Susanna in her bath). Perspective transforms observational relationships of this kind into a universal possibility capable of integrating *new* constellations.

In the seventeenth century, the possibilities of painting on this side-stage of latency observation appear to have been exhausted. They do not penetrate deeply enough into the world of individual motives. Modern society demands that social relationships be motivated, and the need to be guided by motives creates suspicion. Accordingly, the leading role in the development of latency observations shifts to theater and literature, especially to the novel. The figures that populate narrative are no longer legendary heroes of an accepted (biblical or Greco-Roman) history. They are blatantly presented as invented personae. They must be ordinary individuals drawn from real life. (What sense does it make to invent heroes?) The interest shifts from moral, exemplary perfection or cosmic fate to complex motivational structures that appear in a different light depending on whether they are the object of self-observation or are observed from the outside.

There is room for doubt whether the first variants of this technique— the attempts to describe behavior as a consequence of reading (for example, the critique of women's reading of novels in *Don Quixote*)—can already be subsumed under the function of observing latent motives, even though the reader is invited to witnesses what the novel's heroes do not experience themselves. These novels still foreground a transitional syndrome—the problem of the consequences of print—that plays a role in other realms as well, for example, in the reactions to the public revelation of tricks and "secrets" of the state. The depiction of a powerful profit motive that offends morality (*Moll Flanders*) or violates the parental determination of one's profession (*Robinson Crusoe*) partakes in the problematic of second-order observation only to a limited extent. The extensive debate, after 1678, about whether the behavior of the Princess de Clèves— her confession and ultimate renunciation of love—was commendable foregrounds the fissures in contemporary morality but does not necessarily reveal latent motives. With Richardson's *Pamela*, at the latest, it becomes evident that the novel shows the reader—whether intentionally or not—how to land a marriage without acknowledging sexual or social motives.[70] Ever since, the woman who wants to have it her way in arranging her marriage has been considered either a mixture of innocence and *rafinesse* or someone who intuitively follows unconscious motives in a manner that is transparent to the reader.[71]

One might ask whether literature or painting has been more influenced by commercial considerations. Be this as it may, the notion that literature ought to be "interesting" gains prominence in the course of the eighteenth century.[72] Painting, too, wants to surprise and catch the eye, but in a more conventional sense, by pointing to something absent. Moreover, it insists that its aesthetic accomplishment be judged not by its surprise effect but in terms of its artistic means.[73] Literary works can stage second-order observations for the reader much more effectively, and they are "interesting" when they succeed. They invite the reader to observe his own observations and to discover previously unacknowledged idiosyncrasies, prejudices, and limitations.

What makes an artwork beautiful—not only pleasing upon first sight but interesting—is precisely the suggestion that second-order observation is at stake. The lines of this discussion are determined less by the distinction between artistic talent and its effect upon the audience than by the removal of obstacles that stand in the way of sympathy and interest—obstacles having to do with the formalities of a rule-based poetics, with a prescribed social order that determines the relevance of persons and actions, and, above all, with moral obligations. The novel closely follows the theater in establishing a level of second-order observation, and unrelated criteria of literary quality are difficult to detect.[74] The attitude toward such criteria appears to be unstable, something that could be demonstrated empirically by investigating which works were translated and which ones were not.

We shall not elaborate this point—for example, with reference to the practice, transparent only to the reader, of deriving highly individualistic motives from an imitation of competitors.[75] Certainly, the intention of letting the reader speculate about latent motives necessitates structurally more complex characters who have not been flattened by the strictures of morality.[76] The complex narrative structure of the novel paves the way for generalizing the topos of latent motives. In the novel, this process leads to an internalization of signs. One can read the narrative as pointing to what it leaves unsaid but nonetheless belongs to it. In this way, the habit of exploring latent motives can be trained and finally passed on into common knowledge for those versed in psychological and psychiatric research. Despite its interest in mirrors and doubles, romanticism still believed in the "idea" that "holds together the doubles of our knowledge."[77] In the early twentieth century, sociology and social psychology dropped this assumption. The individual exists as a fragmentary self that acquires a representable identity solely under pressure from the expectations of others. The excess of consciousness is repressed into the "unconscious," so that the self becomes habitual and no longer needs to experience consistency as an external necessity.[78] Whatever one may think of such theories, what matters here is that their plausibility no longer depends on their literary, fictional presentation. Instead, they can be "verified" by common scientific procedures or in the successes of therapeutic practice.

In this cultural-historical situation, art begins to discover a new topic, the topic of "authenticity." To the extent to which the observation of artworks as second-order observation becomes normalized, oppositional trends begin to emerge. At bottom, all of these trends point to the problem of authenticity. We shall mention only one example, the cult of the sublime in the late seventeenth and eighteenth centuries, triggered "just in time" by the rediscovery of Pseudo-Longinus, the apotheosis of the sublime rebels, on the one hand, against the "pompous" style that glorified the powers of the social order and, on the other hand, against an aesthetics based on rules.[79] In both respects, the protest concerns positions already rendered obsolete by second-order observation, especially by the emerging critical tendency to observe what other observers cannot observe. The fascination with the sublime cannot be explained in terms of its role as a substitute, since it rejects rules. Rather, the cult of the sublime reacts to the loss of authenticity that occurs (or must be feared) when second-order observation establishes itself and artistic production and art criticism shift to that level. No matter how Boileau might have read Longinus's text, what fascinates him is its autological, self-referential structure. "In speaking of the sublime, one becomes sublime oneself."[80] In corresponding to itself, the sublime is spontaneous and nondeliberate. This is why the sublime defies definition.[81] But it can be demonstrated! The style of the Old Testament, the ruin as a product of incessant decay, death, and what it leaves behind, the cemetery—none of these phenomena is produced for the sake of observation. One looks for remnants of a more archaic authenticity and draws from them inspiration for authentic art. What cannot be observed is integrated into art by representing self-transcending boundary phenomena, that is, by presenting the unpresentable. Representing the renunciation of representation can once again claim credibility—or so one hopes—just as seducers in the French novel, in somewhat different ways, try to be sincere in their insincerity. As a solution, however, the sublime, or *das Erhabene*, cannot convince for long, since it, too, is eventually proclaimed to be a style and becomes subject to observation. For the romantics, such productions have only a single function, namely, to emphasize the incredible, to suggest that there is something worth suggesting. For August Wilhelm Schlegel, the sublime is nothing more than a refined laxative for intellectual constipation.[82] Others ridicule, while shuddering at the thought, the "sweet horror" that propels the baroness to sleep with her maid in the same room.[83] Once the sublime takes shape, it displays a new side, from which it can be observed as both fashionable and ridiculous.

Generally speaking, second-order observation transforms latencies into contingencies, followed by the tendency to replace "what" questions by "how" questions. The result is a gradual dissolution of the constraints and obstacles that used to secure the continuity between past and future. Contingencies exceed their frame conditions. But when everything can be done differently, the self-referential conclusion eventually suggests itself that one might as well continue as before—provided one conforms to the new demand for authenticity.

Contrary to all appearances, authenticity—both as a problem and as a topic—is thematized at the level of second-order observation. The question is now: How can one maintain an immediate relationship to the world while being aware of being observed as an observer, or even while knowing that one produces for the sake of being observed? How, in other words, can one abstract from a system that is fully established at the level of second-order observation and return to the paradise of first-order observation? Usually this happens when the artist allows himself to be captivated by his own work while observing its emergence. But this begs the question of how one can *demonstrate*, or make observable, that one is not irritated, influenced, or manipulated by the fact of being observed.

Perhaps this problem is merely one of the forms in which art reflects, for its own sake and for the sake of other functional systems, on what modern society has rendered impossible.

X

The question of how the world can observe itself is not new, nor can it be traced exclusively to Wittgenstein.[84] With the retreat of the religious world order and the erosion of the observation of God as world observer, the questions arose: "Who else?" and "What else?" At this moment the subject began to announce itself, occasionally under the pseudonym "Spirit." Here, ever since romanticism, art has found its niche. One rejected alternative options for the self-observation of the world, above all, those provided by physics. "Suppose we think of nature as a self-conscious being," writes August Wilhelm Schlegel, "what would it consider the greatest imposition? To study itself in terms of experimental physics."[85] He meant that nature finds its way "blindly." In the twentieth century, one can no longer follow this. Instead, the world's self-observation has fallen primarily into the domain of physics, which must take into account its physically functioning tools, including living physicists, so that the world can observe itself in a manner that is irritating (and therefore in need of reflection). In this situation, can "poetry" still compete? Now that such an epistemological insight is everywhere, how can poetry stand the pressure of reflection it is bound to apply to itself?

In mathematics, physics, biology, and sociology alike, the form of reflection adapts to the radicality with which the problem is framed. A problem of second-order observation is always at stake—how to observe how the world observes itself, how a marked space emerges from the unmarked space, how something becomes invisible when something else becomes visible. The generality of these questions allows one to determine more precisely what art can contribute to solving this paradox of the invisibilization that accompanies making something visible.

The shift to a level of second-order observation radically alters what is presupposed as the *world*. The first-order observer finds his objects amidst other objects and events. He can assume that his observations are linked to other objects and events and together constitute a world. To him, the world is a *universitas rerum*. Since he cannot see everything, he imagines invisible things. This leads to the development of symbols that represent the invisible in the visible world. Among other things, art can take over such symbolizing functions.

The second-order observer, by contrast, observes the distinctions that first-order observers (including himself) employ to emphasize and indicate something. This operation renders the world invisible. First, the world itself cannot be observed. The act of observing, which constitutes itself in the move from an unmarked to a marked space, does not make the unmarked space disappear. (It is not clear how this could happen without a prior marking of that space.) Rather, observation preserves that space as a necessary component of its capacity to distinguish. The unmarked space remains the other side of the form. Second, the distinguishing operation produces a two-sided form that cannot be observed as a unity (unless one employs yet another distinction) and thus remains invisible in the operation. In this twofold sense, the notion of a final unity—of an "ultimate reality" that cannot assume a form because it has no other side—is displaced into the unobservable. With regard to the world, the distinction between inside and outside does not apply. Nor does it make sense to say that the world has an inside but no outside. The inside/outside distinction is a "primary distinction" that must be introduced into the world.[86] If the concept of the world is retained to indicate reality in its entirety, then it is that which—to a second-order observer—remains invisible in the movements of observation (his own and those of others).

From this perspective, art can no longer be understood as an imitation of something that presumably exists along with and outside of art, although both artworks and artists can be found and indicated in the world along with other observers. To the extent that imitation is still possible, it now imitates the world's invisibility, a nature that can no longer be apprehended as a whole and must therefore be represented by emphasizing its curves, its "lines of beauty."[87] Art activates distinctions that operate in a "connexionist" manner, thus hiding the unity of the distinction that guides the observation. Regarding texts (and with a slightly different slant) one might speak with Kristeva of a "zone of multiple marks and intervals whose non-centered inscription makes possible in practice a multi-valence without unity."[88]

Theology initially investigated such issues in conjunction with the notion of God. Inspired by the idea of God as observer, theology began to observe this observer, even though it was forced to concede that an observer who creates and sustains the world by virtue of his observation excludes nothing and hence cannot assume an observable form.[89] By externalizing this paradox and by incorporating the notion of observing the unobservable into the idea of God, one sought to shield the conventional notion of the world as *universitas rerum* from infection by logical paradoxes. To the extent, however, that modern society imbued all of its functional systems with second-order observation and itself ceased to provide a stable counterbalance, the concept of the world had to be altered. The world was now conceived, along the lines of a Husserlian metaphor, as an unreachable horizon that retreats further with each operation, without ever holding out the prospect of an outside.

This epochal turning point results in a shift in the "eigenvalues" that gain stability in the recursive operations of observing observations. With regard to the world, they assume the modality of *contingency*.[90] Whatever exists or is made in the world could be otherwise. At least so far as concerns the world, the counterconcepts of necessity and impossibility are dropped; henceforth they apply only to temporally or regionally limited affairs. The world no longer owes its stability to a scaffold of essential forms that separate the necessary from the impossible. All forms, especially the forms of art, must persist against the challenge that they could be different. They convince by evoking alternative possibilities while neutralizing any preference for forms not chosen.

However, the contingency of forms by no means prevents us from estab-

lishing what is so in everyday life. To the first-order observer, the world remains exactly what it used to be. And any second-order observer is always
also a first-order observer to the extent that he must focus on the observer
he wants to observe. Systems theory, too, needs to establish a system reference from which it can observe how a given system observes itself and the
world. Not everything is other than what it is, nor does the unobservability of the world imply that we can no longer find our way from one place
to the next because there is nothing "in between." But understanding the
specificity of modern society and of modern art requires taking into account that these systems establish their advanced structures recursively at
the level of second-order observation and that they have become so adapted
to this situation that it is difficult to imagine how society could continue to
operate if it were to regress entirely to a level of first-order observation.

   This confirms once again that in the modern world neither consensus
nor authenticity can be taken for granted or presumed to be attainable.
Neither the unobservable world nor the paradox of form can secure these
conditions. It means further that individuals cannot participate "authentically" in matters of consensus and that consensus cannot be justified
simply by pointing out that individuals consent without force (that is, authentically). Such losses must be accepted by a society that carries out its
most important operations at the level of second-order observation. The
notion of the individual has long since adapted to that situation.

   Individuals are self-observers. They become individuals by observing
their own observations. Today, they are no longer defined by birth, by social origin, or by characteristics that distinguish them from all other individuals. Whether baptized or not, they are no longer "souls" in the sense
of indivisible substances that guarantee an eternal life. One might argue
with Simmel, Mead, or Sartre that they acquire their identity through the
gaze of others, but only on condition that they observe that they are being
observed.

   Participating in art (which is neither necessary nor impossible) provides
an opportunity for individuals to observe themselves as observers and to
experience themselves as individuals. Since in art their experience is mediated by the perception of improbable things and events, the chances for
self-observation are greater than in verbal communication. It does not matter whether one acts or experiences "uniquely" in the sense of employing
forms that occur only to oneself and that are inaccessible to anyone else.
How could one, if there is no way to prove it? The point of self-observation

is not to cultivate self-reference at the expense of hetero-reference. It is merely a question of attributing visual perceptions to a perceiver, thus creating an awareness of contingency that relies neither on necessities nor on impossibilities. By no means is the individual free to interpret at will. We learn from participating in art that any attempt at arbitrary interpretation is thwarted, and in what ways. This is why we can remain content with observing ourselves as observers despite the fact that there is no ultimate certainty of the One, the True, and the Good.

XI

The old European tradition explained the nature of society (domestic or political) by appealing to the nature of man. From the very beginning, however, the notion of a common nature contained a time bomb, built into the necessity of distinguishing human nature from other creatures. The rift between human and nonhuman nature continued to deepen—partly because of religious concerns about "souls" and their salvation, partly because of the growing demands an increasingly complex society placed on human resources. In the transition to the modern age, specialized human faculties such as reason and cunning were sharply emphasized.[91] As a result, the natural foundation of society began to erode, and its unity had to be reconstituted on the basis of reasonable motives—hence the escape into a social contract that engages subjects and no longer relies on objects to stabilize society. Even German Idealism, despite its importance for aesthetics, never managed to develop a theory of observation that would acknowledge the dependence of observation on distinctions. Distinctions began to multiply, but they were always taken to be a preliminary step in the inquiry into the ultimate unity or ground proclaimed under the name of the Idea or the Ideal.[92] The trajectory of this line of questioning ends in a rejection of ontological metaphysics and the humanist tradition—in the postulate of an "exemplary Being" or the reduction of society to the anonymity of the "they," as in Heidegger's *Being and Time*,[93] which preserves the traces of the tradition it rejects.

In the course of modernization, previous forms of grounding society in nature lost their plausibility. A normative concept of social unity displaced nature—by transforming natural law into a law of reason, by introducing the doctrine of the social contract, or by advancing the notion, shared by sociologists such as Durkheim and Parsons, that the unity and persistence

of society depend on a moral or, at any rate, a value-driven consensus. Today, this notion still blocks recognition of the unity of a global system or
world society, apparently because of a prevailing need for security, particularly in modern society. Appeals to solidarity seek to compensate for dramatically increasing inequalities that are still interpreted in stratificatory
terms and experienced as unjust. In the face of the inevitable insecurity
and volatility of crucial structures, one holds on to basic expectations,
even though they are frustrated in the particular instance. The obligatory
form of the normative brings this about, although it can promise nothing
but counterfactual validity.

By contrast, many domains lack normative determination, especially
when seen from the viewpoint of the individual. Consider love or money.
Norms cannot prescribe or prohibit whether or not we love and whom.
The economy would collapse (or lose its unique rationality) if rules prescribed how we should spend our money. Some normative constraints certainly do exist in these domains. As one can learn from specific cases or
from the movies, love is no excuse for espionage, and there are countless
legal constraints on business transactions. But the core of these symbolically generalized media eludes normative regulation in much the same
way as the interior of the home once did.

This basic fact refutes any theory that would establish the structure of
society in the normative domain—in a tacitly assumed social contract or
in a moral consensus. No one denies that expectations need to be protected against disappointment. This is indispensable, as are many other
things. Such protection is above all the function of law, and without law
there is no society. But neither the unity nor the reproduction (autopoiesis) of society can be reduced to that function.

All of this concerns the function of second-order observation—hence
this lengthy excursus. Second-order observation takes the place of the su-
pervisory authorities that a normative theory of the social system would
consider indispensable and name as such. The second-order observer may
be a guardian but is not necessarily so. He is not adequately described—
following the tradition of the past two centuries—as a critic who knows
better. Rather, by reducing and increasing the complexity that is available
to communication, his function is to arrive at a level compatible with the
autopoiesis of the social system.

Second-order observation has a toxic quality. It alters one's immediate
contact with the world, eroding the mode of first-order observation, which

it nonetheless retains. It plants the seeds of suspicion within the life-world (in the Husserlian sense) without being able to leave that world. While the first-order observer could still cherish the hope of penetrating beneath the surface and grasping a Being beyond appearance, the second-order observer harbors suspicion about this "philosophical" project. He is not particularly fond of wisdom and know-how, nor does he love knowledge. Rather, he wants to understand how knowledge is produced and by whom, and how long the illusion might last. To him, Being is an observational schema that produces "ontology," and nature is nothing more than a concept that promises a comfortable end and blocks further questioning. Equally toxic is the second-order observer's penchant for questioning the "meaning of life"—for roughly one hundred years, from the mid-nineteenth century to the mid-twentieth, he was intoxicated by this question, only to realize that it, too, must be observed as nothing more than the specialty of a certain epoch.

But this analysis already assumes the position of an observer of the third (and ultimate) order. Or we are second-order observers who draw the autological conclusion and observe ourselves as second-order observers. As second-order observers, we can balance our account, though without hope of finding a resting place or final formula. Second-order observation makes possible various types of communication—both utterance and understanding—that would be inconceivable without it. Modern art is a good example. It cannot be adequately described as supporting the normative pretensions of religion or political power, nor does it progress toward ever more excellent works, spurred on by perpetual self-criticism. Art makes visible possibilities of order that would otherwise remain invisible. It alters the conditions of visibility/invisibility in the world by keeping invisibility constant and making visibility subject to variation. In short, art generates forms that would never exist without it. Whether this justifies the existence of art is a gratuitous question. For sociologists it suffices to take note of the fact that this is happening here and nowhere else.

Our insistence on distinctions as forms of observation adds little that is new. The theory of art has always used distinctions (otherwise, it would have been unable to observe, at least in terms of our theoretical concept), and it distinguished distinctions that play a role in art. This raises the question of what new insights the concept of observation (first- and second-order observation) has to offer. The answer is: it traces the problem of unity back to the ultimate form of paradox.

The tradition did not dare to take this step, despite its sensitivity to distinctions and its oscillation between a skeptical and worldly philosophical taste and a more idealistic one.

To illustrate this point, we select two extreme cases from the final days of rhetoric and of German Idealism. Baltasar Gracián's *Agudeza y arte de ingenio*[94] consists of nothing but distinctions—presented one after the other apparently without any order. Nonetheless, the text is held together by a distinct motive, namely, by the question of how one can cause effects in a world that generates and feeds on appearances. Referring to text-art, his answer is: by arranging the textual body in a beautiful fashion. Karl Wilhelm Ferdinand Solger's lectures on aesthetics are equally chaotic and almost compulsive in assigning distinctions, mainly because he inherits many of his distinctions from an eighteenth-century tradition.[95] But Solger, too, cannot do without a unity that provides meaning. This unity is presupposed in the idea of beauty, which he conceives of as neither a goal nor a product but as a primordial unity that supports and renders possible the *Aufhebung* of all distinctions. In Gracián's text, the meaning of the world is opaque and inaccessible but taken for granted in a religious sense. For Solger, the world recommends itself by virtue of its ultimate values. His argument is interchangeable with religious formulas without depending on them. *In both cases, an unquestioned premise points the argument toward an ultimate unity.* The concept of observation drops this premise. It takes the unity of form, of every distinction, as a self-induced blockage of observation, whose form is paradox. Paradox is nothing more than an invitation to search for distinctions that, for the time being, are plausible enough to be employed "directly" without raising questions regarding their unity or the sameness of what they distinguish.

This shift from unity to difference has far-reaching consequences. It displaces, for example, the metaphysical premise of the world as Being by suggesting that it is always possible (albeit questionable) to focus one's observations on the distinction between being and nonbeing. This means, in the theory of art, that the notion of "beauty" as an ultimate value, a value that excludes only what is inferior and what can be dismissed, must be replaced by the logical concept of a positive/negative coding of the system's operations. One might ask whether it still makes sense to speak of beauty to indicate the positive value of the art system's code. But in view of the paradigm shift at issue here, this is merely a question of terminology.

XII

Second-order cybernetics, the theory of observing systems, has much in common with the critique of ontological metaphysics debated under the name of "deconstruction" in the wake of Jacques Derrida's and Paul de Man's work. Deconstruction has become fashionable above all in theories of literary criticism in the United States. These theories refer to what is given using the concept "text" and designate the operation concerning it "reading." The theory of deconstruction (if it is a theory at all) is thus compelled to draw autological conclusions, because it merely generates texts for readers.

This insight surrounds deconstruction with an aura of radicalism that provokes comparison with the theory of second-order observation.[96] To find a common ground for such a comparison, we must expand the notion of the text to include every object in need of interpretation. This includes any kind of artwork. "Reading" then turns into "observing," or, if one's goal is to produce texts, "describing." Deconstruction questions the "materiality" of objects that suggest the presence of something to be described. The critique of this assumption—of the presumed distinction between a given text and its interpretation, or between a material object and its description—is one of the most crucial insights that has emerged from the context of deconstruction.[97] The distinction between text and interpretation is, for its part, a textual distinction. Like any other distinction, it presupposes itself as its own blind spot, which deconstructive techniques can point out and emphasize as indispensable.

The theory of observing systems has no difficulties with this proposition. What distinguishes and constrains deconstruction is a kind of affect directed against the ontologico-metaphysical premises of Being, presence, and representation. As a result, the dissolution of metaphysics is preoccupied with affirming itself through perpetual self-dissolution. All distinctions can be deconstructed without exception if one asks why they, rather than others, rely on their own blindness to distinguish and indicate something specific. The theory of second-order observation provides more elegant and more rigorous forms for such a project. It can do without the assumption of given (existential) incompatibilities and restricts itself to observing the incompatibilities that arise, at the operational level, among the observations of a given system.[98] It need no longer seek refuge in ontological concepts. But even if we accept this proposition, we still might ask whether some constructions have proven more stable than others, although they, too, can be deconstructed.

At this point, it might be worthwhile to shift our attention away from deconstruction's philosophical radicalism—the heir of ancient skepticism—toward scientific research. In this domain, the theory of self-referential systems has much to offer. It can accept the deconstructive reservation while pointing out the cognitive benefits one gains if one abstains, for the time being, from deconstructing this distinction.

The distinction between (self-referential, operatively closed) systems and (excluded) environments allows us to reformulate the distinction between text and interpretation. The materiality of texts or other works of art always belongs to the environment and can never become a component of the system's operational sequences. But the system's operations determine how texts and other objects in the environment are identified, observed, and described. The system produces references as its own operations, but it can do so only if it is capable of distinguishing between self-reference and hetero-reference, if, in other words, it can determine whether it refers to itself or to something other. The next step is to specify the kind of operation by which the system reproduces itself. The distinction between perception and communication prepares the ground for such a move. Just like the deconstructionists, we can now deconstruct the concept (the distinction) of the "reader" and replace it with the concept of communication, which situates our theoretical design within a general theory of social systems and, in particular, a theory of the social system.

These interventions (all of which, as we point out again, can be deconstructed) connect our findings to empirical research that works with a systems-theoretical design. This holds for the type of research that goes by the name of "cognitive science" but also for the sociology of social systems. With these assumptions in mind, we can set out to explore whether, and in what ways, the historical specificity of modern art can be understood in terms of the differentiation of a specialized functional system of society.

XIII

A final remark will distinguish second-order observation from the cherished *critical* attitude that has been with us since the eighteenth century. A critic knows and makes known what is wrong with others. Although it refers to the external world, critique has a strong self-referential component. This is why it was long hailed as a scientific, if not a political, achievement. The critical attitude—and therein lies its historical significance—launched a search for acceptable criteria and suffered shipwreck in the process, repeating the effort over and over again with ever more abstract means. Armed with philosophical pretensions, aesthetics reacted against this manner of criticizing art and taste. In the wake of the critique of an ontologically grounded metaphysics, a long philosophical tradition emphasized subjective knowledge, the will to power (the claim to master existence through an affirmation of repetition), and finally "Being" itself or writing. In this context, one should mention Kant, Nietzsche, Heidegger, and Derrida. Eventually, identity was displaced by difference, and reasons gave way to paradoxes in an attempt to gain critical distance from preestablished models—until critique itself was recognized as a historical phenomenon, a "sign of the times," a possibility residing in a belatedness that allows for the contemplation of already printed and finished products.

Second-order observation refrains from critique. It is no longer deceived by the inherent ambiguity of the word *krinein* (to separate, distinguish, judge). It resolutely embraces a perspective interested in "how" things emerge, rather than in "what" they are. Evidence for this tendency abounds. Consider, for example, the widely accepted shift from substantive to procedural rationality.[99] The critics, who will probably still be around for a while, tend to respond to this shift with the evasive question: What's the point if one can no longer state the point of one's endeavors?

There is a response to this question. If one cannot deny that there are observers in the world (the critic can do so only in the form of performative contradiction), then a theory that claims universality must acknowledge their existence; in other words, it must learn how to observe observations. And it cannot help realizing that second-order observation has been around for a long time and operates today at structurally important junctions in society.

This is not to silence the critics. Nor are we proposing a paradoxical critique of criticism. Plenty of work remains to be done if one wants to figure out what is wrong—whether with metaphysics or with the system of public garbage disposal. All we want is to raise the possibility for second-order observation so we can ask what kinds of distinctions the critics work with and why they prefer these distinctions to others.

Perhaps the art system is a good starting point for such a revision. As early as the eighteenth century, art critics became targets of a criticism fueled by artistic experience. Critique was soon exiled from art to find a home in philosophy, which at least refrained from criticizing works of art. After the short-lived revival of critique in the romantic notion of reflection, we arrive at an unmatched historicism that exploits the advanced observational possibilities that come with belatedness, focusing on what kinds of distinctions have been used in the past and feeling the urge to cross their inner boundaries. The observation of previous limitations leads to the possibility—as if on its own—of doing things differently. Or better—who could tell? That is beside the point.

§3 Medium and Form

The art system operates on its own terms, but an observer of art can choose many different distinctions to indicate what he observes. The choice is his. Of course, there is an obligation to do justice to the object and its surrounding distinctions. It would be wrong to say an object is made of granite if it is really made of marble. But what about the distinction granite/marble? Why not old/new, or cheap/expensive, or "Should we put this object into the house or in the garden?" Theory has even more freedom in choosing its distinctions—and this is why it needs justification!

In the first chapter we introduced the distinction perception/communication in order to keep distinct system references separate. We further distinguished operation/observation and system/environment. When one deals with multiple distinctions, their relative significance becomes a theoretical problem that can be resolved only through further investigation. Any somewhat complex theory needs more than just one distinction, and whether it makes sense to arrange distinctions hierarchically (by distinguishing them in rank) is doubtful, although familiar terms such as *systems theory* might suggest a conceptual hierarchy.

This chapter is about the distinction between medium and form as exemplified in the domain of art.[1] That distinction is meant to replace the distinction substance/accidence, or object/properties—a guiding distinction, crucial for any object-oriented ontology, that has long been criticized. The question is: *With what can we replace it?* By defining properties in terms of object determinations (colors, for example, as determinations of paintings) this distinction separates the "internal" too sharply from the "external," or subject from object. The distinction between primary and secondary qualities was meant to correct this bias. However, it ended up dividing the problem between subjects and objects rather than suggesting the compelling consequence that *both* entities, subjects *and* objects, must be thought "ecstatically." Nor does the distinction between being and having,[2] favored by many critics of modernity, point beyond this impasse.

The distinction between medium and form suggests another primary distinction designed to replace and render obsolete the object-oriented ontological concept of matter. In traditional notions of matter, one thinks of the wax mass that suffers the engraving and erasure of inscriptions.[3] From a systems-theoretical standpoint, by contrast, both media and forms are constructed by the system and therefore always presuppose a specific system reference. They are not given "as such." The distinction between medium and form, just like the concept of information, is strictly internal to the system. There is no corresponding difference in the environment. Neither media nor forms "represent" system states of an ultimately physical nature. The perceptual medium of "light," for example, is not a physical concept but rather a construct that presupposes the difference between lightness and darkness. Accordingly, the internally projected distinction between medium and form is relevant exclusively to the art system (just as monetary media and prices are relevant only to the economy), even though the distinction can be applied not only to art but equally well to nature, in a manner that transcends the boundaries of both.

What both sides of the medium/form distinction have in common, and what distinguishes this distinction from other distinctions, lies in the notion of a coupling of elements.[4] The term *element* does not refer to natural constants—particles, souls, or individuals—that any observer would identify as the same.[5] Rather, it always points to units constructed (distinguished) by an observing system—to units for counting money, for example, or to tones in music. Furthermore, these elements cannot be self-sufficient in the sense that they could determine or in-form themselves.[6] They must be thought of as dependent on couplings. They would be invisible as pure self-references, since one can observe them only by using distinctions. Certain media employ the same elements but distinguish themselves with regard to the coupling—loose or tight—of their elements.

Let us begin with the notion of medium, which applies to cases of "loosely coupled" elements. The choice of terminology is awkward, but since the concept has been introduced in the literature, we adopt it here.[7] Loose coupling has nothing to do with a loose screw, for example. Rather, the concept indicates an open-ended multiplicity of possible connections that are still compatible with the unity of an element—such as the number of meaningful sentences that can be built from a single semantically identical word.

To decompose further whatever functions as an "element" in specific media is to broach the operatively impalpable—just as in physics, where the question of whether we are dealing with particles or waves boils down to a matter of prejudice. There are, in other words, no ultimate units whose identity would not refer back to the observer. Hence, there is no indication without a sufficient (observable) operation that executes it.

Loose coupling, which leaves room for multiple combinations, can be understood in both a factual and a temporal sense. Factually, it means that a number of tight couplings are likely and selection is inevitable. Temporally speaking, a medium is often understood as a condition for transfers. In addition, there are close ties to the theory of memory, if memory is understood in terms of a delay in the reactualization of meaning. An observer must employ modal-theoretical terms to describe such media.

This explains further why media can be recognized only by the contingency of the formations that make them possible. (This insight corresponds to the old doctrine that matter as such, as sheer chaos, is inaccessible to consciousness.)[8] Observed from within the schema of medium and form, all forms appear accidental; or, to put it differently, no form ever expresses the "essence" of the medium. This is another way of formulating the insight that what matters is the *distinction* between medium and form; we are dealing with two sides that cannot be separated or thought of in isolation. This leads to the realization that the distinction between medium and form is itself a form, a form with two sides, one of which—the side of the form—contains itself. The distinction between medium and form is a paradoxical construct insofar as it reenters itself and reappears within one of its sides.[9]

Forms are generated in a medium via a tight coupling of its elements. This process, too, presupposes two-sided forms, and our two-sided concept of form remains valid here. The forms that emerge from the tight coupling of a medium's possibilities distinguish themselves (their inside) from the remaining possibilities contained in the medium (their outside).[10] Of course, we are dealing with a special case of distinguishing rather than with its general form, for which the other side is the surrounding unmarked space.

The specificity of the medium/form distinction points to the emergence of distinctive features of such forms. This specificity depends on evolution. Forms are always stronger and more assertive than the medium. The medium offers no resistance—words cannot struggle against the formation of phrases any more than money can refuse to be paid at specific prices. Of course, media impose limits on what one can do with them. Since they consist of elements, media are nonarbitrary. But their arsenal of possibilities is generally large enough to prevent fixation on a few forms. If this happened, then the medium/form distinction would collapse.

We can further elucidate the medium/form distinction by means of the distinction between redundancy and variety. The elements that form the medium through their loose coupling—such as letters in a certain kind of writing or words in a text—must be easily recognizable. They carry little information themselves, since the informational content of an artwork must be generated in the course of its formation. The formation of the work creates surprise and assures variety, because there are many ways in which the work can take shape and because, when observed slowly, the work invites the viewer to contemplate alternate possibilities and to experiment with formal variations.[11]

It is worth noting that forms, rather than exhausting the medium, regenerate its possibilities. This is remarkable and can be easily demonstrated with reference to the role of words in the formation of utterances. Forms fulfill this regenerating function, because their duration is typically shorter than the duration of the medium. Forms, one might say, couple and decouple the medium. This feature highlights the correlation between the medium/form difference and a theory of memory. The medium supports the retarding function (which regulates the reuse of elements in new forms) that underlies all memory. Memory does not store items belonging to the past (how could it?); memory postpones repetition. The creation of forms, by contrast, fulfills an equally important function for memory, namely, the function of discrimination, remembering and forgetting. We remember the elements we frequently employ when creating forms and forget the ones we never use. In this way, a system memory can delimit itself by adapting to the incidents the system experiences as chance events.[12]

The difference between medium and form implies a distinctly tempo-

ral aspect as well. The medium is more stable than the form, because it requires only loose couplings. No matter how short-lived or lasting they
turn out to be, forms can be created without exhausting the medium or
causing it to disappear along with the form. As we noted earlier, the medium receives without resistance the forms that are possible within it, but
the form's resilience is paid for with instability. Even this account is far too
simple. It disregards the fact that the medium can be observed only via
forms, never as such. The medium manifests itself only in the relationship
between constancy and variety that obtains in individual forms. A form,
in other words, can be observed through the schema of constant/variable,
because it is always a form-in-a-medium.[13]

Finally, let us return to the notion that media and forms consist of
(loosely or tightly coupled) elements. Such elements always also function
as forms in another medium. Words and tones, for example, constitute
forms in the acoustic medium just as letters function as forms in the optical medium of the visible. This terminology does not allow for the boundary concept of matter as defined by the metaphysical tradition, where
matter designates the complete indeterminacy of being regarding its readiness to assume forms. Media are generated from elements that are always
already formed. Otherwise, we couldn't speak of their loose or tight coupling. This situation contains possibilities for an evolutionary arrangement of medium/form relationships in steps, which, as we shall see
shortly, entails an essential precondition for understanding art.[14] But before turning to art, let us consider yet another example that illustrates the
generality of this step-wise arrangement. In the medium of sound, words
are created by constricting the medium into condensable (reiterable)
forms that can be employed in the medium of language to create utterances (for the purpose of communication). The potential for forming utterances can again serve as the medium for forms known as myths or narratives, which, at a later stage, when the entire procedure is duplicated in
the optical medium of writing, also become known as textual genres or
theories. Theories can subsequently be coupled in the medium of the
truth code to form a network of consistent truths. Such truths function as
forms whose outside consists of untruths lacking consistency. How far we
can push this kind of stacking depends on the evolutionary processes that
lead to the discovery of forms. The logic of the distinction between medium and form cannot determine the limits of what may be possible in
this regard. It does, however, permit judgments concerning chains of de-

pendencies that point to the kinds of evolutionary achievements that must be present so that further, more and more improbable constellations can arise. Most likely, we will be able to demonstrate sequences of this sort in the evolution of art as well.

II

The most general medium that makes both psychic and social systems possible and is essential to their functioning can be called "meaning" [*Sinn*].[15] Meaning is compatible with the temporalized manner in which psychic and social systems operate. It is compatible, in other words, with the way these systems constitute their elements exclusively in the form of events that are bound to a certain point in time (such elements are unlike particles, which possess a duration of their own and can be altered, replicated, or replaced). Meaning assures that the world remains accessible to the events that constitute the system—in the form of actualized contents of consciousness or communications—although they vanish as soon as they emerge, each appearing for the first and for the last time. The world itself is never accessible as a unity—as a whole, or totality, a mystical "all at once"—but is available only as a condition and domain for the temporal processing of meaning. Each meaning-event can lead to another. The question is: How?

Initially, the problem presents itself as follows: no matter how distinct, how obtrusive and indubitable any momentary actualization may be, meaning can represent the world accessible from a given position only in the form of a referential surplus, that is, as an excess of connective possibilities that cannot be actualized all at once. Instead of presenting a world, the medium of meaning refers to a selective processing. This is true even when concepts, descriptions, or semantics referring to the world are generated within the world. Actualized meaning always comes about selectively and refers to further selections. It is therefore fair to say that meaning is constituted by the distinction between actuality and potentiality (or between the real as momentarily given and as possibility). This implies and confirms that the medium of meaning is itself a form constituted by a specific distinction. But this raises the further question of how to comprehend the selective processing of meaning and in what ways it is accomplished.

At this point, we will have to rely again on the (paradoxical) notion of reentry. The meaning-producing distinction between actuality and potentiality reenters itself on the side of actuality, because for something to be actual it must also be possible. It follows that the distinction between medium and form is itself a form. Or, considered in terms of meaning: as medium, meaning is a form that creates forms in order to assume form. Meaning is processed via the selection of distinctions, of forms. Something specific is indicated (and nothing else): for example, "This yew-tree is nothing but itself, and it is a yew-tree and no other tree." The two-sided form substitutes for the representation of the world. Instead of presenting the world as phenomenon,[16] this form reminds us that there is always something else—whether this something is unspecified or specific, necessary or undeniable, only possible or dubitable, natural or artificial. The form of meaning is at once medium and form, and is such in a way that the medium can be actualized only via the processing of forms. This shows clearly that, and in what ways, one can speak of meaning (as we are doing right now) and that the actual infinity of the unreachable, intangible world of Nicholas of Cusa can be transformed into, and set in motion as, an infinite process. As a self-reproducing (autopoietic) process, meaning must always begin with the actual, a historically given situation in which it has placed itself.[17] It follows that systems constructed in such a manner cannot observe their own beginning or end and that they experience whatever constrains them temporally or factually from within a boundary they need to transcend. In the medium of meaning there is no finitude without infinity.

These observations go far beyond the specific domain of art. Considering, however, that art possesses meaning, they are relevant to art as well. This is true especially for the realization that we will have to cope with paradoxical but structured phenomena whenever we inquire into *meaning* or into *the world* as such, while at the same time we must give a *specific* meaning to this inquiry *in the world.* In art, too, world can be symbolized only as indeterminable (unobservable, indistinguishable, formless), for any specification would have to use a distinction and confront the question of what else there could be.[18] In the end, suggestions of this sort lead nowhere. One thing is certain, however: the distinctions we have at our disposal to raise such questions cannot be selected arbitrarily (although they can be criticized in each case), and any decision in this realm limits the selection of forms in ways that may be fruitful for an observation of artworks.

The case of art clearly shows that, and in what ways, a form can be used as a medium for further formations. *As* form, the human body can be used as a medium for the presentation of different postures and movements. A play can count as form to the extent that it is determined by a script and stage directions; at the same time, it functions as a medium in which different productions and individual performances can assume a specific form. (We see clearly that, and how, this difference emerges along with the evolution of the theater.) For its part, a medium—the material of which the artwork is crafted, the light it breaks, or the whiteness of the paper from which figures or letters emerge—can be used as form, provided that this form succeeds in fulfilling a differentiating function in the work. In contrast to natural objects, an artwork's material participates in the formal play of the work and is thereby acknowledged as form. The material is allowed to appear as material; it does not merely resist the imprint of form. Whatever serves as medium becomes form once it makes a difference, once it gains an informational value owing exclusively to the work of art.[19] At the same time, the emergence of more demanding forms remains dependent on the primary medium and ultimately on the medium of perception. There is no other way to render perception as a form that can bring about communication.

The question of whether there is a special medium for what we experience as art today—an art-specific medium with corresponding forms— poses a significant challenge. Several primary media capable of fulfilling this function already exist in the realm of perception for seeing and hearing, and, dependent on these, in the realm of language. One immediately notices a number of striking differences between these media, which raises the question of whether one can speak of a unified artistic medium at all and, if so, in what sense. This situation has a unique explanatory force, however: after all, a plurality of artistic genres traceable to these different media does exist—sculpture and painting, music and dance, theater and poetry. We must therefore radicalize the question and ask whether there is a "unity of art" in this multiplicity (as we have assumed naively) and whether this unity may reside in the specific logic of medium and form, that is, in the evolution of derived medium/form differences that attempt to realize analogous effects—with regard to a special function of art, for example—in different media. This line of questioning abstracts from individual media of perception and regards even language merely as one form of artistic expression among others, which shows how improbable this question, this way of drawing internal or external boundaries, really is.

The beginnings of a theory of a special medium of art date back to the late sixteenth and seventeenth centuries, before the arts began to emerge as a unified subject matter in the mid-eighteenth century. The notion of a special artistic medium was still concealed behind the idea of "beautiful appearance," a counterconcept that referred not only to theater and poetry but also to the visual arts and even (as in Baltasar Gracián) to the beautiful self-presentation of human behavior. "Beautiful appearance" may be an illusion, as in perspectival painting or the stage theater; but if it is, one can see through it. It is an illusion whose frame or stage ensures that one does not mistake it for the real world. Including the entire range of human behavior, as in Gracián, requires a functional equivalent for the external frame, a special *desengaño* (disillusionment), a clever strategy for seeing through the deception, which, in this case, equals self-deception. The problem is that the reality of the artworks, the actual existence of the paintings and texts, of the stage and its productions, can hardly be denied. The differentiation of beautiful appearance does not remove art from the accessible world. This is why the artistic medium must be constituted by the double framing of an illusion that, at the same time, is recognized as such on the basis of specific clues. It is constituted by an internal medium that shapes materials—paint, language, bodily movement, spatial arrangements—within an external medium that isolates the forms in their striking particularity and guarantees that they are perceived as art rather than as wood, a coat of paint, a simple communication, or human behavior. One hundred years later, Diderot will speak of the paradox of the comedian who must simultaneously perform and disrupt the illusion.[20]

The technique of double framing for the sake of illusion and disillusionment separates the medium of art from other objects and events, from nature as well as from commodities and utilities of all sorts. It places high demands on the observer, demands that require special arrangements—the stage theater, for example, as opposed to the merely symbolic religious plays of the Middle Ages—but may also have emerged in response to the truth claims of an ever more hectic religious activity in the post-Reformation period, to the new sciences, or to profit hunger in the world of trade.[21] The dissolution of the religiously nourished, unified cosmos of the Middle Ages favors bifurcations of this sort; but we still need to show how this double framing comes about in the case of art. The stage theater and perspectival painting may have provided models capable of illustrating the general concept of "beautiful appearance."

The other arts, in particular poetry, the spatial arrangements of baroque architecture, and eventually the modern novel could follow these developments. At the same time, however, the internal formative media of these genres were still too disparate to allow for a unified concept of the arts.

III

Before turning to the diversity of artistic genres, we must clarify a basic distinction that needs to be integrated into the theoretical context we are proposing here: the distinction between *space* and *time*.[22] Any further differentiation or evolution of artistic genres is based on this distinction, even if some artistic genres, such as dance, deploy both space and time.

Whatever one might suppose their "underlying" *hypokeimenon* (substratum) to be, we understand space and time to be *media of the measurement and calculation of objects* (hence not forms of intuition!). By measurement and calculation we do not have in mind culturally introduced criteria; rather, we are thinking of the neurophysiological operation of the brain.[23] On the one hand, space and time are always already attuned to the brain's quantitative language; on the other hand, neither consciousness nor communication can follow the brain's computations. They must presuppose the relevant achievements on the basis of structural couplings and permit their interpenetration. In this way, consciousness is free to develop its own procedures of measurement, which rest on comparisons and are used only sporadically, not in a constitutive manner. From the internal viewpoint of conscious operations or communications, the world is always already temporally and spatially disclosed. They have no power to control, let alone prevent, the operations that bring about this disclosure; only in positioning objects within these media do they have a certain freedom. This accounts for a certain *uniformity* of space and time that is presupposed in any meaningful constitution of objects and that can be used as a medium. This uniformity is needed to apprehend discontinuities, caesurae, and boundaries, as well as to estimate distances in both space and time.

The ability to identify places independently of the objects that occupy these places generates space and time. This is true even when the destruction of an object implies the loss of its "ancestral" place (which is not a loss of space as such). Differences between places qualify the medium, whereas differences between objects define its forms. Places are coupled differently from objects but by no means arbitrarily. Again, the medium "as such" is inaccessible. Only forms make it perceptible. Objects, one might say, are based in space and time in order to supply the world with variety. But variety requires redundancies, that is, nonarbitrary relations between positions in space and time, as well as between the two media.

In this regard, space and time are in agreement. They are both generated in the same way, namely, through the distinction between medium and form, or, more accurately, between place and object. They do, however, differ considerably, which makes it impossible to impoverish the world by reducing one to the other. One essential difference between the two concerns the way in which space and time manage variety, the alternation of forms: in space, places can be recognized when they are occupied by objects. At the same time, space and time emerge isotropically (and thus redundantly), whereas the places occupied by objects can alternate (in this sense, space and time are variable). One cannot do without the other, and this is why variety remains bound to redundancy. In time, the same formal accomplishment is tied to the identity of objects that can be recognized and confirmed in new situations, even though the temporal conditions may have changed. Space makes it *possible for objects to leave their places*. Time makes it *necessary for places to leave their objects*. In this way, contingency is furnished with necessity and necessity with contingency. The separation of the two media thus permits the unfolding, in the world, of the modal-theoretical paradox that the necessary is contingent and contingency necessary—this is already accomplished by perception, independently of any modal-logical solution to the problem.

An occupied space creates an atmosphere. Atmosphere is always what the individual objects that occupy places are not, the other side of their form, what perishes along with them. This explains the "invulnerability" of atmosphere, along with its dependency on a given occupied space.[24] Atmosphere is a kind of excess effect caused by the difference between places. It cannot be analyzed by describing places, nor is it reducible to places. It comes into being each time an object occupies a place and creates an ambiance that is neither identical to the object nor able to exist without it. Atmosphere makes visible both the unity of the difference that constitutes space and the invisibility of space as a medium for the creation of forms. But it is not the same as space, which, as a medium, can never become visible.

So long as the differentiation of society needs stable spatial boundaries—this is true especially in segmented societies but also holds for advanced societies in which stratification or city/country differentiation still rests on household economies—spatial symbols can be used to mark boundaries or other ambiguous sites, such as markets.[25] Since their spatial position is unambiguous, it supports and tolerates the transitory nature of events, the movement from one side to the other at a position determined as a crossover point. With the decreasing significance of spatial boundaries—for example, as a result of the universalization of a money-based economy and the dependency of the average household on monetary incomes—entrenched symbolizations presumably lose their power to convince and must be replaced by a semantics of signs. We shall return to this point.

Time articulates its necessity in terms of a *simultaneity* of all conditions and events—a kind of self-negation. Whatever is actualized at a given moment occupies *only one* position in time. All other positions momentarily withdraw and hence cannot be accessed; in this sense, they suggest a stable world. Instability correlates with actuality, stability with nonactuality—which is a manner of unfolding temporal necessity. The principle of space allows a place to be occupied *only* by one *single* object. (Depending on the kind of object, this place can be either reduced in size or enlarged.) From this unique position, however, *any other place is accessible* within the structure of places. Only the objects themselves make movement difficult. The stability (a temporal notion!) of space relies on each object having its place and remaining there so long as it doesn't move (movement always equals a loss of place, securing a new place is the exception.) Nor does this necessity exclude contingency; on the contrary, it includes it. The spatial position or place is precisely what is identified as world-place, the position *from which* other places are accessible. Both space and time thus require a place as a starting point that enables access to other places. The world itself remains inaccessible, because one can access the world only by moving from one place to another.

As perceptible objects, artworks must use the media of space and time so that they can exclude, from their unique position, other spaces and times. As artworks, these objects simultaneously create imaginary spaces and times. The imagination constitutes itself by including the exclusion of the world that is always given here and now, in real space and time. (This is how the imagination remains real and can be fixated in a work of art.) In the imaginary world, the medium/form structure of space and time replicates itself together with its unique unfolding of contingency and necessity. In art, however, this structure leaves varying degrees of freedom that can then be exploited for the self-limitation of art.

In the imaginary world of art, just as in the real world, a spatial position defines itself by providing access to other places. Architecture determines how the context of the edifice is to be seen. A sculpture defines its surrounding space. Temporal positions in art, above all in music, are determined by their own vanishing, and the artwork must define what remains significant and what can follow—a momentarily fixated and vanishing where and whence. It is always the difference, the boundary, that makes a difference and is turned into information by the work of art.

The most important contribution of the media of space and time to the evolution of art is perhaps the possibility *for tightening up redundancies and thus securing a higher degree of variety.* If the artwork can be successfully based on the unity of space and/or the unity of time as a means of ensuring redundancy—the formal sameness of all places—then it can assimilate much more variety. Yet the observer never loses the overview. He can still proceed step by step without running the risk of considering the work a failure. This effect can be accomplished by any optical, acoustic, or narrative means that ensures *everything* can be painted or narrated, so long as space and time provide the necessary stability. The most telling example is the invention of unified perspective. Others include temporally synchronized transitions in narrative[26] or the suggestion of tone sequences via melody, rhythm, the dissolution of dissonance, or retardation in music.

In this sense, the wealth of artistic possibilities rests on an imitation of the differential structure of space and time—not, as common belief has it, on an imitation of objects in the world of real space/time. Even "abstract" art creates and places objects. Otherwise it could accomplish nothing. But abstract art takes the liberty of unfolding these objects according to the logic of space and time and leaves it to the individual artwork to create a convincing arrangement.

Finally, we must keep in mind that space and time, both of which are media for calculating objects, do not yet provide a basis for classifying artistic kinds.[27] It would be wrong to think of spatial arts, on the one hand, and temporal arts, on the other. This fails to do justice to narrative, dance, or the theater. Even genres that tend toward one of these media might use the other as well. We think of sculpture as arrested in its movement[28] and organ music as clearly related to space. There is no hierarchical or bifurcated order in art—in the sense that the world could be split into space and time, and each of these media would subsequently divide to produce further artistic kinds as if by a Ramist logic. The evolutionary "accident" that led to the emergence of different perceptual media accounts for generic differences, and these media cannot afford to specialize exclusively in spatial or temporal observations.

The distinction between ornamental and figurative (representational, illusory) components of artworks seems more appropriate to guide our investigation. Ornaments organize space and time directly and supply these media with redundancy and variety. They presuppose a self-defined space that is closed off, as it were, from within. The same is true when time becomes ornament (in dance, or in the ups and downs of tension in narrative). From the viewpoint of the creative process, such an enclosure must first be created in the form of a partial space prepared specifically for this purpose (such as the facade of a building or the surface of a container), or as a slice of time with a self-determined beginning and end.[29] Representational art, by contrast, begins by projecting an imaginary space or time in order to gain a free hand in employing this self-created medium for purposes of ornamentation and representation. Since the early Renaissance, European art has preferred this option, relegating ornament to the function of decoration, of placing accents and emphasizing the essential. A closer look, however, reveals that the ornamental is always the work's infrastructure, even in deliberately representational art forms, for the following reason: if one employs space and time (how else could an artwork appear?), then these media must be organized, whatever might subsequently be represented in them.

IV

No matter how we place the accents, no matter how much a work's figurative or ornamental aspects may capture our attention at first, we must assume that the forms that constitute the work by virtue of their distinguishing force diverge, depending on which medium of perception or intuition they deploy.[30] There is no commensurability between painting and music, or between sculpture and dance, or between the lyric and the novel—which is not to say that there can be no "onomatopoeia" in music or that dancers cannot become sculptures. These formal differences are conditioned, not by the *choice* of form (if they were, then they could be avoided), but by the medium that underlies each form and that, by virtue of its loose coupling, makes tight couplings possible. Perceptual media do not display a spectrum as broad as that of artistic genres. Painting and sculpture, theater and dance, depend on light—a visual medium—whereas the lyric, like narrative (the epic, the novel), relies on language as a medium of fixation for intuition. But the manner in which art shapes and makes use of perceptual media differs in each genre. To radicalize our previous question: How can one speak of the unity of art, or of the unity of an artistic medium in view of such diversity?

In anticipating this question, we have taken great care to elaborate the distinction between medium and form. We can start from there. Perceptual media are media of the psyche in Heider's sense, rather than of a social or communicative nature. No one can share the perception of others, although one can perceive that others perceive or that others perceive one's perceiving. We shall make the controversial claim that the same is true in the realm of intuition, that is, in the realm of imagined perception. It is true when language is used for the purpose of stimulating intuition (rather than communicating information) and thus holds also for artworks created in language, especially the novel. No one knows what another experiences intuitively when reading about Odysseus and how he had himself tied to the mast, or about Siebenkäs, who searches for his own grave only to find the woman he will eventually marry.[31] No one knows how others imagine Robinson's surprise when Friday appears, or how Napoleon (in *War and Peace*) is struck by the events of the Russian campaign. One tends to speak of "fictional" literature in these cases. Whatever that means, the fictional medium is primarily constituted by the private nature of an intuition that requires no "continuation of communication" and therefore no special effort on the part of consciousness and memory, but instead allows them to operate freely.

How, then, is art nonetheless possible as communication? And what, in this case, would be the medium of communication?

The key to this question may well reside in the intentionally created observational relationships we analyzed in the previous chapter. Once someone (no matter who) recognizes, from the manner of presentation, an arrangement that is produced for an observer, a social medium has come into existence—whether or not this aspect is communicated in the work of art. Literary texts in particular often distinguish themselves by self-referential clues of this sort. (Incorporating the text's production into the text, addressing the reader, attacking the reviewers in the manner of Jean Paul are still rather crude stylistic means, aimed at differentiating the text at the level of an observation of observations.) In the wake of these developments, it becomes possible to establish an "artificial" form that simultaneously serves as a medium for forms within the form—such as the space contained in a painting, the potential movement of a sculpture arrested in time, or the realm of possible events in which a narrative establishes sequences that present in tightly coupled forms—in this and no other way—what might well turn out otherwise. Or consider the deceptive maneuvers of baroque architecture, which are enjoyable only when seen through, or dance, which does not take the direction of its movement from ordinary life but instead presents it so that it appears, from moment to moment, as if it had been selected only for the sake of the dance.

Although perceptual media and artistic genres differ greatly with regard to their concrete materialization, they share a common ground in the manner in which they construct novel medium/form relations that are intended to be observed and are intelligible only when this is understood. The unity of art resides in that it creates for the sake of observation and observes for the sake of being observed, and the medium of art consists in the freedom to create medium/form relations.

The possibility for combining forms and thereby tightening the work, as it were, from within, suggests another parallel between individual genres. We recall that forms are always two-sided. No matter what they indicate and fixate in the work of art, they always simultaneously present another side that must cooperate in rendering visible what is determined by the work. This is true if the artwork itself is meant to be recognized as a specific object (and nothing else). It holds for every detail that constitutes the work in collaboration with others.

The unmarked space is the indispensable other side, a reference to possibilities that, for their part, point to an infinity that cannot be contained in one place.[32] The first step in the making of an artwork leads from the unmarked space into a marked space, and it creates a boundary by crossing that boundary. Spencer Brown speaks of "drawing a distinction." At the same time, a difference between medium and form comes into being, an enclosed, specially prepared marked space, in which the artwork follows the pull of its own distinctions and determines its own forms.

The determination of one side does not entirely leave open what can happen on the other side—this accounts for the specificity of individual art forms. While it does not determine the other side, it renders it nonarbitrary. What can happen there must "fit" or it will cause dissonance, a flaw, or disruption (which can, of course, be intentional, in which case it requires a balancing fit on its part). The determination of one side, as we just stated, does not determine the other. But it facilitates decisions and the observation of decisions concerning what can happen or has been established on the other side by the artist. If an indication is to become a work of art, then the other side must remain *accessible*—which assumes that one can demarcate another unmarked space in relation to this other side.

Whenever an object is intended to be a work of art, the indication does not refer merely to itself (to this and no other object). It also refers to the crossing of the boundary that divides the form into two halves and instructs the observer to search for and fix what has not yet been decided. This holds for the artist as well as for the observer of art, and ultimately for any observation that depends on time. The indication, we might say, is used as meaning. Crossing the boundary never leads into the unmarked space, never into the world as such, but always executes an indication, a new indication. As we know, indications can only be executed as distinctions. They specify only one side of (another) distinction that, for its part, has its own other side. This is why an artwork cannot reject the world.[33] To do so, it would first have to indicate and distinguish the world, that is to say, it would have to execute operations that can occur only in the world.

In this sense, the artwork forces both the artist and the observer to advance from one form to the next in order to return eventually to the form from which they began, which is now the other side of another form. Forms play with forms, but the play remains formal. It never arrives at "matter," it never serves as a sign for something else.[34] Each formal determination functions simultaneously as an irritation that leaves room for subsequent decisions, and advancing from one form to the next is an experiment that either succeeds or fails. This is why, as we shall elaborate below, a "code" emerges in art, a continuously maintained binary orientation concerning the "fit" or "lack of fit" of forms. This is why every artwork contains "information" in Gregory Bateson's sense—differences that make a difference.[35] And all of this holds for *any kind* of art!

Accordingly, for all genres the medium of art is the sum total of possible ways of crossing form boundaries (distinctions) from within toward the outside and of discovering fitting indications on the other side that stimulate further crossings by virtue of their own boundaries. The medium of art is present in every artwork, yet it is invisible, since it operates only on the other side—the one not indicated—as a kind of attractor for further observations. The process of discovery transforms the medium into form. Or else one fails. In working together, form and medium generate what characterizes successful artworks, namely, *improbable evidence.*

Does this always have to be *another* distinction with *another* side? One may well imagine an artwork that has two components but only one form (or, more accurately, a precise congruence of two inverse forms that overlap one another). In this case, one focuses on the side that is the other side of the other side and vice versa. The formal asymmetry necessary for observation is canceled in symmetry. One can only oscillate between the two sides. Any further dynamic is blocked. We have, in other words, the precise image of a logical paradox, a kind of time trap that compels the observer to move back and forth between its poles in the shortest possible instance. This is not meaningless, nor is a logical paradox meaningless. But the meaning of such a figure—of its form—must be sought in the clue that allows for unfolding this paradox and reintroduces asymmetry into the form.

Paradoxes present the world in the form of a self-blocking observation. It is certainly possible to stage works of art as paradoxes, but only in order to demonstrate what doesn't work, only to symbolize the unobservability of the world. Works consisting of only two components are not yet genuine artworks. But to the extent that they carry along the other side of the form as an empty form, as mere exteriority, they are works of art after all.[36] This is particularly true where paradox becomes the work's theme—as in Escher's etchings, in Magritte's work, or in certain forms of sixteenth- and seventeenth-century lyric poetry, especially that of John Donne.[37] In these cases, the paradoxical oscillation of truth is introduced deliberately—not to represent the world, but to invite the viewer or reader to search for an innovative exit that remains undetermined in the work and about which even the artist himself may have his doubts.[38] While several aesthetic forms may work together to accomplish this effect, paradox remains the superform, the frame suggestive of what remains unsaid in the work and what is only marked as unsaid.

Let us return to the ordinary. What remains open as the other side of a form is generally determined by an indication that actualizes another distinction for which the same is true. This process keeps going until a system of references closes itself off, in which nothing remains undetermined. Occasionally, things may go wrong in the process, and the remaining discord must be covered up or minimized. This is a fact of life. Our concern here is not art criticism but the principle of form, the process of observing (the making and observing) of artworks.

It should be clear by now that this analysis precludes comprehending an artwork in terms of the relation between a whole and its parts. Dividing a work and judging the relationship between parts misses its internal nexus. Nor are we concerned with the primacy of the whole in relation to its parts.[39] If one wants to isolate parts, then one discovers that their contribution to the work consists in what they are *not*, what they make available for further elaboration. The artwork closes itself off by reusing what is already determined in the work as the other side of further distinctions. The result is a unique, circular accumulation of meaning, which often escapes one's first view (or is grasped only "intuitively"). Eventually, it may turn out that a determination plays a role in several distinctions at once, that it is multifunctional and therefore not interchangeable. This creates an overall impression of necessity—the work is what it is, even though it is made, individual, and contingent, rather than necessary in an ontological sense. The work of art, one might say, manages to overcome its own contingency.

Several more or less standardized, genre-specific formal models are available for this process. The basic form for generating forms from other forms is the (misleadingly so called) ornament.[40] All ornaments are based on the problem of broken symmetry, on the problem of form. At stake here is the projection of asymmetries that still exhibit traces of the symmetries from which they emerged. Ornaments are recursions that keep going by recalling previous and anticipating further forms. They display the unity of redundancy and variety.[41] Transitions are effaced; at least they are not emphasized as breaks, since each place in an ornament is at the same time the place of another place. This includes the repetition of forms at other points in space or time, whereby their positional difference suggests nonidentity within the ornament's overall identity. Continuation is the principle that integrates what is excluded at first, that defines the excluded as a motif, reiterates it, or connects other motifs. This clearly shows that art is neither a sign for something else nor the mere form of the material. The ornament generates its own imaginary space by continuously transforming formal boundaries into transitions that have more than one meaning. It prevents the work from falling apart into isolated figures, on which one can focus or from which one can turn away. The ornament, in other words, holds the artwork together, precisely because it does not partake in its figurative division. One can call this "mere decoration" only in social situations in which the differentiation of art is already under way, whereas decorative ornaments also adorn utilitarian objects, jewelry, sacred objects, or "crafts," so that mere decoration must be distinguished from art. In such a situation, the ornamental structure can be granted only a subordinate role.[42] Gombrich speaks of an "explanatory division" and supplements his observation by referring to the masking function of decoration:[43] on the one hand, decoration renders the information more distinct and enables faster comprehension; on the other hand, it suppresses contradictory, confusing information. The ornament accomplishes all this with a luxurious excess that tends to become an end in itself.

The basic idea is still one of "hierarchical opposition," of a contrast between balanced proportion and mere adornment. One expects art to keep decoration under control. This places the burden on the dominant side of the distinction, on what is supposedly balanced proportion or is later called symbolic meaning. But the inability to resolve the problem of hierarchy eventually "deconstructs" the distinction itself. The ornament, initially meant to fulfill a secondary function, takes on the burden of supplying meaning. If one wants to observe artworks as art with reference to their play of forms, then one must pay attention to their ornaments.

Only then can one return to the question of how the work is made and which secondary meanings serve the ornament while receiving from the ornament the electrical charge that accounts for their artistic quality. Painting, too, eventually pushes its ornaments to the margins or into the background—which needs to be filled anyway—in order to foreground its figures. Assisted by unified perspective, painting develops the background into an open space—a landscape, for example—only to discover the need to compensate for the ornament's function by filling its imaginary space with nonarbitrary objects until, in the end, even the landscape is no longer necessary.[44] While the ornament is marginalized as mere decoration that can also adorn nonartistic objects, a functional equivalent of the ornament emerges from within artworks themselves—an inner "line of beauty"[45] that joins what has been separated figuratively, a line that is more distinctly curved and of much greater condensation than any natural line. Even as ornamental adornment is excluded from art, the ornament is reborn within the work. Similarly, in poetry sound and rhythm are more easily replaced by meanings, which requires that the play with distinctions be reproduced as a formal nexus among narrative elements. By indicating an action, narrative, for example, can serve two distinctions at once: it characterizes the agent and moves the plot forward.[46] The *au-thor* arranges the events, that is, he shapes the medium in such a way that the *reader* can infer the changing mental state of the hero. The *fictionality* of the arrangement hides behind the *contingency* of events and actions that must serve as the starting point for the reader who follows the narrative.

The intense use of these possibilities leads to the modern novel of the individual. "Flat" heroes become "round,"[47] their motives become trans-parent, the strength of motives is demonstrated (typically those preferred by the author, such as the profit motive in *Robinson Crusoe* or *Moll Flan-ders*). At the same time, narrative can induce changes in a character; it can motivate learning, religious conversion, or regret; and it can recommend its result to the reader as a laudable attitude. This development allows the novel to free itself from moral guidelines, and the reader is confronted with live models and experiences that could be his own.[48] Once the for-mal combination of character and plot by means of actions—a combina-tion that informs both of these distinctions—has established itself and guides the reader's expectations, it becomes possible to write narratives that still present themselves as novels but break with this combination. These narratives seek to distinguish themselves by precluding any infer-ences concerning the character and motives of the hero or by refusing to move the plot along by means of actions. This development begins as early as Flaubert's *L'éducation sentimentale* (1869).

The internal ornament serves the artwork's self-description; it beautifies because it is beautiful.[49] It absorbs as much variety as possible, as much as it can bind. On the one hand, the form combination that is selected indi-vidualizes the artwork and qualifies it as a distinct object. This allows for technical reproduction, which neither affects the work's recognizability nor "damages" its individual form, but instead makes it more accessible. Technical reproduction, in turn, generates a new form: the distinction be-tween original and copy. On the other hand, observing how the work is made yields an observation of a more general type often called "style."[50] At the level of stylistic forms, the art system is able to evolve; it can replace form combinations that have already been tested or derive new forms from the rejection of what has become all too familiar. Moreover, the sys-tem can turn rejection itself into a form that is intelligible only to those aware of what used to be customary and what, accordingly, is the expec-tation to be disappointed.[51] The movement that, strangely enough, calls itself the avant-garde has taken this backward-looking manner to an extreme—like oarsmen, who face the direction they are coming from and have the goal of their journey behind their backs.

We will not elaborate on these reflections. Instead, we would note that situations of this sort—in any artistic genre—presuppose the artwork as a specific combination of forms, no matter how this presupposition is then attacked in the search for new forms. This protest is possible only when (and so long as!) a loosely coupled medium is available for the creation of possible forms. If the previous reflections hold, then this medium may well reside in the need for another, yet undefined side on the other side of the indications that make up an artwork. This need would explain why an artwork, in closing itself off and in determining its open side by means of other distinctions, coagulates the medium in such a way that a tightly coupled form emerges, though the medium always reproduces itself at the same time—that is, the question of what lies on the other side of the form is posed anew in each instance.

V

We began with the medium of perception, mentioning the medium of language only in passing. But in order to demonstrate the unity of art and the formal similarity of all artistic genres, we must pay attention to the verbal arts as well, especially to poetry. Here, we are dealing with *words* as medium, as a loosely coupled set of elements. Words serve not only as elements to be coupled but also as a means for the artwork's self-description, a means of bringing about the unity of the description and the described.[52] Accordingly, the creation of poetic form consists in a special formal combination of words that calls upon words to display an unusual meaning—whether or not it relies on the structure of grammatically correct sentences. This can happen only if distinctions are placed *in* words. There is no need to paraphrase these distinctions; nor can they be paraphrased, for to do so would create the possibility for rejection—just what art wants to avoid.

Ordinary language uses the same words in multiple contexts and therefore relies on wearing down their meanings and on phrases as an aid to understanding. It seeks to establish unambiguous denotations and accomplishes this goal via naming and the construction of abstract objects, conceptual correlates, or ideas. Poetic language operates in reverse—with or without the aid of phrases. It reflects on the usage of language—as if language were one material among others that one finds in the world.[53] Poetry has no use for denotations. Instead, it relies on connotations,[54] employing words as a medium in which the connotations that select one another assume form. Rather than forcing the diffuse referential richness of words into the most unambiguous relation to facts in the world, poetry posits this richness (including the resonance of what remains unsaid) over against the facts. Just as atoms alter their internal electronics when combining into molecules, poetry modifies the meaning of words. It may generate striking new nuances or create estrangement, but it can also surprise by restoring the original meaning of everyday words. Overgeneralized forms are pried open and reconstructed. Poetry contextualizes such forms so that they become structurally determined and can no longer easily be recognized. Like any use of form, this strategy aims at what it excludes. Other words can pick up what remains unsaid, but they can also serve as a reminder that many important things must be left unsaid. The other side of the form always plays along—as a boundary that can either be crossed by further guided observations or else is fixed, again and again, as the same boundary, as the unmarked space of different words.

Poetry shifts from a denotative to a connotative use of words because of its need for poetic closure—a closure for which the poetic genre does not choose the form of narrative. Referential meaning would refer the reader into the world, where it would lose itself among the multiple references that make up the meaning of reality.[55] The poem becomes a unity only at the level of connotation, by exploring the liberties that come with using words exclusively as a medium.[56] This means that only temporary forms can be secured at this level, forms one must relinquish when moving from one poem to the next. Poetry requires an intensification of memory, that is, a retroactive reading (if one still wants to call this "reading"[57]). Author and reader must leave behind the linearity of the text and apprehend its structure in a circular manner; they must be able to take apart the network of multiple circles that makes up a text. But such an effort is feasible and can be accomplished only within a single poem.

Connotations start out from the familiar meanings of words, truncating only their hetero-reference so that opposites, for example, can appear as a unity, even though and even because this is not how they appear in the external world. This technique requires a suspension of the ordinary referential meaning of words, which catches the reader off guard. Last, but not least, this is possible because of the *ornamental* quality of verbal constellations. This quality may reside in the sound of words (*nevermore* and *vast* [English in the original] are well-known examples), or it may be an effect of the relation between short and long syllables or of repetitions, echoes, stereotypes, contrasts, anagrams. In *Finnegans Wake*, the ornamental quality of language, the resonance between sounds and *other* words, overwhelms the text to an extent that intelligible words communicate only that they do not matter. Rhythms are complicated to the point where they escape reading altogether and require recitation to be apprehended. To convince, poetry appeals to perception, not to thinking. And the function of the ornament, in poetry as elsewhere, is to intensify redundancy and variety in ways that would otherwise hardly be possible.

Poetry, then, is not just rhymed prose. If one reads poetry as a sequence of propositions about the world and considers the poetic only as beautification, adornment, or decoration, one does not observe it as a work of art. Nor can one apprehend in this way the formal combination the poet uses to compose his work. Only at the level where symbols,[58] sounds, meanings, and rhythms conspire—a level that is difficult to "read"—do poems refer to themselves in the process of creating forms. They generate contextual dependencies, ironic references, and paradoxes, all of which refer back to the text that produces these effects. Supported by the text, poetic self-reference may eventually articulate itself explicitly[59]—not as a flat, abrupt statement, but as a form within the nexus of forms that constitute the text.

The problems presented by the materiality of words have often been discussed, at least since Mallarmé and frequently with reference to him. It seemed plausible to locate the problem in the relationship between consciousness and language, in the poet's access to language, or in the self-sacrifice commanded by the shaping of language. This general insight, which ultimately points to the distinction between psychic and social systems, can be supplemented by the distinction between medium and form. This distinction is a projection of art, here a projection of poetry, a form of its autopoiesis. It is given neither as matter nor as Spirit. It has no ontological substrate, which makes it tempting to observe how observers handle this distinction.

All of this needs further elaboration. William Empson and Cleanth Brooks brought these problems to the attention of a literary theory that calls itself "critical."[60] But instead of producing a general terminology of form, this awareness yielded only the formal analyses of the New Literary Criticism and subsequently led to the critique of what these analyses ignored.[61] Caught in the conventional division between the visual arts and literature, the promise of a unified theory of artistic kinds went unfulfilled. Currently, however, literary theory is sufficiently receptive to interdisciplinary suggestions that this separation is unlikely to prevail. Thus after this excursion into the special domain of the medium of language, we return to more general analyses.

VI

The medium of art renders the creation of forms at once possible and improbable. The medium always contains other possibilities and makes everything determined appear to be contingent. This improbability is emphasized when everyday purposes and utilities are bracketed as the guiding principles of observation. Artistic form (backed by aesthetic reflection) goes out of its way not to appear useful.

In this way, the artwork directs the beholder's awareness toward the *improbability of its emergence.* If attention is drawn to poetic constructions, then it is only because they do not seem very likely, whereas the likelihood of using other constructions is, on the contrary, very high. "Poetic is that which has not become law," writes Julia Kristeva.[62] Especially for poetic texts, one might add that their improbability must not be based on their informational value, which always implies a certain quality of surprise, but consists in their renunciation of information in the sense of mundane utility.

During the past two centuries, a number of doctrines derived from this enforced improbability surfaced in poetic reflection—the rejection of a rule-based poetics, for example, or the emphasis on the individuality and originality of an authentic artwork, and eventually the search for an alternative explanation of the improbable that points to the "genius" of the artists. But these are collateral circumstances, secondary phenomena that accompany efforts to come to terms with the improbable. When focusing on the improbability of form itself, one is primarily concerned with the observer's fascination, his staying-put-with-the-work in a sequence of observations that attempt to decipher it.

One might expect the sequence of medium-form-medium-form formations progressively to constrain the medium's possibilities, thus leading to an increase in redundancy. Many potential sculptures come to mind if one considers only the media of space and material. When one represents a mobile living being, the limitations of its body constrain what can be rendered. Lessing's analysis of the *Laocoön* shows that the artist is not entirely free in selecting the moment from which the before and after of movements can be rendered visible. Once we are dealing with the *Dying Gaul* or with stage productions of *Lucia di Lammermoor*, very few performances are conceivable that could give form to precisely this medium. The improbability of the composition must be wrested from these limitations. This may result in a "structural drift" within the art system that turns into an end in itself not only the artwork but above all its improbability. Eventually, one begins to experiment with the idea of declaring everything a work of art so long as an artistic claim can be asserted and maintained. The work's probability then boils down to the credibility of such a claim.

But artistic credibility is still a relationship between medium and form. The difficulty of creating forms shifts to the difficulty of claiming a work as art and maintaining this claim. Yet the medium remains a medium of art by virtue of its ties to the history of art; it continues to function as a medium that propels the historical machinery of the art system beyond its current state with new and ever more daring forms. The medium might absorb decontextualized historical references, as it does in postmodernism, whereby the improbability resides precisely in this decontextualization, in free selection from a historical reservoir of forms. What used to be bound historically is now up for grabs on the condition that it remain recognizable as such. One might equally well continue the project of the avantgarde in an effort to expand, via the production of art, the concept of art itself. In both cases, art turns into the artistic medium insofar as, and so long as, it is capable of making the observer recognize the improbable as improbable. In the end, the observer might even be challenged to comprehend the incomprehensibility—created especially for him—of an artwork as a reference to an incomprehensible world.

The recognition that every form is a form-in-a-medium dates back to romanticism. A medium suited for artistic forms had to be sought, discovered, and eventually constructed by dismantling interpretive aids taken from everyday life. The fairytale-like incredibility of backdrops served this purpose and simultaneously indicated that henceforth only absolute self-reflection—a reflection that includes the observer—could be presupposed as the ultimate medium. Fantastic art,[63] by leaving open whether or not the events and forms presented can be explained naturally, is subject to similar conditions. But the general situation was still conceived in terms of the subject, an authority that underlies itself and everything else. In the meantime, the dynamic of the art system has evolved in ways that can no longer be attributed to a subject. The observer—the self-reference underlying all distinctions and the distinctions underlying all self-reference— seems a more appropriate basic figure. From the position of the observer, one can unfold this circle by distinguishing the distinction from the indication of one of its sides, and self-reference from hetero-reference. This distinction specifies the operation of observing as a distinguishing indication and defines the concept of the self-referential system as a system that copies the operatively generated distinction between system and environment into itself and bases its observing operations on the distinction between self-reference and hetero-reference.

Once the "subject" gives way to the observer, we no longer need the counterconcept of an object. Regarding the manner of operation, a wide range of possibilities is now conceivable besides intentional awareness (a state of consciousness). The observer can be a social system, and observation can be communication. The artwork is not necessarily a device that causes the perspectives of producer and observer (or of theories of production and reception) to oscillate. Still, nothing speaks against starting out from references to psychic systems, either to the artist or the observer. But the emergent unity of the art system and its unique medium cannot be grasped in this manner. The art system is a special system of social communication. It has its own self-reference and hetero-references that indicate forms existing exclusively in a medium unique to art. This medium is the improbability of the combinatory structure of form that art wrests from everyday life and that refers the observer to other observers.

These reflections eventually raise the question of whether an artwork has to be difficult and, if so, why.[64] Like everything else, this proposition can be questioned today, and there is a tendency to separate art from craftsmanship. Pushed to its extreme, difficulty might ultimately boil down to the problem of how one can work as an artist in a manner that is still recognizable. Pointing to the essence of art—to the idea of art, the rarity of genius, or the like—is of no help in this matter. The question, rather, is whether and for what reasons the medium's potential for creating forms must be limited, and how this limitation is accomplished.

Within a theory of symbolically generalized media, Talcott Parsons assumed that each of these media, just like money, requires a real backing that can be overdrawn by confidence but not expanded at will. Using the medium below or in excess of its capacities is certainly possible, but it leads to an inflation or deflation of the medium that jeopardizes its functioning.[65] If we follow Parsons's suggestion, then what would be the backing of art, especially of modern art? Obviously, nothing external to the medium can fulfill this function; what backs the medium of art is the work's triumph over its own improbability.

This is why the trend toward facilitating the creation of forms and reducing forms to simple distinctions cannot be countered by judgments of taste or values. Even the concept of art apparently no longer sets limits to what can count as art. But one can know that the medium/form dynamic requires constraints and that expansive trends lead to inflation. How much inflation the art system can tolerate boils down to an empirical question. Sanctions are evident not in the reaction against violations of the norm but in the loss of interest in the observation of observations.

VII

As we suggested earlier, the distinction between medium and form is based on a complex relationship to time. On the one hand, medium and form must be actualized simultaneously. On the other hand, the medium reproduces itself only by alternating the forms that an observer employs as distinctions. The stability of the medium rests on the instability of forms that repeatedly realize and dissolve tightly coupled relationships. Media are constant, forms alternate. In the basic medium of meaning, all other media are subject to variation as well, but only to the extent that they are observed as forms in another medium.

The paradoxical "simultaneity" of invariance and variability corresponds to the general problem of structuring the autopoietic reproduction of systems. Only actualized elements that assume the form of events (operations) can reproduce the system, which requires a recursive recapitulation of the past and anticipation of future events; in other words, nonactualized events must be actualized as nonactual. The actualization of the nonactual requires (and is made possible by) a selectivity that employs the logic of the distinguishing indication. Selections capable of actualizing the nonactual always function as structures—in the moment of their actualization—by virtue of references that transcend the actual.[66]

In art, the work's material substratum guarantees that the observing operations can be repeated. It ensures that the potential for repetition is perceived along with the work and that it actualizes what is momentarily nonactual. At the same time, the work indicates the nonidentity of the repetition. We are aware that we experience the same work (without questioning its sameness) differently each time—for example, as recognizable or familiar, as confirming our attitudes rather than presenting us with astonishing information. Redundancy and variation collaborate in their effects. Repetition alters what is repeated—especially when the repeated content is recognized and affirmed as the same. Identity is necessary—but only to allow for the nonidentical reproduction of the observing operation. Observational sequences can build up comfortable redundancies and suppress provoking irritations; they can search for confirmation in one aspect of the work and find it in another. In the visual arts, the stability of the material secures this process. In texts, writing—and in music, the repeatability of the production (with or without notation)—does the same. We need not pursue the details of this art-external (material, memorylike) anchorage here; what should be stressed is that it requires a *separation of individual artworks.* The horizon of reference must be interrupted in order to allow for recursion, for the return to the same, and for the structuring anticipation of this return. But if this is true, doesn't the art system disintegrate into a disjointed ensemble of individual works?

This question enforces the recurrence of the temporal problem at the level of the system's autopoiesis, a level that transcends the individual artwork. At this level, the temporal paradox of structuring, the paradoxical actuality of the nonactual, recurs at a higher level. It is no surprise that unfolding the paradox once again boils down to a distinction—not between externally secured constants and the fluidity of observation, but between change and conservation in what counts as art.

To observe the changes in a domain common to many artworks, the (historical) concept of *style* has been available since the last three decades of the eighteenth century.[67] Long before that, the concept of style had been used to designate ways in which the elements of an artwork are coupled.[68] Rhetoric, following a general trend of hierarchization, proposed a ranking of styles and prescribed styles according to the dignity of their objects.[69] Not until Winckelmann was the concept of style—which concerns factual differences such as "writing," manner, and presentation—anchored in a temporal dimension and claimed to reveal (and cause) historical differences. The distinctions employed by artworks, the "against what?" of their manner, were subjected to the pressure of innovation. Not only did individual works have to distinguish themselves, but what did not distinguish them needed to be distinguishable at another level of comparison, as being sanctioned by the concept of style. One expected style to legislate itself—not to succumb to a prescribed canon, but rather to distinguish itself by deviating from models. A style prolongs the half-life of the public's interest in a work of art; one is reminded of similarities in other works and can observe each work anew with reference to similarities and differences. Style respects tradition by deviating from it. Deviation is a specific form of acknowledging relevance; it is not indifference or ignorance. Deviation requires knowledge of the subject matter, circumspection, and precision in selecting aspects where deviation matters, and often it is necessary to reformulate the unity of the preceding style with disregard for what was relevant and accessible to this style. The procedure is a typical case of recursive reconstruction!

At the same time, there is the opposite trend: to hold on to what is worth preserving, precisely because of deviation. Objects are put into museums or, when this is not possible—as with textual art—they are identified as "timeless" classics.[70] Museums grow out of processes that decide what is and what is not accepted. Today, even the most recent art can be defined as given (= already dated) by the mere fact of being accepted and displayed in a museum. The decision observes observers, that is, it belongs to the level of second-order observation. Classicism, too, is a construct, created by observers for other observers,[71] and the intent of this construct has always been to reverse time: in contrast to other works, classical works improve with time.[72] Museums and the classics symbolize an art removed from stylistic change, which is of no significance whatever unless there is something against which the preservation of worthy objects is directed, namely, the perpetual historicization of styles. The notion, implicit in the idea of style, "that one is no longer able and will never again be able to work that way" reinforces the conservation of resources that are no longer reproduced, and each loss becomes an "irreplaceable" loss. One needs institutions of mourning, of the "nevermore" [English in the original].[73]

This diagnosis shows that even at this level the paradoxical unity of the distinction between medium and form seeks identifications, plausible distinctions that can be carried on and prove one another. Style as form, the museum as form, classicism as form: all of these forms respond to the same fundamental situation (concealed by forms themselves), namely, that loose

and tight couplings are reproduced simultaneously in a manner that is invariant and invisible in the medium and variable and visible in the form.
What reacts to this situation is not a supermeaning, a principle of art, an
ultimate, convincing idea, but yet another distinction plausible enough to
enable convincing identifications. The form of "style" processes the burden of innovation and along with it the temporality of all forms while cast-
ing a secret glance toward an eternal life beyond its own time. The form of
the museum and the form of classicism live off a work's ability to outlast
changing styles and find therein its meaning.

Although art collections have been around for a long time and there
have always been preferred authors and composers, the museum and classicism as forms of conservation presuppose an art system that operates at
the level of second-order observation. It is therefore no accident that these
forms, along with a historicized concept of style, appear in the final decades of the eighteenth century—at a time when the differentiation of the
art system reaches the level of second-order observation, when it establishes itself and begins to solve its problems at this level. Now one begins
to inquire into the unity of the arts regardless of the different media of
perception in which they realize their primary forms. Only now is art, no
matter what kind, defined in temporal and historical terms. This period
also introduces a reflexive concept of culture: it situates culture within the
context of historical and regional ("national") comparisons for the purpose of self-evaluation. Once the game of observation is played at this
level, it finds rules and opportunities for self-affirmation, which, for the
time being, provide sufficient orientation. An "analytical" terminology capable of more rigorous analyses is nowhere in sight. At any rate, such a
terminology would only reveal the paradox that informs any operation
with distinctions.

§4 The Function of Art and the Differentiation of the Art System

I

One of the few constants in the century-old academic history of sociology is the assumption that modern society is characterized by a certain degree of social differentiation and by some unique form of differentiation.[1] Historical development, it turns out, is subject not only to differentiation but also to de-differentiation.[2] Moreover, the elaboration of systems theory and the theory of evolution have altered the manner in which the theorem of differentiation is justified and how it is conceptually framed. Today, one no longer works with analogies based on the paradigm of the division of labor, which was believed to occur spontaneously whenever there was an opportunity, simply because of its yields or its productive rationality. It is doubtful that more differentiation, or differentiation at the level of the division of labor, is generally desirable. (Adam Smith already pointed out its disadvantages.) Currently, an overall critical, more skeptical, and doubtful attitude prevails. This does not change the fact that the theorem of differentiation posits a crucial accent, if not the main criterion for distinguishing modern society from its predecessors. However, if differentiation in its specifically modern form turns out to be not as beneficial as was previously assumed, then one needs to revise one's judgment of modern society. Many indications point toward this.

A first step—which hardly improves our relation to the tradition—is to describe modern society as a functionally differentiated system. Generally speaking, this means that the orientation toward specific functions (or problems) of the social system catalyzes the formation of subsystems that

133

dominate the face of society. If one wants to investigate the consequences of this development and wants to know how differentiation affects the subdomains of social communication (in this case art), then one must focus one's conceptual apparatus more accurately. Most importantly, one must clarify how functions can serve as evolutionary "attractors," and in precisely what sense subsystems constitute systems in their own right.[3]

A description of the art system that takes these background assumptions for granted and analyzes the form of social differentiation in general systems-theoretical terms yields consequences that will accompany us from now on. Today, systems theory is a highly developed, albeit controversial, analytical instrument. It requires theoretical decisions that do not directly concern art. (This, of course, holds for other—for example, semiological—analyses of art as well.) In conjunction with the thesis that society is a functionally differentiated system and is in this form historically unique, a systems-theoretical orientation has further consequences. It means that the different functional systems are treated in many respects as comparable. The terminology we introduced earlier demonstrates this in remarkable detail. Issues such as system formation and system boundaries, function, medium and forms, operative closure, autopoiesis, first- and second-order observation, and coding and programming can be investigated with regard to any functional system. As these investigations take shape and yield answers, a theory of society emerges that does not depend on discovering a unified meaning behind society—for example, by deriving societies from the nature of man, from a founding contract, or from an ultimate moral consensus. Such propositions may be treated as part of the theory's subject matter, as different forms of self-description available to the system of society. What ultimately characterizes society, however, manifests itself in the comparability of its subsystems.[4]

In a domain such as art (just as for law, science, politics, and so on), we discover not unique traits of art but features that can be found, *mutatis mutandis*, in other functional systems as well—for example, the shift to a mode of second-order observation. Art participates in society by differentiating itself as a system, which subjects art to a logic of operative closure—just like any other functional system. We are not primarily concerned with problems of causality, of society's influence on art and of art on society. (Such issues are of secondary importance.) Nor do we advocate the defensive attitude that the autonomy of art ought to be upheld and protected. Modern art is autonomous in an operative sense. No one else does what it does. This is why questions concerning the independence or dependence of art can arise in a causal sense. The societal nature of modern art consists in its operative closure and autonomy, provided that society imposes this form on all functional systems, one of which is art.

We base the following analyses on a distinction, namely, on the distinction between system/environment relations, on the one hand, and system/system relations, on the other. When dealing with system/environment relations, the system constitutes the internal side of the form, whereas the environment is its unmarked space. "The environment" is nothing but an empty correlate of the system's self-reference; it provides no information. If, however, we are dealing with system/system relations, then the other side can be marked and indicated. In this case, art no longer deals with "everything else" but with questions such as whether and to what extent the artist is motivated by political convenience or by wealthy customers.

Insofar as system/environment relations are concerned, system differentiation merely replicates the difference between system and environment within the system, that is, it reenters the two-sided form system/environment into the system.[5] The decisive question is whether, and in what ways, other autopoietic systems, endowed with their own autonomy and their own operative closure, can emerge within the autopoietic system of society (which is closed with regard to its own operation of communication). The answer lies in the problems that occur in the system at large, problems that take over the subsystems as their own functions, because these functions can be fulfilled nowhere else. Older social formations provide examples of such operative closure—urban communities based on center/periphery differentiation, and aristocratic societies based on stratification. But if at times centers of privileged life partially differentiate themselves, this does not mean that autopoietic, operationally closed subsystems are established within society at large—except within the dominant framework of segmentary differentiation. Only given functional differentiation do the subsystems generated according to this principle become operationally autonomous, because none of these systems can fulfill the function of the other.[6]

In system/system relations, the concept of form becomes relevant in a different way. Only in such relations can one speak of a "form of differentiation" in the sense that a system's type of differentiation informs the system of the other systems it must expect in its environment: systems of the same type in the case of segmentation, systems of a different type in the case of a center/periphery differentiation, and both similar and different systems in the case of functional differentiation. The differentiation of a functional system already indicates that there must be other such systems in its environment—whatever else the environment might contain—for the simple reason that all the necessary functions of the system as a whole must be taken care of in one way or another.

These reflections suggest a certain developmental logic in the evolution of forms of differentiation. This is not a matter of decomposing a given whole into its parts. Forms of differentiation are not principles of decomposition. If they were, then the transition from one form to another would be difficult to imagine. Rather, the system of society as a whole involves the possibility for differentiating operatively closed subsystems. When, and only when, this happens, the subsystem assumes a form that presupposes another side. The specific system type suggests what kinds of other systems can be expected on the other, external side of the form: other settlements if the form is a settlement; systems of lower rank if differentiation rests on a claim to higher rank; and eventually other functional systems if the differentiated system specializes itself along functional lines. In this way, religion was crucial for the development of the early modern state, first as ammunition for civil wars and later—after reorganizing itself during the tridentium and within the corresponding structures of a state church that evolved in the Protestant world—as a partner in another, political function.

The relations between art and stratificatory differentiation are certainly more complex than one might expect in retrospect. When one distinguishes individual genres and then asks how they can be connected, the problem presents itself as one of hierarchical ranking[7]—that is, in the terms in which the unity of society or of the world is described. Hierarchy makes people look upward—even if it increasingly conflicts with the self-image of art. On the one hand, the nobility certainly did commission artworks. Art finds appropriate objects, persons, and destinies only in the highest social circles.[8] There is a connection here to the moral-pedagogical function of art. At the bottom of the social hierarchy, there is not enough room for free action, hence no example for excellence. Stylistic forms of rhetoric and poetry vary accordingly, depending on the rank of the persons depicted.[9] According to Henri Testelin, even drawing must take social status into account and draw rustic country folks with rough strokes while using clear lines to represent grave and serious people.[10] In Ludwig Tieck's novels, princes and dukes are still indispensable, but poverty contributes equally important possibilities for action. On the other hand, the indispensability of social rank for the novel does not necessarily mean that the upper classes developed an understanding or interest in art. The nobility in the Roman republic was said to consider poetry *supervacua* (or, in an older expression, *supervacena* [superfluous, unnecessary]) and turned to law for intellectual stimulation.[11] Apparently, the development of art was motivated less by the private interests of the upper classes than by the presentation of public-communal affairs of a political or religious nature; art, in other words, developed with an eye toward certain functions. From very early on, certain structures in the theory of art address *every* (appropriately trained) observer and no longer anticipate a bifurcation along birth rank.[12] Theory prepares art to think itself independently of social status and to decide for itself who understands something about art and who doesn't.

We are all the more justified in asking: What happens to art if other social domains, such as the economy, politics, or science, establish themselves as functional systems? What happens when they focus more narrowly on a special problem, begin to see everything from this perspective, and eventually close themselves off with an eye toward this problem? What is art if in fourteenth-century Florence the Medicis support art as a way of politically legitimizing money acquired in dubious ways, which they subsequently invest in consolidating their political position? What happens to art if the functionally oriented differentiation of other systems pushes society as a whole toward functional differentiation? Will art become the slave of other functional systems, which dominate from now on? Or does —as indeed we shall argue—the increasing automatization of functional systems challenge art to discover its own function and to focus exclusively on this function? The developments leading to the Italian Renaissance appear to confirm this hypothesis.

II

Investigating the function of art requires clarification of the systems-theoretical relevance of this line of questioning. Contrary to popular belief, the notion of function has nothing to do with the purpose of actions or institutions. Unlike purpose, function does not serve the orientation of first-order observers—of the actor himself, his advisors, or his critics. An operation needs no knowledge of its function; it can substitute a purpose

(for example, the making of an artwork). The advantage is a temporal limitation of the operation, a formation of episodes that come to an end
when the purpose is accomplished or turns out to be impossible. A purpose is a program that seeks to diminish, if not to cancel, the difference
between a desired condition and the actual state of the world. In this respect, purpose, too, is a two-sided form. It fixes a condition that carries
the world along as its external side until the purpose is accomplished.

A function is nothing other than a focus for comparison.[13] It marks a
problem (one speaks of a "reference problem") in such a way that multiple
solutions can be compared and that the problem remains open for further
selections and substitutions. In this sense, functional analysis is a methodological principle that can be applied by any observer to any problem (including purposes). The arbitrariness of functional analysis is reduced when
the observer selects a system reference—here, when we restrict our focus
to reference problems within society. Thanks to this restriction, we can observe a number of circular relationships. The reference problem is marked
in the system that looks for solutions by marking the problem. This happens only when solutions to the problem suggest themselves. In this sense,
the solution creates the problem it helps resolve. The observational terms
problem and *function* serve only to reproblematize established institutions
in view of possible alternatives or to find out how far one can go in exploring variations without exploding the functional context.

Unlike traditional doctrines of the division of labor, social theory assumes that the grounds for the existence of particular institutions never reside in their functions—as if Aristotle's older teleological explanation could
be replaced by a functional explanation. The theory of evolution offers explanations for historical changes in the societal system that draw on the
notion that functions—as evolutionary "attractors"—can influence the direction of the evolutionary process and the possibilities of verification they
entail. Orientation with respect to functions evolves, too, whether it remains latent (hence visible only to a second-order observer) or directly influences the functional systems' testing of possibilities.

The question about the function of art is therefore the question of an
observer who must presuppose an operatively generated reality; otherwise
it would never occur to him to raise this question. This observer can be an
external observer, such as a scholar or a sociologist. But the system in
question can also be an observer: it can observe itself and raise the question of its own functioning. This does not do away with the necessity of

distinguishing between operation and observation. The operation of artistic communication does not depend on whether the function of art is problematized, let alone clarified. The operation occurs when it occurs (and doesn't if it doesn't), and if it needs motives, then it can find them anywhere.

Like all other functions that occur in society (whether or not they are differentiated as systems), the function of art can be traced to problems of meaningful communication. Meaning serves as the medium not only of communication but also of consciousness. One must therefore conceive of the specificity of this medium in very general terms without assuming a psychic or social-system reference.[14]

The formal specificity of meaning, whose formative capacity qua medium we introduced earlier, manifests itself in phenomenological as well as in modal-theoretical analyses. Both types of analysis presuppose a temporal restriction of meaning, a time-related actualization of meaning in an instant of experience or of communication. To the system operations that employ this medium, meaning always presents itself as actual. But actuality frays (William James) and refers to other, at the moment unactualized possibilities of actualizing meaning (Husserl). Actuality exists only as a starting and connecting point for further references. In modal-theoretical terms, the *unity* of the medium of meaning resides in a *difference*—the difference between actuality and potentiality. Under conditions of meaning, systems always operate on the internal side of this form, that is, in the mode of actuality. They cannot operate "potentially." But since an operation is an event that vanishes immediately after it is produced, any operation that is controlled by meaning must move beyond actuality toward what is otherwise possible. Something pertaining to the realm of potentiality must be actualized, which in turn requires that the difference between actuality and potentiality occur at the heart of experience and communication—formally speaking, the form "reenters" the form. At the same time, transcending the boundary between actuality and potentiality in actual operations requires a specific indication of the possibility to be apprehended, an indication that can occur only selectively and contingently, by pushing aside all other possibilities.

For the time being, this short description must suffice.[15] It suggests that all the problems to be solved in the system of society are directly or indirectly related to the structure of the medium of meaning. When functional systems differentiate themselves, the corresponding reference problems are abstracted to the point where existing institutions can be presented as solutions, while other, functionally equivalent solutions come into view. Religion, for example, initially struggles with the problem that meaning references point toward an unfamiliar terrain and eventually lose themselves in indeterminacy. A differentiated science focuses on research and on actualizing as yet unknown truths or untruths for the sake of structuring the realm of possible propositions by means of the true/untrue code and on the basis of decision programs (theories, methods) related to this code. At the same time, science treats currently improbable or rejected perspectives as a reservoir for findings that may turn out to be tenable after all. The economy seeks to secure supplies for a sufficient (albeit in principle unlimited) amount of time in the future, even though it cannot operate in the present except on the basis of actual states of affairs. In politics, one wants to ensure, via collectively binding decisions, that others are bound by such decisions, even if they did not consent or are in no position to retract their consent. In law, one seeks to create a security of expectations that persists and promises social support in the face of actions that contradict such expectations.

But what about art?

We are not missing the mark if we assume that in earlier societies the objects we retrospectively perceive as art and store in museums were produced as supports for other functional circles, rather than in view of a special function of art.[16] This holds especially for religious symbols, but also for the playful transgression of the necessary in producing objects of ordinary utility. In retrospect, we describe the intricate, specifically artistic form combinations of such works as incidental, as ornamental. In any event, the link between functional specification and the differentiation of functional systems constitutes a sociohistorical nexus, which long remained protected by familiar contexts. Not until artistic possibilities of this sort reached a high degree of evidence and independence did the specific function of art take hold as an attractor for creating forms that now followed their own dynamic and began to react to their own realization. This apparently happened for the first time in classical Greece and then again during a period that deserves to be called the "Renaissance."

But where is the orientation toward a special function of art headed? The distinctions we used earlier to characterize the artwork yield no direct answer to this question. In accordance with the literature on the subject, we established that an artwork does not grow naturally but is an artificially manufactured object, and we emphasized its lack of utility for social contexts of any sort (whether economic, religious, or political). The question "What's the point?" remains an open, self-canceling question. To pursue it further, we must formulate more radically the difference that art establishes in the world.

One might start from the assumption that art uses perceptions and, by doing so, seizes consciousness at the level of its own externalizing activity. The function of art would then consist in integrating what is in principle incommunicable—namely, perception—into the communication network of society.[17] Kant already located the function of art (of the presentation of aesthetic ideas) in its capacity to stimulate thinking in ways that exceed verbal or conceptual comprehension.[18] The art system concedes to the perceiving consciousness its own unique adventure in observing artworks—and yet it makes available as communication the formal selection that triggered the adventure. Unlike verbal communication, which all too quickly moves toward a yes/no bifurcation, communication guided by perception relaxes the structural coupling of consciousness and communication (without destroying it, of course).[19] The freedom of movement entailed in the world of perception is recovered in language and against the narrow focus of language. And the encapsulation of perception within the psyche prevents one from subjecting one's perceptions to a test for consensus. Consensus becomes an issue only in verbal communication, in commentary, where it is raised in an entirely inadequate manner.

An independent relation between redundancy and variety characterizes perception. In a manner that is matched neither by thought nor by communication, perception presents *astonishment and recognition* in *a single instant*. Art uses, enhances, and in a sense exploits the possibilities of perception in such a way that it can present the *unity of this distinction*. To put it differently, art permits observation to oscillate between astonishment and recognition, even if this requires worldly media such as space and time as a means of securing continuity.[20] This is not a matter of indulging in the automatic recognition of what is already known—the kind of pleasure produced by the "culture industry" that was so arrogantly rejected by Horkheimer and Adorno.[21] Rather, the pleasure of astonishment, already described in antiquity, refers to the unity of the difference between astonishment and recognition, to the paradox that both *intensify one another*. Extravagant forms play an increasingly important role in this process. Such forms reflect upon the problem without drawing on the mundane familiarity of objects: for example, by quotations from other works that render repetitions at once familiar and strange; or by a self-referential gesture by the text that calls upon the reader to understand the allusion when the text is mentioned within itself. However, a more precise analysis would show very quickly that the identification of repetition relies on perception rather than on conceptual abstraction. Art specializes in this problem, and this distinguishes it from ordinary efforts to cope with small irritations in everyday perception.

This also explains why the art system must, in principle, distinguish itself—indeed, distance itself—from religion. Religious communication is concerned with what is essentially imperceptible, and it is marked by this concern. For art, the question remains whether it suffices to think of its function in terms of integrating a specific section of the environment into communication—that is, in terms of a "reentry" into communication of the difference between perception and communication—or whether one should expect the function of art to reside in its relationship to the world as such, that is, in the manner in which art establishes in the world a reality of its own while making this reality a part of the world. This appears to be precisely what art accomplishes when it describes the world as such (and not just spectacular instances) from the perspective of astonishing redundancies.

The work of art, then, establishes a reality of its own that differs from ordinary reality. And yet, despite the work's perceptibility, despite its undeniable reality, it simultaneously constitutes another reality, the meaning of which is imaginary or fictional. Art splits the world into a real world and an imaginary world in a manner that resembles, and yet differs from, the use of symbols in language or from the religious treatment of sacred objects and events. The function of art concerns the meaning of this split—it is not just a matter of enriching a given world with further objects (even if they are "beautiful").[22]

The imaginary world of art offers a position from which *something else* can be determined *as reality*—as do the world of language, with its potential for misuse, or the world of religion, albeit in different ways. Without such markings of difference, the world would simply be the way it is. Only when a reality "out there" is distinguished from fictional reality can one observe one side from the perspective of the other. Language and religion both accomplish such a doubling, which allows us to indicate the given world *as real.* Art adds a new twist to this detour, which leads via the imagination away from and back to reality—art realizes itself in the realm of perceptible objects. Any other doubling of reality can be copied into the imaginary reality of the world of art—the doubling of reality and dream, for example, of reality and play, of reality and illusion, even of reality and art.[23] Unlike language and religion, art is made, which implies freedoms and limitations in the choice of forms unknown to language and religion. What accounts for the peculiar originality of Greek art might well be its courage to push aside any scruples of religious hubris and count on technical-poetical realizations that *made* their intent perceptible.

Only within a differentiated distinction between a real and a fictional, imagined reality can a specific relationship to reality emerge, for which art seeks different forms—whether to "imitate" what reality does not show (its essential forms, its Ideas, its divine perfection), to "criticize" reality for what it does not want to admit (its shortcomings, its "class rule," its commercial orientation), or to affirm reality by showing that its representation succeeds, in fact, succeeds so well that creating the work of art and looking at it is a delight. The concepts imitation / critique / affirmation do not exhaust the possibilities. Another intent might address the observer as an individual and contrive a situation in which he faces reality (and ultimately himself) and learns how to observe it in ways he could never learn in real life. One thinks here particularly of the novel. The novel is an imitation that, rather than referring to reality directly, copies one imaginary reality into another such reality.

It is generally true, for art as well, that the function of a communication system is not equivalent to its positive code value—the function of law is not simply being legal. Nor is it the business of art to manufacture beautiful, successful, interesting, or spectacular objects and present them for the sake of pleasurable consumption or admiration. The function of art is difficult to detect, even when one takes into account that the positive code value must be distinguishable from its opposite to reveal its preferential status. This may suffice as an orientation for the coded communication of everyday life. Sociological interest in the notion of function goes further. In art, it aims at the "other side" of the distinction that art introduces into the world. The question might be rephrased as follows: How does reality appear when there is art?

In creating a double of reality from which reality can be observed, the artwork can leave it to the observer to overcome this split—whether in an idealizing, critical, or affirmative manner, or by discovering experiences of his own. Some texts are meant to be affirmative and oppose the hyper-critical addiction to negativity[24]—yet they can be read in an ironical or melancholy mode or as mirroring one's own experiences with communication. The artwork commits the observer to fixed forms. Within the context of modern communication, however, this constraint leaves room for applying the formally established difference between imagined and ordinary reality in multiple ways. Because it embeds its forms in objects, art need not enforce a choice between consensus and dissent, or between an affirmative and a critical attitude toward reality. Art needs no reasonable justification, and by unfolding its power of conviction in the realm of perceptible objects, it demonstrates this. The "pleasure" afforded by the artwork, according to traditional doctrine, always also contains a hint of malicious joy, indeed of scorn, directed against the vanity of seeking access to the world through reason.

All of these attempts may be directed at discovering and realizing various possibilities of order on the basis of an increasing freedom and a growing distance vis-à-vis an established reality. In ancient Greece—which may have been the first culture to reflect upon artworks as independent realities—a problem of meaning might have been at stake, created by the discrepancies between religion, urban politics, a new monetary economy, and a state of knowledge that needed to be fixed in writing. As Arthur Danto suggests, art may have developed parallel to philosophy in ways that could still be adequately described as imitation (like the search for truth in philosophy).[25] Further developments created an entirely different situation for the relationship between art and religion, however, especially in conjunction with the return to the artistic endeavors of antiquity in the Renaissance. An independently developed sense of form in art leads to gains in autonomy, especially when art develops its own dynamics and begins to react to itself. The supporting function of objects defined in religious, political, or stratificatory terms diminishes and is eventually cast off as inessential. Everyday life becomes worthy of art, and what used to be significant is subjected to distorting misrepresentations. In painting, this development began around the second half of the sixteenth century, in narrative, somewhat later. Common values were not just negated or turned on their head; they were neutralized and rejected as distinctions for the sake of demonstrating possibilities of order that had nothing to do with them. This is how art of the sixteenth and seventeenth centuries reacted to a new social situation marked by the erosion of a unified religious worldview, a monetary crisis of the nobility, the imposition of order by the territorial state, and the new rationalism of mathematical-empirical science with its geometrical methods. Against these trends, art developed procedures and principles of its own—novelty, obscurity, style-consciousness, and eventually a self-description that thematizes the various artistic genres and sets them apart from the new rationalism.

The transitional motives that contributed to this trend must be established via detailed historical investigations. At a time of rapid social change, one strove to make visible a new order that was described much later as the order of bourgeois society. Profit motives became worthy of literature, and peasants became suitable for portraits. In the second half of the nineteenth century, technology became a legitimate topic in artistic genres of the most diverse kind. In a sense, art projects a society unable as yet to experience and describe itself adequately—especially in the nineteenth century. Persistent validities are subverted by irony—as in Flaubert's *Madame Bovary*—and reflected upon in the tragic destiny of the hero or heroine.

In the twentieth century, one encounters artworks that seek to cancel the difference between a real and an imagined reality by presenting themselves in ways that make them indistinguishable from real objects. Should we take this trend as an internal reaction of art against itself? Or is it an indication that confronting a reality that is the way it is and changes the way it does no longer makes sense? There is no need to answer this question, which is bound to fail anyhow and would prove only that this failure has become the object of reflection. No ordinary object insists on being taken for an ordinary thing, but a work that does so betrays itself by this very effort. The function of art in such a case is to reproduce the difference of art. But the mere fact that art seeks to cancel this difference and fails in its effort to do so perhaps says more about art than could any excuse or critique. Here, what we learn to observe is the inevitable and ineradicable rule of difference.

The theory of art produces reflections that accompany these developments. According to traditional doctrine, art was meant to evoke a feeling of astonishment and admiration (*admiratio*).[26] It placed the soul into an otherwise unattainable contemplative state, distanced from daily routines, and pointed it toward the essential. This was accomplished by a realistic depiction of improbable and yet possible events[27]—after all, the gospel teaches nothing else. The question of whether poetry is suited for this purpose remained controversial until the sixteenth century, due to a long ped-agogical tradition of relying on Aristotle.[28] In the eighteenth century, the theory of literature adjusted to a (positively valued) fictionality. One then demanded that the work be "interesting."[29] Romanticism considered (transcendental) poetry to be the core of art. A trend becomes apparent, but a function of art was still lacking.[30] We can establish that this function turns on creating a difference between two realities or, to put it differently, on providing the world with an opportunity to observe itself. There are several ways to accomplish this goal; religion is one of them. Moreover, this difference assumes historically different forms. This is why we insist on the question of the specific sense in which art can function as an evo-lutionary "attractor."

Even when dealing with art, we cannot help constructing an everyday world. The difference between actuality and potentiality, which produces meaning and shifts from one moment to the next, is projected onto a sta-ble reality, an ontological world that is presupposed as invariant.[31] Even though things move and some are subject to change, the world remains as it is; otherwise one could distinguish neither movement nor change. This certitude is reaffirmed in the formulas of religion and natural philosophy. The skeptical humanism of the sixteenth century and the seventeenth cen-tury's questioning of certitude raise doubts at this level. But the everyday assumption of a reality—one now speaks of "moral certitude" or "common sense"—cannot be shaken by such doubts. Nor can one do without it.

This is why art searches for a relationship to everyday life that differs from the rationalist philosophy of Descartes or from the mathematical physics of a scientist such as Newton or Galileo. Unlike philosophy, art does not search for islands of security from which other experiences can be expelled as fantastic or imaginary, or rejected as a world of secondary qualities or enjoyment, of pleasure or common sense. Art radicalizes the difference between the real and the merely possible in order to show through works of its own that even in the realm of possibility there is or-der after all. Art opposes, to use a Hegelian formulation, "the prose of the world,"[32] but for precisely this reason it needs this contrast.

This leads us back to the ancient topic of astonishment, which affects not only the observer of art but also the artist. The observer may be struck by the work's success and then embark on a step-by-step reconstruction of how it came about. But the artist is equally struck by the order that emerges from his own hands in the course of a rapidly changing relationship between provocation and possible response, problem and solution, irritation and escape. This is how order emerges from self-irritation, which, however, requires the prior differentiation of a medium of art to decide that this order differs in its stakes from what occurs elsewhere in reality.[33]

The real world is always the way it is, nothing otherwise. It interferes with human purposes in its own way, but always with reference to the specific differences established by these purposes. Once the choice of purpose ceases to be self-evident and becomes subject to varying preferences (interests), purposes cannot be ordered unless they are subsumed under general purposes. Art opposes not only the status quo but also any attempt to introduce purposes into the world. The artistic rendering of the real solidifies reality in order to contrast the possible as a realm capable of order, of an order without purpose.

One such possibility is to show that striving for purposes ends in tragedy. Another is to render in a comic light what others take seriously. Such moves convince only if they succeed aesthetically and as form, that is, when they manage to offer an alternative order. In the language of a tradition that is still effective today, one might say that the aesthetic means, not the objects of art, must elicit conviction.

So long as art is bound by a reality that guarantees the compatibility of objects and events, the problem is solely one of imitation. To the extent, however, that art begins to work with feigned realities, it becomes difficult if not impossible to decide whether the objects depicted—blue horses, talking cats, dogs with nine tails, an irregular time that leaps forward or does not move at all, or other such "psychedelic" realities—can coexist side by side. When reality can no longer secure their coexistence, art must supply aesthetic guarantees of its own. This is relatively harmless so long as art is concerned with altering the color of objects in the manner of expressionism or with presenting unrealistic narrative contexts. But such strategies already suggest that hetero-references merely serve as a pretext for displaying alternate possibilities of order. One can go even further and reduce hetero-reference to the material—color, wood, stone, or garbage— thus demonstrating an improbable order at the material level.

Within the gravitational field of its function, modern art tends to experiment with formal means. The word *formal* here does not refer to the distinction, which at first guided modern art,[34] between form and matter or form and content, but to the characteristics of an indicating operation that observes, as if from the corner of its eye, what happens on the other side of form. In this way, the work of art points the observer toward an observation of form. This may have been what was meant by the notion "autotelic." However, the social function of art exceeds the mere reconstruction of observational possibilities that are potentially present in the work. Rather, it consists in *demonstrating the compelling forces of order in the realm of the possible.* Arbitrariness is displaced beyond the boundaries of art into the unmarked space. If, following Spencer Brown's injunction to draw a distinction, one transgresses this boundary and steps from the unmarked into the marked space, things *no longer happen randomly.* From now on, the dichotomy of success or failure governs every move. It generates a sense of proportion, which, like a calculus, gets caught in its own logic. This is true even if there is no preestablished idea, no essence or natural purpose to guide the process (whatever motive consciousness or communication might suggest).

Taking one's direction from possibilities rather than relying on the world's natural drift becomes a problem, because one knows, nonetheless, that the world is the way it is and not otherwise. Why count on a deviating course by placing one's stakes on purposes? Whence this courage? Wasn't Prometheus's gift of fire considered a violation? And what about the *technē* of the Greeks? What about the boundless striving for wealth or the current obsession with technological innovation? In the old world, one could hope to counteract such trends by invoking an ethics of justice and modesty or by practicing an aristocratic distance—modern society's awareness of risk invites us to think of similar remedies. But once risk is thematized, such remedies cease to convince.[35] This is why art replaces this problem with a different one. Art raises the question of whether a trend toward "morphogenesis" might be implied in any operational sequence, and whether an observer can observe at all except with reference to an order—especially when observing observations.

From this perspective, the *formal complexity* a work is *capable of achieving* becomes a crucial, indeed, the decisive variable. Whatever functions as the other side of a form requires decisions about further forms that generate other sides of their own, which raises the problem of how much variety the work's recursive integrity can accommodate and keep under control. A number of traditional formulas describe this situation—such as the (pre-Leibnizian) notion of a harmonious relationship between order (redundancy) and variety.[36] Contrary to widely held notions, the function of art is not (or no longer) to represent or idealize the world, nor does it consist in a "critique" of society. Once art becomes autonomous, the emphasis shifts from hetero-reference to self-reference—which is not the same as self-isolation, not *l'art pour l'art*. Transitional formulations of this type are understandable. But there is no such thing as self-reference (form) without hetero-reference. And when art displays a self-positing order in the medium of perception or imagination, it calls attention to a logic of reality which expresses itself not only through the real but also in fictional reality.[37] Within the difference real/fictional reality, the unity of the world (the unity of this difference) escapes observation by presenting itself as the order of the distinction's form.

Art has no ambition to redeem society by exercising aesthetic control over an ever-expanding realm of possibility. Art is merely one of society's functional systems, and even though it may harbor universalistic ambitions, it cannot seriously wish to replace all the other systems or force these systems under its authority. The functional primacy of art holds exclusively for art. This is why, protected by its operative closure, art can focus on its own function and observe, from within ever-expanding boundaries, the realm of possibility with an eye toward fitting form combinations.

Art makes visible only the inevitability of order as such. That it draws on transhierarchical structures, on self-referential circularities, on different versions of a transclassical logic, and on overall greater degrees of freedom corresponds to the conditions of modernity and signals that a society differentiated along functional lines must do without authority and representation. Contrary to what traditionalists might suspect, art demonstrates that modernity does not necessarily imply a renunciation of order.

The function of art, one could argue, is to make the world appear within the world—with an eye toward the ambivalent situation that every time something is made available for observation something else withdraws, that, in other words, the activity of distinguishing and indicating that goes on in the world conceals the world. It goes without saying that striving for completeness or restricting oneself to the essential would be absurd. Yet a work of art is capable of symbolizing the reentry of the world into the world because it appears—just like the world—incapable of emendation.

The paradox unique to art, which art creates and resolves, resides in the observability of the unobservable. Today, this no longer means that art must focus on Ideas, on ideal forms, on the concept in the sense of Hegel's aesthetics. To our contemporary sensibility, it makes no sense to show the bright side of the world. Even the self-reference of thought is no longer directed toward perfection (in an Aristotelian manner). But it does make sense to broaden one's understanding of the forms that are possible in the world. Emphasizing such an understanding requires suppressing any hint of utility, for the world has no utility. Rather, the world displays all the qualities that Nicholas of Cusa ascribed to his God: it is neither small nor large, neither unity nor diversity, it neither has a beginning nor is it without beginning—and this is why the world needs forms.

III

Our previous considerations assumed the (anthropological) constancy of human possibilities of perception. We focused on seeing, hearing, and to a certain extent on tactile perceptions. Accordingly, we located the function of art in its capacity to supply perception with other objects and to harness these objects for a special type of communication. Astonishment, surprise, and admiration were believed to occur in the realm of hetero-reference, in the external world, and were meant to enrich this world. Accordingly, the function of art was to show the return of order even under conditions of improbable artistic variation. Although around 1800 art focused strictly on the effectuation of sensations and feelings, an external motive was always presupposed.[38]

In the meantime, several attempts have been made to dissolve the anthropological conditions of perception (along with traditional art forms). On the one hand, one knows that perceptions are constructed in the central nervous system under conditions of operative closure. Consciousness must "justify" its belief that the world it perceives *is* indeed the external world. What appears to be an external world is, in fact, generated not by the resistance of an external world but rather by a resistance of the system against the operations of the system. On the other hand, opportunities for creating fictional worlds of perception abound—via drugs or other suggestive interventions, or by means of complex electronic devices. From the perspective of a traditional world semantics, such possibilities would seem to create illusory realities—comparable to the option of occasionally interrupting one's ordinary life with play. But when normality is a construct and the schema natural/artificial is no longer applicable or is perceived to be an implicitly hierarchical opposition in need of deconstruction, one faces the question of how the order of certain structures can still be justified as primary. The notion of a "virtual reality" insinuates that a reality that can be apprehended by a natural human apparatus is out there after all, while at the same time one is at pains to show that this "natural apparatus" realizes only one possibility among many.

The literature on "cyberspace," virtual reality, imagination machines, and so forth is growing rapidly.[39] The same holds for attempts to investigate the proximity of these recent developments to art. It is unclear what exactly about such trends is specific to art. The mere fact that we are dealing with artificially created perceptions that deviate from "nature" is not a sufficient indication of their artistic quality. The striking expansion of visual possibilities, their increasing capacity for dissolution, and the possibility for switching back and forth, without further consequences, between real and artificially generated realities—none of these trends proves that we are dealing with works of art. It should strike us as odd that virtual worlds can be purchased and that their descriptions always also serve commercial purposes.[40] It is currently difficult to decide whether works of art in this domain are characterized, as before, by a convincing combination of forms, or whether much more general concerns are at stake—to show, for example, that even after the deconstruction of anthropologically grounded schemata of perception, order continues to emerge whenever perception finds a reason to follow other perceptions.

IV

The differentiation of art as a system is most apparent in the internal blockage of hetero-references. In comparison with other functional systems, this strikes us as characteristic of art.

Blocking hetero-reference is not a matter of eliminating causalities. Colors need to be mixed. Not every voice can sing. The theater needs a place for its performances, and we recognize the effects of differentiation in the isolation of certain spaces or buildings where a theatrical production takes place at agreed upon times.[41] Many things need to be paid for and simply do not happen when there is no money. Everywhere we see boundary-transcending causalities. Yet this is not the problem. When we speak of a blockage of hetero-references, we have in mind the requirement that the *internal* operations of an observing activity, when focused on a work of art, *must be intelligible without hetero-reference*. These operations are produced solely for the sake of observing observations.

Following Plato's (?) *Greater Hippias*, one tends to say that the artwork does not want to be understood in terms of its utility. "It is essential to art that it does not want to be useful. In a certain sense, the beautiful is the antidote to utility; it is that which is liberated from utility."[42] The work of art is produced with the intent of not being useful, or, stated paradoxically, it is a "an end in itself without purpose."[43] The same idea is expressed by the formula "disinterested pleasure."[44] This demand is radical enough to exclude even the artist from those who might benefit from his work. Whereas an architect may eventually build a house for himself or a farmer grow vegetables for himself in his own garden, an artist does not produce a work of art (not a single one) for himself. He may fall in love with some of his works and refuse to sell them. But this does not prevent him from showing these works to others. This is particularly evident in literary texts, which are never written to be read by the author, not even in singular cases.[45] The argument can be generalized. It holds for any work of art.

So long as the formulas of differentiation were content to reject utility, they could benefit from a general reluctance to identify humanity with utility. The aristocratic tradition of distinguishing between *honestas* and *utilitas* already opposed such an identification. But there are more radical claims—for example, when Schiller maintains that there is no path from aesthetic pleasure to other pursuits.[46] The break with the tradition of *imitatio* might again be mentioned in this context, or Solger's idea that the concept of nature covers only everyday perception ("the appearances of objects that can be perceived in the manner of common knowledge") and therefore cannot be binding for art.[47] Generally speaking, the focus on the (individual) human being as subject, characteristic of humanistic aesthetics, resists a more accurate formulation of the societal differentiation of an art system and confines theory to searching for something "higher" *within* mankind.

Within the humanistic-anthropological context of the tradition, the topos of rejecting utility was initially meant to exclude cognitive understanding and reason from aesthetic judgment. In the course of a barely registered development, however, the rejection of utility turns into a semiotic path to block hetero-reference and direct the search for meaning inward. This is why one was content with an oppositional concept such as lack of utility, which remained vague and open to anything. A lack of utility cannot be refuted, even if the work is used for utilitarian purposes, for example, as a gift to pay off a debt or as a security for obtaining new credit.

Such applications remain external to art. They contribute nothing to our understanding of the work, nor do they interfere with it. They are placed "orthogonally" in relation to the autopoiesis of art. The motives behind proclaiming something useless that might turn out to be useful after all must have other, deeper reasons, which obviously have to do with the function of art.

The "other world" of art is communicable only if all references to our habitual world are cut off. But the observer, at home in this world, is sophisticated. It is necessary to block *every* return path into ordinary life and to prevent any speculations about intentions other than the ones the artist presents in the work.

This, however, does not answer the question of how art can possibly benefit from being told that it ought to be useless. Rejecting utility is not a recipe that makes much sense. The attempt to steer an opposite course by deliberately producing useless objects gets caught in the gravitational field of utility, since lack of utility is only the other side of the form of utility. Like the emphasis on autonomy, this is an entirely fruitless demonstration; moreover, it says nothing about whether an artwork (in the sense of the system's code) is successful or not.[48]

In order to escape the distinction useful/useless and to circumvent the paradoxes that arise from it, or from formulations such as an "end in itself," we translate the problem into the language of information theory. Now we can say: an artwork distinguishes itself by virtue of the *low probability of its emergence*.

The work of art is an ostentatiously improbable occurrence. This follows from the specific relationship between form and medium that is realized in the work.[49] A recognizable purpose would explain why the work was created—no more and no less. When this interpretive aid is eliminated, we are plunged into the open, undetermined space of a medium's possibilities. Neither context nor an apparent purpose can motivate us to expect a work of art endowed with specific forms. That it is recognized as a work of art nonetheless is due to the art system and its internal redundancies, and, in principle, to the work itself.

Under a hierarchical world architecture, supreme positions were rare and therefore improbable. Being close to someone at the top created distance from everyday life, which required no further evidence. In a society that is no longer differentiated along stratificatory lines, such benefits are no longer available. This leads—as we cannot emphasize strongly enough—

to the autonomy of art. But it does not sufficiently document the visible improbability of art. The frame established by the autonomy of art must somehow be filled. One way of doing this is by exploiting the temporalization of the hierarchical world order[50] and by searching for the improbable in novelty and eventually in the avant-garde. Under the conditions of autonomy, this means that art must surpass itself and eventually reflect upon its own surpassing of itself. This increases the demands on the observer and favors the development of new kinds of skills in the realm of artistic production. In a society based on stratification, this trend manifests itself in a revalorization of the artist's social status, as one can show for Renaissance Italy. Artists came from wealthy families (Brunelleschi, Ghiberti, Donatello, Masaccio, Alberti), or they were integrated into the circle of the prince's *familiares*. They received the patent of nobility, or they were honored in other ways, sometimes by receiving gifts. It became important to show through one's lifestyle that one did not work for money. The biographies of such artists became the object of literature. Their social advancement always also documented independence and individuality. And when the nobility did not recognize their equal status, as was generally the case, they sought different criteria based on accomplishment and merit.[51]

Of course, such a move requires expertise on the part of the upper classes and, at the same time, places limits on the extravagance of artistic activity. In the twentieth century, a new trend began to emerge. One insulted the clients one portrayed by exposing the limits of their understanding, and finally, when this trend became the object of reflection, one moved on, sacrificing in a spectacular (again, surprising) way the need to demonstrate one's skill and to confront difficulties.

This strategy works only if one can show that the object in question is, in fact, art. Secondary forms of making the improbable plausible become necessary: in other words, one needs an art industry. The art system supplies institutions in which it is not unlikely to find works of art—museums, galleries, exhibitions, theater buildings, social contacts with art experts, critics, and so forth. But this is merely the first step in approaching art. Institutions (in Goffman's terminology) supply only the "frame" for condensed expectations; they generate a receptive attitude for observing striking objects as art.[52] The artwork must provide its own configuration of redundancy and surprise; it must deliberately create and resolve the paradox that information is at once necessary and superfluous. The artwork, in other words, must indicate itself as a concrete and unique object in order to demarcate the frame for displaying universal or exemplary truths. (Logicians might insist on distinguishing multiple levels of analysis, or be forced to accept "self-indication" as the third value in the analysis of the distinctions displayed in art.[53])

Redundancies, in the form of the system's own constructions, are reintroduced in two stages—via frames and works.[54] Possibilities of intensification thus created are unthinkable in the unprepared everyday life of social communication. From the perspective of the artwork, this does not mean that hetero-references lose their significance. On the contrary, as we mentioned earlier, they acquire their function qua *hetero*-references precisely within the protected differentiation of a unique domain for creating and elaborating information. Within this domain, actors on stage or in the novel can be endowed with motives, and paintings acquire representative functions that are not confused with ordinary social reality, even though they refer to reality in a manner that implies both proximity and distance.

This explains why rejecting utility is not the same as rejecting hetero-reference—if it were, self-reference would collapse for lack of a distinction. Rather, the form of self-reference—the distinction between self-reference and hetero-reference—must be reconstructed internally. In science, this happens via the combination of methodological (internal) and theoretical (external) considerations, but also by differentiating linguistic levels: at a certain level, science always employs a socially given linguistic material that might be used in other contexts as well (this is the well-known "ordinary language" argument).[55] In art, we see a comparable trend. As we noted earlier, art remains dependent on materials that can be used outside of art as well, albeit in different ways. Art works with stone, wood, metal, or other materials to create sculptures; it employs bodies in dance and the theater, colors in painting, and ordinary words in poetry. The point is to highlight within the material—which is indispensable for perception—a difference in usage. It is crucial that art dissolves the all-too-compact references to the environment that were still common in the eighteenth century in accordance with the notion of art as imitation. Not even the principles and rules of (an otherwise valid) morality can be inherited in uncontrolled ways, lest the impression arise that the work of art serves moral instruction and edification.[56] Still, a clear tendency toward releasing art and literature from its ties to reality cannot be identified yet, especially not as a principle. A certain type of English literature—such as

Pamela—still teaches that morality may turn out to be quite useful in practice. One has the impression, however, that every restriction to a specific relationship between morals and art/literature is now taken note of and provokes objections, especially when it can be described in a national comparison as typically English or typically French. As a result, art eventually meanders toward autonomy after all. Hetero-references are not allowed to affect the forms that art must select freely if it is to accomplish operative closure. They are restricted to the elements that serve as the medial substratum of art. The medium's capacity of dissolution, which underlies the loose coupling of its elements, adjusts to the work's formative intent. The more abstract the form combination that is to be presented, the more the medium must be dissolved. But even then the medial substratum continues to support the hetero-references against which the work's self-reference must stand out.

V

The differentiation of the art system has been observed from within the system itself and has been described in terms of various semantics of distance. We have shown this in the previous section. We tacitly assumed that works of art present discrete sections of the perceptible world (which is certainly true). Works of art are objects. One can recognize them as works of art (as distinct from other objects or processes) and can see how, at least when they occur in an artistic manner, they give rise to a distinct system almost spontaneously. This account, however, ignores the analytical resources we introduced in previous chapters; besides, other theoretical sources encourage us to go further.

Psychic and social systems create their operative elements in the form of extremely short-lived events (perceptions, thoughts, communications) that vanish as soon as they occur. In the same way, in creation and observation works of art unfold as a sequence of events. But how? In the course of producing or encountering an artwork, one moves from one operation to the next. One must be capable of generating both continuity and discontinuity, which is easier in reality than in theory. What happens during this process?

Following Spencer Brown's terminology,[57] one might speak of a double requirement of condensation and confirmation. On the one hand, identifications must be generated to observe the same in different situations and allow for repetitions and for the recursive recall and anticipation of further events. Meaning must be condensed into forms that can be employed repeatedly. On the other hand, such condensations must fit ever new contexts and, when this succeeds, be confirmed as fitting. In this way, condensations become replete with possibilities. What results from this process can no longer be fixed or accessed by definitions. Using it requires experience gathered within the same system; it presupposes "implicit knowledge."[58]

Jacques Derrida's analysis of writing,[59] though informed by a different approach, arrives at similar conclusions. Derrida asks how repetition (*itération*) is possible in different situations. The objects of repetition are ruptures that are posited together with signs. These ruptures must be mobile; they must be capable of shifting (*différance* of the difference), which requires that the object of the sign (*référent*) and its indicating intention (*signifiant*) remain absent.[60] Translated into the language of systems theory, this means that the sequentialization of events and the recursivity necessary to identify discrete events generate and presuppose a separation between system and environment. A distinct art system differentiates itself because the observations that produce and contemplate artworks are processed sequentially. Only under these conditions can artworks function as bearers of communication.

In another terminology, the condition of operative closure might be described as *autonomy*. Autonomy implies that, within its boundaries, autopoiesis functions unconditionally, the only alternative being that the system ceases to exist. Autonomy allows for no half-measures or graduation; there are no relative states, no more or less autonomous systems.[61] Either the system produces its elements or it does not. A system that partially relies on external elements or structures because it cannot operate without them—a computer, for example—is not an autopoietic system.

This is not to say that the system's size or its boundaries might not be subject to variation. Nor does it follow from our terminology that there can be no evolution, that autopoietic systems have no history. Changes in structure and, all the more so, gains in complexity—an increase in the number and variability of elements—are certainly possible; indeed, they are typical of autopoietic systems. But any "more or less" refers exclusively to the system's complexity. In this sense, autopoiesis and complexity are conceptual correlates, and it is the task of the theory of evolution to trace the connections between them.

Assuming that the system's autopoiesis is at work, evolutionary thresholds can catapult the system to a level of higher complexity—in the evo-lution of living organisms, toward sexual reproduction, independent mo-bility, a central nervous system. To an external observer, this may resem-ble an increase in system differentiation or look like a higher degree of independence from environmental conditions. Typically, such evolution-ary jumps simultaneously increase a system's sensitivity and irritability; it is more easily disturbed by environmental conditions that, for their part, result from an increase in the system's own complexity. Dependency and independence, in a simple causal sense, are therefore not invariant magni-tudes in that more of one would imply less of the other. Rather, they vary according to a system's given level of complexity. In systems that are suc-cessful in evolutionary terms, more independence typically amounts to a greater dependency on the environment. A complex system can have a more complex environment and is capable of processing a greater amount of irritation internally, that is, it can increase its own complexity more rapidly. But all of this can happen only on the basis of the system's opera-tive closure.

When presenting the history of the art system, we must take these the-oretical foundations into account, lest we switch to an entirely different theory. Historically, the differentiation of a system always occurs on the basis of independent system achievements, that is, under the condition of autopoietic autonomy (how else?). Within this framework, however, dif-ferentiation occurs in the form of a rapid increase in internal complexity. Evolution presupposes a self-generated nucleus of autopoietic autonomy, which is recognized and utilized only in retrospect. Evolution, in other words, is a form of structural change that produces and reproduces its own preconditions.[62] If evolution suggests a gradual process that occa-sionally makes a leap forward, the question is always how much complex-ity may still be compatible with the autopoietic autonomy of a system whose irritability by the environment increases accordingly. More accu-rately, differentiation means nothing other than the increase in complex-ity within a fully differentiated system.

VI

From a sociological standpoint, the differentiation of a social subsystem can be inferred from what it demarcates and specifies as relevant in the en-vironment. Certain environmental relationships become more important;

as a result, others are treated with indifference. This distinction presupposes that autopoiesis is well established, in other words, that the stakes of art are readily apparent. In the late Middle Ages, this means that art was no longer a matter of skillfully carrying out the instructions of a client. In a somewhat more suitable terminology, one might say that a self-oriented art system searches for "supporting contexts" that leave enough room for its own autonomy and its own choices.[63]

What we retrospectively identify as art in the Middle Ages, in antiquity, or in non-European cultures fulfilled subordinate functions in those other contexts. A first decisive step toward differentiation had already been made via the shift from a magical to an educational use of the visual arts in the context of Christian religion. In retrospect, we recognize the tremendous difficulties involved in such a shift. We can imagine how hard it must have been to guide viewers, especially the lower classes, from a magical to a representational understanding of images, which focused on recounting familiar narratives. We recognize these difficulties in clerical taboos against images or in efforts to adapt older visual motifs,[64] and above all in the attempts to supplement the treasure house of forms by elaborating the most important themes of Christian religion and clerical history.

Apparently there was never a direct transition from a magical understanding of art to artistic autonomy. Artworks of the Middle Ages (more accurately, works that we would identify as art) were meant to highlight certain religious or other social meanings; they emphasized such meanings and ensured that they could be experienced repeatedly. Within a well-ordered cosmos, created for the sake of the Good and the Beautiful, art took on memorial and educational functions. Its task was transmission, not innovation, and the only freedom it claimed (a freedom nonetheless) was ornamentation (we assume that *ornamentum/ornatum* was understood in the sense of the rhetorical tradition, as expressing the perfection of the creation, rather than as mere adornment). Not until the late Middle Ages can one speak of a situation in which art follows internal criteria. As Hans Belting has shown in great detail, "the aura of the sacred gives way to the aura of art."[65] Within the context of a sociological theory of evolution, the enormity of this transition is astonishing, as is typical of evolutionary leaps. Sufficient skills and experience in the most diverse realms were certainly available, as was a sense for an ornamental play of forms familiar to the ear and the eye. So-called preadaptive advances had already been made. But how could one conceive of art-specific criteria if art was not evaluated independently of the contexts that made it meaningful? And how could the observation of art as art get off the ground, if such criteria did not yet exist?

With European history, the Italian courts provided exceptional start-up conditions for this. During the Middle Ages either guilds or individual monks were in charge of artistic activities of the most diverse kind. As early as the fourteenth century, the culture of the courts began to free itself from these constraints. The stimulation to do so arrived in Italy via Paris and Naples, then throve in the special conditions that existed in small territorial states. After an initial time of confusion, relationships of domination ceased to be defined by social rank. Within city-states or small territories, including the Vatican, such relationships were oriented by political oligarchy (in Florence, for example) or the court. The absence of a centralized state was crucial for the political use of money. On the one hand, Italy (especially Florence) played a leading role in developing a monetary economy (in an export-oriented textile industry, in trade and banking, and in the administration of church income). On the other hand, Italy did not produce a centralized state. In other parts of Europe, income from trade lost its political function for cities and was channeled into larger units—via the purchase of political positions, the acquisition of patents of nobility, or credit. In Italy, such efforts remained focused in the significantly smaller courts, after larger military ambitions (by Milan, for example) had failed. The form of the new territorial state, especially the courtly state, was not yet secured. Whether a new prince belonged to the category of "rex" or "tyrannus" and whether he would build a palace or a fortress on the city's territory were open questions. In this situation, politically motivated patronage developed (or, in Venice, patronage based on a republican oligarchy), and patrons began to compete with one another. The value of artworks, which in the trades was based on material (gold, expensive blues) and labor, shifted toward artistic skill.[66] As a result, the fine arts and individual artists were endowed with new value,[67] especially in the domains of architecture, painting, sculpture, and poetry. The first treatise on painting, Alberti's *Della Pittura*, claimed *nobilità* and *virtù* for the best (not all!) painters, thus elevating their work to the rank of the *artes liberales*,[68] and this goal required the presentation and evaluation of their abilities. Unlike those caught in patron/client relationships based on land ownership, artists were mobile and could take their skills and reputation elsewhere if local conditions were unsatisfactory. According to the conventions of bourgeois theory, such a gain in prestige is described as "advancement," but it might be more accurate to emphasize the emergence of new and enthusiastically cultivated *differences* in rank. One began to demarcate lower domains that came to be considered mechanical rather than belonging to the liberal arts.[69] Legally, this demarcation liberated art from its close ties to the guilds, integrating it into the personal, insecure, and corrupt relationships that characterized the courts.

Under the circumstances, all hopes for advancement of the arts, for the recognition and support of innovations, for one's share of social prestige and a privileged lifestyle had to be based on the system of patronage, especially on the courts. Although, starting in the sixteenth century, print was commonly used to discuss the features and intentions of various artistic genres, and poetry benefited from print, it would have been absurd to expect support for a differentiated art from "the common people" or to entrust the arts to "public opinion." What could be perceived as a trend toward autonomy was restricted to interactions within the system of patronage and to the insistence on internal criteria for evaluating art. At the same time, the patronage provided by the courts created a mechanism for protecting the arts from regulation by guilds and from integration into the ongoing stratification of households. The courtly state was about to leave behind the difference between the nobility and the people—which was based on social rank and was responsible for the failure of classical ideas of republican "liberty." The artist, now held in high esteem, no longer found his place in the order of stratification (although some did receive the patent of nobility[70]). Despite his common birth, the artist could gain recognition.[71] Although the pattern was already moving toward functional differentiation, semantics, especially in the debates about artistic genres and artists, was still completely dominated by considerations of rank.[72] This schema generated a need for criteria enabling the attribution of superior rank,[73] indeed for criteria that could not be derived from the contemporary discussion of nobility, which was flourishing for perhaps the last time.[74]

Today it may strike us as puzzling that the first impetus to differentiation should have been brought about by a high-ranking system of patronage. The most important consequences may have been motivated by patronage's need for decisions—not only decisions that concern a particular edifice, a certain purchase or commission, but also decisions of a new kind that are difficult to grasp, since they require judgments about artists and artworks. Recommendations and court intrigues might have played a role in such decisions, but in the end the work itself had to show whether or not one could attain recognition by presenting oneself as having commissioned it. In order to make decisions of this sort, one needed criteria, and criteria had to be elaborated in writing and publicized. All of this needed to be developed in retrospect and was waiting, so to speak, for the arrival of the printing press.

In the sixteenth and seventeenth centuries, the theory of art developed against this background. Theory inquired into the idea of beauty and, from this position, degraded ornament to mere adornment. Via concepts such as *concetto* [conceit], *disegno*, and *acutezza* [wit], the discussion moved away from the doctrine of harmonious proportion and increasingly embraced irrational concepts of taste or ventures into the realm of the *no so que*. One continued to adhere to the ancient principle of imitation while making room, within this principle, for opportunities to go beyond what was given in nature. One appreciated spontaneity, inspiration, deviation from models, ingenious innovations. Sketches, drafts, and unfinished projects were hailed as artworks of a special kind[75]—perhaps because they initially served as a basis for interacting with the prince or for recommending certain projects or the artist himself, and only later turned out to be pleasing in their own right. (There are reports of princes who visited artists' studios.) But such tendencies presupposed sufficiently well-established criteria of selection. In the course of an extended self-observation, on the level of composition and style the art system gained independence vis-à-vis its clients. It could now take the criteria of evaluation into its own hands and make them more dynamic.[76] On the one hand, this meant that one could afford to exaggerate, because one was aware of the limits of what was tolerable. At the other end of the spectrum, the same trend manifested itself in the late-seventeenth-century appreciation of "sublime" simplicity, which no longer risked being mistaken for a lack of artistic skill. Apart from that, we find a highly developed technical literature that provides instructions, and with Veronese and Rubens we see the beginnings of a workshop organization, in which the bearer of reputation had the function of outlining projects, giving instructions, and signing the works. We shall return to this point in conjunction with the self-description of art.

The next leap forward in the development of art occurred toward the end of the seventeenth century, motivated by changes in the supporting context and by the shift from a courtly system of patronage to the market.[77]

During the collapse of the Roman patronage system around the mid-seventeenth century, a remote patronage for Italian art emerged throughout Europe, depending on expert mediators who knew the right people.[78] A basic stock of tradable art could be found in the tremendous art collections of individual patrons—which often comprised several hundred paintings and occasionally were liquidated—and to a lesser extent in the studios of artists. These collections contained a stock of ready-made products. The market regulated acquisitions and sales by means of prices. There was plenty of wealth, thanks to the rapid development of capitalist agriculture in the wake of the restoration, although in the eighteenth century wealth consisted predominantly of real estate rather than liquid capital. The market reflected limited means in the form of enormous price discrepancies, which subsequently—but presumably only much later—motivated speculative acquisitions as a financial investment. These price differences mirrored the internal dynamic of the market rather than artistic quality (even though unsuccessful works were eliminated). Producing for a certain client (portraits, buildings, and so on) was not impossible, but was determined in part by market estimates—in the sense that negotiations about commissions concerned prices rather than the content of the work (the client had to be interested in acquiring a typical work of a particular artist). Increasingly, market yields became a symbolic equivalent of an artist's reputation. They replaced oral recommendations within a circle of high-ranking patrons and their followers; and they substituted for the tedious personal negotiations with a patron, which always included irrational values such as aristocratic generosity and symbols of the artist's reputation.[79]

Once again, a peripheral situation in European developments provided the decisive impetus that triggered the shift toward market conditions in Italy. The first major market to specialize in the acquisition and sale of artworks emerged in England, which depended on imports.[80] Here, too, money had to be available for investment. Patronage, which had been based on personal relationships,[81] was replaced by large art collections. These collections tended to consist in acquisitions from abroad, frequently from auctions, and they were liquidated again when the occasion arose (for example, with hereditary succession).[82] The value of such collections and the decisions that motivated individual acquisitions depended on experts who knew how to handle the distinction between original and copy and how to attribute a work to a certain artist. This distinction had been around for quite some time; it now took over the function of generating scarcity and guaranteeing prices.[83] At the level of general criteria of taste, one still demanded and sought to develop the competency of judgment that supposedly distinguished the upper classes.[84] The patron no longer defined himself by social rank and aristocratic generosity but based himself instead on his expertise, that is, on function-specific capabilities.[85] While interest in collecting artworks no longer depended on the internal hierarchy of the upper classes, insistence on objective criteria created the fatal side effect of differentiating socially, on a rather shaky basis, between experts and nonexperts.[86] The expertise required by the market could no longer be expected from the upper classes; indeed, it could no longer be located within a stratified order at all. Art became a business that involved risk. Artists began to resist the pretensions of "connoisseurs" and experts who themselves were incapable of producing artworks and thus had no hands-on experience in creating art.[87] In Paris, the establishment of periodic art exhibitions in "salons" (beginning in 1737) triggered a flood of public commentary attacking the irresponsible criticism of the salons.[88] Instead of being justified by (in principle fulfillable) demands on the upper classes, art criticism became a parasite, feeding off the relationship between artist and recipient (buyer). In a sense, criticism took the insecurities that accumulate in this relationship and reworked them from within the art system. In this way, art criticism lost its secure ground; it had to give up its pretensions to represent the only correct view, and it could no longer appeal to truth. At most, it could claim coauthorship of the work in a manner that anticipated romantic criticism; Scottish moral philosophy would later do its part in historicizing the problem in the domains of law, morality, and aesthetics. National differences regarding artistic production and taste could be as fascinating as historical ones. One sought ways to classify art that no longer depended on unconditionally correct criteria.

The economic orientation granted art much more freedom than reliance on patrons such as churches, princes, or leading aristocratic houses. It furthered an evaluation of artworks that was independent of subject matter,[89] and it required less interaction, although the market did generate specialized institutions of interaction and mediation. No longer dependent on a patron's decisions and on negotiations with him, art found itself in the double grip of the demands raised by the art market and a public art criticism. To the extent that the art market relied on economic trends, it was unstable. But it offered two advantages. On the one hand, the market could use the general economic medium of money, while on the other hand, it operated without competition and without the threat of being displaced, which facilitated its isolation from other markets within the economic system. (This is less true when people become concerned with "conspicuous consumption" and art is replaced by coaches, yachts, servants, and so forth—or vice versa.) But the market also generated deception and the need to protect oneself against fraud. It created networks of influence that differed from courtly intrigues, and, thanks to a stronger dynamic of its own, it cared little about what art thought of itself. As a result, economic dependencies were felt more painfully and could no longer be balanced by shifting one's allegiance to another patron; instead, such dependencies had a systemic effect. The relationships between the art system and the economic system could no longer be controlled via the notion of generally accepted criteria. Buyers no longer needed to legitimize themselves by their expertise, and if they made fools of themselves, they were certainly no fools on the market.

The tendencies in painting we have discussed can be observed, several decades later, in poetry as well.[90] The market, with its agents, readers/buyers, publishers, and reviewers, turned into a generalized patron, but one could not respond to the market as one responded to a person. In Parsons's terminology, this change can be described as a shift, within a given set of pattern variables, from the particular to the universal. On the one hand, a market orientation allows more specialized offerings, while on the other hand, it provokes defensive reactions—a written polemic against publishers and reviewers (for example, Jean Paul), a rejection of productions that might stimulate sales (for example, Ludwig Tieck's *Peter Lebrecht*),[91] and, at a more general level of self-description, a contrastive revalorization of art as culture: "At a time when the artist is being described as just one more producer of a commodity for the market, he is describing himself as a specially endowed person, the guiding light of the common life."[92] The fact that the debate about good taste eventually subsides must be seen in the same context: when sales are at stake, public models of taste are no longer acceptable; and in the final third of the eighteenth century they gave way to the idea of the genius *who disciplines himself*—a notion that revives the old nexus between melancholy and discipline.

Academic philosophy in Germany reacted to increased uncertainty in the realm of evaluative criteria by developing a specialized aesthetics that pursued theoretical projects of its own.[93] This high-level conceptual effort tended to gloss over its own failure to register the fact that the social situation of the art system was undergoing yet another fundamental, and by now obviously irreversible, transition toward functional differentiation. Around 1800, however, the situation was still far from clear. Processes of bifurcation at odds with hierarchical structures began to distinguish themselves, especially vis-à-vis politics ("the state") and the economy ("commercial society," "system of needs," "society"). In the meantime, it had become evident that religion was not a science in the usual sense and that the family, bound by love, was not a contractual relationship (despite Kant). Hopes for a "culture state" that would offer education and artistic taste as a preemptive measure against revolutionary aspirations had quickly become obsolete.[94] It had become clear that no functional system can substitute for any other. As a result, the internal criteria of individual functional systems lost their plausibility within society at large. There was a vague awareness of these changes, but a new concept of society that would provide an explanation was still lacking.

When Hegel speaks of the end of art, "In all these respects, art—according to its highest determination—is, and remains, for us a thing of the past,"[95] he can mean only one thing: art has lost its immediate relation to society and worldly affairs and must henceforth acknowledge its own differentiation. Art can still claim universal competence for almost everything, but it can do so only *as art* and only on the basis of a specific mode of operation that follows its own criteria.

The notion that art, as represented by artists, can find a knowledgeable and sympathetic counterpart somewhere else in society must be sacrificed as well. A supporting context—if this is what one is looking for—is no longer available. A model based on complementary roles for artists and connoisseurs can no longer represent the couplings between the art system and society. Rather, it represents the differentiation of art as communication in society. The interaction between artists, experts, and consumers differentiates itself as communication, and it takes place only in the art system, which establishes and reproduces itself in this manner. What romanticism called "art criticism" is integrated into the art system as a "medium of reflection,"[96] and its task is to complete the artist's work. In fact, romanticism was the first artistic style to embrace the new situation of an autonomous art system. Starting with romanticism, the only social support of art is that each functional system deals with its own function, claims priority for its own function, and develops no further competencies that point beyond the system. This also means that each system produces an excess of communicative possibilities—mainly because of the in-difference of other systems—and therefore requires self-limitation, that is, "auto-nomy." The romantic movement intuitively grasped this situation, for which it compensated by focusing on self-reflection, by embracing the temporal difference between subjective reflection and what appears to be the objectively given world, by emphasizing writing as an absence that symbolizes absences, and by counting on concepts such as self-possession, sobriety, and irony. The semantics of romantic reflection was still search-ing for itself in the sense of searching for a goal displaced to infinity. What it actually reflected upon, however, is the autonomy imposed upon art—the functional differentiation of society. This situation seems to have re-mained unchanged for the past two hundred years. Only the extent to which the system provokes itself has been perfected.

When artists can no longer derive stimulation from tradition—or from a patron or the market, indeed, not even from art academies—new kinds of alliances begin to form within the art system. These alliances attract like-minded individuals and compensate for the lack of external support by providing self-affirmation within the group. One thinks of the Pre-Raphaelites, the Blue Rider, Bauhaus, the Gruppe 47, the Art & Language group, and countless other formations. Such organizations are not formal associations, nor do they depend on condensed interactions in the form of regular meetings. Instead, they are loose alliances, which create a sense of belonging and leave it up to individuals how long they want to commit themselves. Socially, these groups appear to be motivated by the desire to find support in similar efforts for unusual programmatic decisions, so that they do not come across merely as idiosyncratic moves by individuals.

VII

The differentiation of the art system—a process characterized simulta-neously by continuity and discontinuity—allows the relation between sys-tem and environment to be reintroduced into the system in the form of a relationship between self-reference and hetero-reference. As we recall, there can be no self-reference without hetero-reference, for it is not clear how the self can be indicated if it excludes nothing.[97] When the unity of self-reference and hetero-reference becomes an issue, searching for the common denominator in the meaning of reference suggests itself: What is the reference of "reference"?

Depending on how the relationship between self-reference and hetero-reference is applied, we shall distinguish an art that is primarily *symbolic* from an art that thinks of itself as a *sign*, and we shall further distinguish an art that specializes in experimenting with *form combinations*.[98] Prior to its differentiation, art was considered *symbolic* if it searched for a higher meaning in its condensed ornamental relationships. In the course of the court- and market-oriented phases of its differentiation, art turned into a *sign*. The sign, by virtue of what was believed to be its objective reference, stood for what the artist, the connoisseur, and the lover of art had in common. But once the differentiation of this community was realized as communication, the only remaining option was to observe the continual balancing between self-reference and hetero-reference in the operations of the art system. Under these conditions, one finds the nexus between self- and hetero-reference in the *formal combinations* of artworks that facilitate an observation of observations.

Semantics follows sociostructural ruptures while glossing over discontinuities and thereby providing for recursions and transitions within the system. These evolutionary changes tend toward tolerating, indeed, toward favoring, the artwork's individual uniqueness. Under the regime of symbolic art, this would have made no sense. But when art is considered to be a sign, thinking of art in terms of its uniqueness becomes an option, and when art is understood to be a form combination, uniqueness becomes imperative—enforced by the mode of production and by the requirements of understanding. At the same time, the trend toward individuality requires sacrificing all external support. It correlates with the social differentiation of the art system, which in turn motivates the perpetual renewal of the relationship between self-reference and hetero-reference. In similar ways, mathematics develops from a symbolic understanding of numbers (as late as Agrippa von Nettesheim[99]) via Descartes's notion of numbers as mental signs of space and infinity[100] to the formalism of self-limiting constructs in modern mathematical logic. The parallel development of art and mathematics suggests general sociostructural transformations, which are outside our present scope. Instead, we restrict our focus to the art system.

We shall term *symbolic* an art that seeks to render present, within the accessible world, what is inaccessible (unfamiliar, unobservable). Symbolic art is always concerned with the unity of a difference,[101] in this case, with the unity of the specific difference between the accessible and the inaccessible. The symbol marks the inaccessible within the realm of the accessible; we are therefore dealing with a form of reentry of a distinction into what it distinguishes. The symbol contains a reference to its own origin, which grounds the representation in its "given" form. This origin does not refer to a distant past that retreats further as time goes by. On the contrary, it is a presence that must be continually reactualized.[102] If the concept of the symbol is understood in this way (as a symbol of hospitality or of belonging to a secret cult), then the symbol *is*, or *brings about*, this unity by virtue of its suggestive power. If the symbol is defined as a sign (*signum*)—as was common in the Middle Ages—then it is a sign that *itself brings about* access to the signified.

The representation of unity in the form of symbols reached a climax in the twelfth century. A (written) theology, increasingly concerned with consistency, might have been troubled by the notion of a "beautiful" God.[103] But visual and poetic symbolizations could develop freely so long as theology could be assured that they did not present simulacra but instead symbolized the unpresentable. In opposition to the effort to integrate traditional elements from antiquity, a new cultural form thus began to establish itself,[104] the origin of what we recognize today as "Western" culture. A differentiation of art was inconceivable within this formal model (even though, at the level of roles, a differentiation of specialized roles and skills did occur). Art remained strictly focused on the problem of unity as it presented itself in a monotheistic (Christian) religion. The unity of the world —a unity of God and his creation—could be shown *in the creation*. This demonstrated that the world is ordered and beautiful. One could trust the world, even though abuse, corruption, and sin abound. For this reason, symbolic art found itself in close proximity to religion, which originated precisely in the desire to overcome the difference familiar/unfamiliar.[105] At first, art turned to the (ontological) distinction between the visible and the invisible for orientation; its task was to activate the invisible within the realm of visibility without actually being able to render it visible. In a sense, art became the sister of magic. A doorway, for example, or an elaborated portal facilitated entrance into an order of higher meaning.[106]

The symbol must be "condensed" in this world (*hic mundus*). Under the condition of such a *contractio*, art could not *be* the supernatural, it could only *represent* the supernatural. In relation to what it intended to show and to what exists without *contractio* in the form of the transcendental God, art marked itself as difference. In so doing, it had to avoid elaborating the kind of illusion that was later called "beautiful appearance." Art did not yet form a medium of its own.[107] At the same time, *contractio* facilitated relationships between symbols, creating a symbolic "language," which had to adapt to the regulations of theology. This required direction and supervision by the church and assigned to those who carried out the work (only) the status of craftsmen. At this level, the paradox of observing the unobservable, the paradoxical marking of differences, could unfold. According to Kristeva: "The function of the symbol in its horizontal dimension (where it articulates the relationship between significant units) is a function of escaping paradox; one might say, the symbol is horizontally *anti-paradoxical.*"[108]

But if the ultimate responsibility for dissolving paradoxes is left to religion, art cannot distinguish itself from religion through this task. Although essentially art is not a religion (not "Spirit" in the full Hegelian sense), it is the servant of religion. Yet the moment the symbol is communicated as a symbol, it raises the suspicion of being a "simulacrum" that exploits the means of visual plausibility to create a deceptive unity. The symbolic relation thus carries within itself the seed of its own dissolution, and once the church deemed it necessary to decide which forms of symbolization are correct and which are false, the symbol's demise was inevitable. This development parallels a mnemotechnical, artificial use of images that was meant to establish a transmittable cultural space and persisted through the decline of this art in the wake of the invention of print. The *concettismo* of the seventeenth century announced the end of this tradition and the beginning of a modern, nonreferential use of signs (which at first lacked connectivity).[109]

Once the ties between art and religion began to relax,[110] art could expand its competency to include "allegories" of common universals or "emblems" that present complex states of affairs in a condensed form.[111] Apart from painting and poetry, the courtly theater of the fifteenth and sixteenth centuries staged allegories supported by an elaborate machinery, which had to compensate for its lack of information and depth. Stage productions of this sort remained subordinate to the regime of the symbol— the point was to render visible something that is essentially invisible—but they now included an awareness of their own exteriority, of the discrepancy between sign and signified, and they gave up the notion that they could bring about unity by virtue of their own operative means. Aside from religion (or within religion), a cosmos of essences established itself, equipped with invariant universals—with virtues and vices, with time, or with good or bad luck. But whatever art signified had to already be familiar. The theater stage, which followed in the second half of the sixteenth century, was a decisive step forward. Productions no longer took place among the people or as elaborate courtly festivals but instead occurred at self-determined times. Space was divided into the stage and the audience. One had to pay to "get in." The actors and the audience no longer shared the tangible symbolization, the "representation" of the invisible in this world—a representation that, in a religious sense, transcended life as a world of appearances. Now both actors and audience participated in projecting appearances; they both knew how to see through appearances and how to read signs as signs for something else—which now meant that signs stood for the fatalities of individuals who had to learn to deal with their own fate.[112] At the formal level, art was free to experiment with new ideas, but at first its representations still presumed familiarity. With the growing supply of signs, the recognition eventually sunk in that there were too many of them, and that one could not rely on the "nature" of signs but had to proceed selectively. As Kristeva points out,[113] this requires a *quantitative restriction* in the amount of available symbols as well as a sufficiently frequent *repetition* of these symbols. This is how the idea of compiling allegories lexically arose, so that correspondences between meanings and images would be accessible to those who wished to produce accurate copies.[114] But more and more art offered the opportunity—especially in the theater and later in the modern novel—to substitute *narrative plausibility* for the *quantitative limitation* of symbols and to generate the necessary redundancies within artworks themselves rather than drawing them from the real world.

But all allegories were still mere signs. In a sense, the artwork debased itself unless it aspired to more than allegory; it excluded itself from participating in the essence of things. In so doing, art gained an important advantage: the true/false schema broke down. Allegories were neither true nor false, or they were both true and false, depending on how one looked at them. Following the rationalistic tendency of modern thought, the realm of the symbol was consumed by the allegorical. Conceptually, it became increasingly difficult to distinguish between the two, until the limited repertoire of conventional allegories was experienced as too restrictive. In the eighteenth century, one gave up the quasi-lexical standardization of allegorical forms (in Alciat and Ripa) and left it to the artist to discover suitable topics and forms of creativity.[115] Kant acknowledges this situation by reestablishing the concept of the symbol on the basis of a new distinction—the distinction between schematic and symbolic—*both* of which he takes in an *operative* sense and posits against the concept of the sign.[116] This conceptual arrangement allows for the devaluation of the schematic and for the "expansion of the concept of the symbol toward a universal principle."[117] Solger reduces the symbol/allegory distinction to the distinction between existence and indication and distinguishes the symbol from a merely signifying function.[118] At such a level of abstraction, however, the concept of allegory loses its relationship to intuition.

Even in earlier times, allegorical art was unable to cover the entire realm of art. The mere fact that art had shifted its hetero-reference from symbols to signs was a step beyond the limitations of allegory.[119] In the wake of this shift, forms could become "classical"; they could strive for perfection and accomplish it on their own. It became possible to draw a meaningful distinction between the sign and its material basis and to treat the latter as interchangeable. Only much later did the questions arise of whether the material substratum of the sign might not in the end be more meaningful than a pure semiotics had assumed, and whether it might communicate something in its own right.[120]

The gradual, more implicit than explicit shift from symbol to sign (which could draw on a semiology that originated in antiquity) may be related to the fact that the concept of the sign facilitates the elaboration of complex patterns of distinction. In modern terminology, the sign mediates both between subject and object and between subject and subject; or, to put it differently, it mediates between the factual and the social dimensions of meaning. The use of signs for the purpose of signification subjects itself to social observation; indeed (just like language) it is necessary only if one wants to communicate one's intention to others. When one uses signs rather than symbols, there is no need to mention the unity of the distinction subject/object and subject/subject so long as a common reservoir of signs can be taken for granted and the selection is situationally motivated. Sociostructural and sociohistorical (evolutionary) conditions apparently confront communication with a complexity that has become more intense and yet is still restrained rather than internally open, so that an orientation toward signs is already necessary and still sufficient. This is why the seventeenth century succeeded in staging, one more time, the unity of the political order of society in a theatrical ceremony that included all the signs related to that order (for example, the king's body and his actions) and could take for granted that the signs of representation would recruit the players.[121] Signs signify the order of signs. Only much later could one accept that the sign user must be observed as an observer and that the signified is not the object itself but a correlate of sign use, a *signifié*.

Signs point toward nonpresence. An experience that can be actualized opens itself toward the nonactual. This includes symbolic art,[122] but it expands its realm toward immanence. As always with evolutionary steps, it is difficult to see why this happens and where it is going. This became plausible in portrait painting, for example, which was meant to preserve the memory of the person portrayed. The early modern apotheosis of nature may have fostered the notion that the entire world was worthy of duplication. Compared to the symbol, the sign supported creative freedom, since it remains external to the signified. Unlike symbols, signs may be used ironically within the limits of intelligible contexts; they can be used in a laudatory sense when one intends to blame someone and vice versa.[123] Unlike the symbol, the sign liberates the facts signified for the tasks of scientific analysis and explanation. As a result, science and art could now begin separate careers in one and the same world. As a kind of compensatory measure, art required an additional component to be meaningful: a work of art must be well made; it must be skillfully crafted. In order to justify its referential access to the external world, art depended more than ever on system-internal criteria, and this provoked an effort of reflection that would eventually transform itself into a theoretical aesthetics.

But the freedom of artistic creativity still remained restricted. Between sign and signified there is no natural relationship of the kind one observes, for example, when the changing colors of the leaves and fluctuating air temperatures indicate the approach of winter. This is why the signifying relation needed another guarantee, which resided in the artwork's resemblance to what it signifies—in the imitation of nature. To put it differently, an artwork could be understood or "consumed" with pleasure only if it allows recognition (or, in information-theoretical terms, if it provides a sufficient number of redundancies). This requirement, along with the concept of imitation, is coupled to hetero-reference. The work of art must bear sufficient resemblance to phenomena familiar from a realm of experience outside of art. The essence of things guarantees their representability, as it were, from within, and this is why art is capable of signifying this essence.[124] Already in the era of courtly art, compromises were inevitable. Representations of the sovereign and his family in portraits, on tombstones, or in texts had to bear a certain resemblance to their objects, and yet one could not exclusively focus on how they looked in reality.[125] Such deviations had to be justified within the doctrine of imitation. Once one produces for an art market, this requirement loses significance. The eighteenth century defined artistic license in ways that permitted, indeed demanded, an imitation of nature while rejecting the imitation of art—the mere copying of other works—in the name of originality, innovation, and progress.[126] This rule was directed against the notion of a self-imitation of art—an imitation that sought to emulate classical perfection—which had earlier served to justify artistic claims to autonomy.[127]

So long as the semantics of the sign dominated notions about art, a balancing mechanism was needed to compensate for the increasing ambiguity of the signifying relation. We find this mechanism in the theory of taste. But with the idea of taste art opened itself up once again to social reference. The displacement of social reference by, and in the name of, autonomy triggered an effort of reflection that replaced the sign relation with the distinction between the universal and the particular and defined art as the appearance of the universal in the particular—art, in other words, was once again defined as symbol, albeit in a nonreligious sense.

In a parallel development, eighteenth-century narrative no longer represents exemplary cases but seeks instead to activate the reader's self-experience. Excessive amounts of detail (in Richardson's *Pamela*, for example) suggest proximity to real life while displacing the exemplary into motivational structures that remain below the level of consciousness. The relationship of such works to reality is beyond doubt. The sign stands in for something that really exists. And yet, the premise of a common world is no longer self-evident. Displaced into the realm of latent motives, it requires a shift in level to become visible, a move toward second-order observation. The reader can see what the hero cannot see. The sign, now fully secularized, takes over the symbolizing function of rendering visible what is invisible. In the meantime, one's understanding of the symbol has changed as well.[128] The entire artistic production is now staged within the world and for this world, and the mystery the symbol sought to apprehend has been displaced to the mode of functioning that characterizes the subjective faculties in their dealings with the world. This shift provided the starting point for the nineteenth-century resurrection of the symbol.

The structure of the sign remains dualistic, like that of the symbol (which is considered to be a special kind of sign). The form of the sign is a difference. But what is the unity of this difference? This question does not arise so long as the problem is posed in terms of a distinction between real objects that one observes as either art or nature. After all, landscape paintings coexist with landscapes and narratives with event sequences in reality. The difference between art and reality is bridged via the demand for resemblance—it must be possible to recognize one in the other. This presupposes, of course, that the signified itself is not a sign, and this assumption limits the complexity that is possible under these circumstances. But what are we to make of the fact that the world is now divided into two kinds of reality—a world of singular events and a world of statistics (or of inductive inferences), a reality out there and a fictional reality? And what happens when this difference is radicalized, when resemblances are deconstructed, when it becomes doubtful whether there is a bridge between these two worlds, and when one is eventually forced to admit with Saussure that "the sign is arbitrary"? Has trust in the sign and its relation to a primary reality become no more than a "habit" of the sort Hume saw in induction or John Austin in legal norms? Is it, as Kant suggested, merely a reflex of the pressure to act, of the need to engage oneself before one's cognitive possibilities are exhausted? Do signs always refer only to other signs—even if their relationship to reality seems "immediate" and thus unquestionably and uncritically plausible?[129] Or is it in the end nothing but the inevitability of a cut, of "writing" (Derrida), the need to draw a boundary without which no observer can observe?

We do not raise these questions in order to provide answers. We take them only to indicate trends. In the second half of the twentieth century, the art system has found itself in a society that can raise such questions—in a manner far removed from the old debate about universals, which was concerned only with the primacy of one side or the other. In his transcendental critique of the empirical world relation, Kant, for example, goes beyond the notion that aesthetics should concern itself with a factually correct use of signs. Earlier we mentioned Kant's reformulation of the concept of the symbol. The authority of aesthetic judgment is now referred to as "Spirit" (in contrast to reason), and its criteria are called "aesthetic Ideas" (as opposed to Ideas of reason).[130] Their function, however, is not to symbolize a hinter-world but to "stimulate the mind,"[131] which Kant describes theoretically in rather vague terms. Subsequent developments went well beyond this conceptualization, not least by radicalizing the problem of the relationship between self-reference and hetero-reference.

This is why romanticism can speak of the symbol as well as of allegory —with a certain preference for the symbol. Romanticism is no longer concerned with an analogy of being, nor with a naturally secured (possibly erroneous) use of signs. Romanticism already reacts to the excesses and insecurities of communication that result from the differentiation of the art system. Its problem is intersubjectivity, a problem that lies at the heart of the subject's self-relation. This relation, and nothing else, is reflected in romanticism's relationship to nature.[132] In the course of the nineteenth century, a symbolism emerged from such notions that tended to present itself as self-sufficient.

In a society that cultivates a doctrine of the sign without reference in the epistemology of a "radical constructivism" and in semiology (including the theory of language), art can no longer justify its choice of forms by hetero-reference, not even by "abstracting" from hetero-reference. German Idealism took measures to animate art via reflection from the idea of beauty, which was a step toward a self-referential grounding of art, even though it did not yet concern art in general but only its core, poetry. The artwork's symbolism now referred to the difference between itself and an Idea that is unattainable and expresses itself in the sensible realm through this difference and in the agony over it. The formula of "Spirit" anticipates the notion of "autopoiesis"[133] but lacks sufficient informational content. A solution must therefore be sought in the art of formal combination, in the work's ability to sustain an internal balance under extenuated circumstances, in the manner in which it creates distinctions that fit other distinctions.

Under such radically altered circumstances, the concept of the symbol acquires a new meaning. Despite repeated attempts to enter into an unholy alliance with religion—which profits from such "revivals"—one begins to formulate, in more current terms, the problem of difference that lies at the heart of the symbol. This problem concerns the difference between signifier (*signifiant*) and signified (*signifié*). Following Peirce or Saussure, one adopts either a pragmatic or a structuralist perspective and analyzes the difference between signifier and signified. To the extent that this difference can be bridged neither operatively nor via the resemblance of images, the sign (*signe*) becomes the unity of signifier (*signifiant*) and signified (*signifié*). But what is the "sign" itself? Is it a difference or a unity? Is it merely a condition that allows us to take the next step? A passing moment in an ongoing process?[134] If so, then how does one copy the signified unity out of the unity of difference (in contrast to copying it into this unity in the form of a reentry)?[135]

So long as signs still referred, one could imagine "differences between levels"—for example, between syntax and semantics. The classical structure of narrative facilitated such a separation and combination of levels, namely, between the narration and the narrated plot. One could project into this difference what the work left invisible. One could use the distinction between levels to render invisible the unity of this distinction (that is, the world). By collapsing these levels and by creating deliberate confusion of the sort we find in *Tristram Shandy*, one could show that this was indeed the case. The dark profundity of the world was no longer symbolized in the old sense; it vanished in the difference between levels and could be represented only by collapsing these levels, that is, by paradox. The distinction between levels remained intact, albeit subject to subversion, and it accomplished precisely what we expect from art, namely, that it make the world visible by making it invisible. Yet this solution remained tied to the distinguishability of levels as well as to the reference of signs and their related arrangements. But where does one stand when the difference between the separation and subversion of levels becomes too obviously a part of the normal artistic repertoire (when the narrator appears in his story *because* he is not supposed to do so)?

Once this difference becomes the object of reflection, the concept of the symbol again suggests itself. The symbol is a sign that reflects upon the signifying function; it appropriates the place of paradox and secures the operation of signification. If we look ahead toward this solution, then we understand why the nineteenth century once again favored the concept of the symbol. The return of the symbol in romanticism was not an invocation of God—in the meantime, God had become a topic of religion.[136] Rather, it evoked (unattainable) unity in such a way as to render the use of the symbol self-destructive.[137] The romantic symbol indicates a combination of forms that rules over its own distinctions, and in so doing refers to something it cannot signify. What it attempts to symbolize is, in the final analysis, the reentry of the form into the form. The symbol not only stands for what it excludes but also signifies the impossibility of signifying the excluded, even though there is more room, internally, to choose one's distinctions. In this sense, the symbol stands once again for the observation of an unobservable world.

One now experiments with intricately nested distinctions in the hope of eliciting "synergetic" effects and tolerates the free choice of form combinations, even though they are subsequently subordinated to the idea of harmony. It is currently difficult to decide whether experiments of this sort yield a higher degree of complexity or whether they eliminate much of what was previously possible in art. After such bursts of complexity, evolution tends to start all over again on a smaller scale, exploring new possibilities on a relatively simple basis without any evolutionary guarantee of success. The current reduction of art to form, its minimalism and radical simplicity, cannot satisfy in the long run. Sooner or later, one might once again demand a maximum amount of complexity from the individual work.

VIII

Hardly any other functional system can compare with art when it comes to integrating the most heterogeneous modes of operation into an autopoietic functional nexus. This is due to the variety of its material basis—in the visual arts, textual art, and music, for example. The assumption of a primordial unity of art that later dissolved into different forms is pure speculation.[138] On the contrary, the history of art suggests that one starts from the difference between genres and never thinks of art in the singular, that is, in terms of an overarching unity. From the Middle Ages to the Renaissance, one employed the same symbolism in different genres so as to invoke a realm that transcends art.[139] Apart from such explicit references, one finds covert references to meanings that are secret (and withheld as esoteric), such as the cosmological-mathematical theory of proportion that (until Palladio) not only played a role in music and architecture but also served as a theme of poetry. One recalls the much quoted formula *ut pictura poesis erit* (Horace), which provoked the competition between poetry and painting,[140] as well as the widely accepted definition of some of the arts in terms of *mimesis/imitatio*. Such correspondences are not all-determining, nor do they concern only the realm we identify as "art" today. They draw on the relationship of art to an external harmony of the world that is partly explicit and partly "esoteric" and that remains imperceptible in the artwork—a notion that had to be sacrificed after its final climax in the hermeticism of the Renaissance.

None of these tendencies stands in the way of a technical differentiation of the arts (as craft), but they hold art at this level. Art is considered a "habit" of artists rather than an island of meaning isolated from the external world.[141] Even today, the notion of a unified art system meets with skeptical resistance, mainly because of manifest differences among the arts, especially when it comes to the question of whether or not literature ought to be considered a part of the art system.[142] Academic honors, disciplines, academies, and faculties tend to be at stake in this dispute; they cannot tolerate that someone simultaneously studies to become a painter, a sculptor, a musician, a dancer, and an actor.

Yet, we cannot ignore correlations that are no longer legitimized in religious or cosmological terms but instead are rooted in the art system itself. They suggest that the unity of art emerged in the wake of a differentiated art system and is now grounded in differentiation. Historically, the notion of a unified art system did not emerge until the second half of the eighteenth century, subsequently altering the referential situation of reflection. Only then could one speak of the Beaux-Arts or of the beautiful in art and describe the product in terms that simultaneously indicate its production.[143] The project of integrating morality was sacrificed, together with the idea that the purpose of art is imitation. Only then did the reflection theory of the art system establish itself as an "aesthetics."[144]

This epochal turnabout in adjoining relationships led to the emergence of features that justify speaking of modern literature or modern painting,[145] or call attention to correlations owing to the speed of artistic development and to the drive of art to surpass itself—the correlation, for example, between atonal music, cubist painting, and a textual production that disregards the expectations and the reading pace of the average reader, even deliberately subverts such dependencies. When the romantics speak of "poetry," they mean something entirely different from what the older poetics had in mind. Though the textual arts might seem to be claiming leadership here, the real issue (as postclassical music and painting demonstrate) is the general problem of fictionality, the exclusive rule of art over the difference between reality and fictionality.

When the history of art is written, caesuras tend to be placed at varying points, especially when they concern artistic genres. In painting, it might be relevant that everyday scenes become worthy of art in the manner of Dutch painting; in eighteenth-century literature, it might be important that the novel emphasizes individuality by presenting "round" characters—a tendency that provokes the romantic flirtation with the double.

Certainly such developments assimilate tendencies indicative of large-scale sociostructural changes. What is at stake here is the subversion of traditional social distinctions of rank or the hierarchical order of households, client relationships, and regions. But this does not sufficiently account for the fact that eventually everything can be painted and narrated. The tendency of the work of art to become unique while its thematic meaning can be generalized presupposes the differentiation of an art system. And this *system*—which is both unique and thematically open, concrete in its operations and yet undetermined—is copied into every single *work* of art. Once the system accomplishes this task via reproducing its boundaries, which happens with *each* individual work (with *every* art-specific operation), it no longer matters to the system's reproduction how the observation materializes itself. Material possibilities might still be distinguishable and might yield more or less evident opportunities for the realization of art. But if distinct systems differentiate themselves in literature, music, and the visual arts, then they can do so only as subsystems of the art system.

Such a view offers the advantage of allowing us to trace how different genres alternately take the lead in the differentiation of the art system. It makes sense to assume that text-art (poetry) takes the initiative in differentiating itself against the truth claims of early modern science (even though mannerist painting, with its formal distortions, makes the same point—that it doesn't care about truth in the ordinary sense). The literary front vis-à-vis scientific texts is the realm where expectations concerning truth are most likely to arise and where they must be rejected in the interest of a domain of utterances unique to art.[146] Conversely, around 1900 music and painting apparently led the battle against the narrowing of what was artistically admissible, introducing the notion that binding traditions (as opposed to a mere history of forms) must be rejected—for example, tonality in music or figurative verisimilitude in painting. If hypotheses of this sort can prove themselves, then one might attribute a supportive role to the diversity of genres in the evolutionary process of the art system's differentiation. As in the differentiation of states in early modern Europe, a segmental differentiation of the art system provides the opportunity to experiment with ideas that can lead further. There is no need to burden the system as a whole with transitions and possible failures; one can begin in areas where success is most likely. The move toward sovereign states throughout Europe does not happen everywhere at the same time. The modern empirico-mathematical method does not revolutionize the entirety of human knowledge in an instant. Some genres dissolve their ties to imitation sooner than others. But at the same time, the unity of the respective functional system proves and reproduces itself in such avant-garde advances: less forthcoming segments are seized by processes of diffusion and are encouraged to experiment with possibilities of their own.

For a segmental differentiation of the art system, generic differences offer a natural starting point that requires little by way of presupposition—in this, the differentiation of art resembles the process by which politics establishes territorial differences or science creates divisions between object realms. However, one can speak of segmental differentiation only if one can take a segmentally differentiated system for granted. External and internal differentiations condition one another. Moreover, one needs to give up the idea—which developed in conjunction with aristocratic notions about education—that there exists a hierarchical relationship between artistic genres: for example, between forms pertaining strictly to the crafts, on the one hand, and higher forms, such as (Latin) poetry, on the other.[147] Along with the functional differentiation of the art system, the internal relationship among genres shifts from a hierarchical order—corresponding to social coordinates—to concerns with equality and difference. The move toward internal segmentation permits the system to block structural correspondences with its environment and paves the way for a functional differentiation of art. It eventually leads to a condition of society in which the differentiation of politics along the lines of separate states no longer finds support in the differentiation of other social systems, such as the differentiation of genres in art, of disciplines in science, or of markets in the economy. As a result, each system can test its own differentiation only internally rather than in view of corresponding divisions in the environment. When such an order of breaks in symmetry has established itself, it is no longer possible to think of the world in cosmological terms as "dividing itself." This shift generates the conditions for a poly-contextural semantics, with which each functional system must now come to terms on its own.

IX

Art has very few direct effects on other functional systems, and this is why society rarely responds to the differentiation and autonomy of the art system. It tends to attract attention when certain functional systems fail to recognize or accept their own specificity and therefore consider developments within the art system to be an encroachment or mistake that needs to be corrected. A notorious case is the reaction of the Catholic Church in the wake of the Counter Reformation or, more accurately, in the wake of the Council of Trent.[148] Other examples are the political reactions of twentieth-century totalitarian regimes, especially in the Soviet Union and in Germany under National Socialism.

In the Middle Ages, the topics of art were predominantly religious in nature, focusing on biblical scenes or the legends of saints. Such themes could be presupposed to be familiar. The primary task of the visual arts was to instruct the people, to preserve and refresh their memory.[149] The same holds for sacred scenes staged by the church—the birth of Jesus, Gethsemane, his crucifixion and resurrection. Those who knew and recognized a scene could supply their own details, but occasionally these details needed to be refreshed by images. This required an unambiguous production that individualized the figures and their surroundings only to a minimal degree and left out confusing details.[150] Attempts at innovation or experiments with aesthetic effects were bound to disrupt the predominantly religious purpose of these images. (The same might be said about courtly poetry—the lyric and the heroic epic—which continued to be recited even after written versions were available.) As early as the fifteenth century, the beginnings of the differentiation of the art system and the increasing personalization of artists in terms of their names, their reputations, and their views about art gave rise to problems that, in the system of patronage, were addressed case by case.

We can observe similar changes in the realm of text-art. In the Middle Ages, debates about artistic topics or controversial issues in rhetoric and poetics were strictly internal religious disputes, for the simple reason that clerics were the ones who could read and write. Christianity had to defend itself—with an eye toward popular belief in magic and miracles—against the claims to credibility of ancient mythologies, at least insofar as these mythologies were known. All of this changed with the rediscovery of antiquity. One began to recognize that a perfection worthy of imitation had existed before *in this world*. Other factors that contributed to this change were the invention of print and the subsequent anonymity of the reading public, as well as the Renaissance penchant for literary debates about topics such as the proper understanding of Aristotle's poetics. The controversy about the poetic status of *meraviglia*[151] no longer posed a threat to religious belief. Under the umbrella of system-internal criteria, one could still follow Tasso and debate whether the poetic rule of *verisimilitudo* could tolerate pagan mythologies, or whether it required restricting oneself to the (unquestionable) Christian tradition. Bishop Minturno wrote his response to the problem of a poetics during his participation in the Council of Trent,[152] which shows that he was perfectly capable of distinguishing between religion and poetry. Religion condemned "enthusiasm" as self-deceptive about divine inspiration and as a cause of conflict, whereas in the literature about literature, a positive attitude prevailed without fear of possible religious conflicts (at most, one invoked the muses).[153] Inner-theological disputes tended to be replaced by concern about possible interferences between the systems of religion and art, especially with regard to the seductive tricks that painting and music play on the senses.

The church did not respond in a focused political fashion until the second half of the sixteenth century. Religious upheavals and schisms within the church had focused its attention on confessional differences and thus on the problem of education. "True belief" had to be consolidated and subjected to organizational surveillance. In the Catholic domain, such efforts were backed primarily by the Jesuit order. One could decide to resist the pressure to innovation exerted by the art system. By the sixteenth century, however, the differentiation of the art system had become irreversible. Despite the religious critique of the invention of new images, a return to the old cult image as the predominant form was out of the question; one had to accept the fact that art was *not* a religious phenomenon. This realization raised the question of the appropriate art for religious service; the answers varied, depending on whether they came from the Protestant or the Catholic side.[154] The idiosyncratic willfulness of art was not yet described in terms of autonomy. The debates, in which the church intervened, were still carried out at a programmatic level. Even in the literature about art, one finds opposition to the liberties taken by Michelangelo and to mannerism, which was emerging then. The interventions of the church, however, went far beyond that. They insisted on a rigid morality and demanded that art follow the themes of a history prescribed by the church.[155] What artists called *invenzione* and *disegno* was restricted accordingly. The kind of music permitted in churches was strictly controlled so as to preclude any pleasurable stimulation of the senses. In addition, one distinguished sharply between sacred and profane art—presumably in reaction to a development that had become irresistible and was applauded with too much enthusiasm.[156] As a result, the kind of sacred art that remained committed to devotion was excluded from the historical and stylistic dynamic of the art system.

This antagonism was bound not to last. Very soon, religion and art discovered a common interest—at least in Catholicism—in creating an affective basis for experience and action. This project relieved the burden of reaching agreement about details in the depiction of figures, so long as the boundaries of proper conduct (decorum) were observed. Maintaining decorum is the seventeenth-century formula for restricting—*without religious grounding*—the whims of illusion, the willfulness of art, and also the arbitrariness of the market. Decorum could once more assert the divisions of segmentation. But toward the mid-seventeenth century, the notion of decorum dissolved, to be recast in the form of the contract, which was the only way to protect the social order against the danger that people might change their "person" and turn out to be other than what they appeared. What remained of *imitatio* in the old sense now referred to human emotions and to the impression created by the unusual despite its recognizability.

What we retrospectively describe as "baroque" is in many respects a combination of church directives and a sense of art aiming toward autonomy, toward form.[157] Secondary motives such as eroticism, asceticism, ecstasy, and heroism, which could be exploited equally well for religious and artistic purposes, paved the way for a rapprochement. Church-political measures that sought to influence the artist via legal and organizational constraints, supervision, and force led to artworks that, in retrospect, were nevertheless classified in art-historical terms as expressing an *artistic style*. Even in the more restricted domain of church painting, one finds a degree of technical expertise likely to raise doubts about its religious inspiration.[158]

The state-political interventions of the twentieth century did not repeat these measures. Political attacks on modern art confronted an entirely different situation. The autonomy of art had been historically established; it was now part of a history that lives through art, either by continuing the tradition or, more typically, by turning its back on it, by overthrowing tradition in search of new beginnings. In order to forestall the internal dynamics of art, one can resort to political force and permit only politically correct productions that no longer impress the art system. Society has settled for autonomous functional systems, however. In the meantime, the art system has discovered an antidote to infringements by religion, politics, or industrial mass production: namely, the distinction between art and *kitsch*.

§5 Self-Organization:
Coding and Programming

I

We speak of self-organization whenever an operatively closed system uses its own operations to build structures that it can either reuse and change later on, or else dismiss and forget. Computers depend on external programming, although computer-generated programs may be developed eventually. By contrast, autopoietic systems produce their own structures and are capable of specifying their operations via these structures (structural determination). This mode of operation does not exclude causal environmental influences. Some of Munch's paintings bear traces of water damage because they were left outdoors. While some people might consider this beautiful, no one would argue that the rain completed the painting. Nor would anyone try to prove the appropriateness of the rain's decisions with regard to the altered formal structure of the painting. Rather, the impression is that a painting was not and could not have been painted in this manner.

Self-organization owes its possibilities and its room for play to the differentiation of the system. Accordingly, art observes itself by means of the distinction between a reality "out there" and a fictional reality. The doubling of reality generates a medium of its own, in which the fixation of forms becomes not only possible but necessary, if the medium is to be reproduced. The opportunity and the need to do something go hand in hand. This conceptual model will guide the following analyses.

In functional systems, we call the system's basal structure—a structure that is produced and reproduced by the system's operations—a code. In contrast to the concept of code in linguistics, we think here of a binary schematism that knows only two values and that excludes third values at the level of coding.[1] A code must fulfill the following requirements: (1) it must correspond to the system's function, which is to say, it must be able to translate the viewpoint of the function into a guiding difference; and (2) it must be complete in the sense of Spencer Brown's definition, "Distinction is perfect continence,"[2] rather than distinguishing just anything. The code must completely cover the functional domain for which the system is responsible. It must therefore (3) be selective with regard to the external world and (4) provide information within the system. (5) The code must be open to supplements (programs) that offer (and modify) criteria to determine which of the two code values is to be considered in any given case. (6) All of this is cast into the form of a preferential code, that is, into an asymmetrical form that requires a distinction between a positive and a negative value. The positive value can be used within the system; at the least, it promises a condensed probability of acceptance. The negative value serves as a value of reflection; it determines what kinds of program are most likely to fulfill the promise of meaning implied in the positive code value.

Whether "tertium non datur" holds for the logical analysis of artworks as units is debatable (but this is true for any unity of distinct objects).[3] According to Kristeva, the work of art either does not exist at all, or it is a processing of distinctions—it is either a "zero" or a "double," but not a simple unit that can be negated in a single instance. This formulation may be premature, for one can certainly negate a double or treat it as a basis for excluding third possibilities. The question of how autonomy can be understood in logical terms leads further. Whenever a system (or a work) claims autonomy, it must entail the possibility for negating autonomy; in addition, it must be able to negate this possibility. If the system claims more than autonomy, if it wants to observe and describe itself as autonomous, then it must take additional precautions to ensure that its code is accepted rather than rejected.[4] This is because society anticipates a variety of differently coded functional systems and therefore can operate, as society, only "poly-contextually." As we shall see, this condition affects the classical status of the idea of "beauty," which does not distinguish between disjunctional and transjunctional operations. As a result, the difference between "beautiful" (positive) and "ugly" (negative) is grounded in the idea or the value of beauty itself, which implies that the beautiful is simply beautiful.

For the time being, we shall deal with straightforward binary coding. According to our understanding, a code is a structure among others—a structure that makes it possible to identify operations as belonging to a certain system but is not necessarily capable of representing, without paradox, the unity of the system within the system. The question remains whether the art system is aware of a code that permits it to recognize what is or claims to be art and what is not art.

Codes are distinctions, forms that serve as observational devices. They are mobile structures that are applied differently from situation to situation. To speak of a code is not to make a claim about essences. No matter which words we employ to describe the code (we shall return to this point), the code, by virtue of its binary structure and its closure, plays a crucial role in the differentiation of functional systems—just as the yes/no code is indispensable for the emergence of society. The primordial significance of the code has been concealed by an obsession with "hierarchy"— which advanced civilizations tend to regard as a prerequisite for order— and by an acceptance of bivalence that has been reduced to the level of mere logic. Even today, the notion of the code still needs clarification.

The function of codes is to symbolize and, at the same time, to interrupt the basal circularity of self-implicative autopoietic systems. The classical objection against tautologies, the *petitio principii*, is rendered obsolete by this insight. Within the code, the short-circuit of self-reference is symbolized and at the same time treated as a specialized phenomenon. Negation requires a positive operation of "crossing" or "switching," a position that equals a negated negation. The code contains itself and nothing else. At the same time, the differentiation of two values interrupts circularity and creates asymmetries—in short, it generates systems. One needs additional information in order to distinguish between positive and negative values. It is possible, in other words, to condition the system in such a way that it can decide which values are to be selected under what conditions. Such if/then conditionings (which are subject to exception or interpretive constraints) lead to the emergence of self-organizing systems.[5] In abstract terms, the code is nothing but an invariant disposition for interruption. On the basis of this disposition, which is always given with language, the system can grow and increase its internal complexity in a historically irreversible manner—initially through chance events and later on the basis of self-organization.

In the process of rendering itself asymmetrical (which exploits rather than neutralizes circularity) the system generates time.[6] Time is necessary to cross the boundary between two values. The operation that accomplishes this crossing takes time. Once the code is established, the implicitly assumed temporal dimension unfolds into an explicit observational schema. The system needs a memory in order to know its initial conditions at any given time. It establishes a bipolar stability that causes the system to oscillate continuously between both of its values, and that keeps the system's future open by refusing to settle for one of these values. In observing itself, such a system relies on an operatively actualized present that allows it to distinguish between past and future.

It is inconceivable that an art system could emerge without coding. Moreover, the code allows the specificity of a system—in this case, the art system—to be indicated by distinguishing its unique code from the codes of other systems. Codes respond to the problem of how to identify operations as belonging to the system and therefore require certain qualities—this distinguishes codes from other types of distinctions. Above all, codes must be formulated abstractly enough to inform every operation in a given system. The code's reusability must function as the equivalent of the indication of the system's unity, but without obstructing the functioning of the code's mobile structure. The code exists only when it is used to constrain the recursive anticipation and recapitulation of operations in the same system. Compared to other functional systems, the specificity of the art system resides less in the names of the code values than in that the task of rendering these values asymmetrical (via conditioning and via the generation and use of time) is primarily the responsibility of the artwork itself, and that intermediate levels—such as rules or concepts of style—are possible, but to a large extent dispensable.

Despite the difficulties in finding convincing names for the code values of art (for example, values analogous to the true/false distinction in science), distinguishing between problems of coding and problems of reference and their corresponding distinctions is of utmost importance.[7] Problems of reference occur whenever one distinguishes between self-reference and hetero-reference or, in our case, between art and nonart. The unity (form) of the distinction self-reference / hetero-reference supplies the system with a satisfactory conception of the world, thereby concealing the difference between system and environment that is initially generated in the operation. Problems of coding, by contrast, concern the difference between positive and negative values, which the system uses to indicate which operations belong to the system. Problems of coding divide the system's self-reference along the lines of what is acceptable and unacceptable, that is, they always refer to the system itself. So far as the environment is concerned, acceptance is not an option. The environment is the way it is, or, put differently, the system has no freedom in the environment. Distinctions of reference and distinctions of coding—we are always dealing with distinctions!—are positioned orthogonally in relation to one another. This is why reference to the environment cannot function as the negative value of the code.[8] Distinguishing a work of art from something else can only demarcate an observational space and signal that within this space observational relations of a special kind hold, even though it may appear as if the environment is admitted into the system—in the form of a bathtub, for example, or as a noise audible when the music stops playing, or as an almost normal newspaper advertisement.

The art system must be coded. It must be able to presuppose a code of its own that cannot be surpassed within the system; otherwise it would be unable to differentiate artworks as a special observational domain. This is true even if the art system's self-description were to orient itself, in a more traditional fashion, toward "principles." It would still have to decide whether a given work is or is not in agreement with these principles. If everything is acceptable, then it becomes impossible to distinguish art from nonart. Without this distinction, there is no way to dismantle the distinction itself. In order to create possibilities for observation, one must begin with a distinction; if these possibilities are to be specific and distinguishable, then one needs to begin with a specific difference.

The differentiation of the art system manifests itself in the independence and distinctness of its coding. This is evident in the relationship between aesthetics and morality, in contrast to the moral obligation of art that still held for Gottsched.[9] Sexual morality provides a poor testing ground in this regard, because morality, in this domain, is in a state of flux (despite criticism from the French side). The extensive theodicy debates in the wake of Leibniz and Voltaire's *Candide* were more likely to show how badly moral justifications were in need of reform (a problem to which Adam Smith, Kant, and Bentham responded accordingly) rather than indicate a conflict between the codes of art and morality. But the problem is also considered more as a matter of principle.[10] The "beautiful" does not necessarily have to agree with the morally good, and it cannot draw support from such agreement if it doesn't convince as art. Yet there is no such thing as a crosswise identification of codes, as if the beautiful would have to prove itself above all in the realm of moral perversities (such as incest). The distinctions are positioned in an orthogonal relation to each other; they are indifferent to one another. But since one sought to distance oneself from a tradition that thought about this problem differently, the formulations expressing this trend tend to be uncertain and ambiguous. Friedrich Schlegel, for example, writes, "Isn't it true that a certain [! N. L.] aesthetic malice is an essential component of a balanced education?" And he later rejects "the aesthetician's fashionable contempt—a contempt that distinguishes nothing—of everything that is, or claims to be, morally good."[11] The problem is how to deal with the plural coding (or poly-contexturality) of modern society while still insisting on the unity of the (human) subject and on a bivalent logic. A possible solution is to recognize and communicate codings as paradoxes, in aesthetics via irony, in morality, directly.[12]

Demarcations of this kind are of little help when it comes to determining the values of codes. In traditional aesthetics, the code values of art were labeled beautiful and ugly.[13] Nevertheless, aesthetics tolerated the artistic depiction of ugliness. As early as the Renaissance, storms, fires, and so forth were much admired topics of painting (later on, they would be called "sublime"), and in order to paint such things, one drew on the very principles one followed when drawing beautiful objects (without altering the technique of perspective, for instance). In Herder's words, ugliness played the role of an "ancillary idea."[14] The concept of beauty was applied in a double sense (and, in this regard, paradoxically): it was opposed to ugliness and it implied a general judgment about the relationship between the beautiful and the ugly, or, put differently, beauty was applied both at the figural level and at the level of the artwork's unity.

This is why one was not in a position to distinguish between coding and programming. The level at which art represents objects was not distinguished sharply enough from the level of coding, even though the representation of ugliness, evil, and deformity was justified as a contrast, that is, in view of the other side of the difference beautiful/ugly.[15] Apart from that, the principle of imitation suggested that art ought to represent both kinds of objects.[16] And when discussing "appropriateness," "fitness," and so on, one was thinking of the nexus between the parts of a whole rather than of a manner of operating.[17] Lessing already considered ugliness to be no more than a transgression of the medium's possibilities,[18] reserving the concept of beauty for the overall judgment of an artwork. Beauty, in other words, was understood to be a viewpoint of judgment rather than an option that emerges along with the process of artistic production. This is how the contrastive formula beautiful/ugly is still applied in romanticism, despite the trend toward explaining ugliness, the negative side of this distinction, in terms of a "crude" taste or a corrupted moral sense, or in similarly disapproving ways.[19]

It has become increasingly difficult to insist on the labels beautiful/ugly for the positive and negative code values of art over the persistent protest of the system.[20] The reason might be that these labels are applicable not only to artworks but to other objects as well—for example, to people.[21] In order to maintain this parallelism, the beautiful/ugly distinction must be restricted to the figurative level and therefore fails to account for operations of observation (such as producing and observing an artwork), which, as operations, are neither beautiful nor ugly. The problem seems to be that this distinction refers the *criteria* for judging artworks to *descriptively comprehensible features* of individual works, or, conversely, that it infers from such features criteria that can be generalized. Under such conditions, it is impossible to separate the levels of coding and programming in a manner characteristic of the functional systems of modern society and their "positive" programs.

One therefore wonders whether the values "beautiful" and "ugly" were ever meant to serve as code values to begin with, in the sense of indicating a relationship of exchange mediated by negation. Be this as it may, the tradition was unaware of the distinction between function and coding as a way of distinguishing between different forms of specifying a given system. In the idea of beauty, both aspects converged, and even in the early twentieth century one still tended to define distinct arrangements of social life in terms of a priori values. One sought to describe social differentiation by differentiating between such values rather than exactly specifying a countervalue (or an external side of the form). Besides, it remained unclear whether the notion of beauty referred to individual parts (figures) or to the beauty of the work as a whole.[22] The tradition thought of beauty as a form of perfection pertaining either to the work itself or to its representations; beauty singled out the work, it served as a mark of distinction. Works of art simply are beautiful, or else they are not works of art. There was no need to distinguish art from failed attempts at art or from nonart. "Ugliness" could be integrated in the form of grimaces, dissonance, and so on without distracting from the work's beauty—in accordance with a general cosmology, which suggested that a world consisting of perfect and less perfect beings—of angels *and* stones, men *and* women—is more perfect than a world containing only the most advanced forms. While the principle of imitation reigned, it was easy to find a balance so long as art was allowed to represent both beautiful and ugly objects in accordance with the work's internal ornamental structure.[23] Such a frame of mind suggested a notion of art as idealization—of both beautiful and ugly objects—whereby ugliness was tolerated as a means of emphasizing beauty by contrast; accordingly, one spoke of "the fine arts." Along these lines, German Idealism turned the notion of beauty into an Idea or an "Ideal" in which all opposites converge,[24] a notion that was still accepted without question in romanticism.[25]

Perhaps the notion of an ultimate value (and its identification with the code's positive value) was only a precarious transitional solution—presumably modeled on the religious idea of God. After the search for "objective criteria" of beauty had failed, the objectivity of beauty was conceivable only as a tautology, as a circle[26]—and the decision about which forms convince as beautiful was left to history. In this way, one could hold on to a notion of unity, even though concrete forms rest on distinctions. At the same time, one could avoid conceiving the unity of the difference between positive and negative values as paradox. Hegel was perhaps the last to cast this idea into the form of a philosophical system. Today, any logical analysis would insist on separating positive and ultimate values by a difference in level. In Gotthard Günther's terminology (which we introduced earlier), this means that disjunctive and transjunctive operations and their corresponding values must be kept separate. In this regard, the idea of beauty appears "confused" in retrospect, which suggests that its function as the ultimate value of the system was to conceal a paradox.

Defining the problem away in this manner is unacceptable. Instead, we must give up the notion that the art system's operations are structured teleologically, that artistic production strives toward an ultimate end, and that beauty is a criterion for permitting judgments about how a work ought to be made and whether it can please or not. This applies to all cases of binary coding. In the true/untrue code, for example, the value of truth does not simultaneously provide a criterion for truth, as the venerable dictum *verum est iudex sui et falsi* [truth is its own judge and the judge of falsehood] suggested. Rather, the positive/negative structure of code values must be distinguished from the criteria (or programs) that direct the proper choice of one or the other value. The positive value, in other words, does not promote itself; it is nothing but the inner side of a form that presupposes another side and cannot be indicated without this other side. In its traditional sense, the idea of beauty blocked the distinction between coding and programming, and introducing that distinction explodes this idea. If one wants to distinguish between coding and programming, then one must refrain from specifying the content of beauty (even if one thinks of it as the unattainable normative goal of an infinite striving).

Beauty, then, is neither a quality of an object (just as truth is not a quality of propositions) nor an "intrinsic persuader."[27] The abstract bivalence through which an observer observes artistic operations requires a third—what Derrida would call a *supplément*—which simultaneously respects and disregards the fact that the system operates under the logic of the excluded third. There is no way of supplementing the code by adding a third value—for example, along the lines of "beautiful-ugly-tasteful." Among the criteria that regulate the evaluation of successful/unsuccessful operations, there can be a plurality of further considerations, which, however, cannot represent the unity of the system as a form (a two-sided form, as usual) within the system. When Derrida speaks of the *supplément*,[28] he is thinking of the official status of such additions. Within the relevance hierarchy of self-organization, they are considered marginal. They fail to cover all the cases, and they do not apply to every operation or to the unity of the whole. This ranking can be "deconstructed" as a mere dictate of systems logic, because, logically, the operation of the code requires supplements of this sort. In the terminology of Michel Serres, they are the "parasites" of the system[29]—the included excluded thirds.

Starting out from the operations of the system, we can at least account for how a code comes into being and how it is used, how it works. Every operation—whether the artist's or the beholder's—must decide whether a given form does or does not fit, whether it can be integrated into the emerging work (or into the work one is about to inspect) in ways that secure connectivity. Every observation places the detail it indicates into the recursive network of further distinctions and, from this viewpoint, makes a judgment about the success or failure of this detail, thus distinguishing between solutions that convince and are immediately intelligible, on the one hand, and moves that are questionable, incomplete, and in need of correction, on the other. This is how a binary code works—which might include situations that require withholding one's judgment "for the time being" (the same is true in matters of truth). But without coding, there can be no decision; anything goes.

One must be cautious not to construe a fitting operation as a way of facilitating the next move—as if we were dealing with a mathematical task or a technical construction. Adding further distinctions to the artwork's form combination might facilitate connecting operations, but it can also make them more difficult. It might become questionable whether one will be able to continue, or whether one will ever manage to produce a work of art that is closed and rounded off. Often enough, the thrill resides in precisely this risk, in the lack of foresight, in the difficulty of the self-imposed task. The only requirement is to stay clear of two limits: the necessary and the impossible. The artwork must remain within the modality of contingency and must draw its power to convince from its ability to prevail in the face of other self-generated possibilities. Suppose one needs a green color in order to balance two incompatible shades of red. But how about gray, which, if one were to use it instead, would look like green?

The fit or lack of fit, the success or failure of additions, does not affect the boundaries of the art system. Failed works of art are still works of art, if unsuccessful ones. This is why it makes sense to take on difficult projects, to incorporate things that do not fit, and to experiment with possibilities of failure. As the structuralists have taught us,[30] trash is a prime source for recognizing order. Likewise, the negative value of the code serves as a means of self-control, as a value of reflection. This is true even when art questions precisely this distinction—doing *just that*. If one wants to leave the art system, then one must look for orientation in a different code or in no code at all.

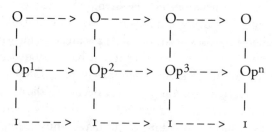

Operational sequences always transport both positive and negative connotations without there being a way to recognize this fact except in the recursivity of operating—it cannot be identified as a telos or a rule. If this proposition holds, it suggests that the code expresses an aggregate of these accompanying valuations. The accompanying diagram explains what we have in mind. The recursive sequence of observations condenses and asserts the system's code by presupposing it in each of its operations as a condition of both the operation's selection and the system's recursive recapitulations and anticipations. In this way, the code is enforced despite the variety of formal decisions. This happens no matter how aesthetics, in its capacity as a reflection theory of the art system, defines this code. There is still no convincing alternative to the labels beautiful and ugly. But this semantics is not to be construed as if art were concerned with "beautiful figures," "beautiful sounds," or other beautiful forms. If one wants to hold onto the semantics of the beautiful, then it might best be understood as a summarizing judgment about what fits / does not fit under added conditions of high complexity, that is to say, in the face of self-generated difficulties.

This does not yet explain how a code, as a component of the art system's self-organization, participates in the system's operations. Individual operations must be recognized as contingent; they must be "motivated" by the work. This suffices as a condition of their intelligibility. Put differently, neither the artist nor the beholder needs the additional specification "coded" in order to observe. Likewise, in research there is no need to mention that truth or falsity is at stake, apart from the theories and methods with which one is working. Invoking the code becomes necessary, however, when the question arises of how art or science distinguishes itself from other functional systems in society. The specificity of coding represents, at a level of third-order observation, the distinction between system and environment. This may be of practical significance if one wants to control the system's recursivity. A piece of raw nature or a slice of unprocessed society might find its way into the artwork—a natural stone in a sculpture or a newspaper ad in a collage. But whatever is integrated in this manner must find its place. Its origin per se does not legitimize its participation in art. Incorporating items of this sort requires no reference to the code—it suffices to be aware what fits in a given instance and what still remains to be done in order to accomplish the integration. That, to begin with, this makes sense and is permitted, and that it can be observed as a distinct process presupposes a higher level of reflection that inevitably reflects upon the code. "Transjunctional" boundaries of acceptance or, more generally, the limits of possible aesthetic forms provoke a definition of art on the basis of its code. Accordingly, the meaning of coding is bound to become more and more abstract, if one can demonstrate that a work's form combinations are still within the realm of the possible.

II

The miracle of recognizability precedes all programs of art. It is an effect of forms that have been distinguished. A figure can be recognized if it is perceived first in nature and subsequently in an artificially created context. A buffalo remains a buffalo when projected against the wall of a cave. Even material differences can be overcome in this way. A human head remains a head—whether it is cast in clay or in stone, whether it is drawn on a vase or on a wall. We can repeat and recognize a melody whether it is sung, whistled, or played on an instrument. Art consolidates identities beyond what nature has to offer, and it does so with a certain indifference to situations, contexts, and materials. Art accomplishes both a condensation and a confirmation of form, thereby ascertaining the hidden order of the world. To borrow a phrase from the ancient Greeks, art allows a glimpse into the essence of things.

This must have been amazing at first. For millennia, the evolution of art has profited from art's capacity to expand and refine its formal repertoire to accommodate recognizability and to detach its forms from natural models, at least to a certain extent. This could be accomplished without differentiating between coding and programming. Whatever "beauty" might have meant, it remained a matter of form, and form was committed to striving for exceptional recognizability. The essential depths thus opened in the world could be considerably intensified; this was, perhaps, above all the accomplishment of the Greeks. But early forms of writing might also be understood in terms of this desire to fix certain contents and to secure their recognizability, especially when presented together with images, so that writing and image illustrate one another and facilitate the recognition of a content that might also be narrated.[31] What was primarily at stake in such representations was the problem of securing the world, and, in view of this purpose, a differentiation of art would have presented an obstacle rather than an advantage. So long as the certainty of the world depended on the recognizability of its forms, its hidden invariance and essences, aligning art with religion, with political power, and eventually with aristocratic genealogies was a commendable course of action.[32]

In the European tradition, a common basic idea was the notion of generalization, which entailed the possibility for drawing, at the level of the universal, distinctions that constituted relationships of exclusion among the objects distinguished. Plato called what was so distinguished *gēnos* and the art of distinguishing it *dihairesis*.[33] In the Greek word *dihairesis* (derived from *hairēo*), it is impossible to distinguish among the activities of reaching out toward an object, of dividing, and of distinguishing the object. The *gēnos*-technique, one might say, constitutes a procedure for gaining access to the world that articulates and divides the world by means of distinctions. The basic rule is to avoid paradox. Although the *gēnos* comprehends a multiplicity within the form of a genre, it is imperative that genres not be confused with one another. The *tō kata gēne diaireisthai* demands that one and the same genre cannot be another and that another genre cannot be the same as the first one. This is a requirement of cognition (*epistēme*), which Plato calls dialectic.[34] It presupposes a clear conception of the ideas that allow for gathering many disparate things into one (despite their diversity). This technique, which Plato illustrates with reference to grammar and the alphabet,[35] is opposed to the Sophists' rhetorical use of paradox; in other words, it is *distinguished against the problem of paradox.*

The desire to exclude paradox constitutes the countertheory to rhetoric. It combines the internal logic of writing, language, and technique with the assumption that, by penetrating to the Ideas, one can arrive at an understanding of how the world is divided, and how one needs to place one's distinctions accordingly. Technique is still understood to be an art of distinguishing bound by nature. Aristotle later supplies the concept of category (= an accusation to which the world must respond) to indicate the primary divisions of being. In his *Poetics*, Aristotle assigns to poetry the task of representing the *Possible* (*dynatōn*) as the *Universal*—that which *by necessity* arrives at its destination unless it encounters an obstacle. To this task corresponds the assumption that the *recognition* of cognitive insights into the essence of things (insights that are difficult to come by) creates pleasure, which justifies *imitatio* as the goal of art. The rhetorical notion of amplification builds on this *gēnos*-technique. Rhetoric values amplification positively, because it tests generalizations and retains successful ones as "commonplaces." This procedure was still common in the Renaissance.[36] The more stringent demands made on rationality and proof in the seventeenth century devalorized this tradition.[37] At first, however, that did not affect the general division of the world according to species and genres, which prevailed until Kant explicitly raised the issue of the possibility for a future metaphysics, finding it difficult to appreciate the distinction between species and genres.[38]

As a result of this *gēnos* technique, the concept of imitation could be broadened significantly, if it not bent entirely out of proportion. Sir Philip Sidney (1595), for example, defines imitation as follows: "Borrow nothing of what is, has been, or shall be, but range (only reined with learned discretion) into the divine consideration of what may be or should be."[39] The demands of a learned (classical) education continued to constrain imitation, while indicating the point where the concept is put at risk by further developments. "Imitation" seems to serve as no more than a cover for a differentiation of art that has already advanced considerably.

Whence the impulse to change this situation? Presumably, the motive was an external incident: the loss and rediscovery of the artistic skill of antiquity, which focused attention on *how* antique art was made. Moreover, print provided an opportunity to proliferate technical literature, thus liberating artistic know-how from the oral doctrine taught in the workshops.[40] Questions of "how" gained prominence, indeed, became primary—at first in the coordination of production and cognition (Bacon, Locke, Vico). This move, however, only expresses what is implied in the technique of *dihairetics* and is later made explicit in Kantian theoretical technique, namely, the desire to pursue into the regions of metaphysics the question of how reality can be reworked by the subject. The transition from "what" questions to "how" questions always indicates a shift from first- to second-order observation, and second-order observation now required programs of its own.

If this assessment is correct, then it should come as no surprise that the artistic programs of the late Middle Ages and early modernity appear in the form of recipes and rules. At stake in these programs is above all the renaissance of antiquity, the recovery of artistic skills along the lines of rediscovered thematic models. With the discovery of perspective in the late Middle Ages, however, second-order observation and the search for its rules went beyond that impulse to rediscovery. Learning the rules sufficed to master this new technique, and if following such rules led to deviations, the sheer demonstration of artistic skill might still count as art. The prime focus continued to be on recognition, albeit within an increasingly expanding, universal realm of meaning independent of thematic models. One studied the rules in anticipation, as it were, of everything that might be considered art. In so doing, art severed its ties to religion, but in a way that included rather than excluded religious art.

Rules formulate a preference for doing things right. They are no longer abstractions of *gēnos*, but they are abstractions nonetheless. Rules anticipate multiple applications in a variety of cases; indeed, this constitutes the regulative meaning of the rule without infringing on its identity. As before, one avoided Plato's *tautōn/hēteron* paradox. To the extent that rules express certain preferences, they do not tolerate a distinction between coding and programming. Following the rules was believed to be the condition for a work's beauty.

A separation of coding and programming (and a reorganization of art in terms of self-organization) did not occur until *novelty* became an indispensable requirement of artworks and copying was no longer permitted.

Upon first sight, novelty is ontological nonsense. Something *is*, although and because it is *not* what was before.[41] As Aristotle was well aware (*Peri hermeneias* IX), this explodes the logical law of the excluded third. Everything excluded must be condensed into a "third value," the value of undecidability. But how can this be, if one must eventually accept that the world itself becomes another world, a new world, from one moment to the next?

A new sense of novelty emerged from a covert revolution in the concept of time and an outspoken polemic against the Aristotelian heritage of the scholastic tradition. It affected the definition of time in terms of the *aeternitas/tempus* distinction and the protection of beings within the presence of the eternal. It concerned the presence of both the origin and the end, the actuality of the ground of being in every moment of its movement. Once one gave up these notions (which happened one by one in various thematic domains), a space was cleared for novelty, for a disruption that requires meaning and selection. The only condition is that novelty must please, and practices of observation and description soon focused on conditions of this sort.

Print might have been another motive for this "transformation of values," especially cheap prints produced for the sake of entertainment and polemics.[42] Novelty became a marketing strategy, since one could assume that no one who knew their content would buy such products.

The criterion of novelty settled an old sixteenth-century controversy. The debate about demarcating poetry from science (or historiography)[43] had raised the question of how poetry can expect to please if it represents falsehoods and fictions.[44] Apparently, only fools and children could take pleasure in such things, and their use was therefore limited to educational contexts. Temporalization, the shift of emphasis from deviation (from truth) toward novelty, created a respectable audience for poetry. As early as the sixteenth century, indications abounded that novelty was considered a necessary condition for the surprising—and pleasing—effect of artworks.[45] At first, this trend responded only to a specific problem in art and traditional poetics—the problem of how to account for art's interest in extraordinary objects and events (*meraviglia* in the widest sense). Because of the experience of religious civil wars in the seventeenth century, innovation still carried negative connotations, especially in the domains of religion and political power and in the classical realms of natural and civil law (but not in the law of the "police," which was just beginning to emerge and claim its own territory). This is why tolerating—or even demanding—novelty could serve as a means of distinguishing functional realms.

Whereas antiquity valued the striking effect of certain objects as a condition of recollection and a source of information,[46] one now temporalized the concept of novelty. One discovered the unique charm of novelty, despite its triumph over what was previously considered beautiful and often for this very reason. Sixteenth-century mannerism illustrates how this tendency became deliberate. (We shall address the question of "style" later.) As a distinctive feature of art, novelty was introduced as a condition of pleasure—and it goes without saying that neither religion nor politics nor law must "please."

The focus on "pleasure" or "pleasurable consumption" suggests that the relationship between producer and recipient, or between art and its audience, was foregrounded in ways unknown in antiquity, in the Middle Ages, or even in the early Renaissance. Generally speaking, this trend strongly indicates that the transition to functional differentiation was under way, emphasizing a function-specific complementarity of roles everywhere (buyer/seller, government/subjects, educator/pupil, lover/beloved). The distinguishing criterion of art, especially in its demarcation from science, was now sought in the manner in which art takes over the hearts of its audience. At the same time, the notion of "pleasure" appeals to individuals; it takes an individual to decide what is pleasing,[47] although at first not every individual was included—not every maid or peasant—but only those capable of judgment, individuals endowed with taste. In retrospect, one recognizes the transitional nature of this formula; it was a compromise that could convince only for a short time during the seventeenth and eighteenth centuries. Only the individual endowed with taste could be stimulated by novelty, for only such an individual could decide what was new, even though one needed criteria to avoid falling prey to everything new.

The demand for novelty implies a retreat of time from all occupied places.[48] There is no need for power struggles, no competition in this displacement, no need to prove superiority. To the extent that the principle of novelty takes hold, history and age no longer legitimate occupying places in a world whose sum remains constant. Novelty pleases because it doesn't need to be regarded as the outcome of some territorial dispute. Rather, novelty seeks to do justice to time itself by surpassing necessity through innovation. Novelty irritates in ways that resemble the delight one takes in paradox, but without proposing mere deviation from the ordinary as a criterion for acceptance or rejection. Just like individuality, novelty challenges the bifurcation of the aristocratic world, of political territories and patron/client relationships, whose origin and age indicate that they have lost their meaning. Long before democracy will prescribe ever new elections, and long before individual destinies are made by careers rather than by social origin (as criterion), a sociostructurally harmless phenomenon such as art could place its bet on perpetual novelty. But how did art accomplish this? How can it bear the demand for novelty? Given the delight one takes in sheer irritation and provocation, how can one arrive at criteria for rejecting some innovations as failures?

On the one hand, one can form an art-specific preference for novelty (against copies). On the other hand, it is not feasible to code the entire art system along the lines of dated/new, thus devalorizing the entire stock of existing artworks—which one collects with great zeal. Nor is novelty suited to serve as a programmatic formula, since it provides no way of recognizing which of the new works qualify as art and which do not. The difference between coding and programming solves this problem. The code remains stable, whereas what fulfills the program function of assigning the correct code value can be left to change, to the spirit of the age, and to the demand for novelty. The novelty postulate functions as a hinge that joins and separates coding and programming. Whatever else it may be, novelty is deviation. The novelty requirement destabilizes both the notion of deviation and the concept of rules. Valuing a work simply on the grounds that it follows the rules no longer suffices; to the extent that one recognizes the work was created by following the rules, it cannot be new and it cannot please.[49]

The code requires abstraction in order to express a preference for an art that is valued positively, and this is why one cannot derive rules from the code for the proper production and evaluation of artworks. And since new works are constantly being produced and exposed to evaluation, the possibility of a program of art that would not be cast in the form of rules becomes questionable. In a sense, the doctrine of taste was the last attempt to answer this question in the affirmative.

III

The task of distinguishing between coding and programming requires distinguishing distinctions—not only objects, rules, or points of view. Abstract coding, which identifies a given operation as belonging to the system, already distinguishes between a positive and a negative value or, in traditional terminology, between beauty and ugliness. But this only secures the general contingency of the system's operations. In addition, one must be able to distinguish, at the level of programming, between correct and incorrect assignments of values to the code. In other words, it is possible to apply the system's programs incorrectly, even though mistakes of this sort do not automatically attract the negative code value in the sense that they would be perceived as ugly. In the doctrine of good taste, these two evaluative levels are not clearly distinguished. A venerable truism states that even ugly objects can be represented artistically (although the theory of art has a difficult time accepting this proposition[50]). Moreover, the doctrine of good taste does not base its evidence on criteria but on the fact that there are clear-cut cases of bad taste. The question is: Can an artwork fail without therefore being ugly? And if so, how?

One might speak of failure when an observer loses control over a work's play of forms, when he can no longer understand how a particular formal choice relates to others on the basis of what this choice demands of the work as a whole. But this can be demonstrated only with reference to a concrete case, not by applying principles or rules.

We might answer this question by considering that every artwork is its own program, and that it demonstrates success and novelty if it manages to show just that. The program saturates, as it were, the individual work, tolerating no further productions of the same kind. At a conceptual level, this excludes the case on which Arthur Danto focuses his aesthetic theory, namely, two objects that look identical and are aesthetically indistinguishable but are "transfigured" via interpretation into two different works of art.[51] (This does not exclude the possibility that a single artwork might be interpreted differently.) Serial painting, which experiments with different versions of the same image, might also be acceptable. But this is a variation on the basic idea of the self-programming artwork—a variation that, compared to a work confined to a single location, permits the display of greater complexity.

The Kantian formulation conceives the artwork's self-programming as the freedom of the observer to let his cognitive faculties play without being guided by concepts. The point in speaking of an "end in itself" or of a purpose without purpose—for Kant, at any rate—is to distinguish art from a conceptually fixed cognition.[52] This version of the problem registers what we call self-programming without explicitly naming the phenomenon. Kant starts out from the cognitive faculties and subsequently directs his critical efforts against every position previously occupied by metaphysics. In this context, art has barely a chance to articulate itself— except by stretching traditional terminology in ways that, even prior to romanticism, were not considered very helpful. What remains noteworthy is that the concept of freedom problematizes the observer, while blocking further pursuit of what the observer's function and role might be with regard to a self-programming artwork.

Then as now, whenever one speaks of freedom, one tends to think of it negatively, in terms of an absence of force; when freedom is defined positively, one thinks of it as oriented toward one's own (yet universally valid) reason. Since the positive determination of freedom is subject to semantic corrosion, only the negative definition remained stable and continues to be propagated today (on the basis of varying notions of force) by liberal and socialist ideologues alike.

Following Kant, Schiller proclaims "that the laws by which the mind proceeds *are not represented,* and since they meet no resistance, they do not appear as constraints."[53] Because it is difficult, on this basis, to account for the necessity that manifests itself in the artwork, one also sought evidence to the contrary. Thus Schiller writes that "the imagination, *even in its free play, orients itself toward boundaries.*"[54] This presupposes a *cognitive* notion of freedom that, under frame conditions it must accept, makes room for possible choices.[55] In this sense, creating a work of art—according to one's capabilities and one's imagination—generates the freedom to make decisions on the basis of which one can continue one's work. The freedoms and necessities one encounters are entirely the products of art itself; they are consequences of decisions made within the work. The "necessity" of certain consequences one experiences in one's work or in the encounter with an artwork is not imposed by laws but results from the fact that one began, and how. This entails the risk of running into "insoluble problems," problems that could never arise on the basis of laws.

The concept of self-programming solves the problems associated with the traditional notion of freedom by relating freedom to self-generated cognitive models. Self-programming does not mean that the individual work is an autopoietic, self-generating system. But one can say that the work constitutes the conditions of possibility for its own decisions, that it observes itself, or, more accurately, that it can be observed only as a self-observer.[56] In order to observe a work of art adequately, one must recognize how the rules that govern the work's own formal decisions are derived from these decisions. It is not clear how to specify such propositions at the operative level. It might suffice to point out that the work delimits the observing operations of any observer (producer or beholder) by suggesting which ones are feasible and successful, and which ones are impossible, obstructive, or in need of correction.

The concept of self-programming is incompatible with the notion that one can get at the work's "essence" by disregarding the "nonessential."[57] This notion assumed that there is such a thing as a distinguishable essence, a remainder, so to speak. Today, this proposition convinces hardly anyone; at best, it gives rise to diverging views about the essence of art and of the artwork. The notion of omission confounds the structural levels of coding and programming. The positive/negative distinction must be executed in applying the binary code to all cases. Without this distinction, nothing comes about. But what is accepted or excluded by the system can be decided only on the basis of a program. The "essence" of art is the self-programming of the artwork.

If the classical formulation emphasizes freedom, then this means that there are no rules or concepts to guide a "critical," cognitive apprehension of beauty. But it also follows that art must operate *without prohibiting the opposite*. In deciding what fits and what doesn't, art follows patterns already established by the work; it cannot rely on independently existing criteria that would prescribe what is permitted and what is not. This seemingly gives rise to a situation in which art can orient itself—and in this sense, art becomes historical—only in its own history, the history of an individual work's production and reception, be it the history of styles, or the intertextuality of the art system itself.

But can self-programming still be programming, if this concept applies, as it usually does, to the conditioning of something other? What would be the identity of the "self" that is the object of its own programming? Furthermore, how can the self-programming artwork distinguish itself, if it is no longer distinguished from the inaccessible domain it symbolizes or from the object it signifies by imitation?

These problems were confronted for the first time in the romantic reflection on art. The distinction that guides this reflection was now located entirely within the art system. The individual work of art identifies itself by its distance from the Idea of art, which the work reflects upon in the impossibility of attaining it. Every work of art must be art as such, art in general; the romantic notion of "art criticism" insists on that. But the Idea remains an idea, whereas the artwork must be concrete. It must be accessible to the senses, and yet it must transcend itself. What is "characteristic" in the artwork can therefore not be apprehended in sensuous experience, nor can it be reduced to the effect of a cause. It aligns itself with the Idea of art without being able to represent that Idea. And the form for this is self-programming—the notion that the work gives itself a form and thereby determines what is possible in the work and what is excluded. In order to express this notion, romanticism has recourse to the symbol and, in so doing, goes beyond Kant.[58]

This means only that difference—in this case the work's distance from the Idea—is understood as a unity. Contrary to the religious tradition, distinction and unity are now located entirely within the autonomous realm of art, reflecting the fact that art has become autonomous. If this paradox is now called "self-programming," does that mean it has been explained?

Let us go further: self-programming is a case of self-reference. Self-reference can be practiced only if it can distinguish what it refers to. It presupposes the distinction between self-reference and hetero-reference. Thus one arrives at the question: What is the hetero-reference of the self-programming artwork?

According to the logic of second-order observation, the hetero-reference of art can only be that which is rendered invisible by the distinguishing schema of first-order observation (as an observation of an observer, second-order observation is also an observation of the first order). Accordingly, hetero-reference refers to that which is rendered invisible when distinctions are introduced into the world: it refers to the irreducible unity of the world as the always operative unmarked space. The program guarantees that the work of art can establish itself at the level of second-order observation, no matter in what concrete form. Or, put differently, it secures the program dependency, the contingency of all the operations that produce or encounter the artwork in a world that as a world cannot be contingent, a world that makes possible the introduction of distinctions for its own observation by withdrawing, as a world, from observation (distinction). In this way, the program prevents the collapse of two distinctions that must remain separate, namely, the distinction between self-reference and heteroreference, on the one hand, and between the positive and negative values of the code, on the other[59]—for it goes without saying that the artwork cannot think of itself as a success and consider the world a failure.

This conception excludes the notion of the world (or society) as a source of directives for the execution of artworks. We have called this exclusion the autonomy of the art system while making the sociological assumption that world autonomy can be accomplished only via societal autonomy. This means that the directives for elaborating and evaluating a work of art must be derived from the work itself.

In many cases, the observational possibilities provided by the artwork can be rendered visible by means of persons: as, for example, in a painting that incorporates unified perspective; in a building that at once offers and denies observational possibilities to those inside and outside the building; in drama, which stages the difference between seeing (knowing) and not seeing (ignorance) in front of an audience; or in the novel, which does the same for the reader. This strategy can be emphasized and brought to an unbeatable conclusion when a play is staged within a play (or, more simply, through lying and deception), or when a novel illustrates how Don Quixote or Emma Bovary creates his or her own destiny through a self-inspiring reading.[60]

The availability of an unambiguous metaperspective that is related to persons and reflects on romanticism must have been responsible for making poetry the paradigm of art in general. But this claim becomes untenable once the observer is conceived in correspondingly abstract terms (as we are doing here) and is defined as an application of distinctions for the indication of one, rather than the other side of a form. The artwork can then be understood as a frame for the observation of observational possibilities that are included or excluded whenever someone uses a distinction.

The world of *dihairesis*—a world that used to be collectively accessible on the basis of given divisions—must be sacrificed. At the level of first-order observation, there might still be error, dishonesty, deception, *machinatio*, and so forth, all of which can and must be corrected *at this level*. At the level of second-order observation, however, there are no longer any divisions, there are only distinctions. The problem no longer resides in the potential need for correction; rather, the problem is that observation remains invisible to itself, no matter what. The self-programming of art is the form of expressing that this is so and that the world, as the condition for introducing distinctions, remains invisible—no matter what kind of operative injunctions are issued by the program.

All of this has consequences for the relationship between program and operation. A first-order observer who has begun working on, or looking at, a work of art (without a beginning there would be nothing to observe) can build on what is already there and search for what fits or might not fit. To such an observer, freedom appears as the constraint on further options. As a second-order observer, he can try to find out whether, and in what ways, other observers might observe his formal decisions. This accounts for the chronic feeling of "being misunderstood." For what could guarantee that multiple observers read the same formative freedom into any given object? An observer of the third order, one in search of theoretical formulations, can only establish the existence of circular relationships. A program is the result of the operations it programs. Nothing else is meant by "self-programming." At the same time, however, the second-order observer can see that the first-order observer might see things differently, so that *for neither of them* does the tautology turn into paradox, and both can tell how it is possible to determine the next step.

IV

The notion of the self-programming artwork remains unsatisfactory in at least one respect. It raises the question of whether one should think of artworks as completely isolated from one another, or whether the programming must be programmed on its part—a notion that amounts to returning, albeit in a different form, to something like a rule-based art. Perhaps it was this unresolved question that prevented the individual work from being released completely into autonomy. Wouldn't one have to conclude that art emerges from chance or, at least, assume a new beginning in each individual case?

Evidence to the contrary was promptly found—in the realm of historical empiricism, so to speak. While observing broader contexts, one discovered that works of art influence the emergence of other works, even when imitation is prohibited. Winckelmann was perhaps the first to exploit this insight for a historiography of art ordered in periods.[61] The *historicization* of the self-description of the art system requires a *periodization* of art history (and vice versa). This move relates the concept of style to distinctions between periods; that is, it temporalizes a concept that had been familiar for a long time and initially referred to something like a type of design (*maniera*) or to genres of such types (like the curial style of text production or the *stilo* in rhetoric.) This is not to say that a certain period is restricted to one particular style, nor does it mean that works of art lose their value when a certain style goes out of fashion. The acknowledgment of a plurality of styles interrupts the relationship between style and social class. The wealth of styles is now open to all observers who, as visitors of exhibitions or museums, are interested in art. From the viewpoint of the observer, inclusion in the art system renders style independent of prior (social) stratification[62] (even though statistics, invisible in everyday life, might well disclose a correlation between the two, though this concerns only the interest in art rather than the preference for certain styles).

The form of style does not affect the autonomy of the artwork; it merely keeps stylistic deviation in check or permits such deviation (if the deviation succeeds). In this way, the canonization of style might encourage the transition to another style, that is, it might stimulate evolution—"defining itself and then escaping from its own definition."[63] Observing different kinds of style supersede one another, one can see—at a macrolevel, so to speak—that art produces novelty and how, then, after exhausting the possibilities of a given style, moves on to the next. One can then recommend stylistic purity, recognize mixed stylistic forms, or register their existence with astonishment.[64] One might even recommend the style of mixing styles as a measure against stylistic purity.

There is an obvious temptation to make works of art converse with one another via their stylistic forms, that is, in view of the limited tolerance imposed by style.[65] This is why a *functional* definition of style suggests itself, one that can respond to the problem of how diverse artworks form a network, so that a system of art can establish itself.[66] By and large, this functional definition covers what has been understood historically as "style"—both in the traditional sense of a design type and in the modern sense of historical styles that have a time of their own and become obsolete once it is over. The paradigmatic significance of individual artworks that served as models to be copied fulfilled the same function, that is, it served as a functional equivalent to style. At the same time, the relationship of functional equivalence indicates that the increasing emphasis on originality—if not on the uniqueness of "authentic works," including the critique of copying—abandons style to this functional realm and encourages the observation of particularly impressive works of art in terms of style. If works of art are not allowed to be copies and have no style either, then they lose their significance as artworks. Singularities resist classification and therefore cannot be understood and observed as art. The act of assigning a work to a certain style signals that the work belongs to art. That is to say, there is a program-related possibility for representing art within the artwork, which exists apart from coding.

Does this amount to metaprogramming? Can one expect or demand that the artist search for and identify a style with which he then aligns his work? And has the classification of styles become indispensable to a competent art criticism?

It is doubtful that such notions can be sustained. The discussion of style, which by the nineteenth century had made a vain effort to clarify its self-understanding, is a clear indication. One sought the programmatic only to use it for restorative purposes.[67] Yet it is difficult to appreciate the notion—especially if the motive is to find one's own style—that style is a matter of applying prefabricated formal decisions that owe their emergence to a work-dependent sense of what is fitting. To the observer and copier of styles, a style presents itself as a synopsis stabilized by habit, while he is aware that this is the side-effect of a spontaneous, merely code-oriented practice that has abandoned itself to the self-programming of the artwork. To emphasize this, one speaks of spontaneity or of an unconscious genesis of style, but spontaneity cannot be expected to occur twice. Choosing familiar styles as programs in an easily recognizable manner amounts to making a rather cheap claim to belong to the art system, and often the works end up not being very convincing.[68] Not accidentally, such degenerative trends are temporally marked as "new" (new gothic, and so on) or, when there is too much of that, as "post" (postmodernism). This seems to say that the demand for novelty, and thus for creativity, is constrained neither by style nor by the imitation of style. Any work of art can search for an as yet unoccupied niche within the context of family resemblances between styles; it can probe new, "impressionistic" light conditions in fields and forests, in cathedrals or train stations. It can also express itself by rebelling against the constraints of style. The classification of styles can be left to the art expert who, like a botanist, consults handbooks on stylistics in order to determine a given style. In this respect, style is not a program but a formal model with which or against which one can work. The outward boundary against the unmarked space of the world is shifted once again. The task of rendering visible the invisible is distributed among two authorities, whose collaboration covers up the fact that this is at stake.

Accordingly, the concept of style is a concept of difference, that is, a concept of form. The limitations of a style yield the possibility for further styles—although at first only in the unmarked space of world possibilities. Historically, just this possibility offers the temptation to make the transition to a new style. The test is that the work must succeed as an artwork. In this manner, one gains the impression of a plurality of styles that have proven themselves in artworks as if by evolutionary selection. This makes possible the ultimate form of reflection—the "postmodern" style of mixing styles—in which the sovereign self-programming of the artwork can be displayed once again. But the combination of diverse stylistic quotations as such does not yet constitute a program. It might succeed or fail. It must confront the code of art. Otherwise it will not be recognized as art.

§ 6 Evolution

I

We know a great deal about the history of art. Ever since the forms and artworks inherited by tradition lost their binding force and ceased to serve as models—that is to say, since the eighteenth century—the historiography of art has amassed a tremendous amount of knowledge. And ever since one began to compare artifacts in an historically and regionally far-reaching manner, there has been "culture"—no longer in the sense of "cultivation of . . . " (of agriculture or *cultura animi*), but as an elevated sphere of reality, a level at which all testimonies to human activity are registered a second time—not with an eye toward their utilitarian significance but in comparison to other cultural testimonies. In comparison, works of art (but also religions, institutions of law, or forms of social order) appear "interesting," all the more so, the more the comparison ventures into realms that are foreign, bizarre, strange, or difficult to comprehend. Considered as culture, art and religion appear to be *universals* of human society, but only on the basis of the *specifically* European and *specifically* historical point of view that is interested in such comparisons and constructs comparative viewpoints. As a result, one now finds art in places where neither the producer nor the viewer knew that art was at stake, let alone culture. This difference is reflected upon, for example, in Schiller's distinction between naive and sentimental poetry.

With art, just as with religion, the observation of culture—a kind of second-order observation—must have had disastrous consequences. In order to compensate for that, culture is emphatically affirmed and celebrated as a value sphere of a special kind. At the same time, culture suffers from a broken heart, reflecting upon its own reflection and registering what has been lost and will never be created again in terms of naïveté. Observing works of art under such circumstances requires blinders that shut out culture, and yet, their benefit is dubious when the works are already infected by culture, when they are produced with an eye to comparison and, as a result, cannot be adequately understood in a naive mode. Or can they? Could it be that including the exclusion of comparative culture has become an essential component in the observation of art?[1]

The differentiation of an academic art history seems to respond to precisely this problem by offering the possibility for distinguishing between an observation as art and an observation as culture. Art historical knowledge in part interprets individual works or masters within their own temporal and historical horizons, in part reconstructs relationships of influence by tracing presumed causalities. Art historians also analyze developmental trends, whether or not they presume a historical progress of some kind. An academic discipline established exclusively for this task has existed only for about a century.[2] For the collection and proliferation of such knowledge, "sources" are significant. These "mouse-eaten records"[3] count only when they appear authentic in the eyes of art-historical knowledge. Authenticity almost suffices to legitimize a source as remarkable. When studying Veronese, one cannot afford to disregard a single work by this painter. Veronese is Veronese.

Following Dilthey, one tends to think that the historian's task is to render totalities in the form of individual figures and to contextualize details. Such a task justifies a selective use of sources, above all a disregard for what happened later and could not have been known when the work was conceived. Of course, the historian has an obligation to investigate the past that was known at the time the artworks of interest to him were created. This explains the inclination (or compulsion?) to see the totalities constructed by the humanities as historical totalities, whose temporal horizons vanished with them but can be rediscovered in the present as our own past. In this way, historiography, as well as the historiography of art, combines the binding force of origins with a (henceforth only) historical relevance. Both disciplines present temporal figures within a reflexive temporal horizon—our own—that modifies temporal horizons in time and through time. In addition, one discovers everyday worlds against which high cultures stand out as esoteric exceptions; or one can demonstrate, by means of quantitative or statistical analyses, "latent structures" that show how knowledge swims in an ocean of ignorance.

All of this is well known and, being current knowledge, it suggests a tempting proximity to our own concerns. What is remarkable forces itself upon us. This makes it all the more necessary to preface our analysis with a clarification: an evolutionary theoretical analysis of history pursues goals of a different sort, and it orders its material in different ways. It rests on a specific theoretical formulation of a problem. In biology, this problem can be stated as follows: How can the one-time biochemical invention of self-reproducing life give rise to such a great diversity of species? For the theory of society, the problem is how to account for the high degree of structural complexity that develops once a continuous, rather than sporadic and repeatedly interrupted communication has been secured—where the structural complexity in question might concern a multiplicity of historical societies or the modern world society. In Spencer's well-known formulation, this implies a "change from a state of indefinite, incoherent homogeneity to a state of definite, coherent homogeneity."[4] What is impressive about the system of society is the diversity of functional systems, and within these systems, the emergence of media that facilitate rich, if unstable, formations—ever new transactions in the economy together with the systems of production that accompany such transactions, or the continual modification of a positive law that remains nonetheless stable. A theoretical interest that goes under the name of evolutionary theory focuses on the conditions of possibility for structural change and, constrained by this focus, on explaining the emergence of structural and semantic complexity. This implies that the description of art, the emergence of a new concept of culture, the cultivation of art as culture, and even the emergence of a theory of evolution must be understood as a result of evolution. The theory of evolution is a self-referential, an "autological" paradigm.

The scientific usage of the term *evolution* is not necessarily so precise. Especially in the social sciences, pre-Darwinist notions prevail. Merely descriptive phase models of social development—in vogue since the eighteenth century (thus long before Compte)—are frequently offered as a theory of evolution. There might be an explanation for this. One might argue, for example, that "social Darwinism" has never been persuasive in the social sciences, that one needs dynamic models capable of explaining why things today are no longer the way they used to be, or that, while evolutionary adaptation to accidental structural changes cannot be denied, such changes might be analyzed more adequately with reference to Lamarck rather than to Darwin.[5] In a rigorous and precise conceptual sense, none of these approaches deserves to be called a theory of evolution. This is why the theory of evolution has been called an "untried theory," and justifiably so.[6] This is all right—at least according to the many social scientists who reject evolutionary theory as a biological metaphor or as an illegitimate analogy to the world of organisms.

Specifying a line of inquiry that might be called evolutionary theory (but could certainly assume other names as well) is an indispensable preparatory step, even though it says little about the research program. The theory of evolution deploys a specific distinction, namely, the distinction between variety, selection, and restabilization. This line of questioning does not focus on a process, nor does it attempt to explain in a historical or causal manner why things happen the way they do. Rather, it is motivated by systems-theoretical concerns. If autopoietic systems are set up in such a way that they must use their own operations to create and modify, or forget and dispose of their own structures, and if this mode of operating always presupposes a potential network of operations—that is, a structure—then the question arises: How is it possible that these structures become increasingly complex? Above all, this tendency is unlikely. What makes it more likely? And how does improbability—the fact that certain phrases are uttered nevertheless, that certain goods are bought, and certain forms are created and admired as art—eventually become so plausible that one can almost count on it? How can society establish its own improbabilities (which require that something specific must be selected from countless other possibilities) in such a way that they stabilize one another, and the sudden failure of crucial accomplishments (for example, the loss of the monetary economy or the police force) would result in a catastrophe whose consequences would be impossible to contain? How, in other words, is it possible that the improbability of emergence continually transforms itself into the probability of preservation?[7]

The theory of evolution is concerned with unfolding a paradox, namely, the paradoxical probability of the improbable. However, we cannot help formulating this paradox in a manner that statisticians will not accept. In statistics, it is trivial that reality, in each of its expressions, is extremely unlikely and at the same time entirely normal. It is therefore not surprising that the statistician fails to register this paradox, precisely because he presupposes its unfolding. The same holds for the theory of evolution. The comparison illustrates, however, that recourse to paradox—no matter how insignificant its methodological benefits might be, and inasmuch as it must be prohibited methodologically—allows one to raise the theoretical question of what kinds of identification facilitate, in one way or another, the unfolding (= rendering invisible) of the paradox. This paradox is ultimately a paradox of self-implication, which resides in presupposing a distinction (here, probable/improbable) whose unity can be indicated only paradoxically. Logicians might object that theory creates this puzzle only to solve it on its own. This is certainly true. The question is: What kinds of comparative possibilities become visible in this manner?

II

One can present the history of society as the history of a general sociocultural evolution.[8] But the system reference of such a history remains the system of society at large. Changes in the realm of art would appear only as instances in the evolution of society. As early as 1800, this problem was discussed—albeit without sufficient theoretical preparation—with reference to Kant's legal-political concept of society and in view of the rising expectations being placed upon art and aesthetic experience.[9] If one assumes an elaborated theory of evolution instead of a theory of consciousness, then the question becomes whether independent (albeit conditioned) subsystems can exist within evolving systems. In order to prove this assumption, one would have to show how, and under what conditions, autopoietic subsystems close themselves off and, by differentiating operational modes of their own, become capable of treating environmental perturbations as chance events that stimulate the variation and selection of system-internal structures.

We have addressed this issue in conjunction with the historical conditions of the art system's differentiation.[10] In that context, our concern was to furnish evidence for special environmental conditions that favored differentiation. In the following, we seek to identify the evolutionary mechanisms whose separation facilitates this process.

Let us begin by recapitulating our analyses of the artwork's form. Already in the individual artwork, we can see how the improbability of emergence is transformed into the probability of preservation. The first distinction, the one from which the artist starts out, cannot be programmed by the work of art. It can only occur spontaneously—even though it implies a decision concerning the work's type (whether it is to be a poem, a fugue, or a glass window) and perhaps an idea in the artist's mind. Any further decision tightens the work, orienting itself toward what is already there, specifying the unoccupied sides of already established forms and restricting the freedom of further decisions. Once the distinctions begin to stabilize and relate to one another recursively, what occurs is precisely what we expect from evolution: the artwork finds stability within itself; it can be recognized and observed repeatedly. The work might still suffer destruction, but any further modification becomes increasingly difficult. Some insoluble problems or imperfections might remain, which must be accepted as a matter of fact. Even in art, evolution does not bring about perfect conditions.

A work might also be conceived more or less according to plan. As in politics or in the economy, the plan becomes a part of evolution. If the artist adheres rigidly to a preconceived program, then he will either produce works devoid of qualitative differences (even if he applies different programs), or he will have to decide between simple acceptance or rejection of the work as a whole. Typically, however, the artist allows himself to be irritated and informed by the emerging work, whatever the program might entail. The typical case is evolution.

It is perhaps a unique feature of the art system that the "intertextual" network connecting works produced within the system is not very tight, and that, to use a strong formulation, chance events are already transformed into necessities at this level. When searching for a theory of how the art system evolves, we must keep this small-scale revolution of the individual work in mind. But the evolutionary mechanisms of variety, selection, and restabilization differentiate themselves only at the level of the system. Only at this level do social conditions emerge that facilitate the production of artworks. If art is not sufficiently differentiated as a phenomenon, then there can be no freedom of beginning, no conception of what is involved in producing or encountering a work of art.

The theory of form combination, which we take as our starting point, suggests that art originates in the *ornament*, under conditions that imply no awareness of a corresponding concept, let alone of an autonomous art system.[11] One might propose a bold comparison: the evolution of the ornament is to the evolving art system what the evolution of language is to the evolution of society; in both cases, there is an extended preparatory stage that yields eruptive consequences once communication has been stabilized to the point where its boundaries become visible. What is emphasized at first, however, is not the difference between object and adornment, but rather the unity of this difference, its meaning. "Cosmos" in the Greek sense means both order and ornament.

In prehistoric times, ornaments emerged independently everywhere in the world (even though the question of whether some patterns emerged independently or by diffusion is a matter of dispute). In premodern societies, the relationship between surface and depth was experienced differently from how it is today. This is evident in the widely used techniques of divination. These techniques are concerned with displaying signs on a visible surface, signs that betray depth. Perhaps ornaments were understood in the same way.

The ornament provided an opportunity to train oneself artistically without depending on demanding social presuppositions. The basis for this trend was a well-developed competence in technique and skill that might have produced ornamental order as a side effect, as a playful addition superimposed on something useful and necessary—as adornment. One could follow the inspiration of existing models or use as guidance the limitations of cult objects or other objects of utility. In this way, one could profit from the integration of such objects in nonartistic contexts and from their evolutionary differentiation. The ornament provided an opportunity to practice observation and to train one's eyes and hands for a type of social communication that could later exploit such skills to create a self-differentiating system.

There might be enough material stashed away somewhere in libraries to write a history of the ornament that could tell what kinds of figurative patterns were used to decorate objects: some ornaments are geometrical, whereas others move in waving lines; some patterns display protruding, recognizable leaves, fruits, heads, and so on; some ornaments are stacked atop each other; whereas others support the formal play of the objects they decorate—a vase, an oven grid, a door, a building—whether for emphasis or to cover up imperfections, whether to make believe or to join figures. Perhaps there are such compilations,[12] but for an evolutionary theory of art, they would serve at best as illustrative materials that one might also find elsewhere.

Distinguishing between a historical account and a theory of evolution is imperative. The prime concern of a theory of evolution is to account for discontinuities and structural changes that suddenly erupt after extended periods of stagnation or incremental growth. Such a theory focuses on the prolonged irritation to which forms are exposed and, above all, on the abrupt occurrence of operative closure, with its chances for autopoietic autonomy.

From this viewpoint, the practice of decoration (in the widest sense) appears to be a preadaptive advance, a development that initially served other functions and to which one can return in the course of the art system's differentiation as if art had existed at all times. Once a system of art begins to differentiate itself, it becomes possible to construct a past; one can redirect a treasure house of forms and continue to use skills one already has. In this way, a structural break in the *social* domain is at first experienced only as an artistic innovation, as an improvement in skill. Under radically new social conditions, art initially sought less radical forms of expression—one returned to antiquity, began to valorize the artist's social prestige, and sought independence from the directives of patrons—and only gradually were novelty and originality demanded from the individual artwork.

The differentiation of the art system must have altered the meaning of ornamentation, in particular by adding a dimension of "depth," so that today only the combination of forms as such is important. In gothic architecture, the ornament was already taken in tow by inventions in structural form, within which it had to prove itself. Subsequent reflections on the limitations of ornamentation and on the primacy of balanced proportion could draw on a history that rendered such developments plausible. The distinction between form and supporting decoration could thus be generalized and adopted later as a theory of the self-differentiating art system. With the emergence of self-conscious artworks that insist on being recognized as such, the traditional domain of artistic skill was divided into two separate realms: one in which decorating objects of utility prevails and where one later turned to certain "crafts" to compete against industrial production; and a realm of art in which works must decide for themselves whether they need or can tolerate ornamentation, and if so, to what extent and in what form. At first, divisions of this kind were necessary. Following Alberti—who introduced the notion of composition[13]— the standard Renaissance literature distinguishes between drawing, composition, and coloration as necessary components of painting.[14] The concept of the drawing, of contour or design, continues the tradition of the ornament in a form reduced to one of its components.[15] The cinquecento in Italy, especially in Florence, developed a theory of *disegno* that covers the entire problematic, stretching the concept to the point where it loses its precision.[16] On the one hand, *disegno* stands for the creative conception (and in this respect, it resembles God's creation of the world, that is, nature in its entirety), while on the other hand it also indicates the artful execution of the work by skilled eyes and hands. *Disegno* involves invention, ingenuity, and intellect (in the traditional sense), while being concerned with a technique of signs, with skills taught in academies, and with the form and contours of the work itself. Since this contradiction could not be resolved, the seventeenth-century discussion of the concept ran out of steam, leaving behind a theory of drawing skills that could be taught.

Poetry follows similar distinctions. Torquato Tasso, for example, divides his *Discorsi dell'arte poetica e in particolare sopra il poema eroico*[17] into *materia, forma,* and *ornamenti,* only to focus entirely on *materia* (choice of topic) and *forma.* In his treatment of *ornamenti* Tasso changes his tone,[18] speaking of *elocuzione* and remaining entirely within the framework of rhetorical distinctions of style, which might equally well be treated as distinctions of form.

Parallel to this discussion, one finds—now under the heading of the ornament—a degradation of the ornamental to mere decoration or adornment. The low esteem in which the ornament was held raises the issue of whether works of art require ornamentation, and if so, why. The solution was to relegate the ornament to a subordinate, merely decorative function in every realm, including the arts, and to distinguish its supplementary function from a more important type of beauty in both nature and art.[19] In this way, one could playfully adjust, at the level of ornamentation, to social changes and develop or adopt forms that did not interfere with the work's thematic focus. One could turn away from a merely religious symbolism and influence the development of styles by drawing on natural forms, interpersonal relationships, heraldry, or models from antiquity.[20] But the distinction between art and ornament (whether in the work of art itself or in other objects) undermines the possibility for indicating the unity of art; if beauty—understood as perfection—requires a supplement, it is not clear what is meant by unity.[21] In the eighteenth century, this master/slave metaphor loses plausibility; besides, the focus shifts toward what holds the work of art together from within. Only linguistic usage stands in the way of responding spontaneously: the ornament.

The distinction, introduced by Hutcheson, between original (or absolute) and comparative (or relative) beauty should not be underestimated.[22] It is a decisive step toward rehabilitating the ornament and toward pushing back the semantics of imitation.[23] Original or absolute beauty is nothing other than (the subjective idea of) the ornamental. Hutcheson defines this type of beauty ("to speak in the mathematical style") in terms of a "uniformity amidst variety" or as a "compound ratio of uniformity and variety."[24] Since this formula—reminiscent of Leibniz—embraces too much (according to Leibniz, it comprehends the entire world), one introduces a principle of intensification that renders a given variety more uniform or adds variety to uniformity. According to the associational psychology popular at the time, even failure and ugliness can be calculated in the form of a disruption brought about by associations that do not fit.[25]

The framing of this concept in epistemology and moral theory (psychology) is limited historically, and a philosophical aesthetics will pursue different goals. But the effects of ornamentation and continued references to the ornament are noticeable, especially in William Hogarth. In his essay *The Analysis of Beauty*, Hogarth still mentions the ornament, but goes on to describe the movement of line as a principle of enhancement, which culminates in "serpentine lines" that present the "inner surface" of the object and its potential movement in its most favorable proportions. This insight into the function of drawing can be translated into technical instructions for producing beauty that are intelligible to *anyone* (not only to "connoisseurs," who operate according to obscure principles), thus accomplishing a *comprehensive inclusion* of observers into the work of art.[26] By and large, the long tradition of statements on the line in drawing remains ambivalent. On the one hand, such statements remain subordinate to an interest in beauty, harmony, and balanced proportion; on the other hand, they gain significance to the extent that the vacuity and redundancy of such a notion of beauty becomes apparent. This is evident not only in Hogarth but also in Moritz and Herder.[27]

To the extent that problems of form acquire a dimension of depth and one began to turn what one had learned from the ornament (for example, under the name of *disegno*) into a theory of the artwork, there are tendencies to rescue the ornament in its exorbitant, if not to say superfluous function, to reinstate it as a kind of supplement, or to use it as a way of transcending the perfection one strives for. This happened in mannerism, which legitimizes capricious and fantastic trends that explode the limits of proportion. Zuccaro presents a theoretical integration of this possibility that explicitly refers to the ornament.[28] The two forms of *disegno*, which combine imitation and perfection, are supplemented by a third—the bizarre, capricious *disegno fantastico*—which adds variety (*diversità*) to the already perfect artwork.[29]

Classicizing theory in the second half of the eighteenth century dealt extensively with the ornament (adornment, arabesque) in the hope of balancing the sterility of forms, on the one hand, and the lack of discipline, on the other, and in order to test the classicist idea of style in the subordinate realm of decoration.[30] In the transition to romanticism, precisely the uncontrolled excess of arabesques and grotesques and their proximity to chaos calls attention to itself, as if the problem of disorder that underlies all creative activity could be harnessed in this undomesticated form.[31] The internal dynamic involved in the rehabilitation of the ornament has been investigated especially by Gustav René Hocke.[32]

If one searches for an analogue to the intensification of the ornamental outside of the visual arts, then one is likely to discover that *suspense* fulfills a similar function of intensifying narrative structure in literature.[33] On the thematic level, the demand that the narration be charged with suspense leads to the disengagement of the hero from the effects of an external fate—a fate that, in early modern times, had functioned as a useful device for increasing variety within the framework of typified redundancies.[34] The narrative development of characters interrupts the nexus between past and future. One needs actions in order to establish coherence, and actions require motives; only toward the end of the story does it become apparent why things happened the way they did. Narrative moves its plot as if in serpentine lines; it fills a space of self-generated uncertainty, so that, in the end, the meaning of the plot can enter the plot (the couple gets married, the criminal is recognized and punished). The narrative—or the play, to speak with Dryden—must be constructed like a labyrinth, in which the spectator can see just a few steps ahead and the conclusion is not recognized until the end.[35] Suspense, in the sense of self-generated uncertainty, draws variety into the work itself, which earlier had to be supplemented from the outside; this means that the author must know what the reader is not yet allowed to know. If suspense secures the work's unity (as an ornament does), then the characteristic features of persons can be rendered more individually without any loss of recognizability. The level of the work where forms are combined permits greater variety while preserving the redundancy necessary to generate information.

What does all this have to do with the ornament? The ornament, too, strives for a complex level of redundancy and variety[36]—in Hogarth's formulation, for "the art of varying well"[37]—as if in "serpentine lines." Redundancy is secured so long as the narrative contains enough detailed references to the familiar world of the reader (short of serving him a story he already knows!).[38] Suspense is created when several potential developments are left open, but only a few of them concern the future (for the mystery novel, this means several possible ways of discovering the past). What is at stake in narrative, in other words, is the combination of connectivity and an open future. The question is which turn the line or the story might take. Prolonging the line under conditions of continued suspense amounts to crossing the boundary of the form while covering up this crossing. It is therefore not surprising that Moritz,[39] when speaking of the "metaphysical line of beauty" in the epic and in drama, emphasizes its strong curvature (in comparison with the line of truth) and what it omits, because it suggests the form of the closed circle. Nor should it strike us as odd that Friedrich Schlegel would call a novel (Diderot's *Jacques le fataliste*) an arabesque and object to the low esteem in which this form was held—according to Schlegel, the arabesque is "a fully determined and essential form or mode of poetic expression."[40] An alternative venue has been suggested by Georg Lukács, who claims that *irony* is the successor of the ornament:[41] irony is the persistently maintained key in which the ups and downs of narrative events are played. We might call suspense, or perhaps irony, the inner forms of the novel's unity, forms that are compatible with, indeed demand, a great variety of narrated events.[42]

In historical retrospect, an art produced in accordance with these principles (and following these injunctions) might strike us as remarkable, perhaps even as the culmination of European art. The second half of the nineteenth century is preoccupied with the question of whether a careful study of decorative style might be able to rejuvenate a style that was evidently lacking.[43] Around 1900 the repertoire of styles expanded once again—one sacrificed the object in the visual arts, tonality in music, and the continuous story line in literature. By now, ornamentation had become what it has always been: a self-directing form combination, the temporality of observation, which is continually in search of what has yet to be decided.

But we still do not know how evolution managed to bring about this state of affairs.

III

The distinction with which the theory of evolution dissolves, displaces, represses, and renders invisible the paradoxical probability of the improbable is the distinction between *variation* and *selection*—that is to say, *another* distinction. One can start all over again, if one can presuppose (which certainly does not go without saying) that variation and selection are separable in reality and can subsequently be distinguished by an observer.

In nineteenth-century theories of evolution, the notion of the "individual" played a decisive role in explaining variation (as a precondition for selection). Of course, one needs to distinguish between two different versions of the individual. Along with the concept of population, a collective individualism established itself against the traditional typological essentialism of the doctrine of species and genres. Populations are capable of evolution because they are made up of individuals. At first, one believes that the diversity of individual forms is the source of the adaptability of populations—that variety is a source of variation. Depending on the course of changing environmental conditions, one or the other characteristic grows stronger and is reproduced in large quantities. Applying this argument to human society, however, transforms it completely. Now, the large number of individuals increases the likelihood that some of them turn out to be creative, innovative, and powerful, and the statistical *normality* of such *exceptional cases* supports the explanation of evolutionary variation. No one would speak of particularly creative flies, birds, or frogs in order to account for changes in the behavior of a specific animal population. But for society, and especially for the realm of art, such explanations do make sense (at least ideologically), though it would be less plausible to focus on the diversity that exists in the form of a "population" of individual artists or works of art.

A long-standing cult of genius paved the way for the explanation of evolution in terms of the individual. In retrospect, one can rephrase Kant's distinction between genius (variety) and taste (selection) as a theory of evolution.[44] Thinking of variation and selection as internal functions of a system's evolution precludes the possibility of attributing the cause of evolution or innovation to "great men and women."[45] An age that was already thinking in historical terms faced the problem of explaining why at certain times geniuses appear in large numbers while at other times they are nowhere to be found. Irregularities of this sort might be treated as a peculiarity of certain historical periods and charged to the account of the times themselves, which sometimes flourish and sometimes don't. It would be more fruitful, however, to invert the relationship between these variables and think of "genius" as the product rather than the cause of evolution. "Genius" stands for the improbability of emergence, and "taste" for the likelihood that works of art prevail. Genius must be admired; taste must be justified.

At first, this distinction appears as sheer difference, without a concept for the unity of what is distinguished. (This difference is accounted for, so to speak, by the creative power of genius). By means of a special trick, however, the theory of evolution can nonetheless come to terms with the unity of the distinction between variety and selection—namely, by positioning this unity and the distinction side by side. The unity of the distinction then assumes the name of a third, namely, *stabilization* or *restabilization.* If there is variation—a positive or negative selection that takes into account or disregards a given variant in the reproduction of systems—then it raises the questions: Under what kinds of structural conditions does the reproduction (of autopoietic systems) take place? How can a system continue to reproduce itself, if it accepts variation, or if it rejects a possibility that offered itself (although other systems might use it[46])? Problems of stabilization are not solely consequences of evolution; they do not solely occur after the fact. A system must already be stabilized if it is to offer opportunities for variation. Stability is the beginning and the end of evolution, a mode of structural change that simultaneously generates instability. This is why the evolutionary theoretical model, which abstracts from time, describes a circular relationship between variation, selection, and (re)stabilization. This is only an indication that the unfolding of the paradox takes time. It explains why, in superficial descriptions, evolutionary theory is presented as a theory of processes. The systems-theoretical concept for this phenomenon is *dynamic stability.*

This abstract theoretical concept can be successfully applied to the empirical realm if one can show how in reality variation, selection, and (re)stabilization each depend on different conditions, in other words, if one can show that they occur in isolation. One tends to assume that the theory of evolution presupposes an accidental coordination of its mechanisms (rather than an integration that is contingent upon the system). The theory of organic evolution has successfully isolated these phenomena with concepts such as mutation, sexual reproduction, "natural selection," or the selection of organisms for the reproduction and the ecological stabilization of populations. We need not concern ourselves with issues that are still debated within this (more or less "neo-Darwinian") theory, such as the notion of "adaptation" to the environment or "natural selection." At any rate, this entire apparatus for describing the functions of separation in biology is inapplicable in the domain of sociocultural or social evolution. This is not to say that a theory of evolution cannot be formulated for society, but rather that functions of separation in this domain must be described differently.[47]

In systems theory, one can distinguish between operations (elements), structures, and the system, that is, one can discern a difference between system and environment. This distinction facilitates an appropriate attribution of evolutionary mechanisms. One can speak of *variation* only where unexpected (new!) operations occur. In these cases, *selection* concerns the structural value of an innovation: the innovation is either accepted as something worth repeating, or it is isolated as a singular occurrence and rejected. *Stability* might be jeopardized in both cases, because new structures need to be integrated, and discarded innovations must be remembered or perhaps become an object of regret.[48] The sheer quantity of operations allows trivial variations to occur on a gigantic scale, variations that, under normal circumstances, vanish as soon as they take place. Occasionally their structural value is recognized. In this case, selection becomes an issue. When this happens, variation can endanger the system, exposing it to a persistent pressure of irritation and forcing it to adapt internally to its own problems.[49]

This theoretical schema presupposes a system of sufficient complexity. Evolutionary mechanisms cannot be thought of in isolation, unless one can assume a "loose coupling" of multiple simultaneous operations, which under normal circumstances ensures that variations are immediately eliminated; otherwise the pressure variation exerts upon structures would be too high.[50] Apart from that, an evolving system must be able to localize and tolerate structural change—in the sense of the older cybernetics, it must be organized in an "ultrastable" manner. Last but not least, evolution is possible only if the system can maintain the stability of prior and subsequent states and if it can distinguish between operations and structures, that is, between variations and selections. All of this precludes considering interactive systems among persons as capable of evolution, suggesting instead that the social system is the primary bearer of sociocultural evolu-

tion. This raises the question—the only one of interest to us here—
whether one can speak of evolution in conjunction with social subsystems
—specifically in conjunction with the art system.

Unlike the domain of evolutionary epistemology or the theory of science, in the domain of art hardly any preparatory work has been done for
such analyses. In the past, evolutionary theories of social subdomains have
typically been developed where, according to the self-understanding of the
domain in question, problems of rationality have come to the fore: in science, for example, on the occasion of the transcendental-theoretical revolution and as a result of the current constructivist revolution; in the economy because of doubts about whether the model of perfect competition
can serve as a valid orientation; in law in view of the obsolescence of natural law and the necessity of coming up with other (not just value-related)
explanations for the selection of current law. It is evident that theories of
evolution are also subject to evolution and that they tend to be advanced
when doubts about rationality cannot be overcome in any other way. Art,
however, has always thrived on the imagination, so that a typical occasion
for evolutionary models of explanation never arose. Social-theoretical models might conceivably be inadequate for applying the theory of evolution in
the realm of art. Be this as it may, the nexus between systems theory and
the theory of evolution outlined above could be an occasion to attempt an
application of this sort with new theoretical tools.

IV

If one wants to apply the theoretical approach outlined above to art, one
must first determine (just as in systems theory) the operation that provides
the point of onset for variations. This must be the operation that supports
whatever happens in art, which must not be confused with other operations—otherwise one might end up with an evolution that has nothing to
do with the system of art. Within the systems-theoretical framework we
presented earlier, we can define this operation in only one way, namely, in
terms of an observation that is focused on art. This notion covers both the
production of art and the encounter with artworks. Formally, it indicates
a specific way of choosing distinctions for the purpose of using one (but
not the other) side as the starting point for further operations. The art-
specific nature of such distinctions is evident in the realization that they
are not placed haphazardly, but are positioned in relation to an emerging

or existing work of art that demands, rewards, or disapproves of certain indications (and distinctions).

The evolution of a separate, art-specific domain within society is occasioned by the fact that the artwork demands decisions concerning what
fits (is beautiful) or does not fit (is ugly), for which there is *no external orientation.* We called the binary form of this unlikely occurrence "coding,"[51]
and we shall use this concept to indicate the "take off" of a special kind of
evolution. We can locate its beginning—which, relatively speaking, is
without presuppositions—in an ornamental staggering of distinctions
that exploit given conditions (for example, in pottery) in order to unfold
a life of its own that is at first harmless, insignificant, indeed playful, and
certainly dispensable. But this early stage already displays the features that
later characterize art. A habitual pattern cries out, so to speak, for variation. A small alteration yields consequences; it requires further elaboration
and supplementation, or else it must be eliminated as inappropriate—and
this happens repeatedly in numerous attempts that might succeed or fail,
establish a tradition or perish. One form seizes the next, the side produced
along with it needs to be filled, distinctions must be established or return
back into themselves—and all of this is driven by an internal dynamic
that propels the execution of these operations without much consideration for the object. Of course, the material must be receptive to such a dynamic, and it must accommodate the purpose for which one wants to use
the material. But the ornament decides for itself what fits and what does
not fit. It creates an imaginary space that is stabilized by external factors
without being determined by them. All of this can happen as a kind of
"preadaptive advance"; there is no need to presuppose a differentiated system of art or specialized roles for artists and connoisseurs.

We argued earlier that even highly developed art forms can be traced to
a kind of "inner ornament," if one pays attention to the connections between its distinctions.[52] The evolution of an imaginary space of art can begin with a sense for ornamentation, because ornamentation does not presuppose a distinct artistic realm, even though it is possible in such a
realm—as if it were a matter of holding in reserve an as yet unknown future. "Ritual is more than an ornamentation of time," writes Jan Assmann[53]
—but it is also just that. Art can start out from its internal ornamental
structures and thus get a taste of what lies ahead. The ornament is a possession, which art can develop further by ever more bold distinctions and
an ever more expanding imagination. From this starting point, self-assured,

art can establish relations to the world and copy familiar or desirable features into itself. From within the ornament, which still dominates the work, human or animal bodies emerge; or poetry creates texts, in which sound and rhythm function as ornament. Works themselves become free to refer to all kinds of meanings. Even when this freedom is restricted, decisions remain; even when adhering to classical models, one must pay attention to what is fitting when representing a *Dying Gaul.* Occasions for reconstructive invention arise more frequently when the material—the techniques or frames—is altered, and one must either determine what kinds of formal combinations are still feasible or else experiment with new possibilities. Such occasions arise in conjunction with the transformation of the mural into painting on canvas, or in the relationship between painting, mosaic, and tapestry; they arise when music that accompanies dance is disengaged from the movement of the body, or when music is played with a different set of instruments: when one stops using wood to create sculptures, then abandons rock and clay for the sake of granite or marble, then finally returns to wood; when large sculptures are replicated on a minuscule scale in ivory; when one considers the relationship between woodblock and lithograph or between pencil and chalk drawings. Examples could be multiplied,[54] but supplying evidence for such innovative thrusts is difficult. It is clear, however, that the struggle with media that impose different kinds of constraints draws attention to the formal correlations that can be realized within these media.

This kind of trial already constitutes an observation specific to art, both with regard to the production of a work and to the appreciation of the work as art. The entire process begins to orient itself recursively, generating a demand for criteria and a need for structure, which stimulate an evolution capable of preserving striking occurrences for the sake of repetition or deviation.

Observation in this sense is the smallest unit in the artistic process. Even when the observational schema is employed repeatedly, the observing operation remains a singularity that vanishes spontaneously and always occurs for the first and last time. This operation focuses on a certain posture in dance (or in sculpture, as in the *Laocoön*), on a single color that has a certain place and intensity in a painting, on how a certain action in a given narrative moves the plot along or clarifies the motives established by the plot. Every time a work of art is produced or understood, innumerable observing operations are necessary. As is typical in evolutionary variations, we are dealing with a massive occurrence of trivial processes that, under normal circumstances, would be of no consequence. At this point, a kind of miniselection already takes place, as well as a test for stability, which resembles the mechanisms at play in the mutations of organic evolution. This raises the question of whether the decisions and opinions that have been established about a given work of art can be sustained in the course of further observation, or whether they have to be sacrificed or corrected.

The trivialization of operations that are sensitive to variation shows clearly that this process cannot yet be called evolutionary selection. If structural change is to yield evolutionary consequences, then it must start from a different level. In general, evolutionary selection presupposes that the adaptive relationship between system and environment is preserved in the course of variations by virtue of the system's autopoiesis (this makes selection possible and constrains it at the same time). But it does not tell us anything about the manner in which selection operates. So far as relationships between meanings are concerned, the problem of selection appears to reside in the reusability of the points of view that guide selection, that is, in an identification that simultaneously varies and confirms these points of view. Such identifications require that operations are observed not only as a series of situation-dependent chance events but also as the realization of a program. The differentiation of evolutionary variation and selection rests on the observational level of (self-)programming.[55] This level of observation constitutes itself only when artworks impress the beholder as successful—whether one prefers the "novelty" of such works or whether they are produced only for the sake of deviation. At first, it might have always been a matter of imitating successful artworks that subsequently served as models for creating variations on a given theme. There is more than one *Pietà*, and what is later diagnosed as a change in style might have established itself in this manner. Certain trends emerge and realize themselves in multiple variants—for example, the trend toward realism in portraits. One further complicates the construction of ornaments that repeat simple basic patterns and therefore react differently to variations. Another example is increasing freedom in the posture of sculptures, which, when they are skillfully crafted, serve as proof of precisely this skill. So far as music is concerned, one could mention the formal impulses that result from the introduction of new instruments or from the fixation of music in musical notation.

Unlike other, more rigidly programmed functional systems, in the evolution of the art system one cannot presuppose the existence of selection criteria in the way one can assume a profit motive in the economy, a criterion of methodological correctness in science, or the distinction equality/inequality in current legal practice. If artworks constitute their own programs, then they can convince only after the fact. Successful art can be observed in terms of criteria only in retrospect, and the question is always whether to imitate or to improve the work, or whether the innovation is based on rejecting all previous criteria. In an extreme sense, this is true of "modern" art, especially when it acts capriciously enough to explode the boundaries of the tolerable and pulls the rug out from underneath all previously valid criteria. Doing so requires a memory that allows the art system to construct and reconstruct its evolution as if it followed an intelligible order. Seen in such a way, it is no accident that the suspension of previous frame conditions and the emergence of an academic art history occur at the same time and that both demarcate an era by virtue of their operations and their observations.

That types are formed in retrospect has been observed in the art system for quite some time, under such catchwords as *maniera*, make, style. At first, such types were considered as a means of distinguishing and classifying styles and of assigning them to appropriate topics; then they served to recognize changes in styles; and finally, since Winckelmann, they have served as a means of art-historical analysis. We can therefore refer to "style" as the formal level where the evolutionary selection of structure takes place. One must keep in mind, however, that the concept of style is by no means unequivocal;[56] the concept has been subject to historical change and is a result of evolution (which is precisely what gives us the license for theoretical abstraction). This leads to the hypothesis we suggested earlier, namely, that the transition to modern art motivated the search for, and the discovery of, an alternative to the freedom of stylistic choice, which resides in the expansion or even dissolution of frame conditions (such as tonality in music or object orientation in painting) that, up to this point, facilitated the emergence of specific styles and their variations. It looks as if evolution motivated the system to introduce concepts that call attention to the difference in level between operation and structure (or variation and selection); apparently such concepts established the boundaries that subsequently provoked their transgression.

In sum, these developments brought about what Darwin sought to explain: a variety of species. Evolution does not guarantee survival; as a matter of fact, most species in life and in art have vanished or are about to vanish. We are not dealing with essences, whether secured by nature or by a cosmos of essences. But evolution remains problematic, and so does the question of how such a proliferation of species is possible to begin with.

In the evolution of artistic genres, the development of types bifurcates in the wake of the differentiation of perceptual media for seeing and hearing and along with the differentiation of space and time. Any further development becomes a matter of additional bifurcations (text-art, painting, sculpture) or of combining seeing and hearing (film, theater). Under these frame conditions, a differentiation of genres occurs, which is culturally and historically important but unstable. Among these genres, the diversity of textual arts is the most impressive—displaying a wide spectrum from the epic to the epigram, from the novel to the short story, from the metric differentiation of the lyric to theme-based narrative genres (such as biography, the historical novel, science fiction, the mystery novel, and so forth). This differentiation of types is not to be understood as a "fight for life" between the epic and the ode (or as a struggle for attention). The principle of competition is supplemented by the insight into the advantages—suggested and facilitated by specific "frames"[57]—of "insulating" innovations, so that they do not immediately transform the entire art system.

The consequences of the separation of variation and selection and their effects are crucial for the differentiation of an art system and for the stability of such a system. From the perspective of the art system, the internal differentiations that establish themselves in this process no longer correspond to those one finds in the social environment of this system: they have nothing to do with the separation between the state apparatus and political parties, let alone with the internal differentiation of the party spectrum itself; nor do they correspond to the differentiation of banking houses and savings banks, grade schools and high schools, or to the internal differentiation of faculties, not to speak of the mega-differentiations of religion, politics, the economy, education, and so on. Any one-to-one correspondence between system and environment (of the kind one observes in tribal societies that practice a totem symbolism, for example[58]) is interrupted. The art system decouples itself from its social environment. To be sure, the social environment does supply certain divisions in the form of neurophysiologically integrated orders that become distinguishable in the form of media of perception. While these "natural" boundaries anticipate the evolution of art, it is easy to see that they present no obstacle to a further differentiation of types, neither in the realm of seeing nor in the realm of hearing. Perhaps the differences among these media of perception provide an indispensable impulse for such a differentiation.

At any rate, the "mismatch" between the system and its social environment isolates the art system from the evolution of society in general. This is not to say that the evolution of society is without significance for the evolution of art. On the contrary! It certainly is, but only for the *internal* evolution of art. For better or for worse, art exploits the evolutionary transformation that leads from a stratified to a functionally differentiated society.[59] But it meets this transition halfway by virtue of its internal evolution. The noncorrespondence between these two types of differentiation forces art to develop criteria for its own affairs. In the shadow of the Aristotelian tradition, one continued to speak of imitation well into the eighteenth century, and the beginnings of a modern philosophical "aesthetics" were motivated by the search for a common notion of beauty in nature and art.[60] Within this framework, Hutcheson already suggested a notion of absolute beauty, which, he believed, grounds all other types of comparative or relative (imitative) beauty.[61] The efforts to determine a universal principle of beauty show that this is not a matter of differentiating between Whigs and Tories; nor does it concern the practices of accounting in firms or of determining a focus for research in the new sciences that were about to develop into disciplines.

Starting in antiquity, guiding concepts such as harmony, balanced proportion, or the notion of a unity that shines through multiplicity served to reconcile a sense of beauty with religion.[62] In evolutionary terms, such concepts guaranteed stability. The cosmos, understood as nature or as creation, gathered a multiplicity (which can be distinguished!) into a unity: *rerum dissimilium convenientia* [the agreement of things dissimilar].[63] The artistic achievements of the Renaissance inherited this notion of beauty but put it to the test, both in texts and in view of what could be represented at all. On the one hand, there were no direct links to an environment ordered along the lines of politics, religion, or households. If art was appreciated, then it was appreciated *as* art. On the other hand, the trust in one's own critical judgment was strengthened through experiences in the workshop, comparison with other artworks, and texts that addressed issues related to art. After the notion of a general mathematical-musical-architectural world harmony was sacrificed in the sixteenth century (because musical proportions could not be rendered in architecture[64]), art had to create its own concept of nature and aim at "another nature."[65] If one conceded that much, then the principle of imitation could survive as a topic for quite some time; but it could no longer guarantee stability in the sense that beautiful forms could be readily repeated and reproduced.

Discussions based on criteria specific to art then began to take place. Art mobilized, as we have pointed out, a memory of its own to orient itself in its own history. The initial impulse was to consider everything according to the schema of rank, as if discussing criteria were a matter of imitating social hierarchy. One debated the primacy of individual artists and genres and, above all, the hierarchical relationship between the ancients and the moderns.[66] The result, in the seventeenth century, was a tightly woven network of rules—especially in texts concerning poetics—from which one violently sought to free oneself. In the sixteenth century, the discussion of criteria was still oriented toward educational tasks. In the seventeenth century, the propagation of "beautiful appearance" in the form of art overlapped with the *science des mœurs*, with the theory of political (= public) conduct, and with the doctrine of passionate love, even though there was no exact correspondence between these realms. Hutcheson still sought a unifying principle capable of comprehending the beautiful, the true, and the good, of uniting the beauty of nature and art, and of reconciling scientific theorems and moral principles.[67] Because of internal developments in these function-specific realms—such as the increasing orientation of politics toward the state and enhanced intimacy in love relationships—such notions were dismissed one after the other. What remained was the problem of how to define criteria, a problem framed as an inquiry into the nature of beauty—that is, in a manner that did not yet distinguish between coding and programming. At least officially, reflection on the art system was cast as the problem of defining beauty. But how could one come to terms with this problem, if experience showed that further differentiation required the generalization of symbols that nonetheless claimed to represent the unity of the system?[68]

We can assume further that the experience of a criterion-dependent selection of art affects the perception of artworks as well. If it is obvious that a work follows injunctions—that is, if rules and works are observed separately, yet simultaneously—the results no longer satisfy. They appear monotonous and uninteresting. Works produced in the classical style are no longer appreciated. Apart from the postulate of originality, the eighteenth century demanded that works fulfill the additional requirement of being "sublime," "interesting," "bizarre," "gothic," "picturesque." Such formulas sought to explode the previous norms of "decorum" or *"bienséance" de rigueur.*[69] If one could no longer rely on generally accepted and stable criteria, one could at least agree on the desire for variation. Then one would be ready to concede that works of art speak to the "lower" senses of the upper classes.

In the second half of the eighteenth century, the concept of style was historicized, along with many other traditional concepts. The emergence of historical thinking uprooted the *querelle des anciens et modernes*—which still relied on universal comparative criteria—and the issues of that debate were displaced by analyses of historical correlations in the emergence and transformation of styles, *especially in art.* Styles were now defined both factually and temporally. They displayed style-immanent criteria—one might say, programs for programming art. Such criteria could no longer be canonized. (Instead, one invented "classicism.") Style provides its own directives for stylistic deviation, which is always justified when the execution of the artwork succeeds. This evolutionary step destabilized the structural factors that secure selection. A selection that concerns a certain style cannot also guarantee the evolutionary restabilization of the structural change it brings about. At that point the evolutionary functions of selection and restabilization separate. As a result evolution gains a momentum that continually surpasses itself. There are parallels in other functional systems: consider the role of profit in the economy, of passion in love, of a context-bound reason of state as a criterion of politics, and of positivity as a criterion of law. From a social-theoretical perspective, such parallels indicate a correlation between functional differentiation and an accelerated evolutionary structural change that affects individual functional systems in different ways, depending on their own criteria of selection. Art criticism can no longer appeal to individually correct insights; instead, it must be content—following the romantics—to reflect upon given accomplishments and merely collaborate in the creation of art. The experience of the system's *internal dynamic* forces one to base its stability on *autonomy* and to ensure that art—by means of "ideas" or by deliberate breaks with tradition—remains distinguishable and observable.

In such a situation, functional systems explore new semantic stabilities that are capable of outlasting such fluidities while still allowing one to formulate the unity and the point of one's endeavor. Typically, one sought solutions in values. Heydenreich already questioned the value of purposes.[70] Along with the claim of a unique, art-specific value formulated initially in terms of an "idea," art made its entrance into the nineteenth century. It is a peculiarity of values to be capable of retaining their identity even under conditions of change. They present themselves as a plurality, undisturbed by the presence of other values that might be preferable in certain situations. On the contrary, displacing a disadvantaged value preserves its memory as a consolation. The notion of value indicates the manner in which the system secures its own stability while attempting to incorporate innovations. Schopenhauer believed that the object of aesthetic contemplation was not the mere objecthood of individual artworks but "the idea that strives to reveal itself in them, that is, the adequate objectification of the will at a certain stage."[71] Hegel still began his lectures on aesthetics by declaring: "These lectures are dedicated to *Aesthetics*; its object is the *vast realm of the beautiful* and, more specifically, *art*, in particular *the fine arts*, constitute its domain." For Hegel, the "object" indicates the moment in which the self-reproducing consciousness experiences its own determination. We can rephrase this insight as follows: the object is the system's memory.

In this way, the perspective of stability is *indicated* as a value. But in the context of a theory of observation and description one wants to know what the value *distinguishes* itself from. It goes without saying that this cannot be the countervalue of ugliness; after all, not everything that is not art (business, for example, or politics) deserves to be called ugly. The debate about criteria thus gives rise to problems within the self-description of the art system, and these problems point to the difference between self-reference and hetero-reference. Problems resulting from the system's need to maintain stability in the face of evolutionary change must be dealt with in the realm of the system's self-description, and this description varies depending on how art distinguishes itself from nonart. That topic deserves careful attention, and we therefore postpone it to the following chapter.

V

After all that has been said, the evolution of art is its own accomplishment. It cannot be caused by external intervention—neither the spontaneous creativity of individual artists, nor a kind of "natural selection" by the social environment, as Darwinian theories would have to assume.[72]

Nor can evolution be explained, as it used to be, by appealing to origins or beginnings. The theory of evolution is designed in a circular rather than a linear manner, because variation presupposes a prior state that, as a result of evolution, is stable enough to absorb variation and perhaps even evaluate it. As our previous analyses have shown, the separation between the levels of variation and selection is a result of evolution. Evolution brings forth its own conditions and hence itself evolves.[73] Recourse to an origin in order to account for evolutionary trends becomes obsolete, indeed, becomes suspect.[74]

In the final analysis, a circular conception of the theory of evolution serves to reformulate the problem of the probability of the improbable or the problem of stability, which is the beginning and end of evolutionary changes in structure. Eventually, one might ask: How can an autopoietic system come into existence, if it must presuppose itself in all of its operations in order to recognize what does and what does not belong to the system?

Gunther Teubner suggests that we give up thinking of autopoiesis in terms of a rigid either/or and adopt a more gradual version of the concept that would solve this problem (or perhaps only make it more gradual?).[75] This suggestion, however, gives away the decisive advantages of the concept of autopoiesis, for no compelling reason. One can solve the same problem via the concept of "preadaptive advances," which has proven useful in the theory of evolution.

Of course, evolution is not possible without presuppositions; it is not *creatio ex nihilo*. Evolution presupposes a sufficiently prepared world, in which autopoietic systems can close themselves off and operate as if they had existed there before. Numerous examples could be cited—such as the emergence of writing,[76] or the emergence of money in the form of coins in the trading houses of Sardinia.[77] Innovations of this sort may or may not initiate the "take off" of a new branch of sociocultural evolution. For the art system, there are good (and goodly debatable) reasons for believing that such a take off—which differentiates the art system from religion, politics, and the economy and initiates an evolution of irresistible structural changes—happened only once in world history, namely, in early modern Europe.[78]

The preconditions for this evolution can be specified with accuracy and situated historically. They reside in the already existent, highly developed artistic skill and literary culture of the *artes* and in a poetics that offers models and allows for imitation and critical appreciation. These conditions established themselves in Europe, especially after, in the late Middle Ages, works of antiquity began to be rediscovered and admired. At first, no uniform concept could cover both the visual arts and painting; nor did one have a sense of art as separate from the outside world. But an admiration of perfection oriented to the work made it possible for the "Renaissance" to assume that art already existed and only needed to be reactualized

Under such conditions, art takes off—epigenetically, indeed, counterintuitively and against all declared intentions. One could just as well have continued to imitate existing models or experiment with new themes in appropriate fashion (*maniera*). In addition, a second factor has to be taken into account. The development of early modern society toward functional differentiation establishes radically new environmental conditions and creates stability conditions of a different kind for the self-differentiating art system. As we indicated in Chapter 4, supporting contexts for art were initially provided by the courts of the new territorial states and later by the emerging art market, both of which allowed art a certain degree of indifference and willfulness in relation to the environment. Moreover, the splitting off of Protestantism from the Catholic Church undermined the certainty of the established religious world order. The intensification of religious propaganda led to a powerful critique of the internal dynamic of the art system—from the Protestant as well as from the Catholic side—which, however, could not prevail and merely ended up radicalizing the problem of art-internal criteria. The development of the modern empirical-mathematical sciences relieved art from competition, especially in the educational sector. Science could no longer interfere with art, nor could art interfere with science. Debates about rank subsided. This development culminated around 1800, when art found itself in a societal system where it had to operate without external support, even if environmental conditions such as economic purchasing power or political nonintervention remained as important as before.

One can discuss this briefly sketched development from a number of different perspectives. For systems theory, it concerns the differentiation of the art system. When treating the self-description of the art system, we shall return to the consequences of differentiation for a reflection on the meaning of art. In the context of a theory of evolution, one can show that changes within socially presupposed stability conditions yield possibilities

of variation and selection that are left to their own internal dynamic and
lead to a rapidly accelerating, self-generated structural change.

When its attention was focused inward, the art system had greater opportunities for variation, and it could expand its own criteria of selection
—indeed, make them more "irrational" (if "rationality" means employing
criteria that are equally acceptable in a scientific, religious, or political
sense). In this way, art could cultivate intuition, imagination, exaggeration,
deception, obscurity, and ambivalence and exploit these means to refer
back to itself. Artistic endeavors that supported religion or politics were
then criticized as "pompous." What one later calls "baroque" aimed at optical illusion, especially in the construction of churches and castles but also
in painting and internal architecture, as if ingeniously to escape the by
now discredited representational demands of religious and political domains of intelligibility by adhering to these demands without fulfilling
them. Another way of eluding such demands was by discovering the everyday life of peasants and burghers. At the same time, allegory provided the
means to represent ideas in the form of abstract concepts and to personify
such concepts. One cultivated paradox in literature with the intent of enforcing a creative, paralogical search for escape.[79] A multileveled structure
of deception and self-deception became the object of poetry, of the theater,
and of the novel. In relation to modern science (for example, of the sort
advanced by Galileo), art no longer thought of itself as opting for false-
hood (as it did in the sixteenth-century *historia/poesia* debate). These issues
no longer mattered. The true/false code was "rejected" as a guiding distinction,[80] and science, for its part, was no longer interested in registering
the representations of the belles lettres and of the arts as "falsehoods."

The debate about criteria took on a dynamic of its own, apparently because it was no longer affected by external factors. One understood that
autonomy, enforced by nonidentity, is a necessity of self-determination.
As early as the seventeenth century, this understanding undermined the
orientation toward proven recipes and rules. The emerging reflection on
art pursued a separatist course that aims at the inexplicable—*no so che, je
ne sais quoi*. Because beauty could not be subsumed under rules or laws,
it could claim a domain of its own. It participated in social communication because it was different. Like the sovereignty of the king and of love,
the sovereignty of art displayed an inexplicability that was nonetheless
not to be understood as arbitrary. One employed analytically charged
concepts such as *acutezza*, cunning, *Witz*, and so forth to characterize and

praise art and the artist. Such concepts promised clarification yet refused to deliver on that promise. All of these trends characterized an autonomy forced upon art, because its claims to engage itself in a religious, political, or scientific sense were denied by the internal logic of these functional sectors.[81]

At the same time, the aristocratic world of stratified society, the world of households and their political alliances, exhibited corresponding signs of crisis. This crisis has often been discussed, and it is well documented with respect to the loss of political power by the nobility and to financial crises (although in places where they were most severe, as in Spain, such crises hardly affected the nobility). We shall focus only on one aspect of these crises. The individual no longer found adequate support in the old ways of life. One searched for more powerful, individual modes of expression—in a stylized amorous passion, for example[82]—but also in an elaborate code of honor, in the provocation of the duel, and in view of one's own (inevitably individualized) death. The semantics of the aristocracy flourished for the last time; but it did so with involuted means that were out of sync with social reality.[83] This meant that art was burdened with the search for its own audience—by turning toward the "common" people, which one now sought to impress, or by valuing artistic expertise and critical appreciation.[84] Since early antiquity, one had taken into account the effects of reception. But now specific complementary roles were at stake, which ran parallel to those in other functional realms (for example, government and subject, plaintiff and court, buyer and seller, lover and beloved, believer and clergy), *and which could no longer be integrated via a stratification of households.*

When we add up all of these changes, it becomes clear that under such conditions art—so far as its mode of operation in producing and evaluating artworks is concerned—began to draw on its own resources and, in so doing, triggered evolutionary sequences unique to art. Reality was robbed of its authority to provide meaning. The rationality continuum that had traditionally joined the nature of action with its natural conditions (as it joined cognition with its object) broke apart. Don Quixote found meaning in his actions and an intense and unperturbed experience in reading, but not in the real world, and this experience was doubled, so to speak, and offered to the reader as the meaning of his own reading. The operations that were now executed as observations specific to art could draw their meaning only from art itself. But this meant that they were subject to the law of variation, that they could no longer pretend to accomplish perfection, but instead had to present novelty. If this was so, however, then the criteria for selection had to be redefined. The artistic effort to surpass itself could not turn into arbitrariness; it had to satisfy criteria of judgment. Ever since Gracián, one has used "taste" to refer to representations in morality as well as in aesthetics, that is, in a sense that encompasses both human conduct and works of art.[85] By doing so, one distanced oneself from rational verification. Taste judged intuitively, directly, and instantaneously. That the judgments of taste were correct could be shown after the fact through reasoning and justification.

The concept of taste joined several distinctions. Initially it rejected the pedantry of applying rules; this was its historical thrust. But it also allowed good taste to be distinguished from bad taste, sorting not only judgments but people as well.[86] Most important in the context of the present argument, however, the concept of taste made possible the separation of variation and selection by rupturing—via such notions as natural perfection or a rule that promises success—the tight coupling between the two, without turning selection into an arbitrary process.

In a parallel development—as if to compensate for the traditionally subjective and indisputable nature of the concept of taste—a notion of classicism emerged in France that offered a history of timeless models to which one could return.[87] Perhaps this explains why French theories of taste propagated during the final third of the seventeenth century and during the first third of the eighteenth century contain a resonance of trust in one's judgments which one finds nowhere else.[88]

Taste exploited the recursive network of anticipations and recapitulations without committing one's judgment about individual works to general and binding perspectives. But the situation in France around the mid-eighteenth century was about to change, precisely because of its ties to classicism. One subsequently spoke of *goût* only to express certain stylistic preferences—for or against color as opposed to drawing, or for or against Boucher. This is what Diderot has in mind when he demands of the critic "all sorts of tastes, a heart that is sensitive to all pleasures, a soul susceptible to an infinite variety of enthusiasms."[89]

The pseudocriterion of good taste—a criterion without criteria—registered that the evolution of the art system was already under way and was subject to perpetual structural change. But such change depended above all on the success or failure of individual self-programming artworks.

There was no ordering hand above this level (in the sense in which the seventeenth and eighteenth centuries appeal to the "invisible hand," if only to deny organized religion and the absolute state jurisdiction over certain domains). Taste was still vaguely oriented toward criteria of social rank (not everyone has taste); however, rank was no longer defined in terms of birth but in terms of an expertise that the art system itself attracted and cultivated.[90] This meant that society was no longer represented in art. But not until the second half of the eighteenth century did corresponding semantic developments affirm the evolutionary autonomy of art and search for explanations of artistic autonomy in art itself—for example, in the historicization of the concept of style or in a new concept of "culture," both of which described evolution from a kind of bird's-eye perspective, but also in what was offered under the name of "aesthetics" as a reflection theory of the art system. At this level, one could claim stability in the face of change. What had thus evolved within a few centuries was a diversity of forms which in retrospect could no longer be understood as nature or perfection and which today cannot even be considered progress. This development began in early modernity; that much we know, because at that time stylistic orientation was already coupled to the production of art. Variation was motivated not only by the production of works but also by work-transcending structures, which could be experienced as contingent—as a *maniera* one could choose—and which could be hypercorrected (thus appearing to the observer of styles as a kind of mannerism or a symptom of stylistic decay). Style legitimized both conforming behavior and deviation—precisely because it was a structural condensation of what was going on in art at any given time. Some theories (for example, of landscape painting) preceded the production of corresponding works, and one demanded of the work, among other things, that it acknowledge the *maniera* it followed.[91]

Art has been condemned to autonomy, and the problems of self-description that arise from this situation are translated into works of art in ways that (still) elude an intelligible theoretical explication. This is evident, for example, in the poetry of paradox and later in romanticism, and it manifests itself forcefully in the avant-garde of the nineteenth and twentieth centuries. We shall return to this point. What interests us here is that this situation does not lead to the collapse of the mechanisms of variation, selection, and restabilization, but rather to a circular network that comprises these different levels of evolution. Evolution is accelerated as a result, and the reservoir of forms expands to the point where the only purpose of constraints is to be challenged.

The nexus between diversification and acceleration corresponds to precisely the kind of hypothesis an evolutionary theory would propose. So far as we can tell, we currently have no other explanation.

VI

An autonomous art system has emerged as the result of an internal evolution within art. The same holds for other functional systems. They all realize operative closure and self-organization, and, in so doing, they increase causal dependencies and independence in selective forms that are typical of modern society. Art, however, bears a special trait which it shares only with religion: participation is optional. Inclusion, whether active or passive, is a matter of individual choice. The low rate of participation in art is astonishing. Only a fraction of the population participates in art, and the idiosyncrasies of modern art often serve as an excuse for staying away from it. Difficulties of observation and understanding abound. On the active side, it becomes increasingly cumbersome for artists to find a niche, a style, a manner of presentation for which they can claim originality. These difficulties seem extravagant and forced, which in turn affects people's readiness to participate passively in art.

There has been much lament over this development. But there is another side to it, an important advantage. Because the art system looks upon participation/nonparticipation as a matter of individual choice, both options are socially possible. No one is forced—as they were in William James's times—to feign a musical self in order to visit the opera in Boston. One abandons conventions of this sort, which were always class specific. The art system thereby gains the advantage of making its mechanism of inclusion/exclusion largely independent of the inclusions and exclusions of other functional systems. Empirical research has no difficulty noticing that the number of people who go to concerts and visit museums and art exhibitions is not a representative selection of the population at large. But this bias cannot be comprehended as a result of a social regulation. Rather, it is a correlate of the evolutionary improbability of equal distribution, which manifests itself differently in mega-events, such as rock concerts, and in classical theater.

In another terminology, one might say: there are only a few, rather loose structural couplings between the art system and other systems. As before, a specialized art market couples the art system and the economic system. But in this market, artworks are traded as capital investments or as extremely expensive individual goods. On the production side, access to this market depends on an established reputation, and the market takes an active role in developing such reputations. However, one should not overestimate the irritating effects of the market on the production of art. Precisely the demand for artistic originality prevents the artist from working with an eye to the market.

Compared to other intersystemic relationships—between law and politics, for example, between the health care system and the economy as an employment system, or between the economy and science—the art system is surprisingly isolated. This might explain why modern art is capable of developing a symbolization of fundamental social problems of modern society that relies neither on an imitation of society's "nature" nor on a critique of its effects.

Art is a "playful" doubling of reality; this is both the result and the condition of its evolution. But what is this enigmatic double? How can it be observed? As a unity? As a boundary one can cross without being able to occupy it? As nothing, and thus once again as something that can serve as an indication of the unobservability of the world?

This situation, which has evolved (unplanned), can be described in several ways, from which society can choose the one it likes best, the one that it finds convincing and that works for communication—whether as a sign for its essence or as a critique, depending on whether society searches for a positive or negative relationship to itself. But if there is a plurality of possible self-descriptions, why not several at once? Perhaps it is the problem of a "postmodern" poly-contexturality of self-descriptions, which society at first explores in the realm of art.

§7 Self-Description

I

One of the incalculable effects of Wittgenstein's philosophy was to raise the question of whether a concept of art can be defined. If the notion of play defies definition, then art should remain undefined as well. This view was widely held in the 1960s.[1] It denies only the possibility for a definition that corresponds to the "essence" of art and holds unequivocally for all observers, however, thus leaving a loophole for the recent theory of operative constructivism, which no longer raises issues of essence or of the consensus of all observers but instead leaves the decision of what counts as art to the art system itself.[2] In relation to this system, all other observers assume the position of second-order observers. Such observers must restrict themselves to reporting what the art system designates as art. They must leave it to the system to determine its own boundaries. This move burdens the theory of self-describing systems with a momentous inheritance. It must salvage a highly encumbered "firm" that has been dealing in "essences" and "referring signs," for which there is no market left.

Moreover, this means that the notion of self-description is not a constitutive operation—in the sense that the system needs to know what art is before it can begin to produce art. Self-description—here and in other contexts as well—is a retrospective operation that requires the prior existence of something it can resort to. This might still leave open the possibility of characterizing self-description as a cognitive apprehension of the "essence" of art, so long as such a terminology is still acceptable. Modern art in particular initially thought of itself as representing a kind of clean, purified essence or quest for truth. But from the viewpoint of self-description, the appeal to "essence" or "truth" is only one possibility among others, which disintegrates under the gaze of the second-order observer. All products of self-description must be treated as contingent, even if they resist contingency at the semantic level. Most importantly, they must be treated as selective choices, incapable of retaining and representing in the system's memory the sum total of what is happening in the system.

This "modalization" of all self-descriptive propositions implies nothing yet about the limits of plausibility to which self-descriptions must adhere. Making concessions to contingency, belatedness, selectivity, or a plurality of self-descriptions does not answer the question of what is accomplished by such self-descriptions. It merely addresses this question to another authority—an authority that is presumably motivated by its own interests to keep arbitrariness under control and is in a better position to do so. Whether it does so remains to be seen. At any rate, works of art must be distinguishable as such. Otherwise they are perceived as objects of utility or, more recently, as trash—or they are mistaken for sacred objects, instructional texts, and so on. As we have shown in detail, society, in order to recognize art, requires a recursive network of observations that makes use of identifiable structures to generate nonidentical reproductions. The artist must anticipate what an observer might observe as a work of art and what kind of additional information one might be able to expect (in terms of theater buildings, art exhibitions, museums, the length of lines in poetry, and so forth). Even the individual operations one performs when observing a work of art must, via *other* operations, refer back to *themselves*. They acquire their distinguishable identity only by a detour through other objects—even when, and precisely when, they are unique. Observations of art occur only in the autopoietic network of the art system. In this sense, one can speak of a basal self-reference at the level of operations that cannot be decomposed further.[3] Without this self-reference, there would be no art. Art, in other words, is not a "composition" made up of preexisting "autochtonous" parts that only need to be put together.

Moreover, the institutionalization of art and the establishment of supporting information (exhibitions and so on) require that works of art "converse" with one another, that art cite, copy, reject, renew, ironize art —that art is reproduced, no matter how, within a referential nexus that transcends the work. Today this is called "intertextuality," which is another way of saying that the art system must have a memory.[4] Memory is presupposed especially when the evolution of artistic communication leads to a situation in which the artwork makes its own laws. We have called this phenomenon the *self-programming of art*. Self-programming requires the specification of such referential networks to ensure that art is still recognized as art, despite the growing tolerance for idiosyncratic artworks. One can now identify the types of form (stylistic levels, symphonies, sonnets) that underlie certain formal constraints. One can identify the styles or "signatures" of a certain artist, or isolate periods in his work in which he draws on his work in a recognizable manner. If one takes this into account, then one can distinguish several levels at which observations of art are self-referentially determined ("level" here does not indicate priority, in the sense that the general would be more important than the particular or vice versa). Under the strenuous conditions of a complexity that increases in the course of evolution, all of these circumstances contribute to the autopoietic self-reproduction of art.

If we speak in the following of the self-description of the art system, then we presuppose these developments. The concept of self-description points in another direction, however. We must presuppose all the operations that produce a difference between art and nonart within the recursive network of these operations. We further assume the basal self-referentiality of observation to be an *operation*. Without it, there would be nothing to be described as art. But the type of reflection that goes under the name "self-description" uses a different distinction. It refers to an other different from the system's basal self-reference, namely, to the environment and specifically to the inner-social environment of the autopoietic system of art. The *theory* of self-description always already assumes the existence of self-descriptions. Theoretical analysis only reiterates the system's own self-descriptions.[5]

In society, all the interpretations generated by communication come together. When art becomes visible as a distinct phenomenon, it stimulates descriptions. One wants to determine what art is all about. Since antiquity, there has been a literature on art. Recognizing works of art as works of art was understood to be a kind of astonishment that provokes curiosity, or a surprise that imprints itself in memory. Such notions lack specificity. One might be surprised on other occasions as well; the narratives of the religious system abound with such reports. Moreover, descriptions of this sort are not localized within the art system. They do not engage in the internal affairs of art, not in the manner in which romantic art criticism engaged itself. They are basically philosophical texts, concerned with one aspect of world descriptions that desire and search for truth. Accordingly, neither in antiquity nor in the Middle Ages was there any concept for what we today call the (fine) arts. What catches one's eye at first are particular differences between media of perception, and also between the visual arts and texts (poetry). August Wilhelm Schlegel still published his lectures of 1801—which were conceived as a comprehensive presentation and certainly belong to the epoch of reflection—in two volumes, under the title *Lectures on the Fine Arts and Literature.*[6]

It was difficult to separate out what, according to our modern understanding, does not belong to art. When representational issues moved into the foreground, as they did in the sixteenth and seventeenth centuries, one felt compelled to include in the realm of art the beautiful appearance of good manners and benevolence (*bienséance*)—everything that was called morality at the time and treated in a *science de mœurs*. Under such conditions, aesthetics and morality became inseparable. The debate about the "beautiful"—whether understood as exemplary perfection, balanced proportion, or a refined sharpening of the intellect (*acutezza, Witz*)—was carried on for several centuries. In these terms, however, it was impossible to separate artistic beauty from natural beauty, the good looks of people, the elegance of their behavior, the eloquence of their speeches, or the dissimulation of their imperfections.

In retrospect one might ask: What was missing? And what would be the theoretical criterion for a self-description of the art system? Approaching the wealth of materials contained in the pertinent literature in the manner of the "intellectual historian" is not enough. We first need to clarify what we mean by self-description.

An understanding of this phenomenon has been obscured by the concept of "culture"—one of the most detrimental concepts ever to be invented. While the concept allowed one to distinguish between objective and subjective culture, both referred to an (artificial) state of affairs that was relativized by attributing it to individuals or groups. The invention of culture toward the end of the eighteenth century—of a form of reflection that subsumed under culture everything that was not nature—presupposed this kind of relativization, which served as a basis for generating historical or national comparisons between cultures—an event staged by "educated Europe," as it was called in those days. Despite its comparative relativization, culture remained an object of essential propositions that could be either true or false. What we mean by "self-description," by contrast, refers to the mode of operation by which systems generate their internal identity, whatever the observers of this process might think of it. One can certainly imagine a plurality of simultaneously generated self-descriptions; but the notion of relativity is completely inappropriate in this case. (Similarly, no relativism whatsoever is involved in making the point that some animals have tails and some don't.) What creates problems is classical bivalent logic, since the description of a self-description projects realities that differ from the ones it describes.

A definition of the concept of self-description can be quickly introduced. As the word indicates, we are dealing with a description of the system by the system. During the years between Baumgarten and Hegel, the theory of art temporarily maintained close ties to philosophy, yielding to theoretical constraints that did not originate in the art system;[7] this is still true for Adorno, at least for his "dialectic."[8] Ever since then, one speaks of "aesthetics." The term alludes to theoretical tools that have nothing to do with art, to imported plausibilities, to an orientation toward what is also otherwise (for example, *geschichtsphilosophisch*) acceptable. By contrast, we consider aesthetics a self-description of the art system to the extent that it reacts to internal problems of meaning and is not just concerned with illustrating general philosophical theories. If aesthetics were indeed a philosophy that covers the entire realm of knowledge about art, it is not clear what kind of independence would be left for art.[9]

In self-description, the system becomes its own theme; it claims an identity of its own. The concepts of self-thematization (if communication is at stake) and self-reflection mean the same thing. And yet, this equation glosses over considerable difficulties. Describing is a kind of observation. Observation is a distinguishing indication. Distinguishing and indicating always go along with a *twofold exclusion*. What is excluded is the unmarked space on the other side of the distinction, that which is not indicated. The unity of the operation that employs a distinction in order to indicate one of its sides but not the other is also excluded. Being an observation, the description renders the world and the operating observation invisible. To be sure, the text indicates that there is more than just a text— an author, for example. The internal side of the description suggests an external, unmarked side. If one wants to cross this boundary, one must be able to distinguish and indicate something on the other side, and the initial problem poses itself again in a different constellation. This might be why the classical theory of the self-reflection of consciousness, or later, of Spirit, preferred to articulate itself within the schema determined/undetermined, without, however, being able to justify its choice of this schema.[10]

The boundary between marked and unmarked, the form of this mark, supplies the starting point for our hypotheses. It raises the question: What is rendered invisible by which distinctions? Or, more precisely: What kinds of distinctions does art employ in order to distinguish (observe, describe) itself? The selection of distinctions for describing art is certainly not accidental (nor are they determined by the "essence of art"). A background process might enforce certain boundaries and block further questioning by way of final concepts. This background process might bring about a reorganization of the domain of social communication or, more accurately, a transition of the social system to a primarily functional differentiation—an order in which art must eventually claim a place of its own that cannot be determined by outside forces.

In all subdomains of society, self-descriptions typically grapple with an excess of possibilities that results from the differentiation of a system within the social system. The emergence of an aristocratic upper class, for example, thanks to a concentration of resources, creates possibilities of cooperation and conflict and allows for dominating a lower class. Such possibilities would not exist without such a differentiation. Therefore it becomes necessary to restrict what is admissible—for example, in the form of a special ethos of the aristocratic way of life. One can observe the same tendency in conjunction with the emergence of functional systems and, hence, also in a differentiated art system. Self-description does not shield the system from constant irritation by excluded excess possibilities. In August 1994, the German press reported that the Federal Association of German Galleries had rejected a proposal to admit artworks (but are these really "artworks"?) by Australian Aborigines to the Cologne art fair, "Art Cologne," on the grounds that these works are merely folk art. One can see here—last but not least because of a long tradition in modern art of attempting to subvert the distinction art/*kitsch* or of presenting forms that are directly and generally intelligible—how strongly the possible rebels against the limits of the admissible, and tends to succeed. Self-description erects a boundary from within a boundary, a "frame" within the "frame" of the system; but precisely because of this difference, self-descriptions remain subject to irritation and become dynamic from within.

II

Already in antiquity, the interpretive description of art had become problematic. One observed that art extends reality in ways that cannot be justified by its utility, by religion, or by a mythical familiarity with origins. There is (alphabetic) writing, a production of texts in which the redoubling of reality surfaces as a problem, simply because one is dealing with writing. The meaning of poetry becomes problematic. The solutions proposed, however, made no claims for an autonomy of art, nor did they maintain that art has a value of its own. They assumed instead that the real world, as nature, does not always appear in its most perfect form. One needed to remember (Platonically) the original Ideas that define the essence of things, or (following Aristotle) to observe nature empirically in its perfect forms rather than in its corrupted forms. Despite differences between these philosophical concepts, the meaning of art resided in a *corrective imitation* that directs the awareness of the observer toward the essential and purges it of imperfections and defects. One could almost speak of an ornamented support and foregrounding of the essence of things, of nature, of the world. Be this as it may, art did *not* find its meaning *in itself* as a realization of its own value.

This situation did not change significantly during the Middle Ages, even though entirely different conditions prevailed. Dionysius (Pseudo-Dionysius Areopagites), who strongly influenced the medieval conception of art, continued to propagate the ideas of late antiquity. A passive notion of cognition prevailed, despite frequent interruptions of this tradition. The world was considered to be a beautifully ordered cosmos, in which the most diverse things distinguished themselves and were fused, despite their diversity, into a harmony that shone even through ugliness, failure, and incompletion. Knowledge did not construct distinctions; it received distinctions. Against this background, the distinctions that determined the conception of art were quite different from the ones we use today.[11] They were determined above all by the guiding distinction between the visible and the invisible and by efforts, inspired by this distinction, to mediate symbolically between the two. Since beauty was considered a property of being or even of matter, all symbolic mediations partook of being; they were made of the same stuff as the Creation rather than signifying something radically other.

This is why a concept such as imitation (which played no central role at all) could move about through creation naively and without bias. This situation did not change until the beginning of early modernity, although a notion of imitation persisted for quite some time. An independent motive for this change might have been the discovery of antique models, by means of which art began to refer to itself. Without referring to the living present and to the infinite distance of God—that is, without religious symbolization—one could now presume *that perfection had earlier existed in this world.* This notion offered the prospect of recapturing perfection solely through artistic means. There was no need to criticize religion; it sufficed to improve one's own work. The contrast *antiqui/moderni* served as the guiding distinction in this regard, and emphasis could vary *within this distinction.*[12] This transition shifted the focus onto the *individual* that brought it about, while stimulating a *critical* discussion that evaluated this transition, initially on the basis of Aristotle's *Poetics.*[13] In retrospect, we can appreciate these trends as first attempts toward a self-description of the art system.

The discussion proceeded initially from premises inherited from antiquity, such as the notion *mimesis/imitatio.* One naively assumed that the object of imitation was already an image that could be perceived. At the same time, this concept signaled a distance from the artistic accomplishments of the original images. Gradually, however, and for different reasons, the notion of constant essential forms became problematic to the extent that the social authority responsible for their interpretation began to crumble. New forms of differentiation undermined former reference points—especially stratification, but also the differentiation between city and country.[14] To be sure, these forms of life continued to persist, and small portions of the population were marked as aristocratic or as living in cities. But for the evolution of the social system, new system formations became more vital: the legal system, the territorial state, the monetary economy, a religion that retreated to orthodoxy, and, last but not least, a science oriented toward provocative experiments and an artificial mathematics. The incipient functional differentiation of the social system created, as if from the outside, a new situation to which the self-description of the art system must respond from a position of *autonomy.*

Correlation between the functional differentiation of the social system, the operative closure and autopoietic autonomy of functional systems that follow from it, and the resulting need for reflection can be traced and concretized at various levels. A strong argument for such a correlation can be made by showing that similar internal reflection theories developed not only in the art system but in other functional systems as well, beginning in the sixteenth and seventeenth centuries and culminating in the eighteenth century. Whereas differentiation has always existed at the level of types of interaction or roles, only the differentiation of functional systems enforced the renunciation of an externally determined identity—of a cosmological-religious nature, for example. It thus created a vacuum that could be filled only by self-descriptions of the respective systems. This qualified self-description as a phenomenon bound to a particular form of social differentiation,[15] rather than a matter of perfecting one's knowledge of things themselves. Yet we are not dealing simply with an arbitrary sequence of "discourses." We refrain at this point from returning to these general social-theoretical arguments.[16]

By 1600 at the latest, one can state explicitly that a special kind of knowledge was required in the realms of painting, sculpture, and architecture—a knowledge that philosophers and theologians were unable to supply.[17] The learned scholastic terminology now seemed useless and gratuitous. The *ars/scientia* debate,[18] which had preoccupied the late Middle Ages, subsided; the reflection of artistic activity now supplied enough material of its own. One resorted to treatises that contained working instructions for artists. For this type of knowledge one still claimed truth. Delight in formulas, especially deliberately obscure ones, did not develop until the seventeenth century. In the sixteenth and seventeenth centuries, the literature about art was not concerned with an overarching system of art, but focused instead on painting and poetry. Apart from technical instructions, it was concerned with evaluating stylistic decisions (for example, by taking a position for or against clearly isolated figures in the critical discussion of mannerism). In this form, the literature on art influenced artistic production in ways that were difficult to evaluate without reference to the system of patronage supplied by the church and the courts; in other words, the influence of the literature on art manifested itself only in its indirect effects.[19]

Another consideration is the question of which *other* specialized functional systems gain significance for the differentiation and self-description of a particular functional system—whether a system relies on the possibility for external support or requires distinction and separation. Rudolf Stichweh has investigated in great historical detail how the university system (the ultimate level of the educational system) gained independence by giving up its reliance on religion and orienting itself toward the early modern territorial state.[20] This analysis is easily supplemented by considering the next impetus toward independence, which became possible in the nineteenth century when the educational system focused its primary orientation on science (on the "unity of research and teaching").[21] Presumably, art gained a similar degree of freedom when it gave up religious patronage and began to rely on the courts[22] and eventually on the emerging art market.[23] Several systems then profited from the same operations and their results, but each system interpreted these operations differently and in the context of different recursive networks, that is, without adversely affecting the operative closure of other participating systems.[24] The effects of symbiotic relationships of this sort on the self-descriptions of systems were mostly negative and restrictive, however. One doesn't bite the hand of one's host, at least not during dinner. This is why the distance that art eventually established from its sponsors did not manifest itself in an offensive way; instead, art emphasized its own accomplishments and its independence with regard to the invention of forms while respecting the sponsor's thematic interests. This situation did not necessarily give rise to a new theory of art or to a self-description of the art system that would be directed explicitly against the environment.

We therefore suspect that a different kind of system-to-system relationship affected the self-description of art much more strongly—indeed, inaugurated this description in the true sense of the word—at a time when the incompatibility of functional systems became apparent. In the early fifteenth century, a new humanistic and scientific understanding of art (based on geometry, perspective, anatomy) freed itself from church supervision. Artists began to rely on their own reason and on their personal access to the world. They claimed a social status that superseded mere craftsmanship.[25] This process of separation initially required that art and the knowledge of nature and human affairs in the widest sense form a unity. In the sixteenth century, knowledge was still as interested in technology and in the explanation of ordinary experience as it was in phenomena that were strange, miraculous, unusual, or astonishing. The former were useful for life, the latter satisfied curiosity and the need for entertainment. Both came together in the double sense of Latin *recreatio*. As late as the sixteenth century, one can still insist that an order striving toward unity was to be valued positively and mere *multitudo* negatively.[26] In the tendency toward unity, everything ultimately leads to God. The representations of art, too, partook of this cosmological evaluation, for which one furnished examples from the world of objects, from the animal kingdom, and from the realm of human life. Beauty was a kind of reflex of an order that strove toward unity; it expressed a preference for unity by order itself.[27] By no means was beauty a criterion that helped differentiate a distinct world of art. But precisely this cultural climate, this insistence on unity, indicated a divergence of heterogeneous tendencies and interests. This was due primarily to dramatic changes and to a wealth of innovations in areas one would classify today as the beginnings of modern science. Cosmology altered its notion of the unity of the world, especially in Italy, abandoning the assumption of an effective unifying principle (read off the paradigm of the soul) and adopting the notion of a dynamic processing of differences for which laws (possibly mathematical ones) must be discovered—all of which boiled down to an empirically and mathematically oriented type of research.[28]

As early as the sixteenth century, the interpretation of art ran into difficulties because it could not keep up with trends that would, in the seventeenth century, aim to consolidate an empirico-rational, experimentally and mathematically oriented system of science.[29] At that time, the need to distance oneself from a truth-oriented science constituted the front on which the early modern understanding of art—primarily of poetry—crystallized. Contemporaries must have been impressed by this move, since previous centuries—the epoch of Alberti, Dürer, Leonardo da Vinci, Palladio, and Cardano—had emphasized the unity of scientific knowledge and an art that strove for beauty.[30] Among the factors that inspired this emphasis was the idea of an *ars magna et ultima*, which could be traced to Ramon Lull and prevailed until the late sixteenth century. Around the mid-sixteenth century, art, including painting, sculpture, and architecture, was still a topic in scientific treatises by famous scholars;[31] a rigorous notion of truth restricted to factual knowledge did not take hold until the seventeenth century. Truth was still bound by expectations of a proper interpretation of the world, which included not only explanations of fact but also fictive representations and, of course, normative validity claims. Only against this common background does the dispute about the truth claims of poetry become intelligible. This dispute staked out the boundaries that would eventually separate demonstrable knowledge from beautiful appearance.

For a long time, poetry continued to exploit a numeric mysticism that suggested harmony.[32] It could do so without effort, since it could emphasize numerical relationships through meter and direct naming. Around the mid-sixteenth century, painting began to resist the scientism of the

Florentine doctrine of proportion,[33] which treated art solely as a mirror of nature. Along with the emphasis on proportion, this doctrine declared redundancy to be the essence of things and reduced variety to an accidental property. One could almost speak of a protest by painters against an attitude that did not differentiate between painting and architecture. Their concerns focused on a more appropriate access to the unique possibilities of painting. Painting was more than mere imitation. "La Pittura è propria poesia, cioè invenzione, la qual fa apparere quello que non è."[34] Eventually, architectural doctrine, too, turned away from the notion of mystical-mathematical harmony and toward more practical purposes. In the wake of Alberti, the doctrine of mathematical proportion—which imitated the hidden harmony of the universe in the form of numerical relationships—culminated in Luca Pacioli's treatise *De divina proportione* (1577).[35] But Pacioli's treatise offers almost no practical directives for applying this doctrine in the construction of buildings. Carlo Borromeo's treatise on the construction of cathedrals (1577) rejects the Platonic, geometrical architecture of centralized construction in favor of a cross construction, which is better suited for liturgical purposes anyway. In addition, one emphasized practical interests. In writing about cloisters, for example, Borromeo elaborates on portions of buildings that existed merely for utility: the lodgings of servants, lavatories, latrines, and prisons.[36] In the wake of the Counter Reformation, religion retreated into itself. Another point of departure for the separation of art was the debate, inherited from antiquity, about the meaning of poetry, which was provoked by the dissociation of poetry from religio-cultic and gentle contexts.[37] The possibility of writing provided a motive for observing the activity of poets and singers "philosophically," that is, in view of their truth content. The effect was twofold: on the one hand, poets complained about being treated poorly by society and bemoaned the lack of recognition of their merits (reading made them aware of their situation).[38] On the other hand, they were criticized by society as useless, if not harmful, in view of the assumption that it was now possible to publish and read up on the truth. The controversies about the proper form of (noble) education raised the issue of whether fictions or stories, even if they were true, could contribute to education.[39] The pessimism of Christianity and the rediscovery of classical skepticism provided the sixteenth century with a new basis for such doubts. Especially in England, one began to emphasize practical utility, and the polemic against poetry and the theater could appeal in an ambiguous way either to the salvation of the soul or to a secular prosperity; in both cases, poetry and performance could be judged to be only a distraction from what really mattered.[40] In the worldview of the Puritans and other religious groups, but also in circles that oriented themselves economically toward the market, there was no place for a function of fictionality.

Moreover, the need to distinguish science from art became more urgent to the extent that art, or the *artes* in general, became incapable of thinking of themselves in terms of a reworking or a recapitulation of classical artistic skill. The unique accomplishments of painting and sculpture—the kind considered modern at the time—began to stand out in comparison with an antiquity that had become increasingly familiar and saturated with interpretation. Mannerism turned deviation into a program. One used one's knowledge of perspective for the deformation of forms. This knowledge, as the saying goes, was applied in paradoxical ways, raising the issue of criteria. As usual, however, the issue of criteria remained secondary in relation to the question of what could function as a binary code whose values could be assigned according to those criteria. At first, traditional models continued to determine the discussion and forced the artistic striving for independence into an unfavorable position. Knowledge remained focused on truth versus untruth, and for ontology or, later, the purposes of actions, the issue was being versus appearance. As long as this was so, art was forced to position itself on the side of untruth and appearance and to affirm this position, if it was to distinguish itself from a knowledge that conformed to reality. Art had to assert itself against the complex alliance of religion, knowledge, and utility.

Thanks to a number of chance events that affected the tradition, this turned out to be easier than it seemed at first. In the discussion about the relationship between (and the pedagogical value of) historical knowledge (*historia*) and poetry (*poesia*), history was at a disadvantage because it was considered to be a collection of real but accidental events.[41] Even though the events might have happened exactly as they were told, this process was obscured by a reality that remained erratic.[42] Poetry, on the other hand, could represent ideal forms—forms that did not exist in the ordinary sense, but defined the goal toward which being strives nonetheless. History only narrated facts that depended on chance, whereas poetry "reduces the thing to the species and to universal nature."[43] In poetry, not only historical details but also fictional supplements were considered accidental; only the latter, however, were needed to represent the essential. The doctrine of *vanitas mundi* could serve as a means of religious justification, which allowed art to distance itself from worldly excess and from pretentious truth claims, even in situations in which art accentuated its own skill (as, for example, in Holbein). Such an attitude could also be symbolized in the form of paradox (for example, by the presence of a skull).

By contrast, religion, which claimed to represent the real world, blamed poetry for taking things too lightly. Moreover, the ancient doctrine still held that only a fraction of knowledge was given in the form of absolutely certain truths (*epistēme*), whereas in many other respects, one had to be content with doctrinal tradition (*doxa*) or with efforts to represent the probable or a "semblance of truth" (*verisimilitudo*), which might also be represented in art, especially in art. The ambivalence of "verisimilitude" glossed over the fact that the distinction between truth and falsity did not matter the least in art, nor was there a need to admit that this was so. Within a clerical context, probabilistic thinking provided an indispensable assistance to knowledge. (Of course, a mathematically founded theory of probability was not yet available; besides, art had no reason to adopt such a theory.) Poetry began to search for its own synthesis of truth and falsity by distancing itself from the specific truth code of science. "The fable . . . is not only false but false and true together; false as to history, true as to its semblance to the truth."[44] Theory could present this notion as an interpretation of Aristotle's text, which left the relationship between truth and astonishment in suspense.

In the context of searching for a code and for artistic criteria, one can easily maintain that art establishes a kingdom of its own in the realm of an artificial-artistic semblance, which seeks to compete neither with the abstractions of mathematics nor with the pedantry of factual knowledge, but rather develops internal criteria of success for its own representations and ought to be allowed to search for ways of affecting its audience. Art, in particular poetry, conceals political allusions behind the notion that art is an activity of *poiesis* which "makes" its own works.[45] In so doing, art can appeal to its own, in the meantime well-established reputation and point to works that are generally considered significant.

When insisting on the rights of beautiful appearance, one means more than just deception.[46] The point is not simply to deceive, but to break apart a simple, bivalent ontology and to reinvent the place of mankind within the cosmos. This requires more complex distinctions, that is, distinctions of distinctions. In the theater, this double framing is fairly straightforward: the spectator is supposed to know that what he perceives on stage is "only" a play, and that within this play, deception—of the self and others—simulates worlds within a simulated world. In narratives, this difference is less evident. Narratives might be presented as fictive from the start and subsequently repeat the fiction within the fiction, as in *Don Quixote*. Or the author might attempt to cancel the distinction between fact and fiction, for example, by feigning (or not feigning?) the presentation of "discovered letters."[47]

An awareness of frames, as well as a sense for their confusion, spread in a variety of ways. This situation enforced the tendency to think of truth and beauty as opposites against a background of social conduct (social situation). Truth concerned being in itself; beauty concerned being for others. To be sure, poetry needed to be defended to the extent that it forsook truth and focused on beautiful appearance. Poetry no longer presented a deficient mirror of reality, nor was it concerned with improving that mirror; on the contrary, what mattered was an appearance that was intentional. When science—in the wake of Copernicus and Galileo, assisted by the telescope and mathematics—set out to explore realities that seemed at first implausible, rhetoric, in alliance with poetry, conceived its task to be finding lasting forms for astonishment and wit. Starting with Vasari, one spoke of *arti del disegno*.[48] In so doing, one elevated oneself beyond mere craftsmanship while being aware of one's historically secure ground. Baltasar Gracián succeeded in formulating this notion as a principle and combining it with wisdom and politics.[49] In a world without certainties, truth accomplished little unless it was concealed.[50] The main issues for Gracián were self-confidence, the ability to assert himself, and social success. Everything occurred in a sphere of self-produced appearance, anyhow. The question of what the world was really like remained unanswered. This was why language, in order to be adequate, had to be obscure, ambiguous, playful, paradoxical, and, in this sense, witty. The genuine achievement of such a language was "to speak where one is not."[51] If one adopts Hegel's notion of Being as being for others (as opposed to Being in and for itself), one immediately recognizes that the enforcement of beautiful appearance hangs together with a subjective individualism that emerges at the same time and provides an opportunity to undermine all previously accepted distinctions. Instead of relying on such distinctions, one now had to construct and defend positions.

Art had greater obligations to social life, and it was much closer to life in an effective, technical sense than a plain and unadorned knowledge. Art alone was formulated in a manner adequate to the world's social intricacies. It did not function as a sign for something other, but instead impressed itself upon its audience. The technological potential of science had not yet come into view; it remained outside the *social* interests of the (Jesuit) order or the Spanish political system. Yet subjectivity developed early in Spain, where it confronted an almost cosmological alliance between politics and religion.[52] In such circumstances, beautiful appearance might have been plausible as a formula for compromise. To it, Gracián adds a shift in emphasis from truth to effect and thus from being to time.

Filling out the negative side of the truth code—untruth and appearance—highlighted both the skills and the difficulties involved in a task that is not exactly favored by Being. Unlike in the Middle Ages, one now demanded that the conception of the artwork be the artist's own. Formerly, works of art were considered works of a client who made use of skilled labor to carry out his plans. Now the artist was considered the author of the work—at first perhaps only for masterworks, but eventually for any work that claimed to be art, whereas clients and observers were expected to contribute only expertise and critical judgment. Such demands were expressed in the notion of *concetto*. In addition, intense efforts and wit (*Witz*) were necessary to produce art. In the Italian literature dominant at the time, one spoke of *acutezza*.[53] The British were praising "cunning" as a quality of superb artists.[54] The thoroughgoing duality of description (*acutezza/concetto, agudeza/concepto, cunning/conceit*) was striking. It implied that life and erudition must coincide. A skill of this sort rendered itself—that is, the illusion—transparent as a deliberately created *surprise*. The *concetto* underlying the illusion was displayed along with it; indeed, the *concetto* was what ultimately mattered. This was how John Donne dragged paradox out into the open—a paradox hidden[55] behind abstract concepts of species and genre in the controversy between realists and nominalists, in Ramism, and in a Platonism that was once again perceived as modern. But Donne did not expect anyone to believe in such deceptions.[56] The point was to reveal the deception, which now included the argumentative mode of theologians and philosophers. Unlike in traditional rhetoric, to which early modern art owed its awareness of tricks, the recipient of the message was not supposed to be deluded or remain in the dark. Rather, he was exposed to a shock, which rendered the deception transparent and elicited *admiration* (*admiratio*). The meaning of *admiratio* shifted toward irritation. In order to accomplish this goal, art had to know its audience, which soon gave rise to a discussion about whether art was meant for the common people or for connoisseurs.[57]

Did the *concetto* draw its force of conviction from erudition? The humanism of the Renaissance tempts us to believe all too quickly that this was so. Several authors expressed themselves in ways that support this claim—and they seemed to be aware that expertise and a knowledge of literature did not depend on social origin.[58] Dryden still spoke positively of "learned plagiary" (with reference to Ben Jonson).[59] However, tolerating the idiosyncrasies of "witty" allusions did not justify sacrificing redundancies embedded in the foundations of knowledge shared by all of Europe. Moreover, we must keep in mind that art depended on patronage and, hence, on contracts. Thematic models were frequently tied to specific expectations, especially in the iconography of the visual arts. If the artist possessed the necessary education (which became possible only in the wake of print), he could balance thematic faithfulness and artistic freedom in ways that avoided potential conflicts with the client.[60] In the second half of the sixteenth century, these ties began to crumble, a trend that seemed to be supported by the fact that the artist took responsibility for his own *concetto*, turning it into a flash of wit. Against every stylistic rule of traditional rhetoric, one "conceived" the improbability of forms, the lack of resemblance, exaggeration, artificiality, skill, and the confusion of signs. Moreover, the notion of *concetto* implied that the flash of wit had no effect of its own accord. "Ogni concetto," writes Pellegrini, "e sempre necessariamente sommistrato dall occorso di qualqu'altro concetto."[61] *Concetti* mutually supported and encouraged one another. They pointed to one another within a recursive network of implicit and explicit references, which served as a precondition for the observation of astonishing and striking appearances. And where an early humanistic erudition still claimed truth to be the entire realm of its awareness, one looked for another kind of fascination within the mutually supporting network of *concetti*, namely, for an intellectual force that convinced by deviating from the familiar.

The notion of *concettismo* renders imitation (*mimesis*) problematic, without overcoming it right away. A contemporary text, written entirely in the spirit of *concettismo*,[62] states that art supplements nature with a second being, elevating it to a state of supremely beautiful perfection. But how could one know such perfection if not through nature? Consequently, the concept of nature dissolved into a multiplicity of meanings—depending on what one wanted to get out of it.[63] The notion of *imitatio* has a long history, which must be taken into account if one wants to understand why imitation prevailed for so long. The beginnings of the concept in Plato suggest an act of liberation—a liberation from the idea that the invisible resides within the (cult) image. The notion of "residing in," which always carries religious connotations, was replaced by a notion of relation, which was subsequently burdened with the entire legacy of religion, and which remained in need of interpretation.[64] *Imitatio* amounts to a liberation from the "simulacra" of the old world, and this is what earned the support of a theologically inspired religion—until it was taken entirely for granted and there was no further need to insist on it.

This tradition still assumed that things themselves preserved a memory of their origin and communicated this meaning to those who perceived them. But this notion conflicted with another assumption running parallel to the former, namely, that the artist himself was the origin of the artwork and that works of art preserved the memory of the artist. In Plato, this contradiction results in a devaluation of art. With the revalorization of art in early modernity, this solution became unacceptable. The demand that artworks had to be original shifted the emphasis entirely onto the (inexplicable) genius of the artist. A process of erosion began to affect all former ties and eventually called into question the notion of imitation itself.

If we base this conceptual history on an analytical scheme that transcends it, then we realize that the concept of *imitatio* combines two components: one of resemblance (to what?), and one of repeatability (redundancy). In one way or another, a sufficient degree of recognizability must be secured; the concept of *imitatio* accomplishes this by referring to an already existing knowledge of the world. The assumption is that redundancy can be guaranteed by resemblance. After all, it is possible that, within this combination, the accent shifts away from resemblance and toward redundancy, especially when the reference of the demand for resemblance becomes increasingly unclear—resemblance can refer to clerical tradition, to reality or to the ideas behind reality, to Being or to appearance, to what exists or to what does not exist but could exist or ought to exist. So long as repeatability is guaranteed, one can grant more room to nonresemblance. What matters, eventually, is nothing more than the repeatability of observation, and this is guaranteed only by the manner in which the artwork is executed.

Long before the final break with imitation, one began to focus on artistic skill. To the extent one becomes concerned with know-how (in the widest technical sense), the notion of art as *imitatio* loses its power to convince. With music, one was forced to relinquish the idea of cosmic imitation for the simple reason that the idea of the cosmos as a harmony of proportions and numerical relationships began to wane.[65] To Sir Philip Sidney, for example, imitation in poetry could still mean imitation of the divine inspiration of what could or ought to be.[66] At the same time, deliberate deviations from the familiar became possible; they were sought out, legitimized, and made conspicuous. According to Aristotle, poetry must also stimulate astonishment.[67] Poetry compares itself to painting and vice versa.[68] The treatises on imitation typically contain contradictory statements.[69] Imitation is too easy and *therefore* no longer deserves admiration; only a more demanding kind of imitation that strives to create an illusion can assert itself as art.[70] Instead of *imitatio* one emphasized *inventio*,[71] which no longer meant discovery but invention. By imitation, art elicits astonishment and calls attention to itself. (Familiar and recognizable objects appear in an unfamiliar context.) Once art is fully differentiated, getting attention becomes *its own* affair. On the basis of the old doctrine of the art of painting,[72] Roger de Piles mentions evaluative criteria of a quite different sort, by which the artist can refer more precisely to his artistic means. "Attracting the spectators" with a successful imitation is henceforth only the gain, the reward of the effort.[73] The same venerable doctrine requires that the means by which art accomplishes its effects remain hidden, that *knowledge and know-how (and accordingly the roles of artist and observer) remain strictly separate.*[74] The function of imitation is subsequently reduced to differentiating between the observational modes of the artist and his audience; but this step does not interfere with the prevailing notion that imitation is the essence of art and the form of its truth[75]—as if the essence of art were to mediate between two different modes of observation, one pertaining to the artist, and the other to the audience.

What most restricted the meaning of imitation—apart from the necessity of displaying skill in order to receive attention—was perhaps the distinction between originality and imitation.[76] This distinction decoupled the meaning of imitation from its cosmic frame of reference and integrated it into a distinction that was valid only in art. The fate of imitation as a counterconcept to originality was sealed, despite initial attempts to salvage the old cosmological reference by distinguishing between imitation of nature and imitation of art.

Sacrificing imitation as the meaning and destiny of art must have been difficult, if not impossible, so long as cosmology still assumed an origin or creation of the world that coexisted with the present in the form of a descent. Creation accounted for the possibility of art and, at the same time, art was bound to the creation.[77] Under these conditions, knowledge, too, had to be understood as an imitation of originally fixed determinations, for example, as a Platonic recollection of ideas.[78] Poetry was the younger sister of knowledge, so to speak, a sister who was brought up more liberally. Both knowledge and art are "pleasing" to mankind because they represent the origin and the essence of things. Kant, in his *Third Critique*, no longer thinks of this correlation as an imitation of products but in terms of a parallel action, an analogy.[79] Kant's contemporaries substituted the subjective endowment of meaning for imitation.[80] Art and nature were decoupled, even though it was difficult to think of the subject without the correlate of a world. One no longer assumed a common origin of subject and world, and yet the origin of artistic skill was still understood to be nature, as genius.

In romanticism, for the first time accounts of the function of art were fully separated from the idea of imitation.[81] To be sure, the word *imitation* was retained. It reemerged repeatedly in the nineteenth century, but it sounded hollow once it was reduced to the function of emphasizing the fact that art operates in the world in a nonarbitrary manner. Imitation was now primarily understood as selection, and selection was understood to be an intensification, which permitted art to "imitate" the opposite of what it found in the real world.[82] The competition with truth became obsolete, and the expulsion of artists from the republic was no longer worth any serious discussion. One spoke of a culture state [*Kulturstaat*]. Only traces remained of the old concern about the exclusive rights of poetry.[83] The problem now was how to fill the empty space of its autonomy.

In the sixteenth and seventeenth centuries, the form in which art displayed its accomplishments was called *disegno*. *Disegno* replaced the scholastic notion of *intentio*,[84] substituting for the immanent teleology of action a concept that clearly distinguished between internal conception and external execution while subsuming both aspects under the same concept.

Disegno, or "drawing" as it was later called, is one of the most interesting notions of the tradition, because it cannot be grasped in ontological terms. According to Leonardo da Vinci, the boundary of an object, just like the boundary between past and future, amounts to nothing.[85] The boundary is neither internal nor external to the object. *Disegno* is the rupture of a continuum; it explodes the world with the consequence that, henceforth, there is one side. It is nothing one can draw from nature.[86] As more value was placed on artistic activity, *disegno* was thought of as artists' *know-how* and was supplemented by other notions. This inevitably raised the issue of criteria for good or inferior *disegno* and opened up an arena for debate and historical development. In and of itself, *disegno* was nothing more than a special case of Spencer Brown's injunction: "draw a distinction." At the same time, it involved more than simply following this injunction "somehow." Ontological nothingness had to be transformed into demonstrable skill that required criteria. Only then did it open up a space in which art could establish itself as a recursive system that creates its own determinations and stands in for itself.

This step established a worldview characteristic of other functional systems as well, a worldview that combined universalization and specification. From the perspective of art, *everything* was *disegno*. The notion was fully backed by theology—after all, God himself created the world on the basis of a *disegno*.[87] Philosophy, the sciences, the art of government, even theology, all had to rest on an underlying *disegno* if they wanted to be effective in the world.[88] The theory of art, however, treated only a partial view of the designed world, namely, the *artes* in the usual sense, the "disegno humano pratico."[89] This concept included everything—and excluded almost everything—because it was specifically tailored to art. It was capable of formulating high demands, which, however, could no longer be decided upon by vote.

As never before, this first wave of reflection on art brought home the point that visibility depends on drawing a boundary against the invisible. In assuming form, art includes what it excludes. Deception deserves admiration as deception, as *arteficium*. The mere fact that deception is possible says something about the world. In this regard, the artistic focus on deception paralleled a simultaneous scientific interest in hallucinations—but rather than aim at a reality behind deception (after all, this was the age of a revived skepticism), art sought to make transparent the worldly fact of deception. The *machina mundi* was copied as *machinatio*. The orientation toward species and genres was reduced to the absurd *as such*. By proclaiming and demonstrating such positions, art asserted—*itself*. This was what the self-description of art had to put into words.

Once the stakes of art were defined in terms of *acutezza*—which deserved admiration for its own sake—one discovered what remained invisible on the observer's side—the inscrutability of genius, the *no so che* or *je ne sais quoi*, which, in the seventeenth century, soon degenerated into a cliché.[90] Art taught how to observe oneself as an observer, and self-observation hit upon the unfathomable. Art demanded a type of admiration that could not fully explain or account for itself. Ambivalent emotional references (admiration, astonishment, terror, pity) entered into the classical topic of *thaumastōn/admiratio*,[91] which, in Descartes, took on the meaning of "deviation, novelty" and eventually came very close to what today one might call *irritation*.[92] This ambivalence concerned observation itself rather than its motives and interests, and it was closely related to the fact that one could analyze existing works according to their manner of presentation (*maniera*) without having the slightest idea of how novelty came about *as novelty* and why only the new could *please*. What remained unaccounted for was not the object itself, but the operation that brought it about. The invisible observer announced himself in the description of his product. At this point, the notion of good (cultivated) taste launched its career.[93]

The seventeenth century invited art (especially poetry, narrative, and the theater) to do what science could *never* dream of, namely, to undermine the distinction between being and nonbeing, or between being and appearance. This is evident in John Donne, in Cervantes, and in Shakespeare, to mention examples pertaining to each one of the above-mentioned genres. The unity of the distinction henceforth appeared only as paradox.[94] Rhetoric had been cultivating the art of paradox for quite some time, thus making paradox available as a means of irritation. Art drew on this familiar practice, but it used paradox in less arbitrary ways, not just for the sake of displaying the art of paradox as an effective skill.[95] To be sure, art played with paradox—for example, by exploiting the linguistic feature of using "nihil," "nothing," "nobody," and so forth as a grammatical subject, as something active, capable of being indicated and determined. The artistic interest in paradox aimed beyond mere trickery toward establishing a terrain on which science could not operate, yet nonetheless yielded insights—a terrain where fatal deception (of the self and others) reigns, where love or a sincerity that comes across as naïveté prevails, or, more generally, where the world presents itself as appearance, devoid of stability and without essences.

Thus art came to emphasize its own obscurity, novelty, and paradox. *Disegno* became blurred; its extension into the invisible, unworked realm of the imaginary space of art could only be guessed at. But what can one hold onto there, except the work of art itself? The illusion it creates predisposes art to serve courtly entertainments and to supply courts with material— for example, in the form of the transparent nonrealism of novels in the style of *Amadis*. Art brought cunning, deceit, and illusion onto the stage, and in this way it copied into itself what it practiced. In the same vein, one expected the hero, since he performed admirable deeds on stage and was admired within its reality, also to be admired by the spectator, even though the audience experienced the stage as an illusory world and its situations as out of the ordinary. *Admiratio* was generated as its own means.[96] The difference between being and appearance, between everyday life and the extraordinary was replicated within the world of appearance. To invoke Spencer Brown once again, the distinction "reenters" the distinguished, a solution to the problem that logic had to accept or, at any rate, could not surpass logic. The observer has no way of knowing how he observes; this insight was at once brought home to him and kept from him.

Art thus established itself on one side of the distinction Being/Appearance or Truth/Beauty and left the other side to science. Both systems codified their sides as true/false or as beautiful/ugly, but the prior distinction was therewith forgotten or treated as a thematic premise for scientific research or artistic representation. In the domain of art, the fiction of the distinction between fiction and reality was not recognized. This primary fiction functioned, rather, as an unapproachable law, a transcendental condition, an unconscious realm in which there was no distinction between fiction and reality, no doubling of reality.[97] In brief, it functioned as paradox.

Beautiful appearance had to legitimize itself against religion and science. But this necessity entailed the opportunity to adapt the relationship between art and politics to changing conditions. After the invention of print, politics was practiced not only in the form of courtly service but also by publishing one's opinions for an anonymous audience in anticipation of a public (political, according to contemporary understanding) effect.[98] We think of such authors as Erasmus, Sir Thomas More, Seyssel, and Quevedo or, more generally, of the use of ambivalent stylistic means and of fictional (difficult to "censor") representations of political views. The topos of the world as a stage made room for inventions in artistic form, while easing the relationship between art and politics. This might explain the sudden transition to modern forms of theater in the second half of the sixteenth century.[99]

The sharp differentiation of truth and beauty (science and art) should not lead one to expect that the old unity of the good and the beautiful (of *honestum et decorum*, morality and art) would be given up as well. Until the sentimental turn in the theory of morality toward the end of the seventeenth century, we can observe distinct parallel developments in the science of social behavior (morals, *science de mœurs*) and aesthetics, *both* of which shared a distance from modern science *and* an interest in beautiful appearance. The smoothing of social relationships required retaining, indeed revalorizing, the rhetorical tradition against the background of questionable and inscrutable religious meanings, in which one continued nonetheless to believe. In antiquity, ethics, unlike art, was expected to apply the guiding distinction virtue/vice to its own procedures.[100] This distinction increasingly lost importance. The production of beautiful appearance was now treated as the production of a work to be judged only from the perspective of its result.

The decisive difference that impelled art toward autonomy appears to have been the difference between art and the rationalism of the new sciences. Religion tolerated this differentiation of art and science, though it had also to accept the differentiation of both domains from itself. Around the mid-seventeenth century, a specifically political aesthetic differentiated itself in the form of the courtly ceremony, which, for roughly one hundred years, made it possible to stage the political reputation of those in power at a sensuous-aesthetic level[101]—and to free the general development of the self-description of the art system for further differentiation. Ceremony was the cornerstone of an order of representation, to which belonged not only bodies and stylized gestures but also gardens, buildings, city planning, theater performances (as microtheater within the macrotheater), historical and poetic texts, as well as other things. These objects functioned as a kind of circle of references, designed to hold together widely distributed codings and structural asymmetries, including those of politics, in the form of a thoroughly planned order of signs. Ceremony in this sense was not a sacred ritual; it was not taken for granted as a proven tradition.[102] Rather, one now distinguished between religious and secular ceremony.[103] Ceremony still tolerated the liberties of an ingenious artistic variation, precisely the kind of liberties which the art system now claimed as its own terrain. Ceremony was presented with an awareness of its artificiality and of its regional differences, and this was why one needed a special science of ceremony.[104] The self-understanding of art, however, was no longer affected by this perishing hybrid. What would later be called "aesthetics" continued to be guided by distinctions within "higher" forms of cognition. Kant still felt the need to emphasize the distinction between ideas of reason and aesthetic ideas, which absolves him from saying any more about aesthetic ideas than that they are representations of the imagination produced without concepts.[105]

No matter what subsequent conceptual efforts accomplished, in view of such an opposition, the self-description of art was forced to abide at the level of nonformulations in the manner of *je ne sais quoi*. This must have felt like a thorn in the side at a time that was preparing for a new rationalism keen on distinctions and for "enlightenment"—at a time, in other words, when individuals were no longer disciplined by class hierarchy, but instead by the supposition that they act rationally.

III

In seventeenth-century theoretical discussions of art, the dimension of time gained significance to the extent that guiding perspectives became more irrational and de-ontologized. On the one hand, this shift in emphasis gave rise to a discussion of rank—whether ancient art was superior to modern art or vice versa. On the other hand, one demanded—as if the matter had already been settled—that art present an original creation, that it be new and astonishing in a pleasing manner.

Regarding technical matters of composition, artistic production remained bound to experience, to what one could learn in workshops and from models that one might occasionally ignore. The semantics of self-description glossed over such matters; it changed more rapidly and called attention to styles and stylistic changes so as to affect the art system. In order to organize and regulate the mediating role of self-description (we think of Colbert), one established academies that cultivated education and communication about art. Temporal schemata such as old/new, original/copy were stabilized and eventually taken for granted.

In the wake of the invention of the printing press, one copied continuously, emphatically welcoming the opportunity to do so. In view of this trend, the simultaneous devaluation of the concept of *copia* was astonishing, especially since in the rhetorical tradition the concept carried the positive connotation of mastery over a great number of occasionally applicable figures and commonplaces (*topoi*). Apparently, the shift in the meaning of *copia* was related to the revalorization of novelty within the dimension of time.[106] The value of novelty stood in an orthogonal relation to the trend that facilitated the distribution of art, which was also received with enthusiasm and from which novelty, for its part, could benefit. One found oneself in the midst of a new era, in which new ideas were communicated faster and spread among a much larger audience.

There is no need to elaborate on the details of this discussion. We will restrict ourselves to a few points that become significant in the transition to the eighteenth century, particularly in the realm of art.

The criteria of novelty and originality asserted and strengthened the differentiation of the art system, especially in relation to the systems of religion and politics, which, during the seventeenth century, remained rather hostile toward innovation, because they feared potential "unrest." Science and education, however, distinguished themselves from art as well. These systems were interested in proliferating new ideas in a different manner, since their capacity for innovation depended on providing the greatest possible number of people with an opportunity to learn quickly about the new trends to which they had to adapt. In these disciplines, copying was the very condition for the increasing probability of innovation. This was different in art, where emphasis was on the originality of individual works.

In connection with these changes, the meaning of the miraculous, of the extraordinary and unusual, of *meraviglia* shifted as well: it was no longer considered a thematic quality of art but referred instead to the accomplishment of the artist. The classical discussion of the role of astonishment, which dates back to Aristotle, came to a close and was transformed into a debate about criteria for evaluating artistic accomplishments. The issue was no longer one of claiming license for extravagant moves in relation to cosmic events; rather, it turned more or less on the question of how an artist could maintain control over variety and bring it to bear on the unity of the work. The miraculous and the new merged with what one expected from art in terms of the originality and the difficulty of its task.

In addition, the temporalization of requirements within the art system affected the possibility of fixing objective criteria of beauty and for doing justice to such criteria in evaluating works of art. For the next one hundred years, one argued about "taste" and expected from this concept an answer to these new uncertainties. From a sociostructural perspective, this turn was related to the fact that the upper classes had lost the certainty of their judgments and now had to demonstrate expertise or at least pretend to do so—in Italy, this situation was a consequence of frequent turnovers in the papacy along with their favorites and clans; in France, it occurred as a result of a court centralism that enforced fashion, and in England it resulted from the upheavals of a long civil war. *Origo* no longer indicated the eternal presence of the origin or the aftereffects of descent. Originality now testified to the unexpected and inexplicable emergence of the new. Things lost their memory, so to speak. Their primary function was no longer to remind the beholder of their own nature or their creator. Now, objects were referred to by signs, or they were fitted out with the name of an author in order to remind the beholder of their origin in time. This happened at a level of communication outside the image or the text. Under such conditions, the artist had to create or at least stylize himself as the origin. In retrospect, he could be described as "genius." After all, originality was not a recipe that provided instructions for being original or for producing original works. Rather, we are dealing with a construct of second-order observation, which indirectly turned into a concern and a topic of art in its attempt to market itself as new and original.

The old system of connoisseurship was gradually replaced by a new system that combined a market-oriented mediation with expertise, and by a critique that had been observing this trend all along.[107] Art had to publicly assert itself both against critical judgment and against the market. In search of criteria for judgment, the eighteenth-century reflection on art clearly responded to a public interest in art and art criticism. In this context, we should mention the discussion, initiated by Jonathan Richardson in England, concerning objectivity and the recognition of the unique nature of painting.[108] In its style of argumentation, this discussion still reflected the effects of rhetoric. One praised the beautiful and the good, and presented in a negative light what one rejected. But the discussion failed to produce analyses of any depth, let alone a theoretically integrated terminology. Because of their didactic mission, the academies founded in the seventeenth century still taught familiar techniques, but one now found this literature more in France than in Italy.[109] One praised works that went against the rules to represent their subject matter in a gracious, delightful, and agreeable manner. But it was not clear, as Coypel complained, how one could derive aesthetic criteria, if art was supposed to please and everybody already knew what pleased him.[110] The emerging public sphere—made up of the noisy, inchoately expressive crowd that visited art exhibitions[111]—was not specific to any one class, and that made it difficult for the reflection on art to sort out its criteria, especially when it lacked a theoretical guiding thread. It became virtually impossible to distinguish art criticism from the mere assertion of reputation.

In retrospect, the failure to determine objective criteria is often simplified as a transition from objective to subjective (sensualist, pleasure-oriented) criteria. Upon closer inspection this view is untenable. Assuming subjective criteria without any grounding in reality makes no sense whatever. (Even Kant is forced to make concessions in this regard.) But it is true that the inside/outside *distinction* as a two-sided form became increasingly significant to the *individual* and displaced previously privileged concepts of order, both in epistemology and in aesthetics. Only against this background does the continued significance of the pleasure/disgust distinction throughout the eighteenth century become intelligible. The distinction was anchored at the internal side of the inside/outside distinction, but since it could not be controlled internally, it referred to *external* motives. The "inside" was elaborated as a counterconcept to the "outside"; it was fitted out with emotions, an imagination, and a desire for individualization; it reigned over pleasure and disgust and was subject to associations that remained to be explained by psychology—and this, in all probability, was the major reason why the idea of imitation ran into such difficulties in the course of the century and had to be either detached from the notion of objective reproduction or abandoned altogether.

Since the inside/outside distinction remained in suspense, it generated further distinctions. The eighteenth century was overdetermined by multiple distinctions—art and nature, the beautiful and the sublime, the simple and the complex, the sensuous and the spiritual, the particular and the general. These distinctions yielded a variety of different hauls from the ocean of tradition, and yet they could not satisfy the self-description of an art system that depended on new formations.[112] The available distinctions made room for semantic experiments urgently in need of theoretical consolidation. In the second half of the eighteenth century, this need was fulfilled by philosophy, which began to establish itself as an academic discipline and was in a position to take on this task. One now spoke of a "philosophy of art" (just as one speaks of a philosophy of history or a philosophy of religion) in a new way, and tried to relate the self-description of art to an object. The most important text in this regard—a text soon to be outdone by its romantic successors, is Kant's *Critique of Judgment*.[113]

In the eighteenth century, reflection on the *unity* of the art system became a problem for the first time. Until then, one spoke of a plurality of *artes* and reflection focused on specific artistic genres, especially on poetry. Concepts such as *disegno, imitatio,* or *verisimilitudo* suggested a wealth of metaphors, analogies, and connections. As we indicated in Chapter 4, however, there was no unambiguous relationship between internal and external boundaries and, hence, no art system to be reflected upon as a unity.[114] Yet the heterogeneity of art did preserve a unity, because the artist's skill was only another, practical kind of knowledge that differed from the contemplative knowledge of theory.[115] This situation did not change until the second half of the eighteenth century. Art began to distance itself not only from science but also from morality,[116] and the realm that partook of the revalorization of a genial artistic imagination became problematic as a unity. The old principle of imitation became untenable; at least, one investigated other, more appropriate alternatives to imitation. One realized that imitation established a difference toward what lay outside, that it amounted to a transgression of the system's boundary, and that it made more sense to work with internal distinctions and inquire into their unity. The goal was to demarcate a realm that pertained exclusively to art (or perhaps to a view of nature trained in art). Starting with Baumgarten, efforts of this sort were called "aesthetics."[117]

In order to appreciate this theoretical proposition, we must keep in mind that throughout the tradition, theory was distinguished, not from practice, but from a type of knowledge grounded in immediate sense impressions. A *theorōs* was someone who observed the festival as an envoy and reported to those at home, or someone who returned from Delphi with a message from the oracle. Theory was knowledge at a distance, so to speak (the kind of knowledge that envoys could bring home from other cities or countries, and to which they could testify in a credible manner[118]). Knowledge mediated by the senses, on the other hand, was a close-up kind of knowledge; it stayed within reach and made no special demands on memory and communicative credibility. One could still count on this semantic disposition when the term *aesthetics* was introduced as a name for the theory of art. At first, aesthetics did not differentiate between the beautiful in nature and in art. It merely assigned a positive cognitive value to sense perceptions directed toward the beautiful. The object of such perceptions could be either the new concept of nature or art.

Contrary to what the concept suggests, aesthetics is not a theory of sense perception—such a theory would have to be carried out as a psychology. Already in Baumgarten and more strongly after him—until Kant and beyond—conceptual efforts aimed at a theory of the *judgment* of sense perception, which paralleled similar attempts to formulate an ethics concerned with the *judgment* of moral conduct. Aesthetics picked up the thread which, during the first half of the century, had led to radical doubts about the possibility for justifying criteria, both in the realm of a publicly oriented art criticism and in the doctrine of taste. One was concerned, in other words, with linguistic procedures of justification, with issues of consensus, and with the possibility for distinguishing between high and low artistic quality, or at least with developing standards of quality. In addition, one sought to supply directives that would allow individuals to participate in a meaningful way in what was happening in art (the viewpoint of perception, by contrast, suggested that individuals should know best what they perceive). No matter which idea might have been responsible for its name, aesthetics was carried out as a theory of art within philosophical reflection, and it occupied the place of the self-description of this particular functional system.[119]

Aesthetics, in treating the relationship between nature and art—which has nothing to do with perception—found itself in a position where, after renouncing the notion of order as imitation, it was forced to take sides. One gained the impression that a change in leadership was taking place. The more the natural sciences followed the model of physics and reduced their representations of nature to mathematical equations, and the more they formulated these representations in terms of long-term processes which, like geological processes, reached back into prehistoric ages, the greater the need for "meaning." The fine arts took on the task of a self-reflection of sensibility.[120] At the same time, the *reflection* upon sensibility transcended the interiority of an exclusively private sphere and exposed it to public view. This was the reason why one could speak of *Bildung*.

Art no longer sought to imitate nature (no matter in how idealized a form). However, art had to present its own order—especially in literature—in such a way that the observer could draw inferences pertaining to his own life and to his own world of experience, whether this experience concerned the private or the public sphere. The individual turned into a subject; he became the constructor of his own history, a history with which he could identify; and the reader was offered an opportunity to try this out for himself. The force of nature was pitched against transcendental philosophy, but it resided within the subject, together with transcendental philosophy: as the experience that not everything obeys one's thoughts and one's own will.[121] The analogy between fiction and reality was reversed: one now exploited this difference in order to attribute to reality the kind of hardships one actually experienced, or one invoked it to stimulate critique, if not reform.[122] Or one pursued the seemingly opposite goal and projected onto nature experiences one derived from art and its pleasurable consumption. This held equally for the "beautiful" and the "sublime." The beautiful in art became the measure of natural beauty. Even after this transition was complete and had become familiar, it was long before art dared to expand the primacy of its self-reference to the point where hetero-reference was reduced to a play with its own, inevitable history, or with a material used exclusively *by art itself.* Eventually, Hegel would restrict aesthetics to a "philosophy of art" that excluded natural beauty[123]—a move that necessitated alternative means of externalization, for example, in the form of "Spirit."

Apart from that, once beautiful appearance had been clearly demarcated, one could again draw on science. With Locke, Berkeley, and Hume, the system of science had developed a reflection theory of its own, an early version of constructivism. Only momentary sensations and impressions counted as a source of reality. All subsequent identifications, including the identity of the observing self and its objects, were declared "fictions" or familiar "habits." It was no longer possible to justify inductive inferences with reference to the essence of things and their correspondence to innate ideas. This situation provided an opportunity for art to play its fictions off against those adopted merely by habit[124]—especially in an era in which fundamental sociostructural changes were pressing toward new semantic formations. In view of the latest philosophical reflection, it was impossible for the reader not to question his identity and his habitual forms (one already spoke of *Bildung*), neither of which were more than "inferential entities." Starting in the Enlightenment, the new reflection on art adopted the imperative to be "critical."[125] This imperative, however, no longer referred to cautious selection within a positive/negative schematism of good/bad, true/false, or success/failure, or to its rhetorical presentation. At stake here was, rather, the imperative to examine critically, and in accordance with the spirit of the eighteenth century, the ties to one's own tradition. Tradition now appeared to be an externally imposed immaturity from which one sought to liberate oneself. The reflection on art was expected to mark its distance from its own tradition; art thereby participated in society despite the autonomy of its self-image. In both society and art, the appeal to descent lost its legitimizing force. It was difficult to give up absolute criteria, even though one knew perfectly well that such criteria were incapable of settling controversies. As transcendental-theoretical or idealist formulations indicated, abandoning the search for absolute criteria appeared almost impossible. Generally, however, one tended to be guided more by the distinction between rationality and tradition and by the demands of the age. One was in a position to risk autonomy, indeed, one was compelled to do so. Once liberated from tradition, the self-grounding of rationality was seamlessly transformed into another kind of interruption of self-reference, namely, into the self-reflection of the present moment [*Jetztzeit*] and later into historical relativism.

Another transformation, which concerned the social component of artistic judgment, took much longer to become effective. As early as the seventeenth century, the relationship between sign and signified had become ambiguous, at least in art. This ambiguity justified the function of the criterion of (good) taste. In the course of the seventeenth century, the notion of taste displaced the notion of the intellect.[126] One insisted on distinguishing objectively between beautiful and less beautiful works, while assuming a subjective position in order to deal with the problem of how one could know and judge such distinctions. Solving such problems required *fantasia, ingenio acuto ed attivo*, and *memoria*,[127] and the prime concern was to eliminate unsuccessful works.[128] One derived the beautiful by exclusion without being able to determine beauty itself. The problem was that the *distinction* could not be denied.[129] So long as the code was beyond doubt, one could tolerate irrational criteria of judgment. Taste was supposed to be "delicate," which was incompatible with the idea of law. Taste judged intuitively.

In a dissolving stratificatory order, the relationship between code and criteria could function as a means of social discrimination and prove itself in this function; but (perhaps for this very reason?) this solution remained theoretically unsatisfactory. It led to the circular argument that taste could be recognized only in an intuitively appropriate aesthetic judgment which, in turn, must manifest itself in good taste. There was no possibility for distinguishing between first- and second-order observation. In order to interrupt the circle, one incorporated time: the judgment of taste was instantaneous and direct, whereas its adequacy became apparent only after the fact.[130] But this begged the question of how one went about recognizing the adequacy of judgment. For a while, the semantics of taste fed off the traditional notion that obscurity was a legitimate property of art, a notion we addressed in the previous section. But appealing to tradition fell short, once it became important that art distinguish itself from other functional systems by virtue of its own identity.

This was all the more true when the art system, in addressing the general public in a specific manner, had to leave room for the inclusion of everybody, just like any other functional system. The eighteenth century still distinguished between different styles, depending on whether they were addressed to the general public or only to a few select individuals.[131]

At the very latest, the stylistic simplifications recommended in the transition from rococo to neoclassicism committed art to opening itself to everybody and to discriminating henceforth solely on the basis of internal criteria, that is, in the process of self-observation. The norms of freedom and equality (equal access to functional systems) became accepted throughout society, thus working against a class-specific definition of criteria. Hogarth's polemic against the cognitive claims and judgments of contemporary "connoisseurs" becomes intelligible against this background.[132] Critique began to criticize itself, declaring war against "the pestilence of our current criticism."[133]

But how do we explain the fact that one eventually ceased to appeal to good taste altogether? Apparently, a well-known trick of evolution was at work in this situation, exploiting transitory phenomena to introduce permanent structural change. Here evolution propelled such changes by supporting the attribution of semantics in national terms.[134] In England, Hogarth chastised the still-dominating principle of imitation for providing simplistic directives that were insufficiently formalized and systematized, and therefore prevented artists from participating in reflection and analysis.[135] According to Hogarth, this led to a situation in which "connoisseurs," along with their mystifications and typifications (distinction of "manners"), dominated the scene.[136] Around the mid-eighteenth century, the focus of the debate shifted to the German-speaking territories, which made it possible to distance oneself from "French" frivolity—in love as well as in art. For Kant, taste was only a matter of sociability.[137] For Ludwig Tieck, it ended up being nothing more than pretense, suitable perhaps for communicative purposes but no longer corresponding to any subjective reality. "Common taste is not the reason why we take delight in works of art; it only invokes a feeling of shame, which is necessary to prevent us from admitting that the works themselves leave us cold."[138] The social imperative of taste served to separate psychic from social reality, and once these realms were separated, criteria no longer mattered; what mattered was solely social convenience.

As a result, one could put aside the quest for criteria of taste and return (if more than just good or bad taste was at stake) to the distinctions by which art distinguished itself. After imitation had reached a final climax, the distinction between nature and art became insignificant. Beauty of nature coexisted with beauty in art. (In Baumgarten, both are of equal cognitive value.) This, however, did not explain what the observer considered beautiful and why (one now wanted to know reasons) he judged the way he did. Art was guided only by the idea of beauty. It abandoned nature (indeed, the entire "world system") to science, and the beauty of nature appeared as a reflex of the beauty of art.[139] What remained relevant were the distinctions *sinnlich/geistig* [pertaining to the senses / pertaining to the intellect] and particular/universal, which proved capable of combination in the course of further theoretical development from Baumgarten to Kant.[140]

Presumably, these distinctions could be combined because they allowed for a reentry of the distinction into what it distinguished. Art was the appearance of Spirit in the realm of the senses, or of the universal within the particular. Upon closer inspection, however, it became apparent that we are dealing with an appearance of the distinction *sinnlich/geistig* within the realm of the senses, or of the distinction universal/particular within the particular. How, if not by a distinction, could the other side be made noticeable on the side that aesthetics is primarily concerned with?

This presentation (which adopts a deliberately noncontemporary perspective) of a theory that began to take shape in Baumgarten under the special term of an aesthetics entailed an important suggestion.[141] Reentry is always a tautological and ultimately paradoxical operation, which presupposes an imaginary space (similar to the space of imaginary numbers). Classical aesthetics failed to recognize and acknowledge this fact. It was led astray by conceiving the relationship between the particular and the universal in abstract terms. This became a problem. To be sure, one recognized that this kind of abstraction was inadequate for a theory of art, and yet, from Baumgarten to Kant, efforts to understand art led straight into the field of cognitive theory. "Aesthetics" thought of itself as a cognitive possibility, as a philosophical science whose task was to demarcate and to investigate its own terrain.[142] Confronted with the need to differentiate itself from science and Enlightenment rationalism, art felt the pressure of self-assertion, and it turned out to be "impossible to salvage art except by rehabilitating the senses."[143] Even in Kant, this disposition remained unchanged; in fact, Kant inferred from it the necessity of expanding his critique of ontological metaphysics into the realm of aesthetics. At the same time, Karl Philipp Moritz made quite clear that artistic production was not a cognitive affair (even though he still published his treatise under the title of "imitation"): "The beautiful cannot be known, it must be either produced or *felt*."[144]

It is remarkable that the theory of art should present itself as "philosophy." This self-image might be related to the fact that this "firm" had just been incorporated as an independent academic discipline. Besides that, classifying aesthetics as philosophy allowed the theory of art to be separated both from the judgment of art and from art criticism. The theoretically gifted philosopher who knew his texts, concepts, and theoretical architectures, and who was caught up in polemics of his own, no longer needed to be able to judge and evaluate works of art. He functioned, instead, as a kind of parasite, who profited from the erosion of the underlying criteria of art criticism and taste, and he established his competence as an expert in distinctions and justifications.

It is doubtful whether such efforts can still count as self-descriptions of the art system, especially when they are part of a general architecture of transcendental-theoretical critique, as in Kant. However, they are closely related, which becomes apparent when one takes into account the difficulties involved in the Kantian project, the resistance of the object to the imposition of theory, and, last but not least, the intense controversies surrounding Kantian suggestions in early romanticism.

In the subsequent phase, German Idealism initially returned to traditional figures, enforcing their renewed and intensified deployment. Philosophy still had enough credit to be able to assign a position of lower rank to art. The great number of available distinctions—now called "opposites"—were still interpreted with an eye toward unity. The indispensable—the ultimate ground of diversity, the final thought that held opposites together—was called either "Idea"[145] or, if it referred to the illusory world of art, as in Schiller, "Ideal." The Idea identified itself with the positive value of the code of art. It thought of itself as the beautiful, thus blocking any reflection on the logical structure of the system's binary coding. How the positive value of the code could be repeatedly applied to indicate the meaning of art as a whole—the unity of the difference between beautiful and ugly—remained as unclear as the naive assumption in contemporary ethics that distinguishing between good and evil was good. The paradox one hit upon along this path remained concealed, and the cultivation of paradox in romanticism responded intuitively but in an insufficiently formalized manner to the problem of the unity of difference.

The Idea of beauty was considered to be an intrinsically necessary unity, and only its realization was believed to generate variation and diversification. Moreover, the ontological orientation of aesthetics was evident in its concern with the opposition between being and appearance and in its efforts to restrict the role of art in realizing the Idea to the world of beautiful appearance. As a result, appearance was once again valued positively in relation to being (which indicates a deep uncertainty regarding the evaluation of modern conditions). The same holds for Schiller's distinction between seriousness and play.[146] The problem, in other words, was dealt with on the basis of familiar (and comprehensible) distinctions. By placing a positive value on the other side of these distinctions, one hoped to find a way for the Idea to reenter reality. Apart from that, the context of the discussion continued to be determined by a philosophical anthropology centered on its "human" object rather than by a social theory. This orientation offered the advantage of using familiar anthropological distinctions—such as understanding, reason, will, feeling, sensuousness, imagination—and thus of starting out from seemingly incontestable facts of human life. Moreover, it preserved the possibility for smuggling in cultural and moral prejudices that went undetected by theory and exploiting such prejudices for the purpose of "approximating" the Idea. "As always, so long as such an idea remains on the horizon, moral law allies itself with empirical culturalism to dominate the field."[147] Neither in the political nor in the economic sector did the contemporary theory of society entail the possibility for substituting society for the reference to "mankind."

IV

After efforts toward reflection in the realm of art had become sufficiently consolidated, reflection began to react to self-generated problems. One demanded that art establish its *autonomy* at various levels,[148] and on the basis of an art-specific system for reflecting the relationship between the individual and society. All traces of heteronomy had to be erased. Art could no longer draw on erudition as it used to do in the Renaissance, nor could it rely on *Bildung*, as erudition was now called, since art forms grounded in *Bildung* had become obsolete.[149] This was all the more true for imports from the sciences, which were acceptable at best as material for artistic forms. Although religion did not date, it raised the question: Which religion? All of these problems disappeared, once art began to insist on autonomy.

We must take the notion of autonomy quite literally here, in the sense of self-legislation; in view of Kant's *Critique of Judgment*, we might perhaps speak of self-organization.[150] Modern self-description started at the structural rather than at the operative level of the production of unity; but this sufficed to establish the notion of autonomy against the outside— against science, morality, religion, or politics. This step established the autonomy of art philosophically—but in a manner that failed to clarify the operative basis of autonomy and led in the nineteenth century to the separation of philosophical aesthetics from a historically oriented type of research. As a result, the autonomy of art was eventually considered to be no more than a kind of regional ontology, governed by its own specialized a priori and its own "value."

The traditional demands of technical expertise—of *acutezza*, of brilliant accomplishment in the sense of Gracián—lost their edge. One no longer cared for these values, but searched instead for a basis of observation and judgment in the autonomous self-legislation of art. In this respect, art shared not only the typical uncertainty of an age of social transition but also the hopes and disappointments triggered by the French Revolution and an emerging individualism. The romantics, foremost among them Jean Paul, reflected upon the failure of communication or, more accurately, upon the disappointed hopes that individuals placed in communication. At the same time, art defined its unique aesthetic qualities in relation to the cognitive offerings of the most recent philosophy. Indeed, it was the notion of a cognitive order, presentable in purely logical terms (despite its need for transcendental-theoretical grounding), which motivated romanticism to distance itself from philosophy. Art refused to practice philosophy.[151] On the one hand, one asserted that the science of art is not necessarily a beautiful science.[152] This brought home the point that a reflection of the system within the system presupposed a special type of differentiation, which required an awareness of the primacy of the part in relation to the whole within reflection.[153] On the other hand, precisely this awareness raised the problem of how reflection could be adequate to its object. The understanding that the theory of art itself could not be a work of art, if it was to fulfill its function, radicalized the questions of whether theory describes the art system from an external or internal standpoint and of how the self-positioning of theory—given that both positions were possible—determines the construction of its object. The question of what reality "is" in itself became undecidable[154]—and was therefore a matter of dispute.

While art was still governed by the demands of mimesis/imitation, it could take the existence of a cosmic design for granted. Art could focus on its unique skills, on whose basis it could strive for and find recognition. In the second half of the eighteenth century, this assumption broke down, due to the increasing complexity and antinomy of descriptions. The collapse of commentary became a topic of art—for example, in *Tristram Shandy*. Art not only had to organize its own resources but to project a world of its own making and to create a convincing nexus between self-reference and hetero-reference (which could no longer be legitimized with reference to Being or nature).[155] These changes, however, did not concern the realm of symbols and metaphors, nor did they surface at the level of taste; rather, they affected the manner in which the work of art claimed its right to exist. Under such conditions, reality no longer functioned as an object of admiration or critique; reality had to be created by the work itself, if it wanted to succeed as a work of art.

From the viewpoint of an operative constructivism and from the perspective of the much-debated theory of self-referential systems,[156] assumptions about reality appeared to be correlates of internal resolutions of operative inconsistencies within the system—particularly of "contradictions" between the system's memory and momentary impulses. Romanticism continued to apply the notion of reality to the resolution of internal inconsistencies that were negotiated with what the system remembered as culture. But the resistance that generated reality was now relocated within the system, so that it could subsequently be externalized again as "nature." Romanticism "hovered" between inside and outside, but it could no longer resolve this paradox in favor of the world as it was. Its own reflection of this difference had to enter works of art themselves, for example, in the form of the incredible or uncanny assumptions it made about reality. The resulting irritation was appreciated as such and communicated to the observer.

The distance from reality, its treatment as a mere backdrop or means for staging art, is one of the most striking features of romanticism. As in contemporary philosophy, any reference to the world remained "speculative" in a positive sense. On the other hand, romanticism resisted—for good reasons—the suspicion that its relationship to reality was governed by arbitrary subjective impulses. One mystified reality so that the observer was not distracted by it. The suspension of disbelief, necessary for understanding fictional representations, was driven to the extreme; it was provoked and brought to reflection in this provocation. The beholder was supposed to focus his awareness on the artwork itself. Once this was accomplished, a new realism could emerge as a correlate to Idealism.[157]

From that moment on, distinctions came to be used in a different manner. Traditionally, society and art assumed that certain phenomena fell outside of any given order and that such phenomena were indeed accessible. One thinks of the devil and his temptations, or of the technique of reversal employed in carnival, or of other such interruptions.[158] But techniques of this sort only managed to traverse the distinction; upon return from the other side, everything would be the same as before.[159] They merely reaffirmed the distinction. This is how one became aware of the distinction between texts (among them fictional texts) and reality, though one treated this distinction in terms of different ontological regions, and confusing these regions was forbidden. One had to be able to distinguish between a narration and something that really happened. This included the possibility, depicted in *Hamlet*, that it becomes impossible to turn this distinction into a decision.

By introducing concepts bound by reflection—self-possession, irony, critique—romanticism changed all this. The novel had paved the way for the reflection of the distinction between fiction and reality within itself.[160] Fictional texts were produced in such a way that readers were tempted to recognize their personal situation in the work and apply what they read to their own needs. This was not simply a matter of duplicating in one's own life the models one found in literature. Preferred topics such as a criminality (regretted after the fact) or (prohibited) sexual liberties were meant to present the reader with situations that called for *decisions*, by means of which he could individualize himself in ways that yield consequences. As long as this was so, it was difficult to avoid moral implications, even though literature learned to distance itself from the obligation of moral instruction. Romanticism took an important step beyond that. It dissolved the ontological reference of the distinction between fiction and reality, which had been tailored to the observer, fictionalizing even what might be taken to be a reality "out there." It duplicated worldly affairs both in the realm of fiction and in reality and shrouded them in the "twilight of romanticism."[161] "If the poet, by virtue of the magic of his presentation," writes August Wilhelm Schlegel, "manages to transport us into an unfamiliar world, he is free to operate in this world according to his own laws."[162] The reference to reality remained in suspense. In his *Nachtstücke*, E. T. A. Hoffmann invokes magnetism as a potentially natural, if dubious, explanation, but the unity of his narration depends on the reader's belief in the miraculous despite this explanation.[163] In the face of such deliberate ambiguities, *everything depends on who, under what circumstances, observes how others observe.*

Each time a negation is introduced into the art system, it generates a different condition that enables and requires new observations. Negation—as reversal, paradox, or parody—dissolves any given determination and, *at the same time, supports the reflection of the system's autonomy, which articulates itself by virtue of the fact that this is possible.* In particular, textual arts such as poetry and the novel thematized themselves and their own literariness and included what until now had been excluded from literature—sexuality, for example (*Lucinde*). The difference between self-reference and hetero-reference, along with the problem of the unity of this difference, became an inevitable by-product of reflection.

Since the distinction between self-reference and hetero-reference rested on the distinction between inside and outside, the problem of its unity could not be resolved in a one-sided manner: for example, by insisting on "pure" self-reference. Just as the subject became aware of an external reality when it ran up against its own boundaries—otherwise there would be no boundaries—art, too could not afford not to distinguish itself. While it might be true that romanticism, and even more so modern art, tend to advocate the primacy of self-reference, neither the semantics of a "purpose without purpose" nor *l'art pour l'art* succeed in denying hetero-reference; they only create a situation in which their references become ambiguous. Works of art began to admit their need for interpretation and became receptive to the idea that consensus might be lacking. And critique no longer meant search for the one true judgment, but rather the perpetual improvement of the artwork itself.

When, in the wake of the French Revolution, one contemplated alternatives, one ran up against the problem of communication. The romantic critique of Idealism focused on the unresolved problem of communication. One preferred "hovering" in a state of undecidability,[164] because communication no longer found stability in the old categories of an ontological metaphysics and because even successful communication could not compensate for this lack. Hovering between the universal and the individual was now considered "interesting," a notion that adequately characterized and at the same time devalued communication. One cultivated humor and irony as forms of communication, as the *presentation* [*Darstellung*] of a "hovering" self-relation. Since *information* (hetero-reference) lacked certainty, one relied all the more on utterance [*Mitteilung*] (self-reference).[165] It is possible to understand the romantics' longing for unity and wholeness as a cipher for a problem of communication, and their experimentation with myth and poetry as an attempt to reach out to the people across social boundaries. Within their own circle, the romantics intensely engaged in dialogue and correspondence, only to run up against the limits of agreement. Worst of all, claiming a separate world of beauty, aesthetics, symbolism, and poetry bifurcated the realm of social communication. The reflection of autonomy faced an excess of *internal* communicative possibilities that resulted from the loss of external reference points and their indifference. The romantics experienced this problem in the self-relation of the subject. But freedom and reason could no longer be identified as the same. This was evident in the realization that oral communication was bound to fail (the couple in Jean Paul's *Siebenkäs* is acutely aware of this failure—as are the twins in his *Flegeljahre*, or the lover in Constant's *Adolphe*, who is no longer in love—and this awareness manifests itself in attempts to live out the liberties of a romantically inspired communication).[166] Communication replicated misunderstanding. As Friedrich Schlegel puts it poignantly in *Lucinde*: "What separates the beings is not hatred . . . but love."[167] Lack of positive affirmation through communication provoked the endless self-reflection of the subject. The individual became the subject of his own being.

   Written communication provides a way out of this dilemma. Texts cannot deny their communicative intent, even when they present themselves as fragments or unfinished utterances that might or might not elicit a response, or when they react to an excess of communicative possibilities devoid of credibility.[168] Text-art caught up with what had been a long-standing practice in the visual arts by including the unfinished, the sketch, and the fragment; and it was no accident that the visual medium of perception was indispensable for the stability of such forms. The fragment allowed for the articulation of self-referentiality; it made room for freedom to decide whether completion was necessary or whether it might be preferable to play with the magic of the fragment;[169] completion would only burden the work with an excess of information. *Communicating* autonomy in this manner avoided the impression that the artist did not know how to go on and therefore left his work unfinished. In order to exclude this possibility, the "fragment" was marked as form and cultivated and reflected upon as such—and it, too, presupposed writing.

In romanticism, art was perhaps for the first time fully acknowledged as writing,[170] and poetry was the name that announced a programmatic form for this kind of writing. What was at stake in poetry was neither rhetoric nor enlightenment, but the attempt to capture the unattainable. This notion yielded the inevitable conclusion (which encountered much resistance[171]) that the theory of literature was actually literature, and that literature inevitably partook of literary theory. It became possible to entertain the notion that the reflection on art should express itself not only in learned treatises but also and above all in works of art. The prototype is Friedrich Schlegel's *Lucinde*.

This shift affected the poetry of nature as well. Nature no longer derived its significance from its own resources or from the fact that humans are natural beings. Rather, it mirrored the infinitely displaced search of the self for itself; a search that appeared interminable, because it no longer encountered a limit in society. "The relationship with nature has been superseded by an intersubjective, interpersonal relationship, that in the last analysis [but only for romanticism, N. L.] is a relationship of the subject toward itself."[172]

The problem became how to deal further with the excess of communicative possibilities and with the interminability (or connective uncertainty) of communication, if *this problem* could not be resolved by the *individual* subject. Romanticism solved it by introducing the notion of *art criticism*. The notion that criticism is an essential component in the perfection of art acknowledged for the first time the status of theory as a self-description of the system within the system.[173]

Classical examples of romantic criticism are Friedrich Schlegel's essays on Georg Forster, on Lessing, and on Goethe's *Meister*, all of which relate works to their authors and present both as a unity.[174] When dealing with

romantic criticism, we must disregard any potential analogies to science,
in particular the notion that the convergence of critical opinions indicates
their truth. This notion must be sacrificed.[175] In romanticism, individual
differences between aesthetic judgments were considered normal and legitimate.[176] There was nothing offensive about disagreement, nor did it
diminish the value of critical judgment.[177] This suggested that the objects
themselves, if they mediate communication in the form of artworks,
served as an equivalent for the kind of security that was accomplished ver-
bally only via consensus or dissent—an equivalent that secured the continuation of autopoietic communication. Criticism was already a program for an observation of the second order—for an ability to distinguish
that, for its part, could be distinguished and did not need to strive toward
convergence. But if this was so, communication had to allow itself to be
supported by perceptible objects in order to compensate for its boundless
insecurity.

Accordingly, reflection turned into a medium for shaping critical judgment.[178] The medium itself continued to stand for the unity of the system, for the underlying idea of art. But this idea could not be realized in
the form of a perceptible work. It remained unattainable. Any attempt to
approach the idea exposed itself to criticism and observation. Every form
infinitely displaced what made it observable, lagging behind its ambition
at the level of realization. Transcending the boundaries of the imagination
was as necessary as it was impossible.

This is why criticism could achieve only a broken—"reflective," "sober"
(attentive to artistic means), "ironic"—relationship to its object. Criticism
did not expect the object to meet its standards of judgment, nor did it
strive, as criticism, for beauty, let alone to surpass itself as a critically conceived work of art. Its goal was neither rejection nor the mere classification of art in terms of whether it succeeds or fails. Rather, the task of criticism was to distinguish the visible from what is rendered invisible by the
visible. As if from the corner of its eye, criticism attempted to catch a
glimpse of the excluded within the included. This is why Jean Paul, unlike
Goethe and Schiller, located the sublime in the finite rather than in the
infinite.[179] For the first time, the self-description of the art system included its own motive: the reflection of unity in the paradox of distinguishing, which constituted the "unmarked space" and the unobservability of observation. Resolute awareness of the chasm between art and the
"real world" was called irony;[180] irony was dead serious, so to speak, about

the fact that it did not take the world seriously; it was a consistently maintained self-assertion.

Criticism renounced the ambition of being measured against artistic standards, and the critic compensated for this renunciation by presenting himself as a member of an elite of reflection—being neither of noble birth nor rich, but competent and full of high self-expectations.[181] As for the negative side—neither noble nor rich—the critic could identify with artists and poets, while distinguishing himself by his role as critic. The sheer amount of emerging talent allowed for a differentiation of functions, if not of persons. To many, among them Goethe and Hegel, the excessive proliferation of differences appeared to be an untenable subjectivism. The refusal to determine identity objectively was certainly one of the features of romanticism. It dispensed with the Idea as the point of convergence between subject and object (even though this Idea was retained in multiple forms).[182] Who is to say that the subject/object distinction matters to the self-description of a functional system?

Another possibility for exploiting the freedom of autonomy while escaping the dead end of transcendental reflection was the dissolution of identity for the purpose of communication.[183] Romanticism was fascinated with *Doppelgänger*, mirror-images, and twins, as well as with narratives from which the informed reader could infer that the author had split himself into two different personae that communicate with one another.[184] As Schlegel puts it, "Nobody can know himself, unless he is both himself and an other."[185] Identities no longer functioned as a means to secure hetero-reference; instead they organized self-reference. Under such conditions, one could exploit the dissolution of identity in order to represent both the difficulties and the failure of the ego's self-reflection as a problem of communication. One did not yet speak of "genius," but there was a general awareness of the fact that the inclusion of artists into the system was the system's own affair and not determined by nature or by birth. One retained the original/copy distinction while knowing—as expressed in the figure of the *Doppelgänger*—that this distinction was not derived from reality, but produced by art in order to commit the art system to the production of "original" works.

These epochal historical changes affected the romantic conception of historical time as well. The erosion of proven methods of inferring the future from the past at first increased freedom in relation to both past and future by allowing for a transfiguration of the past (not just of antiquity but also of the Middle Ages) that left the future indeterminate and turned it into a summons. What became politically an open question after the French Revolution corresponded artistically to the problem of self-confirming form. As Novalis puts it, "We have outgrown the age of generally valid forms."[186]

To the extent that the factual limitations of what is artistically permitted fall away, relevant art forms are defined in terms of a temporal relationship to previous forms. The avant-garde claimed to be ahead of its time. But since, like everyone else, it could not act in the future, this claim boils down in practice to a distanced, critical, and polemical attitude within a shared present. Even the self-descriptions of postmodernism suggest historical periodization. But claiming a historical position requires unambiguous structural decisions of the sort postmodernism refuses to provide. Only postmodern architecture lives up to this claim in some sense, since it succeeds in distinguishing itself clearly from the reductionist style that precedes it (keyword *Bauhaus*). Everywhere else, attempts to define postmodern art lead to a temporal melange of modern, late modern, and postmodern trends. All of these trends converge in the effort to eliminate an excess of communicative possibilities by means of the *form of the utterance* [*Mitteilung*] rather than via the *kind of information* it entails. In other words, one tends to privilege self-reference over hetero-reference. This preference appears to be the decisive factor in the further development of art, especially in the twentieth century. It is astonishing that such a privileging of self-reference should be possible at all, and that convincing forms could be found to articulate it—given that self-reference can be observed only by distinguishing it from hetero-reference. Hetero-reference is reduced more and more to the "unmarked space." Entering that space yields nothing, since the boundary must be crossed again if something is to be accomplished there. However, characterizing modern art in this way highlights the historical contingency of its bias toward self-reference, which raises the question of whether representing autonomy in terms of self-reference is a permanent solution.

Despite all agonizing over the bifurcation of the bourgeois world, and despite the diagnosis of this world as divided by oppositions, the distance that comes with differentiated reflection appears as a structure one must subsequently accept. One might dress up this structure with expectations of a "new mythology" (in the manner of the *Älteste Systemprogramm* of Friedrich Schlegel, Hölderlin, and Schelling), only to provoke self-doubts and disbelief. A "new mythology" requires decisions in place of the models that used to be provided by tradition and by the contractually fixed orders of patrons.[187] Or one can share Schiller's hopes for a moral-aesthetic unity of sociability (= society), only to find oneself out on the limb of a bourgeois interiority.[188] One might indulge in "sublime" experiences and miracles, in magic, ghosts, and dreadful surprises—only to admit that for every one of these phenomena, the modern world offers a trivial explanation.[189] Or one might follow Hegel's belief that unity is henceforth possible only in reflection (with emphasis on "henceforth only"). The observer has entered the scene and subjects himself to observation. Henceforth, one can no longer escape the question of what kinds of distinctions one employs in observation and why just these and not others. With the advent of the observer, philosophical attempts to put down art as a competitor come to an end. Minerva allows more than one owl to fly, and every observer can be observed as someone who constructs a world that appears to him as if it really were the way it appears.

V

There is nothing particularly new in the romantic trend to think of art in terms of a self-generated mystery, of a limit of what can be conceptually grasped. The romantic description of art is work-oriented, even where a description of artistic means would be more appropriate. It does not penetrate to the level of the elemental operations that produce and reproduce the work. This situation changed, at the latest with the advent of impressionism. In the nineteenth century, even more so today, descriptions of art must keep up with the increasing awareness of the operations involved in art, which means that the beautiful can no longer be the goal of such descriptions.

Hegel puts an end, if not to art, at least to a philosophy of art that claims to situate it within the systematic structure of philosophical theory and to determine the range of artistic possibilities from within that structure. There will always be philosophers who deal with art; but the object of interpretation is determined by the rapid development of the art system, which escapes questions concerning its why and whence. When painters, beginning with Manet, began to rediscover the canvas and accentuate its visual space in paintings that are still to be perceived in spatial terms, their rediscovery did not depend on a prior study of philosophy, nor was it motivated by irritations that came from philosophical theories. Rather, it emerged from the artists' reflection upon their own activity, from their reaction to a prior "realism," accompanied perhaps by a sense of the paradox that one at once sees the space of the image, sees it disappear [and become only canvas], then sees it again. No philosophy could evaluate, from the perspective of its own system, what is happening here and why. A description that wants to resonate with the art system must be able to connect to discoveries within the system.

The artistic trends that established themselves as "modern" during the second half of the nineteenth century suggested a renunciation not only of imitation but of fictionality as such. Fictional representations were not supposed to be confused with reality. The reader was meant to react with disbelief, then suspend his disbelief and consider the artwork to be a reality in its own right. The suspension of disbelief—this double negation of the relevance of the real—now became superfluous. Fictionality still presupposes the possibility for discovering what the world is really like, so that fiction can offer a fitting description. To do so, the work of art must supply both contextual similarity and redundancies. Modern art goes beyond these conditions of fictionality. The modern artwork does not imitate (or does so only ironically), nor does it seek to anchor its own reality in the fictional realm. It relies exclusively on its own means to convince its audience, and it assumes that its attempt to surpass previous models is persuasive. This farewell to fictionality might be the ultimate consequence of a differentiated art system, which had to sacrifice the recognizable aspects and redundancies implied in the notion of a fictional reality as distinct from a reality "out there" in order to realize redundancies exclusively as internal suggestions within the work or, in contemporary terminology, as "intertextuality" within the system.

Some observers of the eventful (and nonetheless rich) history of twentieth-century art have returned once again to "dialectical" presuppositions.[190] Dialectics suggests that a process driven by negation must eventually culminate in affirmation. Proving this point, however, turned out to be difficult. We think of Adorno's efforts to find affirmation in Schönberg (but not in Stravinsky). One stereotypically invokes "capitalism" and "bourgeois society." But such cross-references no longer succeed in analytical terms, and there is no concept of society that could explain why art runs into problems with its own autonomy (even though everyone seems to concur that it does). But if dialectics—after the "dialectic of Enlightenment"[191]—

no longer offers any prospects for the future, are we supposed to infer that this holds for art and society as well? Or, given the improbability of this proposition, wouldn't it make more sense to sacrifice dialectics? For this reason (and without referring to other findings) we break with this loosely Marxist mode of argumentation and regard the social modernity of art, like that of other functional systems, to be a matter of system autonomy, which then becomes the theme of self-descriptions.

Self-descriptions of the system within the system, however, do not reproduce the system's operations, only the ideas that guide these operations. This process preserves the differentiation of specific activities of reflection. The theory of art is increasingly applied within works themselves, until the avant-garde eventually seizes the political idea of experimenting with the entire range of the concept of art, if not with the universality of the realm of artistic competence as such. What used to be *ideal* in the idea of art is replaced by a notion of *universality* that is independent of objects and determined internally.

The possibilities for escaping into the exotic or the trivial that used to be available no longer suffice; one now transgresses their boundaries. Everything mysterious is expelled from art—unless it elicits a shock effect[192]—and displaced into the unmarked space where signs are engraved into the empty stage, the white sheet of paper,[193] or the silence that makes tones resonate. This displacement focuses awareness once again on "writing"—not on writing as distinct from what it signifies, but on what writing, understood as graph, fissure, design, or contour, creates and leaves unnoticed as its presupposed other.[194] Signs once again turn into symbols and are called upon to represent their relationship to what cannot be signified—they stand as "pure" forms that no longer signify any content, but function only as difference. Signs become symbols that want to be something they cannot be, symbols for the reentry of the form into the form. Picasso is considered the representative painter of this century, and for good reason; the unity of his work can no longer be comprehended in terms of form or style, but only in terms of an irony which he probes in all conceivable forms and styles.

Abstraction toward pure form is merely an indication that everything is possible. The realm of the permissible and of the artistically possible keeps growing, so long as what saturates this realm can still be observed as a symbol for the fact that the only thing excluded is exclusion itself. Theory becomes the agency of permission. Its general question becomes: What does it mean for the art system to contain its own descriptions, and how can this fact be rendered observable in a work of art?

However, a self-description of the system can also contain a self-negation of the system—for example, as a negation of every boundary and every internal determination, as a negation of the obligation to follow traditional models, or as a negation of the system's future.[195] In each of these cases, negation is a positive operation (here, of communication), which depends on a meaning recursively secured within an actually existing autopoietic system. Self-negation is therefore possible only when the system that executes the negation operates autopoietically, when it disposes over a memory and projects a future—if only in the empty formula of "I have no idea how to go on."

Romantic "criticism" wanted to exhaust the most perfect possibilities and complete the artwork in its unattainable perfection. Now, the challenge was to locate the negation of the system within the system, to perfect the system's autonomy, because autonomy, in its most radical sense, can be thought only in terms of the inclusion of self-negation into the system (or, phrased differently, in terms of the exclusion of hetero-negation). As a result of this development—one already "historical" from today's standpoint—one can see that art can deal with limitations in two ways: it can reject limitations as repression and try to overcome them, or it can accept limitations as necessary working conditions and subsequently treat such conditions as substitutable.

Based on a fundamental notion of negativity, Adorno's aesthetics offers two alternative versions of negativity:[196] a purist version that insists on rejecting any external influence, and a sociocritical version that reflects on the contradiction that art realizes itself positively in society while assuming a negative (critical) position vis-à-vis society. It is difficult to see which common notion of negativity could reconcile these two versions and bring about their dialectical synthesis. Earlier we raised the question of whether one can assume negation at the operative level,[197] or whether there must be a prelogical notion of distinction, which requires the operation of negation only at the level of self-description, that is, the level where self-reference and hetero-reference are distinguished.

At any rate, one can see how modern art, in its more recent developments, transforms its relationship into an extra-artistic reality *in a manner that does not depend on negation*. Initial experiments of this sort were limited; one incorporated chance into the work of art, one allowed raw ma-

terials to appear in the work, or blanks that refer to a future continuation
of the work in interpretation. Suggestions of this sort were supported by
the work itself; they were able to connect to formal models and therefore
appeared as forms.[198] However, when a work of art is determined to call
art as such into question, when, inspired by Gödel, it tries to appear as a
work of art outside of the system art, or when it seeks to accomplish a
reentry of nonart into art in the sense of Spencer Brown and, in so doing,
generates an endless oscillation between inside and outside in an imaginary realm outside of the calculus of forms[199]—when all this makes up the
intended meaning of the work and can be observed accordingly—then
the art-system has definitely arrived at a new level of self-description, a
level characterized by the introduction of self-negation into the system
(and is no longer limited to the calculability of individual forms).

The mathematics of reentry leads to an "unobservable indeterminacy,"[200]
not because it is codetermined by an incalculable environment (by independent variables), but because it is set up in a self-determining manner.
Any further determination must be left to the workings of time. But the
autopoiesis of the system has no place for an ultimate operation that would
negate the system as a whole, because all operations are conceived from the
perspective of reproduction. As a form of practicing autonomy, the self-
negation of the system is only one operation among others, an attempt to
press the system to its limits so as to include the excluded, or to surpass
with its negativity everything that preceded it, or to allow every possible
nonartistic reality to reenter the realm of art. There are many attempts of
this sort. One provokes one's audience by making it extremely unlikely that
art will be noticed as art, for example. One etches a sign into a park bench
in the expectation (hope?) that no one will recognize its artistic quality, but
that one could prove it in court should the need arise. One might "declare"
objects of utility to be works of art (Marcel Duchamp, Andy Warhol) or
inscribe different meanings into works of art that are indistinguishable at
the level of perception.[201] Narratives no longer invoke the incredible, as in
romanticism, but are presented as unreadable[202]—perhaps in order to call
attention to the fact that writing is all that matters. In "happenings," the
observable content is reduced to a minimum and presented to a group of
randomly selected passers-by, just to demonstrate that this is still art. Hope
is invested in the negative provocation of a hopelessly random consensus of
art-specific observations.

But how is this possible socially if not on the basis of autonomy? Any attempt of this sort presupposes the autonomy of art and seeks to realize autonomy in a limiting case. This is true even when autonomy is practiced as a renunciation of autonomy—when one seeks to reconcile art and life or attempts to commercialize art to the point where it no longer claims any specifically artistic form, where its artistic quality is reduced to the fact that it *wants* to abandon itself and this is how it articulates itself as art.[203] Werner Hofmann speaks of the "art of artlessness" and explains this trend with reference to an increasing "unlearning" of art.[204] The reason why a work of art is a work of art to begin with—apart from the mere claim—remains a mystery, as if this mystery were meant to symbolize the unobservability of the world. This is why art is "in need of commentary" (Gehlen), why it depends on a supplementary *linguistic* mediation of its meaning. "Reflection paraphrases production," writes Hofmann,[205] but one might as well claim the opposite by saying that the work of art only paraphrases reflection.

However, negating art as art is not the sole concern of modern art. Important variants take issue, not with the art system, but with the system of society. Art of this sort no longer offers representations or oppositional utopias, nor is it concerned with a social critique that feeds on ideologies. The less one is convinced that a work's novelty can be located on an ascending line surpassing previous art in quality, the more the idea of plotting novelty as a provocation of society suggests itself. Given that provocation cannot be repeated, it is necessary to come up with ever new provocations, until society grows accustomed to this tactic and ceases to respond. This kind of art, too, is no longer possible. If the classics of provocation were still alive today, they would no longer provoke.

Significant opportunities for expression can be understood on the basis of the distinction between inclusion and exclusion. This distinction helps us see that artworks symbolize (the unity of) difference—especially by aesthetically reintegrating the excluded into the realm of inclusion. One significant example is the use of garbage and scraps in the composition of artworks.[206] Another version is the cultivation of an unkempt appearance, which provokes exclusion in order to make the point that exclusion does not matter. Even the aesthetics of slowness, of the easy, laid-back motorcycle ride, is meant to characterize a society that makes inclusion contingent upon speed.[207] Along the same lines, we find a blurring of the distinction between artistic types—the painter, the sculptor, the poet, or the musician—in the figure of the "artist" as such, for whom one can no longer specify criteria of inclusion. The "artist as such" celebrates inclusion as deliberate self-exclusion, as a "neither-nor" in relation to every artistic medium. All of these strategies are meant not to negate art but rather to characterize society as a system that contains its own negation by reproducing inclusion and exclusion through its own operations. Is this art? The question is posed by the artwork itself and turns "art" into an auxiliary concept for understanding its presentation. Art confronts the "unresolvable indeterminacy" of a mathematical reentry, an indeterminacy that points to the end of the calculus and leaves the future to the future.

In music, we find a similar decision, which goes far beyond rejecting the limitations of the tonal system. It focuses entirely on the tone that is actualized at any given moment, thereby destroying any possibility for memory and expectation of the sort provided by melody. Only the present counts, and each new present must come as a surprise. However, since sequentially formed identities require temporally recursive networkings, such a program ends up canceling the distinction between music and nonmusic. The form that is supposed to accomplish this goal is the unexpected noise, a noise that announces its unexpected occurrence only against a background of silence. Even here, one still needs authorization— by John Cage, for example—to back up the claim that it is indeed music.

This development runs the risk of cutting off communication between art and its audience. The audience becomes an invention, a phantasm of the artist, to borrow a phrase from a publication of the Art & Language Group. The audience, in other words, becomes part of the artwork.[208] Earlier one could assume that the artwork signals its own status as a work of art. External frame conditions—such as the stage and the curtain in the theater, or the frame of a painting—have always been used to demarcate art and, at the same time, to indicate "this is art," independently of the aesthetic quality of any particular work.[209] Only within such frames could the question of quality arise. Most recent modern art experiments with eliminating any art-internal signals. As a result, art depends all the more on frames and external signals to indicate that an object not recognizable as art is nonetheless meant to be seen as art. Or one concerns oneself, like the Art & Language Group, with the "redescription" of styles and works, which are produced solely in view of further "redescriptions."[210] There is no longer any reason to stop production. Autopoiesis turns into form, and only the lack of fantasy and imagination can lead to destructive external effects. When this happens, one can talk endlessly about it, which means that this talk, too, must eventually come to an end, like a fashion that becomes obsolete when people embrace a new one. However, if the work of art no longer wants to convince as a work of art, but is merely marked as such, some observers might refuse to see it as art, or they might have recourse to the embarrassing relics of conventional aesthetic criteria.

Perhaps the possibilities for reintegrating the negation of the system into the system are by now exhausted as well. And perhaps there is still room for an inspiration that can overcome even this impasse. At any rate, it has become possible to recognize and describe the inclusion of negation as a strategy. Art is no longer critical, nor is it concerned with theory or with justified judgments at a level of reflection that maintains an observing distance from what goes on in art. Academic aesthetics is dead; it has nothing to say to art (if one asks the artists). Phenomena (of whatever kind) no longer matter; what counts is performative contradiction, a "deconstruction" that turns back upon itself. One looks for ways of staging art at the level of operations that present themselves to observation *as works of art*—this claim remains an integral part of the self-negation of art. Even in "the age of technical reproduction," works of art distinguish themselves from other artifacts in that they do not have to prove themselves outside of art.[211] This is why they can live out their originality, why they can be innovative or disagree without reservation, the only risk being that they might no longer be understood. Without having to take responsibility for further consequences, works of art can focus on irritating the observer. And yet, even the most radical gesture, the most alienating "installation," must submit to the necessity of concretion; a babble of ideas won't do. Something must be "presented," or else the other locations within the system remain beyond reach. Works of art are also logical artifacts, to the extent that they solve a logically insoluble paradox, namely, the paradox of instituting in a singular, concrete object their belonging to the genre of art and to the system of art.[212] For good reasons, the artist does not rely on the communication of opinions that goes on among the elite who reflect on the system. He simply does what he does. The point is not to declare the end of art on the basis of convincing arguments, *thereby setting an end to art.* The self-negation of art is realized at the level of autopoietic operations in the form of art, *so that art can continue.* The much debated "end of art" does not necessarily imply stagnation; art can continue to move along—if not as a river, perhaps as an ocean. The end of art, the impossibility of art, the final sellout of all possible forms assumes a form that claims to be self-description and artwork at once, and this secures the reproduction of art as a perfectly autonomous system, a system that includes its own negation.

The growing pressure to manifest originality as deviation eventually leads to the discovery of the compulsion to repeat.[213] So long as one still believed in taste, one had to make sure that originality could be recognized. Even after the forefront of discussion had shifted to the legitimization of technical reproduction, no distinct criteria for originality came forth. In one way or another, artworks cannot and would not exclude repetition; repetition plays a role in the repeated encounter with an artwork, in a play's repeated performance, or in the notion of a copy that remains true to the original. Indeed, works of art are created as "potential multipliers."[214] The first step is to concede that the artist can be allowed to repeat himself in ever new variations on his original idea. For awhile, this notion continues to invest the code original/copy with corresponding positive and negative values. But eventually one must ask oneself how important this distinction really is, and whether art will tolerate its tyranny. Once the original/copy distinction becomes the topic of "transjunctional" operations and can be accepted or rejected as a distinction, a new description is needed to resist the hegemony of the law of novelty. "Postmodernism" rebels against this law; but in so doing, it only returns to an older law, which states that the work of art, in one way or another, must mediate between variety and redundancy in order for the appeal of novelty to become intelligible.

Undeniably, this development has a certain consistency. Works of art distinguish themselves from other objects by virtue of their self-referentiality: they claim to be art, and they can do so because this claim is an affair of communication rather than a matter of mere objecthood. But when the self-description of the art system focuses on this claim—the claim to be art—and henceforth claims originality exclusively for this purpose, the question of how it can redeem such a claim arises.

The nineteenth century solved this problem by distributing the alternative "self-reference or hetero-reference" among two separate styles. Those who advocated the primacy of self-reference could stick to aestheticizing artistic styles, which emphasized formal decisions. Those who preferred hetero-reference—whether in an affirmative or critical sense—could count on realism.[215] This opposition became programmatic. The distinctions were tested on a stylistic level, but they remained contained within the system precisely as a form of stylistic choice (of which there were many).

This solution, however, could not withstand the increasing radicalization of reflection (which did not exclude the possibility for distinguishing, as before, between stylistic preferences). *L'art pour l'art* was surpassed by *l'art sur l'art*. Self-reference is undermined when the system challenges its own boundaries and when it begins to treat the choice of one or the other type of reference as a system-internal operation. When "everything goes, and only the intention counts," art retreats to self-reference, and this holds even for programs that oppose this opening. Art approaches a boundary where artistic information ceases to be information and becomes solely utterance [*Mitteilung*], or, more accurately, where information is reduced to conveying to the audience that art wants to be nothing more than utterance. Art restricts itself to signing what it subsequently claims to be art,[216] or it produces as "conceptual art" what finds attention only as an element in the autopoietic chain of self-reflections and re-descriptions of the system.

To the extent that reflection on the notion of reentry is radicalized and the distinction between art and nonart becomes increasingly paradoxical, the relationship of art to its own history is affected as well. The diversity of artistic creations is leveled when they are reduced to mere difference. One no longer remembers *what* earlier innovations rebelled *against* and how passionately they were defended and attacked.[217] History becomes dehistoricized and is treated as a reservoir of simultaneously available materials for artistic forms. What goes under the ill-fated title "postmodernism"[218] is therefore a typical product of memory: it has forgotten most of what came before, especially that which will never be repeated, and remembers only a few extraordinary events.

"Postmodern" architecture and its surrounding literature provide perhaps the most convenient access to the postmodernism debate, because in architecture the contrast to "modern" architecture is most clearly visible. In reacting to the essentialist simplifications of modern architecture, postmodernism does not simply follow principles but also attempts to copy a differentiated, diverse environment into the artwork and thus into the system[219]—it seeks to create a kind of "requisite variety" in the cybernetic sense (Ashby). The same can be said of the heterogeneity of tastes and stylistic expectations. It also holds for the difference between the expectations of a critical elite and what the population at large is able to understand,

and it applies to the relationship between the equally justified demands for recognizability and innovation, as well as to the (conspicuous!) adaptation of obsolete styles to modern technology. In order to highlight the heterogeneous demands placed upon the work, "quotations" become indispensable—mere copying no longer suffices. "Requisite variety" requires "requisite simplicity." The questions become whether, and in what way, the work can claim unity, and whether it can assert itself against its own (!) "requisite variety." The "purist" and "essentialist" emphasis of modernism is surpassed by a reflection upon variety. Unity is displaced by a reflection on the unity of heterogeneous distinctions.

If one wants to derive from this special case a general formula that can be applied to other artistic genres as well, then such a formula might be found in the problem of "reentry," that is to say, in the question of how the environment can enter into the system without losing its character as an unknown, unattainable environment. How, in other words, can the art system reflect upon its own differentiation, not only in the form of theory, but also in individual works of art?[220]

This problem also arises in response to the increasing tempo of change and to the self-reference perpetually stimulated by this change. One of the striking features of postmodernism is an extremely rapid alternation between "more or less fabricated movements"[221] that impress themselves upon the observer by the imaginative nature of their self-descriptions.[222] If art is capable of infinitely expanding its boundaries in order to facilitate innovation, hetero-reference is eliminated as a result. It becomes important to rely on self-reference as a principle for generating forms. The operations of the system are reflected upon as system-generating operations, and "works" are reduced to being temporary manifestations of this process. This change requires the incorporation into the artwork of distinctions internal to the art system, distinctions that derive either from the history of art or from the formal repertoire available as art. When there is no longer a binding tradition of form, and yet every form is still within reach as a (recognizable) quotation,[223] everything depends on how the work is put together.

From the viewpoint of art, this radical break with tradition entails above all an irritation, the need to search for forms, to make decisions, and to accept the primacy of self-reference. Art henceforth quotes itself, selecting stylistic elements only to reintegrate stylistic selectivity into the selection and to take into account alternative styles, so that the artwork documents the choice of a style as choice. Individual works, especially in architecture, create local observer positions, from which things look different than from other positions, which are also taken into account rather than being rejected as incompatible. Works of art, in other words, are conceived in a poly-contextural manner. Transitions take the observer by surprise, and this is the point. Works of art were always meant to elicit astonishment, but now the astonishment is incorporated into the work via a kind of reentry. Given the abundance of possibilities, there is no end to astonishment. Accordingly, the criteria for qualifying a work as art must be stricter than ever. Presumably, the tightening of standards also increases, in an unprecedented manner, the risk of failure and the difficulty of recognizing failure.

Efforts to reproduce the reflection theory of the art system in the form of art indicate the end of the aesthetic era in the self-description of art—the end of all attempts to come to terms with the problems of reflection. It is clear by now that the *unity* of the distinction between self-reference and hetero-reference is an *operative* problem of any given system. The synthesis of information and utterance is reproduced from one moment to the next as communication. The constative and performative components of texts require, to borrow a suggestion from Paul de Man's literary theory, a rhetorical symbiosis without support in a prior unity. The ramifications for sociology are less evident, and it is not clear what will come next. We suspect that one possible solution might consist in *operationally focused* analyses that do not deny their own status as operations, operations which exclude, by virtue of the forms they select, what cannot be observed on the basis of these forms, and which include this very exclusion.

To summarize in retrospect efforts to describe the social significance of art, we can identify two distinct tendencies. On the surface, art continued to be preoccupied with the "beautiful" until well into the nineteenth century. Art presented itself to society in the form of its positive value. (And who would want a society devoid of beauty? Marcuse still used this argument to counter the agitated students of the 1968 movement.) What was intended to be a positive code value was meant to describe the function of art in relation to the outside and, at the same time, to serve as an internal criterion for judging artworks. As it turned out, this placed too heavy a semantic burden on the concept of beauty, and artists themselves refused to adhere to the concept. To reconstruct the issue in formal terms, one sought to express in one final thought both the hetero-reference of art (its relationship to the external world as a social accomplishment) and its self-reference (as a criterion or formula for the unity of programs). But if this project entailed formulating the difference between hetero-reference and self-reference as a *unity*, it amounted to rendering invisible a fundamental paradox, namely, the paradox of the unity of the distinguished, or the systemic paradox of the unity of system and environment.

In a concurrent but more or less underground tradition, this paradox emerged: more accurately, what emerged was the effort to erase its traces— "the trace of the erasure of the trace," to formulate the issue by referring to Derrida's paradox of the presence of the absent.[224] Crucial evidence can be found in the Renaissance poetry of (cognitive) paradox, which assumed that the business of art was to undermine pretentious knowledge claims and methods of acquiring knowledge without offering a solution that would provide a better knowledge. A corresponding strategy was to make transparent (and thus to legitimize) the production of illusion, to disrupt the illusion within one's own domain, and, generally, to resist the demand for consistency and to qualify one's sources and intentions as irrational. We found similar intentions in romanticism, especially in its play with doubles, counterconcepts, and incredible events. And eventually, the so-called avant-garde turned the transgression of boundaries into a program.

From Baumgarten to Hegel reflection theory appears to have treated the guiding distinctions of aesthetic theory—especially the distinction between the universal and the particular and between the intellect and the senses—along the same lines. Officially, the goal was to define the place of the fine arts; one was concerned with demarcating art and with dialectical synthesis. A second analysis, however, shows that the real issue is the "reentry" of the form into the form, of the distinction into what it distinguishes. The difference between the universal and the particular is replicated within the particular, and the difference between the intellect and the senses recurs within the sensuous realm. The artwork, so to speak, takes on the burden of paradox and dissolves it in its own formal arrangement; one then sees quite concretely: it works!

One can treat a number of distinctions in this manner. When the distinction between system and environment is reintroduced into the system in the form of the distinction between self-reference and hetero-reference, then used within the system to determine the self (for example, as effort and beauty), this, too, is an operation of reentry, whose function is to provide the observer with a workable distinction. And reentries are always forms, that is to say, distinctions, on whose other side paradox is not to be seen.

The self-description of a system is a paradoxical undertaking from its very beginning. Observation and description presuppose a difference between the observer/describer and his object, whereas the intent of *self-description* is to negate precisely this difference. In other words, the operation of self-description yields the distinction between describing and the described *within the same system*. This distinction generates an excess of possibilities. As a distinction, however, and as an excess that allows for multiple possibilities, it raises the question in what sense the unity of the system can still be the object of description. From the beginning to the end, the self-description of the art system is concerned with this problem, a problem that can be observed only as a paradox (and must therefore be concealed). This is a deconstructive insight. Deconstruction, however, is not the same as destruction. The analysis does not suggest that everything is arbitrary or senseless. Rather, it demonstrates that, and in what ways, the difference between the paradox and its unfolding—which renders the paradox invisible by constructing sufficiently plausible identities and distinctions—functions so as to integrate the system of art into the "course of history," or, considered from a sociological perspective, to adapt the system to the results of social evolution while preserving its autopoietic autonomy.

VI

Post-Hegelian philosophical aesthetics had tremendous difficulty grasping the semantic consequences of the differentiation of the art system, especially in its modern variant. On the one hand, philosophical aesthetics raised hyper-dimensional expectations that aspire to leave out nothing, not even nonart; on the other hand, it created a peculiar milieu that was preoccupied with itself above all and kept rebelling against its own history. Whether one follows Gehlen or Marquard in assigning to art a role of release and compensation, or sides with Adorno in attempting to reduce purist and sociocritical ambitions to the common denominator of negativity, the problematic relationship between art and society remains unresolved. If, however, one starts out from Parsons's pattern variables or from a theory of social systems differentiation, then it becomes immediately clear that universalism and specification do not contradict, but rather condition one another. For Parsons, this is a matter of combining *different* pattern variables.[225] For an elaborated theory of modern social differentiation, it means that, in modern society, *universality claims* presuppose functional differentiation and hence a *specific* system reference. Indeed, only subsystems can claim universality, and only with reference to their specific function.

Making such claims requires a system-internal memory, that is, a system-internal history and a distinction between self-reference and hetero-reference that refers to the system. The history of modern self-descriptions of the art system from romanticism via the avant-garde up to postmodernism can be subsumed under one perspective, as a variation on a single theme. What is at stake in all of them is the question of how to relate to the past within a system that has become autonomous, how to mediate between past and future, between memory and the freedom to change sides, in all of the system's distinctions.[226] In early modernity, a new conception of genius established the rule that the artist should follow his own genius rather than adhere to preestablished models.[227] The *concettismo* of the seventeenth century signaled that the artwork was more than itself.[228] The art of the past was no longer a model, an exemplary standard, or a reservoir of *paradigmata* or examples. Instead, it offered *the possibility for a hetero-reference that does not interfere with the autonomy of art*. The art of the past has become history. This precludes the simple repetition of existing works or styles. By losing the self-evidence of its binding force, the art of the past relinquishes its forms and styles as material to be exploited. Museums (and, in a different way, libraries) now serve as a system-internal context against which the new can distinguish itself *and which is indispensable for this purpose*. Given this situation, and given that the idea of a universal and, hence, binding museum could not be realized, one can have recourse to this contextual function and generate novelty by selecting or even creating the context against which the new can appear as such.[229] This operation, too, involves crossing a distinguishing boundary. One operates on the other side of the new, on the side of the system's memory, in order to select the background against which the works that are currently produced and positioned can appear to be new.

Even if, under the signature "postmodernism," insistence on the novelty of the individual work has been replaced by the freedom to combine traditional forms, the self-historicization of art remains bound to the distinction between the new and the old (otherwise, this self-historicization could not be understood in difference-theoretical terms). One must choose one of these forms: either the form of quotation or the form of recombining heterogeneous stylistic elements. Or one can take the past to be an ensemble of established expectations about art in order to provoke—and disappoint—these expectations. This strategy, too, keeps art dependent on the old/new distinction, even in reflection. Only new works can make history (which leads some people to infer an "end of history," because the possibilities appear to be exhausted). But this also implies that the unity of the old/new distinction is not available to reflection. And the fact that one does not reflect upon this difference facilitates the use of anachronisms in an explicitly modern fashion, namely, as forms that absorb contingency.[230] The old/new distinction becomes the blind spot of the system's self-description; and an observation of the third order is required—a description of a self-describing system—if one wants to know what this distinction is all about and how the art system reflects upon itself by means of *just this* distinction.

The hypothesis that every fully autonomous system requires an external reference might provide a starting point. Gödel as witness. Selecting the dimension of time for the purpose of externalization provides the greatest possible freedom for a specifically social, communicative self-determination of the system. As a concrete reality that cannot, indeed must not be treated *as binding any longer*, the past fulfills its function as a guarantor of autonomy. The past is thus neither insignificant nor dispensable. But it can henceforth fulfill its function only paradoxically: as the presence of an absence, as the inclusion of an exclusion, as the trace that, according to Derrida,[231] is left by the effacement of the trace—in short, as a parasite that thrives on the paradox that the unity of the distinction (old/new), which is used by an observer, cannot be indicated in the observation itself.

Even if one follows Nelson Goodman and places on art the burden of contributing to the creation of the world,[232] a world can be created *operatively* only *within the world* and, in observation, only *from another world*. In this way, the world accompanies all operations as a continually reproduced "unmarked space." At the observational level, however, it is possible—in science as well as in art—to make transparent the premises behind previous ways of world making. Doing so inevitably marks the previously valid world and thereby cancels it as a world. Subsequently, earlier theories, styles, works, and so forth can no longer function *as world* (no matter how such concepts as reality, objectivity, Being, and so on are treated at the level of philosophical terminology). In this way, the degradation of the world through signification perpetually regenerates new unobservabilities. This is why the generation of the new is ultimately inexplicable.

But what happens, exactly, when postmodernism tolerates the return to a traditional reservoir of forms? One would think that the old/new distinction becomes obsolete once the continued employment of old forms is tolerated or even recommended. The opposite is true. What is at stake is not merely copying old forms, but rather trying out new combinations. It appears as if, under the title of postmodernism, the system claims autonomy even with regard to the old/new distinction, which is to say, it claims autonomy in crossing the boundary between the old and the new, whereby the new eventually becomes obsolete as well. If this is true, then the old/new distinction must be decoupled from the distinction between self-reference and hetero-reference. The art of the past cannot be treated as something external simply because it is past and operatively unattainable. Presumably one learns that only the system can guarantee the reality of its own world. Therefore reference to reality resides exclusively in the resistance of the system's operations to themselves—some form combinations simply won't work!—and in the fact that the world, whether one likes it or not, remains unobservable.

Classical thought sought to solve this problem by *generalization*, following the schema of species and genres. In this way, one would arrive at ultimate principles that were continually reaffirmed in all distinctions involved in the practice of distinguishing. In German Idealism, particularly in romanticism, this hope faded away, withdrawing into a distance that, while it could still be localized, could no longer be reached by reflection. The hope for ultimate principles was preserved as a direction without an end, and in this sense one could still speak of the ideal of beauty. But by *stating* the issue in such terms, one has reached the point where even this is no longer possible. One can refuse to acknowledge this fact and keep rebelling against it. At that point, the temporal dimension of the art system turns into its reflection dimension. The goal is not to affirm the present, the moment, the decision as the sole guarantee of reality; quite the opposite: one perpetually rebels against the present to the extent that it still contains traces of the past. The present revolts against itself, and what is at stake in this revolt is the inclusion of the system's negation into the system. The present is reduced to a mere caesura, a temporal "nothing," where art cannot reflect but only operate. The future represents the self-reference of art, and the past, because it cannot be altered, represents its hetero-reference. The parasites[233] generated by this distinction force their way unnoticed into the system and take over its invisible government. The invisible hand (the metaphor indicates the paradox) remains invisible, because it knows only a timeless present. Whatever happens, happens. One begins, places a difference, draws a distinction, and then abandons oneself to what can no longer be altered, only destroyed.

Once reflection shifts to the primacy of the temporal dimension, its self-description as an "aesthetics" becomes meaningless.[234] And yet, even after the reference of the term—the difference between forms of knowledge guided by theory and forms of sensuous knowledge—had long been forgotten, its reference to the phenomenal world remained the distinguishing feature of aesthetics. Even when art was no longer a matter of imitation, one still assumed that the communicative intent of art had to appear in the artwork itself. A name for a theory that can do without this assumption has not yet been found, and the undertaking is dubious. But under the catchword *deconstruction*, one already debates the dissolution of the "phenomenological" meaning of literature, if not of art in general.[235]

If we compare the situation of the art system in the present century, outlined above, with the situation of other functional systems, then we notice the collapse of the internal boundary between the self-reflection or theory of the system and the system's productive operations. Everywhere else this boundary is respected. Theology does not need to produce results that can be presented in a sermon. The interdisciplinary and internationally oriented self-understanding of legal theory distinguishes itself from the generalized decision rules that must assume forms capable of functioning as law. Pedagogy, rather than being taught, stages the professional self-understanding and the mission of a profession specializing in education. The theory of knowledge is not a scientific method; it may present itself as a scientific theory about a specific object, science, but it is not meant to be applied in this realm. The self-description of the art system appears to have developed in a different way. One might ask: Why?

More than any other functional system—religion, politics, science, or law—the art system is able to accept multiple descriptions of complexity. More than any other functional system, it is in a position to demonstrate that modern society and, from its perspective, the world can be described only in poly-contextual terms. In this sense, art makes the "truth" about society appear in society, while demonstrating (if it can!) that under precisely such conditions formal constraints emerge, that what fits and what doesn't becomes an issue, and that the common fear of arbitrariness, of "anything goes," is unfounded. A shift in guiding distinctions—in "contextures" in Gotthard Günther's sense, or in observational "frames"—requires a sufficient degree of transparency. One must be able to recognize where such leaps are heading and how continuity is secured under the conditions of a shifted "frame."

The reflection theory of the art system presents itself in and through works of art—no longer (if it ever did) as an aesthetics.[236] Prior to any textual fixation of the meaning of art, famous names and masterworks already exist—Dante, Giotto, Raphael, Michelangelo, Palladio, Shakespeare, Goethe—which must be included in any "discourse" about art. This makes expert competence in evaluating artworks indispensable. The trend begins with artists who write; then, with the emergence of art academies in the seventeenth century, we find artists who teach; finally, there are art professors who seek to make a name for themselves as practicing artists. There is a need for expertise and consultation in decisions about acquisitions. Exhibitions must be conceived and put together. The quality of poetry, or at least its capacity to catch the reader's attention, must be evaluated before poems are published. All of this remains a "critical" business, because the system generates more possibilities than it can accept.

The need to establish a frame within the frame of the art system generates a parasite, an art-specific establishment of more or less significant experts, which is capable of responding positively or negatively to new publications—whereby the distinction between positive and negative judgments becomes of little significance, because both can establish a given topic in the mass media. Controversies stimulate business, although certain rules of belonging must be respected. Moreover, the rapid establishment of possible but initially excluded works prevents the establishment of experts from being disrupted by every dispute. In order to highlight one's critical competency, it is important to lack a specific organizational affiliation. No particular organization monopolizes the art scene—neither galleries nor museums, neither the theaters nor the concert halls, neither the journalists that specialize in art nor the professors of the art academies. In this regard, the claim to expertise does have a professional aspect, even when membership in a number of different organizations takes care of the necessary income. At the same time, artworks begin to emerge that reflect upon the context facilitating such success and along with it upon the "system." As early as the seventeenth and eighteenth centuries, one finds ironic (?) paintings of art collections or art exhibitions that depict entire walls filled with paintings—paintings that are ruined by the fact of being exhibited. The degradation of the paintings by the much desired exhibition becomes a topic of art; it is displayed as art. Today one can even find exhibitions entirely dedicated to paintings that depict exhibitions.[237]

This world of art criticism, which is affected by art and reflected upon in works of art, is the true source of the art system's self-description. Such criticism filters and puts together what is written about art with a claim to scientific status, a careful choice of terminology, and a sense for theoretical consistency. Criticism is where intellectual fashions affect the art system. To be sure, it is difficult to ignore the marginal position of recent theoretical trends—structuralism, poststructuralism, "literary criticism," hermeneutics, reader-friendly reception theory, or psychoanalytical thought —but none of these theories can establish itself as the dominant paradigm. Such frequently used labels respond to the seemingly irresistible urge of academic intellectuals to categorize themselves in terms of such trends.[238] Names facilitate communication. They may inspire artists to produce works "in tune with the times," but offer little help when it comes to relevant formal decisions. At least in one respect, however, recent trends in art and theory do converge, namely, with respect to the dimension of time. Artworks demonstrate their independence from tradition and play with the traditional reservoir of forms. They not only announce the end of European art but also want to be this end. They challenge the distinction between art and objects of utility in order to demonstrate, as works of art, the universalization of art, the inclusion of the world in art, in order to make the point that this is how things are. But can one perceive this intent? Is it possible to see, to hear, to experience it in an imagination stimulated by literature? Or can one only *know* and *understand* that this is *intended*?

When the artwork turns into genuine philosophy[239] and intellectuals restrict themselves to commenting on this state of affairs, how can things go on? Should we expect the art system henceforth to trade primarily in derivatives of the intellect, just as the financial market trades in derivative financial instruments? Are the consequences for the art system as unpredictable as they are in the realm of finance? Or is it possible to channel operations and self-descriptions once again into different tracks, so they can stimulate one another without merging? Too much identity inevitably means: no future.

More than any other functional system, art appears to succeed—or at least has the intention of doing so—in representing modern society within society—or, to borrow a fitting formulation by David Roberts,[240] to realize the "emancipation of contingency" as a model of society within society. Art demonstrates, so to speak, this is how things are, or this is a possibility! The paradox, which art cannot represent but only unfold, consists in the necessity of contingency. But does this mean that art must give up its art-specific manner of presenting its intent in such a way as to allow the observer to observe observations along the lines of distinctions internal to the work?

No one familiar with the art scene will deny that art can realize the emancipation of contingency in many different ways. It can adapt its operations, even its existence, to this situation and thus put itself at risk. Whether a strict self-limitation of the possible, of the *potestas in se ipsum*, can emerge from this adaptation remains to be seen. Simply doing without self-generated necessities is not enough; this strategy certainly does not incorporate society into society or the form into the form. Renouncing necessity always sacrifices that which is distinguished from necessity, namely, freedom. The necessity/freedom distinction is replaced by the distinction necessity/contingency.

By staging and perpetually restaging a form of self-reference that reflects upon itself, the art system can do without distinguishing between affirmative and critical attitudes toward the external world. It does not need a "political function," which it never had any chance of successfully occupying anyway, at least not "democratically." Instead, the art system symbolizes conditions that, at the level of society and its functional systems, established themselves as a consequence of functional differentiation and leave open what one thinks of them, because it no longer matters. The appropriation of the topics of social movements by the functional system of the mass media is one among many examples. The art system realizes society in its own realm as an exemplary case. It shows things as they are. It demonstrates what society entered into when it began to differentiate individual functional systems and abandoned these systems to autonomous self-regulation. Art exemplifies a situation in which the future, no longer guaranteed by the past, has become unpredictable. Operative closure, the emancipation of contingency, self-organization, poly-contexturality, the hypercomplexity of self-descriptions, or, simpler and less accurately formulated, pluralism, relativism, historicism—all of these trends offer no more than different cross sections of the structural fate of modernity. By suffering its own condition, art shows that's just how it is. Whoever perceives this can see in modern art the paradigm of modern society. But this situation only raises the question: What difference does it make?

VII

From the very beginning, it was our intention to treat art as a unified topic, disregarding differences that result from different media and their sensuous or imaginary realization. No one will dispute that this is a historical task. The question is whether it can be carried out by an external observer who can take as his starting point a latent function invisible to art or proceed from "deep structures" that cannot be transformed into premises useful to art.[241]

Before investigating the problem more thoroughly, one should not insist on an insurmountable communication barrier between external and internal description. Indeed, the unity of art is thematized in the history of the art system's self-description—if initially only under the "patronage" of philosophy, so to speak. It is generally assumed that this self-thematization did not occur until the eighteenth century and that it followed a singularization of the concept of art and its reduction to the realm of the "fine arts," which made such a singularization possible. But this assumption is too simple. Ever since Aristotle, the concept of imitation has covered more than one artistic genre, applying not only to the imitation of objects but also to the imitation of actions, not only to the visual arts but also to drama and poetry. The real difficulty, however, could not be resolved within the Aristotelian framework.[242] The formula of imitation aims at representation; it seeks to embrace the world by replicating it in another medium. This purpose requires entirely different presuppositions, which might be captured in a concept but not in a unified theory. The visual arts could be significantly improved with regard to their technology of representation, especially through the invention of perspective, by representing light and shadow, and by capturing movement in a significant position. In drama and poetry, this kind of progress was inconceivable. Instead, the discussion ran aground in the old problem of truth and deception. The relationship to nature remained as vague as the concept of nature itself. One could define the task of imitation as mirroring the better part of nature, or simply as manifesting a brilliant capacity for deception, which presented a transparent deception in a highly artful fashion while obscuring the manner in which this effect was accomplished.

In the eighteenth century—for a relatively short period from Baumgarten to Hegel—the guiding principle of imitation gave way to the guiding principle of aesthetics. The problem became a problem of cognition, a cognition that used the senses—hence the term *aesthetics*—and that therefore had to renounce the highest rank in the hierarchy of cognitions. Sensuousness dragged one down, while the idea was uplifting—this was the tension that art sought to express and that it had to realize as "beauty." From Hegel's historicizing perspective, art could only represent a transitional stage in the self-realization of Spirit. But if the task of Spirit was to process distinctions—one called them "oppositions"[243]—it had to culminate in the perfection of the self-reflection of Spirit. Since art could not claim the highest relevance, this process ended a little earlier. Processing distinctions ended in identity. And, as usual, identity meant: no future.

Today, the theory of art continues to be irritated by the idea of the end of art,[244] and efforts to break entirely with the traditions of imitation and aesthetics, or even with the relation to sensuousness as a distinguishing characteristic of art, only confirm this prognosis. When the artwork is forced to reflect upon the end of distinguishing, indeed, must be this end, differences among operation, program, and self-description collapse, and one arrives once again at an identity, thus, at no future.

Notions about "postmodernism" remain bound to the legend of an end of art, emphasizing a break with the formal traditions of history. Such notions make forms belonging to *different historical periods* available *simultaneously* and thus abstract from the sequentiality and periodization of history emphasized by historicism. At the same time, however, they exploit the past for the purpose of authorizing forms—as a source of authority, so to speak, that does not prohibit the opposite. The difference that guides attempts of this sort is the question of whether artistic forms are bound to the context of their emergence and must perpetually overcome this context, or whether these forms, precisely as belonging to the past, can be divorced from their context and exploited for any arbitrary form combination. A tradition that has come to an end, has exhausted its possibilities, can think of its "aftermath" only in terms of willfulness, of offering quotations to a learned audience, of parody.[245] But the end of art is a distinction that, for its part, points to an unknown "beyond." From the viewpoint of a theory of observation, one must ask who distinguishes that way and why. The history of reflecting upon the unity of the art system provides an answer to this question. All attempts to determine unity as such have always also reflected on the reference to another side of the form— whether this side is occupied by a nature perfected in itself or by a cognition that has become fully reflexive. But these counterconcepts do not necessarily prevail; they could be exchanged for others, if one only knew which ones to use instead.

Thematically, the history of the self-description of art was concerned with determining the meaning of art, and changing answers to this question were determined by the differentiation of an autonomous art system and its operative closure. This development rendered all boundaries problematic, canceling the distinction between the map and the territory (in thought) and favoring attempts to realize this cancellation as a work of art. Art arrives at a point where "the end of art" comes into view, where the programmatic rule of innovation not only demands distance from existing art but also seeks to surpass even this distance by enforcing a distancing from this distance from tradition. The reintegration of the tradition into an art that no longer accepts tradition is called "postmodernism." The sociologist can observe all of this as an existing reality.

But the historical reconstruction of the self-description of art raises the question of whether there might have been a submerged, other history, a history concerned not with unity but with difference. Pursuing this question suggests that the theme of reflection does not define the meaning of the autonomy of art, but the meaning of the doubling of reality in which this autonomy established itself. The program of imitation would appear to be a kind of conciliatory gesture, which assumes a reality that is more beautiful (better, more perfect, and permeated by the Idea) than it presents itself. Reversing this is easy but doesn't lead very far. One would merely have to show that the world (icy, bathed in cold light, nearly everywhere uninhabitable) or society is much worse than our idyllic notions of nature and culture would have it. Making this point today is once again called "sublime." As early as romanticism, however, one was potentially aware of other, more far-reaching possibilities for disrupting the illusory reference to reality, namely, by incorporating the doubling of reality into art itself. If this strategy were successful today, then one could dispose over the doubling of reality in art—whether through the one-sided accentuation of artistic means, of the "script" of art, through self-sabotage, or through presenting the elimination of difference. But isn't the "end" reached in this way perhaps just the end of an identification of art with a certain style of self-description, with a reflection on unity rather than a reflection on difference?[246]

One must therefore ask oneself how and to what purpose one distinguishes between reality and fiction, and what reality must be in itself that it can tolerate this distinction. The artificiality of this distinction becomes evident if one considers the difficulty of introducing it and rendering it plausible in the seventeenth and early eighteenth centuries. Statistics, which emerged roughly at the same time, was confronted with the same problem (the same distinction). Employing the distinction between reality and fiction begs the question of what reality itself must be like in order to assume both a real and a fictional form, while leaving open the possibility for crossing the internal boundary of this distinction. We have based our investigation on a theoretical concept capable of answering this question; we presupposed an operative system that draws this distinction and, in so doing, renders the world invisible. When communication (rather than perception, for example) is at stake, society is the system that makes it possible—for itself and for art—to distinguish between reality and fiction. One could then pursue the suggestion that art tests arrangements that are at once fictional and real in order to show society, from a position within society, that things could be done differently, which does not mean that anything goes.

Along these lines, reality might still be defined in terms of a resistance, which is no longer the resistance of the external world to attempts to grasp it by knowing and acting, but a resistance, within one and the same system, of internal operations to the operations of the system. In the system of society, one might think of the resistance of communication to itself, a resistance that ends up constructing a genuine reality (one must keep in mind, of course, that there are structural couplings between communication and the perceptions of individuals and that individuals tend to intervene in communication when claims are made that contradict their perceptions[247]). In the art system, this resistance has to do, as we suggested earlier,[248] with incongruities in the formal arrangement of artworks or with disturbances in communication through art and about art that can be traced to the lack of fit between the components of an artwork. If a work manages to pass this test, then it creates what we have called a fictional reality. The more demanding the manner in which the problem of form is posed, the more unlikely it becomes that communication occurs at all and the more impressive is the manner in which the work testifies to the reality that is processed within the art system.[249] Given the problematic state of the current self-description of the art system, who would want to exclude the possibility that this might still happen in the future?

However, our description remains external and has no control over whether, and in what ways, the art system, together with its works and self-descriptions, will venture into this future. To do so, the art system will have to proceed in a manner specific to form, that is, by using distinctions. One will have to avoid the trap of identity. In this regard, at least, art must break with the kind of modernity envisioned by Adorno, or even the one propagated by Habermas. The future of art depends on whether it opts for difference and whether it can make use of constraints to expand the room for further distinctions.

VIII

We can summarize the results of our elaborate investigations in one question—a question that cannot be answered by sociology or by any other academic discipline, but only by art. Society has differentiated an art system at an operative and structural level. As a result, that system remains dependent on its social environment, and such dependencies (of an economic nature, for example) may increase. At the same time, however, the environment cannot determine what counts as art and how artworks will be judged. The overabundance of communicative possibilities that· emerges from this state of affairs can be processed and put into form only within the art system. This includes the problem—which did not present itself until the twentieth century—of how the distinction between art and nonart is to be controlled; how, in other words, the paradoxical unity of art and nonart can be dissolved within the art system itself.

If this is the question, then everything depends on determining more precisely what contributes conceptually—eventually through the direct observation of artworks as "form"—to the operative closure of the art system. In this regard, highly abstract mathematical and systems-theoretical considerations suggest the need to pay attention to distinctions and to think of form as a boundary that separates two sides. This notion can be elaborated under a factual or a temporal aspect. Factually, each determination of a form excludes something—the world, on the one hand, and the observer (the artist, the beholder) who uses the distinction, on the other. Under the title "conceptual art," the individual artwork, although indispensable, was relieved of the burden of answering for itself, and the problem was displaced onto the recursive network of the art system. In this situation multimedia modes of presentation flourished. But the question of how the work is made, how it is represented, remains. Temporally, each form determination generates an indeterminacy transcending the form, which, if one wants to retain the form (rather than destroying it and starting from scratch), can no longer be filled at will. Art therefore always demonstrates the arbitrary generation of nonarbitrariness or the emergence of order from chance. In addition, it displays the difficulties that occur in the creation of connecting forms, and it shows how established forms are altered by "redescriptions" of the sort suggested by the Art & Language Group.

An external (in this case sociological) description of the art system can establish this much—and, if necessary, revise it in the course of further development of the discipline. But such a description says nothing about how the art system handles self-generated uncertainties and difficulties. The avant-garde has raised the issue and put it into form. It remains to be seen whether and how the art system will deal with this challenge. With growing freedom, the uncertainty of criteria will increase, and distinguishing between success and failure in art will become more difficult. Some may doubt whether the traditional task of creating more redundancy for a greater amount of variety is still binding for art. However, so long as the autonomy of the art system prevails, there will always be a medium that motivates the search for convincing forms. If anything is possible, then the criteria for selecting what is admissible must be tightened. In the long run, handing out commuters' passes instead of a selection can hardly satisfy. Only the overcoming of difficulties makes a work significant: *Hoc opus, hic labor est.*[250]

Reference Matter

Notes

Preface

1. Niklas Luhmann, *Soziale Systeme: Grundriß einer allgemeinen Theorie* (Frankfurt, 1984); trans. as *Social Systems*, trans. John Bednarz, with Dirk Baecker (Stanford, Calif., 1995). Concerning the social system, currently only a short text written for Italian universities is available; however, a more comprehensive publication is in preparation. See Niklas Luhmann and Raffaele De Giorgi, *Teoria della società* (Milan, 1992).

§ 1

1. This distinction has since been relativized on the basis of neurophysiological research. See Gerhard Roth, *Das Gehirn und seine Wirklichkeit: Kognitive Neurobiologie und ihre philosophischen Konsequenzen* (Frankfurt, 1994).

2. As Derrida has pointed out repeatedly, this move has turned the philosophical tradition against itself. Assuming the primacy of thought, it treats writing as something external, although the tradition itself could only exist as writing!

3. We speak of "double closure" in the sense that the brain, in separating levels of operation, puts itself in a position to coordinate the coordination of its primary processes. See Heinz von Foerster, "On Constructing a Reality," in his *Observing Systems* (Seaside, Calif., 1981), pp. 288–309 (304ff.).

4. This reverses the common Cartesian doctrine (hetero-reference is doubtful; self-reference is certain). Kenneth J. Gergen, *Toward Transformation in Social Knowledge* (New York, 1982), p. 66.

5. Here and in the following, we disregard the neurophysiological correlates of perception. At this level, perception must be understood as a kind of measurement that functions selectively in that it cannot measure everything when it

measures something. See Howard H. Pattee, "Cell Psychology: An Evolutionary Approach to the Symbol-Matter Problem," *Cognition and Brain Theory* 5 (1982): 325–41; A. Moreno et al., "Computational Darwinism as a Basis for Cognition," *Revue internationale de systémique* 6 (1992): 205–21. See also Roth, *Das Gehirn und seine Wirklichkeit.* Regarding this process, consciousness begins with a delocalization, that is, by erasing all information about the location where the perception actually takes place.

6. On this topic, see Heinz von Foerster, "Das Gleichnis vom Blinden Fleck: Über das Sehen im allgemeinen," in Gerhard Johann Lischka, ed., *Der entfesselte Blick* (Bern, 1993), pp. 14–47.

7. On space and time as media, see Chapter 3, section III, below.

8. One can arrive at different results only if one fails to distinguish between brain activity and consciousness. For a typical example in the realm of neurophysiology, see Gerhard Roth, "Erkenntnis und Realität: Das reale Gehirn und seine Wirklichkeit," in Siegfried J. Schmidt, ed., *Der Diskurs des radikalen Konstruktivismus* (Frankfurt, 1987), pp. 229–55. Roth even ascribes "semantic" capabilities to the brain.

9. One reason for this may be that the neurophysiologist occupies the position of an external observer for whom the internal/external difference defining his object of research is already given. Then the only question remains how the brain enables itself to perform representational or semantic functions. On this topic, see: Paul M. Churchland, *A Neurocomputational Perspective: The Nature of Mind and the Structure of Science* (Cambridge, Mass., 1989), esp. p. 77; Gerhard Roth, "Kognition: Die Entstehung von Bedeutung im Gehirn," in Wolfgang Krohn and Günther Küppers, eds., *Die Entstehung von Ordnung, Organisation und Bedeutung* (Frankfurt, 1992), pp. 104–33. Consider further the distinction between "reality," from the perspective of an external (second-order) observer, and actuality, from the perspective of the brain or consciousness, in Gerhard Roth and Helmut Schwegler, "Self-Organization, Emergent Properties and the Unity of the World," *Philosophica* 46 (1990): 45–64 (56ff.).

10. See George Spencer Brown, *Laws of Form* (1969; rpt. New York, 1979), pp. 56ff., 69ff.

11. For good reasons, Benny Shanon has argued against this prevailing view. See Shanon, "Metaphors for Language and Communication," *Revue internationale de systémique* 3 (1989): 43–59. In his theory of language, Maturana rejects the metaphor of transmission as well—but only because he conceives of language in terms strictly internal to the organism as a structural coupling of the nervous system with itself (which may be justified but is of no help for a theory of social communication). See Humberto R. Maturana, *Erkennen: Organisation und Verkörperung von Wirklichkeit: Ausgewählte Arbeiten zur biologischen Epistemologie* (Braunschweig, 1982), esp. pp. 54ff., 154f. On transmission as one of many meta-

phors that have influenced our understanding of communication, see also Klaus Krippendorff, "Der verschwundene Bote: Metaphern und Modelle der Kommunikation," in Klaus Merten, Siegfried J. Schmidt, and Siegfried Weischenberg, eds., *Die Wirklichkeit der Medien: Eine Einführung in die Kommunikationswissenschaft* (Opladen, 1994), pp. 79–113.

12. See, e.g., Paul de Man, *Blindness and Insight: Essays in the Rhetoric of Contemporary Criticism*, 2d ed. (Minneapolis, 1983), pp. 232f.—but in a somewhat different terminology, replacing reference by constitution.

13. See Roth, *Das Gehirn und seine Wirklichkeit*, pp. 250ff.

14. For Husserl, as we know, this meant that conscious activity and phenomenon were strictly the same thing (this is why he called his philosophy "phenomenology") and that intention was the form of the act that continually reproduced this unity.

15. From this insight follows an epistemological "constructivism" that finds its equivalents in the realms of biology and psychology—that is, in the world of Jean Piaget, Humberto Maturana, and Heinz von Foerster. See Niklas Luhmann, *Erkenntnis als Konstruktion* (Bern, 1988); Luhmann, "Das Erkenntnisprogramm des Konstruktivismus und die unbekannt bleibende Realität," in Luhmann, *Soziologische Aufklärung*, vol. 5 (Opladen, 1990), pp. 31–58 (trans. as "The Cognitive Program of Constructivism and a Reality That Remains Unknown," in Wolfgang Krohn et al., eds., *Self-Organization: Portrait of a Scientific Revolution* [Dordrecht, 1990], pp. 64–85); and Luhmann, *Die Wissenschaft der Gesellschaft* (Frankfurt, 1990); see further Helmut Wilke, "Systemtheoretische Strategien des Erkennens: Wirklichkeit als interessierte Konstruktion," in Klaus Götz, ed., *Theoretische Zumutungen: Vom Nutzen der systemischen Theorie für die Managementpraxis* (Heidelberg, 1994), pp. 97–116.

16. Quite differently, Wil Martens, "Die Autopoiesis soziale Systeme," *Kölner Zeitschrift für Soziologie und Sozialpsychologie* 43 (1991): 625–40. See also the subsequent discussion in *Kölner Zeitschrift* 44 (1992): 139–45.

17. See Heinz von Foerster, "Für Niklas Luhmann: Wie rekursiv ist Kommunikation?" *Teoria Sociologica* 1/2 (1993): 61–85. His answer is that communication is recursion or, more accurately, that "Kommunikation ist das Eigenverhalten in einem rekursiv operierenden, zweifach geschlossenen System" (p. 83).

18. The significance of the "unfinished" in Leonardo da Vinci and Michelangelo was already debated in the sixteenth century. On the intentional use of ambiguity, often to the point of infinite interpretive possibilities, see Umberto Eco, *Opera aperta* (1962), 6th ed. (Milan, 1988). See also the notion of "blanks" [*Unbestimmtheitsstellen*] in Roman Ingarden, *Das literarische Kunstwerk* (1931), 4th ed. (Tübingen, 1972), pp. 261ff.; see further William Empson, *Seven Types of Ambiguity* (1930; 2d ed. Edinburgh, 1947).

19. On the Parsonian distinction between simple and double contingency,

see James Olds, *The Growth and Structure of Motives: Psychological Studies in the Theory of Action* (Glencoe, Ill., 1956).

20. For a similar argument, see Peter Fuchs, *Moderne Kommunikation: Zur Theorie des operativen Displacements* (Frankfurt, 1993), pp. 15ff.

21. The notion of "reading" may become questionable here, although it generally includes reading poetry. At any rate, artistic perception blocks our habitual, hasty, carefree reading, or we are not reading the text as literature.

22. "See "Blüthenstaub," no. 19: "Der Sitz der Seele ist da, wo sich Innenwelt und Außenwelt berühren. Wo sie sich durchdringen, ist er in jedem Punkt der Durchdringung," quoted from Hans Joachim Mähl and Richard Samuel, eds., *Novalis: Werke, Tagebücher und Briefe Friedrich von Hardenbergs*, vol. 2 (Darmstadt, 1978), p. 233.

23. When guided by thought, perception can distinguish between *movements* and *changes*. While driving to the gas station, I see someone climbing a ladder and changing the price tag. The man's movements are one thing, his changing of the price, in relation to before/after, is another. The man might fall off the ladder, the prices cannot. But both can be seen! The same capacity for discrimination must be present whenever we participate in communication and, once again, already at the level of perception.

24. A longer quotation is warranted here. In Jonathan Richardson, *A Discourse on the Dignity, Certainty, Pleasure and Advantage of the Science of a Connoisseur* (1719), quoted from *The Works* (London, 1773; rpt. Hildesheim, 1969), pp. 241–346 (247), we read that works of art are suited "to communicate ideas; and not only those which we may receive otherwise, but such as without this art could not possibly be communicated; whereby mankind is advanced higher in the rational state, and made better; and that in a way easy, expeditious, and delightful." See also p. 250: "Painting is another sort of writing, and is subservient to the same ends as that of her young sister." Richardson goes on to emphasize the temporal advantage of painting over the much slower sequentiality of words.

25. Baumgarten, the founder of aesthetics as a special branch of philosophy, introduces the topic as follows: "Aesthetica (theoria liberalium artium, gnoseologia inferior, ars pulchre cogitandi, ars analogi rationis) est scientia cognitionis sensitivae." Alexander Gottlieb Baumgarten, *Aesthetica* (Frankfurt/Oder, 1750), § 1, p. 1. Baumgarten considered beauty the goal and perfection of sensuous knowledge (as if we looked into the world to discover beauty, and only occasionally encountered deformities)—a figure burdened with tradition that propelled aesthetics toward its later development. See *Aesthetica*, § 14, p. 6: "Aesthetices finis est perfectio cognitionis sensitivae qua talis, § 1. Haec autem est pulchritudo." Baumgarten does consider other possible orientations of perception, but when sensuous *cognition* searches for its *own* perfection, beauty is the exclusive goal.

26. See also Moreno et al., "Computational Darwinism."

27. See also Niklas Luhmann, "Wie ist Bewußtsein an Kommunikation beteiligt?" in Hans Ulrich Gumbrecht and K. Ludwig Pfeiffer, eds., *Materialität der Kommunikation* (Frankfurt, 1988), pp. 884–905 (trans. as "How Can the Mind Participate in Communication?" in Hans Ulrich Gumbrecht and K. Ludwig Pfeiffer, eds., William Whobrey, trans., *Materialities of Communication* [Stanford, Calif., 1994], pp. 371–87); and Luhmann, *Die Wissenschaft der Gesellschaft*, pp. 11ff.

28. We are not investigating, in Kantian fashion, the conditions of possibility for language, nor are we conducting a Darwinian inquiry into the evolution of language.

29. In the realm of alphabetic writing. Ideographic writing in China and Japan has preserved the connection between art and writing in the form of a cherished artistic genre.

30. See Horst Wenzel, "Visibile parlare: Zur Repräsentation der audiovisuellen Wahrnehmung in Schrift und Bild," in Ludwig Jäger and Bernd Switalla, eds., *Germanistik in der Mediengesellschaft* (Munich, 1994), pp. 141–57.

31. See Hans Ulrich Gumbrecht, "Stimme als Form: Zur Topik lyrischer Selbstinszenierung im vierzehnten und fünfzehnten Jahrhundert," ms. 1992.

32. This idea is not entirely new, as a quotation from David Hume would show. Compare Peter Jones, "Hume and the Beginning of Modern Aesthetics," in Peter Jones, ed., *The "Science of Man" in the Scottish Enlightenment: Hume, Reid, and Their Contemporaries* (Edinburgh, 1989), pp. 54–67. See also n. 24 above.

33. "Blüthenstaub," no. 23, Novalis, *Werke*, p. 237.

34. For variations on this problem, see Niklas Luhmann and Peter Fuchs, *Reden und Schweigen* (Frankfurt, 1989).

35. See esp. Pierre Bourdieu, *La distinction: Critique sociale du jugement de goût* (Paris, 1975); Bourdieu, *Ce que parler veut dire: L'économie des échanges linguistiques* (Paris, 1982).

36. In other words, Bourdieu's analyses make it possible to converse about Bourdieu and his analyses—but in the host's home we would be reluctant to comment on Dürer's rabbits hanging above the piano.

37. Heinz von Foerster calls this capacity "memory." See his "What Is Memory That It May Have Hindsight and Foresight as Well?" in S. Bogoch, *The Future of the Brain Sciences* (New York, 1969), pp. 19–64.

38. This conclusion is supported by quite different theoretical foundations. For Lyotard, a "phrase" is a language event that makes a difference and vanishes if it is not linked to other events (*enchaînement*). See Jean-François Lyotard, *Le différend* (Paris, 1983). Regarding the consequences for aesthetics, see, e.g., the essay "Newman: The Instant" in Jean-François Lyotard, *The Inhuman: Reflections on Time* (Stanford, Calif., 1991), pp. 78–88. There is no need for a subject that "supports" and "grounds" the event. It realizes itself: "Occurrence is the instant which 'happens,' which 'comes' unexpectedly but which, once it is there, takes

its place in the network of what has happened. Any instant can be the beginning, provided that it is grasped in terms of its *quod* rather than its *quid*" (ibid., p. 82).

39. An entirely different question is whether there is a kind of meditation, a motionless standstill of consciousness without reference that refrains from making distinctions—e.g., in the perception of artworks, in the gardens of Zen monasteries, or in the contemplation of landscapes. But none of these types of meditation would qualify as communication related specifically to art.

40. This crucial difference between communication through art and communication about art is often overlooked (e.g., by Gerhard Plumpe, *Ästhetische Kommunikation der Moderne*, vol. 1, *Von Kant bis Hegel* (Opladen, 1993). As a result, the differentiation of an autonomous art system is treated only in terms of the differentiation of a particular topic of communication about art.

41. Compare *Kritik der Urteilskraft*, § 21–, which is a strange text in need of clarification. On the one hand, the text glosses over the question of whether perceptions are communicable, or, to put it differently, how that which is communicable can be sorted out of what is perceived. Furthermore, the text leaves open what is currently discussed under the topic of intersubjectivity, namely, the question concerning the transcendental conditions of possibility of an alter ego. In both respects, the text operates naively. It almost looks as if transcendental controls could not be introduced at all via the inner reflection on facts of consciousness but only by (reflecting on) how and in what ways these facts are mediated. Let me provide an excerpt: "Erkenntnisse und Urteile müssen sich, samt der Überzeugung, die sie begleitet, allgemein mitteilen lassen; denn sonst käme ihnen keine Übereinstimmung mit dem Objekt zu; sie wären insgesamt ein bloß subjektives Spiel der Vorstellungskräfte, gerade so wie es der Skeptizismus verlangt." The problem of perception is covered up by Kant's sole concern with the (even more problematic) communication of a mental state, that is, with "die Stimmung der Erkenntniskräfte zu einer Erkenntnis überhaupt, und zwar diejenige Proportion, welche sich für eine Vorstellung (wodurch uns ein Gegenstand gegeben wird) gebührt, um daraus Erkenntnis zu machen."

42. For an older account of the disposition concerning awareness/unawareness in museums, see Roger de Piles, *Course de peinture par principes* (Paris, 1708), pp. 12–13. The painter gets annoyed or specializes in capturing the viewer's attention. In a similar vein, and roughly at the same time, Jonathan Richardson complains that gentlemen "overlook the beauties which they do not expect to find" and searches for a new science of connoisseurship that would rectify this problem. *A Discourse on the Dignity, Certainty, Pleasure and Advantage of the Science of a Connoisseur* (1719), quoted from *The Works* (London, 1773; rpt. Hildesheim, 1969), pp. 241–346 (244). Baudelaire begins his famous essay "Le peintre de la vie moderne" with exactly the same observation about preinformed observers (*Œuvres complètes*, Pléiade ed. [Paris, 1954], p. 881).

43. On the notion of the "in sich selbst Vollendete" and the idea of purpose without purpose, see Karl Philipp Moritz, *Schriften zur Ästhetik und Poetik: Kritische Ausgabe* (Tübingen, 1962), p. 6. Moritz retains the category of purpose because "das Unnütze oder Unzweckmäßige [kann] unmöglich einem vernünftigen Wesen Vergnügen machen." The naturalized anthropology of teleological orientation does not keep up with the development of the art system. Giving up this view would require a radical revision of what it means to be human.

44. This may be why Hegel considered a *concept* of immediacy indispensable, although in retrospect, immediacy presents itself to thinking always as mediated.

45. "Erst durch das Kunstwerk erfährt er [der Künstler, N. L.], was er mit seiner Thätigkeit gewollt hat," we read in Karl Wilhelm Ferdinand Solger's *Vorlesungen über Ästhetik*, ed. Karl Wilhelm Ludwig Heyse (Leipzig, 1829; rpt. Darmstadt, 1973), p. 115. And on p. 122: "Dem Künstler *entsteht* das Kunstwerk mehr, als es von ihm *gemacht* wird. Er lernt seinen vollen Vorsatz und seine Idee selbst erst dann ganz kennen, wenn das Kunstwerk vollendet ist."

46. Using Franz Erhard Walther's conception of art as example, Michael Lingner shows that artists themselves not only see but also want to see their role in such terms. "Kunst als Projekt der Aufklärung jenseits reiner Vernunft," in Michael Lingner, ed., *Das Haus in dem ich wohne: Die Theorie zum Werkentwurf von Franz Erhard Walther* (Klagenfurt, 1990), pp. 15–53 (42ff.). See also the other contributions in the same volume.

47. Specifically on this point, see Winfried Menninghaus, "Genie und Unsinn: Zur Poetik Immanuel Kants und Ludwig Tiecks," quoted from ms., 1994.

48. According to Friedrich Schlegel, poetry, too, ought to be treated as art. See his *Gespräch über die Poesie*, quoted from *Werke in zwei Bänden* (Berlin, 1980), vol. 2, p. 155. Obviously, Schlegel's demand does not go without saying, or else there would be no need for it.

49. Cleanth Brooks arrives at this conclusion on the basis of thoroughgoing interpretations. See his *The Well Wrought Urn: Studies in the Structure of Poetry* (New York, 1947). For a summary of Brooks's position, see pp. 192ff.; for an abbreviated version, see p. 74: "The Poem says what the poem says," and it cannot be said in any other way. And p. 201: "to refer . . . to . . . a paraphrase of the poem is to refer . . . to something outside the poem." In the meantime, this view has advanced to the level of textbook knowledge. See, e.g., John Ciardi and Miller Williams, *How Does a Poem Mean?* (1959; 2d ed. Boston, 1975).

50. See Christoph Menke-Eggers, *Die Souveränität der Kunst: Ästhetische Erfahrung nach Adorno und Derrida* (Frankfurt, 1988), pp. 45ff.

51. Experts in modern literature are aware of explicitly unreadable texts. Such texts, however, only intensify a limitation that has always existed.

52. For an elaboration of this point, see Chapter 3, below.

53. See Dietrich Schwanitz, "Zeit und Geschichte im Roman—Interaktion

und Gesellschaft im Drama: Zur wechselseitigen Erhellung von Systemtheorie und Literatur," in Dirk Baecker et al., eds., *Theorie als Passion* (Frankfurt, 1987), pp. 181–213.

54. In order to elucidate the self-reference of poems (as opposed to hetero-reference), Earl R. Wasserman, *The Subtler Language: Critical Readings of Neo-Classic and Romantic Poems* (Baltimore, 1959), p. 7, speaks of "the interactive capacities of any of the properties of words . . . including connotation and the capacity of a word to carry more than one reference as a symbol, metaphor, ambiguity, or pun; position and repetition; word order; sound, rhyme; even orthography."

55. For an older formulation of this principle (comparing it to the outline in the visual arts), see Moritz, *Schriften zur Ästhetik*, pp. 99f.

56. Umberto Eco, for example, defines the concept of form as "un tutto organico" (*Opera aperta* [1962; 6th ed. Milan, 1988], p. 22.)

57. See, e.g., Abraham Moles, *Information Theory and Esthetic Perception* (Urbana, Ill., 1966), p. 57: "By *form* (Gestalt) we mean here a group of elements perceived as a whole and *not* as the product of a random collection. More precisely, a form is a message, which appears to the observer as *not* being the result of random events."

58. Wassily Kandinsky, *Concerning the Spiritual in Art and Painting in Particular* (1912; Engl. trans. New York, 1947), p. 47.

59. Ciardi and Williams, *How Does a Poem Mean?* p. xxii (authors' emphasis).

60. Spencer Brown, *Laws of Form*, p. 1.

61. Gilles Deleuze, *Logique du sens* (Paris, 1969), pp. 37, 41.

62. We shall encounter this insight again under the name of "autopoiesis."

63. Stephan Mussil, "Literaturwissenschaft, Systemtheorie und der Begriff der Beobachtung," in Henk de Berg and Matthias Prangel, eds., *Kommunikation und Differenz: Systemtheoretische Ansätze in der Literatur- und Kunstwissenschaft* (Opladen, 1993), pp. 183–202. Mussil points out correctly that the world prior to all distinctions (for which Spencer Brown has no concept) must be distinguished from the "unmarked space" that emerges when a "marked space" is severed. Initially, Spencer Brown uses only the second concept, which designates the space accessible from the marked space by crossing its boundary. This conceptual limitation, while it serves the purposes of a calculus, does not exclude an inquiry into the state of the world that is severed by the injunction "draw a distinction." Nor does it prevent us from thematizing the unity of the distinction between marked and unmarked space. Spencer Brown acknowledges this by introducing the concept of the "unwritten cross" during a later phase of his calculus. (Spencer Brown, *Laws of Form*, p. 7.) See also, Matthias Varga von Kibéd and Rudolf Matzka, "Motive und Grundgedanken der 'Gesetze der Form,'" in Dirk Baecker, ed., *Kalkül der Form* (Frankfurt, 1993), pp. 58–85 (69f., 77); as well as Hegel's distinction between the infinite as the opposite of the finite and as true infinity in his

Vorlesungen über die Philosophie der Religion I, quoted from *Werke,* vol. 16 (Frankfurt, 1969), pp. 178f. For the purpose of distinguishing these two concepts, we shall speak of the unmarked state when referring to a state of the world prior to all distinctions and of the concept of the unmarked space when referring to the opposite of the marked space.

64. "And, if such a verse as this / may not claim another kiss." From "Claiming a Second Kiss by Desert," quoted from Ben Jonson, *The Complete Poems* (New Haven, Conn., 1975), pp. 131f.

65. The internal rhetoric of the Art & Language Group uses the term *redescription* but primarily for styles or exemplary works. See Michael Baldwin, Charles Harrison, Mel Ramsden, "On Conceptual Art and Painting, and Speaking and Seeing: Three Corrected Transcripts," *Art-Language,* n.s. 1 (1994): 30–69. However, the full significance of a continual reactualization of "redescriptions" becomes apparent only when it is referred to individual acts arranged as a form. Then we recognize that we are dealing with attempts to objectify double contingency, to observe works of art as conversations. Baldwin et al. (p. 63) speak of a "dialogic aura" (where "aura" could be taken to imply a reference to the unmarked space). I am grateful to Christian Matthiessen for arranging a meeting with the members of the Art & Language Group.

66. For an analysis using modern theoretical means, see, e.g., Friedrich Cramer, "Schönheit als dynamisches Grenzphänomen zwischen Chaos und Ordnung— ein neuer *Laokoon,*" *Selbstorganisation* 4 (1993): 79–102.

67. Spencer Brown, *Laws of Form.*

68. Michael Riffaterre, *Semiotics of Poetry* (Bloomington, Ind., 1978), p. 26, understands the poetic value of neologisms in terms of a "a relationship between two equivalent forms, one marked and one unmarked. The unmarked form antedates the text, the marked one does not." See also his "Poétique du néologisme," in Riffaterre, *La production du texte* (Paris, 1979), pp. 61–74.

69. Ranulph Glanville and Francisco Varela tackle a similar question in "'Your Inside Is Out and Your Outside Is In' (Beatles, 1968)," in George E. Lasker, ed., *Applied Systems and Cybernetics: Proceedings of the International Congress on Applied Systems Research and Cybernetics* (New York, 1981), pp. 638–41.

70. Spencer Brown begins with the phrase: "We take as given the idea of distinction and the idea of indication, and that we cannot make an indication without drawing a distinction" (*Laws of Form,* p. 1).

71. Hegel raises a similar issue—that one needs to distinguish *oneself* in order to distinguish—but he treats the problem as the beginning of universality and in this specific sense as the beginning of a reflection that, in its final stage of Spirit, reaches a perfection that no longer has an outside. See, e.g., Hegel's *Vorlesungen über die Philosophie der Religion I,* p. 125: "In der Tat aber ist diese Entzweiung, daß ich *Subjekt* gegen die Objektivität bin, eine *Beziehung* und *Iden-*

tität, die zugleich *unterschieden* ist von diesem *Unterschiede*, und es beginnt darin die *Allgemeinheit*."

72. For an elaboration of this point, see Niklas Luhmann, "Die Paradoxie der Form," in Dirk Baecker, ed., *Kalkül der Form*, pp. 197–212; trans. as "The Paradox of Form," in Baecker, ed., *Problems of Form*, trans. Michael Irmscher, with Leah Edwards (Stanford, Calif., 1999), pp. 15–26.

73. See Elena Esposito, *L'operazione di osservatione: Costruttivismo e teoria dei sistemi sociale* (Milan, 1992).

74. That the exclusion can be observed or can captivate a narrator's interest to the point where he makes it collapse by intervening as narrator into his own narration only affirms the necessity of exclusion. According to the well-known presentation of this problem in Lawrence Sterne's *Tristram Shandy*, the intervening narrator must be distinguished from the narrator who narrates the narrator's intervention. It seems no accident that Jean Paul's *Die unsichtbare Loge*—an early work in which the narrator is identical with the protagonist's educator and interferes with the action in all sorts of ways—remained unfinished, and that the problem is toned down in his following work, *Hesperus*. On this problem and on Jane Austen's solution via stylistic forms that combine self-reference and heteroreference, see Dietrich Schwanitz, "Rhetorik, Roman und die internen Grenzen der Kommunikation: Zur systemtheoretischen Beschreibung einer Problemkonstellation der 'sensibility,'" *Rhetorik* 9 (1990): 52–67. See also Schwanitz, *Systemtheorie und Literatur: Ein neues Paradigma* (Opladen, 1990). Only writing leaves the narrator free to appear in his narration or refrain from doing so. In oral narration, the author is present anyway.

75. A variation on this drawing of a boundary can be found in opera performances, when ovations interrupt a scene and bring the performance to a halt while the audience is in an uproar. The reason why this tends to happen in opera is that the actor's vocal performance can easily be separated from his role in the play. After all, it is remarkable that an experienced opera audience is not bothered by the sudden change from the most delicate music or bravura to the noise of clapping hands, whereas one would expect a frightened reaction from an audience participating in the mode of everyday experience.

76. "Signature Event Context," in Jacques Derrida, *Margins of Philosophy* (Chicago, 1982), pp. 307–30. Signing the text (in print) is of little help in this matter.

77. In literary theory, Paul de Man expounded the idea that the unity of the world is unattainable and nonrepresentable—but through textual analyses rather than an elaborated conceptual vocabulary. See Paul de Man, *Blindness and Insight: Essays in the Rhetoric of Contemporary Criticism* (1971; 2d ed. Minneapolis, 1983), and his *The Rhetoric of Romanticism* (New York, 1984).

78. See Eva Meyer, "Der Unterschied, der eine Umgebung schafft," in *ars electronica*, eds., *Im Netz der Systeme* (Berlin, 1991), pp. 110–22.

79. See Bernard Willms, "Politik als Erste Philosophie oder: Was heißt radikales politisches Philosophieren?" in Volker Gerhardt, ed., *Der Begriff der Politik: Bedingungen und Gründe politischen Handelns* (Stuttgart, 1990), pp. 252–67 (260, 265f.).

80. See Yves Barel, *Le paradoxe et le système: Essai sur le fantastique social,* 2d ed. (Grenoble, 1989), pp. 71f., 185f., 302f.

81. See, e.g., David Daube, "Dissent in Bible and Talmud," *California Law Review* 59 (1971): 784–94; or Jeffrey I. Roth, "The Justification for Controversy under Jewish Law," *California Law Review* 76 (1988): 338–87.

82. So in Jacques Derrida, "Form and Meaning: A Note on the Phenomenology of Language," *Margins of Philosophy,* pp. 155–73, p. 172, n. 16. On the notion of "ichnography," see also Michel Serres, *Genèse* (Paris, 1982), pp. 40ff. and frequently throughout. One could cite further evidence for this basic idea, which underlies the critique of ontological metaphysics and its dependence on the premise of presence.

83. See Arthur C. Danto, *The Transfiguration of the Commonplace: A Philosophy of Art* (Cambridge, Mass., 1981).

84. Friedrich Schlegel emphasized the work's isolation as the essential step on which everything else depends: "Das Wesentlichste sind die bestimmten Zwecke, die Absonderung, wodurch allein das Kunstwerk Umriß erhält und in sich selbst vollendet wird" (*Gespräch über die Poesie,* pp. 157f.).

85. According to the "law of crossing" in Spencer Brown, *Laws of Form,* p. 12: "The value of a crossing made again is not the value of the crossing," and "for any boundary, to recross is not to cross."

86. In response to questions raised by Georg Stanitzek at the Center for Interdisciplinary Research, Bielefeld: "Was ist Kommunikation? Vorlage für das Kolloquium 'Systemtheorie und Literaturwissenschaft'" (January 6–8, 1994).

87. David Roberts, "The Paradox of Form: Literature and Self-Reference," *Poetics* 21 (1992): 75–91.

88. See Theodor W. Adorno, *Ästhetische Theorie, Gesammelte Schriften,* vol. 7 (Frankfurt, 1970). See also Chapter 7, section V, below.

89. For more on this, see Niklas Luhmann, "Zeichen als Form," in Dirk Baecker, ed., *Probleme der Form* (Frankfurt, 1993), pp. 45–69; trans. as "Sign as Form," in Baecker, ed., *Problems of Form,* trans. Michael Irmscher, with Leah Edwards (Stanford, Calif., 1999), pp. 46–63.

90. See also Stanley Fish's critique of a "reception theory" which, despite its proclaimed emphasis on one side, has failed to disengage itself from its opposite—production—and is therefore unable to make distinctions. "Why No One's Afraid of Wolfgang Iser," in Stanley Fish, *Doing What Comes Naturally: Change, Rhetoric, and the Practice of Theory in Literary and Legal Studies* (Oxford, 1989), pp. 68–86. Fish's critique falls short, however, because of its own reluctance to make distinctions.

91. "We see now that the first distinction, the mark, and the observer [whom we had assumed "outside," N. L.] are not only interchangeable, but, in the form, identical" (Spencer Brown, *Laws of Form*, p. 76). We are dealing here with the "reentry" of the form into the form and, in this sense, with a binding of the imaginary space that cannot be thematized.

92. There is no need to derive this—by no means novel—insight from the radicalism of Spencer Brown's formal calculus. Husserl analyzed how determination is gained through a variation of shades, and these analyses, too, ground a common precondition of experiencing and acting in the conditions of possibility for determination. See especially § 41 in Edmund Husserl, *Ideen zu einer reinen Phänomenologie und phänomenologischen Philosophie*, vol. 1, *Husserliana*, vol. 3 (The Hague, 1950), pp. 91ff. See further his *Erfahrung und Urteil: Untersuchungen zur Genealogie der Logik* (Hamburg, 1948), and Maurice Merleau-Ponty, *Phénoménologie de la perception* (Paris, 1945), esp. his analyses of Cézanne on the search for identity, pp. 372ff. On the same topic, see Gérard Wormser, "Merleau-Ponty—Die Farbe und die Malerei," *Selbstorganisation* 4 (1993): 233–50.

93. For fitting formulations, see Lodovico Dolce, *Dialogo della Pittura* (1557), quoted from Paola Barocchi, ed., *Trattati d'arte del cinquecento*, vol. 1 (Bari, 1960), pp. 141–206 (170). For an overview, see Luigi Grassi, "I concetti di schizzo, abozzo, macchia, 'non finito' e la costruzione dell opera d'arte," in *Studi di onore di Pietro Silva* (Florence, 1957), pp. 97–106.

94. While this recognition does not put an end to the elaborate and rather confusing debate concerning a reader-oriented text theory, it does displace its problematic.

95. See Henri Focillon, *The Life of Forms in Art* (New York, 1992), p. 103.

96. According to a formulation of Z. W. Pylyshyn, "Computation and Cognition: Issues in the Foundation of Cognitive Science," *Behavioral and Brain Sciences* 3 (1980): 120; quoted from Klaus Fischer, "Die kognitive Konstitution sozialer Strukturen," *Zeitschrift für Soziologie* 18 (1989): 16–34 (24).

97. We are following the observation that perception requires the repression of neurophysiological information, a "forgetting" of the operative closure of the nervous system. See section I, above. Once again, this condition cannot be lifted; the work of art cannot be experienced as a mode of information processing within one's own brain—it remains "outside." Instead, perception is transformed into a process of reflection, at least into more persistent viewing or more concentrated listening.

98. Ciardi and Williams, *How Does a Poem Mean?* p. 6. See also Menke-Eggers, *Die Souveränität der Kunst*, pp. 77ff.

99. In response to this question, Shaftesbury, among many others, suggests that the artist can be interested only in an audience that is critical, competent, and capable of judgment, or, as it was put in the eighteenth century, in an audi-

ence that possesses "taste." See Anthony, Earl of Shaftesbury, *Characteristicks of Men, Manners, Opinions, Times,* 2d ed. (n.p., 1714; rpt. Farnborough Hants., 1968), vol. 1, pp. 243f. But this idea is by far too general and begs the question of how a work of art can be created, if not in view of rules, at least in anticipation of taste. To respond adequately, one would have to say that the artwork must create generalized expectations in order to specify these expectations via information. After all, we are dealing neither with a declaration of norms nor with a functional equivalent of law or morality.

100. Usually this point is expressed—though not forcefully enough—with reference to the permanent need of significant artworks for interpretation.

101. *This* beginning *before* all differentiation is, upon closer inspection, no beginning at all—despite Hegel's formulation—but rather a *permanent precondition* of all the operations of "Spirit." On Hegel's mode of presentation, see, e.g., the following excerpt from Hegel's *Vorlesungen über die Philosophie der Religion I,* p. 94: "Aber beim Anfang hat man noch nicht unterschiedene Bestimmungen, Eines und ein Anderes: beim Anfang ist man nur beim Einen, nicht beim Anderen."

102. On this problem, see also Niklas Luhmann, "Sthenographie und Euryalistik," in Hans Ulrich Gumbrecht and K. Ludwig Pfeiffer, eds., *Paradoxien, Dissonanzen, Zusammenbrüche: Situationen offener Epistemologie* (Frankfurt, 1991), pp. 58–82. A logical concept of paradox is not at issue here. Logic, no matter how it presents paradox (e.g., as a necessary collapse of the distinction between levels), considers paradox as something to be avoided. By contrast, we suggest that operations that observe, even those of logic, cannot avoid only unfolding paradoxes, that is, replacing them with distinctions.

103. For one of many examples, see Giovanni Paolo Lomazzo, *Idea del Tempio della Pittura* (Milan, 1590), p. 43: the *tempio* itself cannot be seen. On "imitation" as the downscaled reproduction of a nature that cannot be grasped as a whole, see Moritz, *Schriften zur Ästhetik,* p. 92.

104. Jacques Derrida, *Of Grammatology,* trans. Gayatri Chakravorty Spivak (Baltimore, 1974), p. 70.

105. See, e.g., Antoine Coypel, *Discours prononcez dans les conférences de L'Académie Royale de Peinture et de Sculpture* (Paris, 1721), p. 72.

106. Within an ontologically inspired frame of observation, one could only say that the boundary is "nothing." See, e.g., Leonardo da Vinci, *Notebooks* (New York, n.d.), pp. 61, 73f.

107. Perhaps we should abandon the word "object" altogether and return to the "thing" (in the sense of *res*). However, we retain the "object" since in English and French literature the reconstruction has concerned this word. See also, in German translation, Ranulph Glanville, *Objekte* (Berlin, 1988).

108. One would have to add that *symbolization* is necessary because the presupposed simultaneity of other consciousnesses *blocks access* to these conscious-

nesses. See especially George Herbert Mead, "The Social Self," *Journal of Philosophy* 10 (1913): 374–80; Mead, "A Behavioristic Account of the Significant Symbol," *Journal of Philosophy* 19 (1922): 157–63; and Mead, "The Genesis of the Self and Social Control," *International Journal of Ethics* 35 (1924/25): 251–77.

109. Serres, *Genèse*, p. 146.

110. von Foerster, *Observing Systems*, pp. 273ff.

111. Another well-known example from religion is persons transported into ecstasy, whose *public* obsession points to transcendent powers without there being a need for verbal communication. For biblical evidence, see Michael Welker, *Gottes Geist: Theologie des Heiligen Geistes* (Neukirchen-Vluyn, 1992), pp. 79ff.

112. Serres, *Genèse*.

113. This conceptual choice requires a distinction between meaning and information. See Donald W. MacKay, *Information, Mechanism and Meaning* (Cambridge, Mass., 1969).

114. Umberto Eco, too, in *Opera aperta*, e.g., p. 119, considers the increase in information to be a general poetic principle; but not until today does art explicitly aim at this principle and press it to its limits. According to Eco, artworks should therefore remain "open" to further information.

115. On this concept, see Humberto R. Maturana and Francisco Varela, *The Tree of Knowledge: The Biological Roots of Human Understanding* (Boston, 1992), pp. 75ff., 181ff.

116. See Alfred Gierer, *Die Physik, das Leben und die Seele* (Munich, 1985), esp. pp. 121ff.

117. For a semiotic theory, see, e.g., Menke-Eggers, *Die Souveränität der Kunst*, pp. 61ff. Aesthetic experience defines its own signifieds as significant.

118. Disregarding this distinction regresses to the epoch of the cult of genius, which—although it formulated for the first time the radical temporality of art as opposed to its mere historicity—went too far in inferring the rank of an artwork from its unexpected appearance and the genius of the artist from the suddenness of his insights. See Karl Heinz Bohrer, *Plötzlichkeit: Zum Augenblick des ästhetischen Scheins* (Frankfurt, 1981).

119. Critics might suspect that this is stilted nonsense: How is a tautology (art communicates by means of artworks) supposed to sound less trivial when backed up by theory? Precisely this must be shown. The formulation may prove fruitful to interpretation, or it may be capable of synthesizing insights (of a historical and systematic nature) that would otherwise remain isolated.

120. For a special perspective on this question, see Niklas Luhmann, "Das Kunstwerk und die Selbstreproduktion der Kunst," in Hans Ulrich Gumbrecht and K. Ludwig Pfeiffer, eds., *Stil: Geschichten und Funktionen eines kulturwissenschaftlichen Diskurselements* (Frankfurt, 1986), pp. 620–72.

121. The notion of clearly defined artistic genres has become increasingly prob-

lematic. Genres do not constitute autopoietic systems in their own right, but they obviously facilitate the autopoiesis of art by making possible an observing that is restricted and trained, including the recognition of astonishing but intelligible deviations from given formal models. On the integration of genre distinctions—literature feeds off literature, representing nothing beyond itself—see, e.g., Tzvetan Todorov, *The Fantastic: A Structural Approach to a Literary Genre*, trans. Richard Howard (Cleveland, 1973).

§ 2

1. This differs from Fichte: the observer does not begin by positing *himself.*
2. The question whether such observers "exist" and who they are must be left to sociology.
3. See Chapter 1, section IX.
4. See Humberto R. Maturana, who limits his analyses to living systems: *Erkennen: Die Organisation und Verkörperung von Wirklichkeit: Ausgewählte Arbeiten zur biologischen Epistemologie* (Braunschweig, 1982), pp. 34, 149f.
5. Negations are thus no longer primary operations as in classical logic. We shall return to this point when discussing modern art—an art that negates art. See Chapter 4, section II, and Chapter 7, section V, below.
6. As does Novalis in his *Fichte-Studien*: "Wie wird das absolute Ich ein empirisches Ich?" (quoted from *Novalis: Werke, Tagebücher und Briefe Friedrich von Hardenbergs*, ed. Hans-Joachim Mähl and Richard Samuel, vol. 2 [Darmstadt, 1978], p. 31).
7. See the corresponding propositions in George Spencer Brown, *Laws of Form* (1969; rpt. New York, 1979), p. 105.
8. As insiders will notice, we are thinking of Paul de Man.
9. See Jacques Derrida, *Margins of Philosophy*, trans. Alan Bass (Chicago, 1982), p. 66.
10. A selection of the above-mentioned literature includes: Heinz von Foerster, *Observing Systems* (Seaside, Calif., 1981); Humberto R. Maturana, *Erkennen*; Maturana, "The Biological Foundation of Self Consciousness and the Physical Domain of Existence," in Niklas Luhmann et al., *Beobachter: Konvergenz der Erkenntnistheorien?* (Munich, 1990), pp. 47–117; Dean MacCannell and Juliet F. MacCannell, *The Time of the Sign: A Semiotic Interpretation of Modern Culture* (Bloomington, Ind., 1982); Spencer Brown, *Laws of Form*; Gotthard Günther, *Beiträge zur Grundlegung einer operationsfähigen Dialektik*, 3 vols. (Hamburg, 1976–1980); Rino Genovese, Carla Benedetti, and Paolo Garbolino, *Modi di Attribuzione: Filosofia e teoria dei sistemi* (Naples, 1989); George W. Stocking Jr., ed., *Observers Observed: Essays on Ethnographic Field Work* (Madison, Wis., 1983); Ranulph Glanville, *Objekte* (Berlin 1988); Niklas Luhmann, *Die Wissenschaft der*

Gesellschaft (Frankfurt, 1990), esp. pp. 68ff.; and the entire literature on artificial intelligence. For an overview, see also Francisco Varela, *Kognitionswissenschaft— Kognitionstechnik: Eine Skizze aktueller Perspektiven* (Frankfurt, 1990).

11. In the sense of Hans Ulrich Gumbrecht and K. Ludwig Pfeiffer, eds., *Materialities of Communication*, trans. William Whobrey (Stanford, Calif., 1994).

12. See also the strange active/passive ambiguity of "impression" in Raymond Roussel, and on this Julia Kristeva, *Semeiotikè: Recherches pour un sémanalyse* (Paris, 1969), pp. 216ff. (and also pp. 181ff.).

13. For a different account, see Glanville, *Objekte*.

14. See also Louis H. Kauffman, "Self-Reference and Recursive Forms," *Journal of Social and Biological Structures* 10 (1987): 53–72.

15. See the distinction between natural and artificial restrictions in Lars Löfgren, "Some Foundational Views on General Systems and the Hempel Paradox," *International Journal of General Systems* 4 (1978): 243–53 (244). This distinction must be accepted as a distinction, since there is no further observer who could say whether something is "in truth" natural or artificial, necessary or contingent.

16. See Bruno Latour and Steve Woolgar, *Laboratory Life: The Social Construction of Scientific Facts* (Beverly Hills, Calif., 1979); Karin Knorr-Cetina, *Die Fabrikation von Erkenntnis: Zur Anthropologie der Naturwissenschaften* (Frankfurt, 1984).

17. On the history of specialization that led to the production of "papers" and on the corresponding irrelevance of the presence of other observers in science, see Charles Bazerman, *Shaping Written Knowledge: The Genre and Activity of the Experimental Article in Science* (Madison, Wis., 1988). On the cycle of exaggeration and criticism and the increasing "sensitivity to mistakes" in the wake of these developments, see Michael Mulkay and G. Nigel Gilbert, "Accounting for Error: How Scientists Construct Their Social World When They Account for Correct and Incorrect Belief," *Sociology* 16 (1982): 165–83.

18. See Rudolf Stichweh, "Die Autopoiesis der Wissenschaft," in Dirk Baecker et al., eds., *Theorie als Passion* (Frankfurt, 1987), pp. 447–81 (459ff.).

19. See Dirk Baecker, *Information und Risiko in der Marktwirtschaft* (Frankfurt, 1988), esp. pp. 198ff.

20. Simpler societies organize their economies along constant prices that are independent of scarcity or abundance, or supply and demand, because for a first-order observer this kind of information is too difficult and too risky to obtain. See Elisabeth Cashdan, "Information Costs and Customary Prices," in Cashdan, ed., *Risk and Uncertainty in Tribal and Peasant Societies* (Boulder, 1990), pp. 259–78.

21. See Machiavelli, *Discorsi II*, Chap. 24 and *Principe*, Chap. 20, quoted from *Opere*, 7th ed. (Milan, 1976), pp. 288 and 110, respectively.

22. Hegel, *Phänomenologie des Geistes* (1807), quoted from the edition by Johannes Hoffmeister, 4th ed. (Leipzig, 1937), pp. 141ff.

23. This, of course, is not Hegel's terminology.

24. See Niklas Luhmann, "Gesellschaftliche Komplexität und öffentliche Meinung," in Luhmann, *Soziologische Aufklärung*, vol. 5 (Opladen, 1990), pp. 170–82; Luhmann, "Die Beobachtung der Beobachter im politischen System: Zur Theorie der öffentlichen Meinung," in Jürgen Willke, ed., *Öffentliche Meinung: Theorien, Methoden, Befunde. Beiträge zu Ehren von Elisabeth Noelle-Neumann* (Freiburg, 1992), pp. 77–86.

25. See the two essays "Sozialsystem Familie" and "Glück und Unglück der Kommunikation in Familien: Zur Genese von Pathologien," in Niklas Luhmann, *Soziologische Aufklärung*, vol. 5, pp. 196ff., 218ff. On communication routines, see also Alois Hahn, "Konsensusfiktionen in Kleingruppen: Dargestellt am Beispiel von jungen Ehen," in Friedhelm Neidhardt, ed., *Gruppensoziologie: Perspektiven und Materialien. Kölner Zeitschrift für Soziologie und Sozialpsychologie*, special issue 15 (Opladen, 1983), pp. 210–33.

26. In Spencer Brown, *Laws of Form*, we read: "Call the space cloven by any distinction, together with the entire content of the space, the form of the distinction." It is crucial that the concept of form embrace the entire realm ("the entire content of the space") occupied by a distinction. Form refers not just to one side, to a shape as such, or merely to an object or a system. Rather, the indication of a system makes the distinction between system and environment possible.

27. For a pertinent critique of this notion, see Martin Heidegger, "Der Ursprung des Kunstwerks," in Heidegger, *Holzwege* (Frankfurt, 1950), pp. 7–68.

28. See also Niklas Luhmann, "Kontingenz als Eigenwert der modernen Gesellschaft," in Luhmann, *Beobachtungen der Moderne* (Opladen, 1992), pp. 93–128; trans. as "Contingency as Modern Society's Defining Attribute," in Luhmann, *Observations on Modernity*, trans. William Whobrey (Stanford, Calif., 1998), pp. 44–62.

29. On the parallel problem of pedagogical intent, see Niklas Luhmann and Eberhard Schnorr, eds., *Zwischen Absicht und Person: Fragen an die Pädagogik* (Frankfurt, 1972).

30. In the tradition, *novus* initially means simply deviation (see Johannes Spörl, "Das Alte und das Neue im Mittelalter: Studien zum Problem des mittelalterlichen Fortschrittsbewußtseins," *Historisches Jahrbuch* 50 [1930]: 297–341; 498–524; Walter Freund, *Modernus und andere Zeitbegriffe des Mittelalters* [Cologne, 1957]). Indeed, novelty without factual discontinuity is unrecognizable. The shift of emphasis toward a temporal dimension does not occur until the beginning of modernity. At first, the emphasis on novelty is apparently motivated by an adherence to the principle of imitation—as codified in Aristotle's *Poetics*—which, at the same time, sought to deflect the suspicion of slavish imitation. In Sir Philip Sydney, *The Defense of Poetry* (1595; Lincoln, Nebr., 1970), p. 9, we read, e.g., "Only the poet, disdaining to be tied to any such subjection lifted up with the vigor of his own invention, does grow in effect into another nature in

making things either better than nature brings forth or, quite anew, forms such as never were in nature, as the heroes, the demigods, cyclops, chimeras, furies, and such like." The issue here is evidently still novelty of deviation rather than historical novelty.

31. See Charles Sterling, *Still Life Painting from Antiquity to the Twentieth Century*, 2d ed. (New York, 1981).

32. On the history of the concept, see Wolfgang Binder, "'Genuß' in Dichtung und Philosophie des 17. und 18. Jahrhunderts," rpt. in Binder, *Aufschlüsse: Studien zur deutschen Literatur* (Zurich, 1976), pp. 7–33; and G. Biller and R. Meyer, "Genuß," *Historisches Wörterbuch der Philosophie*, vol. 3 (Stuttgart, 1974), columns 316–22. In the seventeenth and eighteenth centuries, the concept maintained a distinct relationship with possession ("jouissance, jouir, c'est connoitre, éprouver, sentir les avantages de posseder," we read in the *Encyclopédie ou Dictionnaire raisonné des Sciences, des Arts et des Métiers*, vol. 8 [Neufchastel, 1765], p. 889). At the same time, however, the relationship to the present is emphasized, and above all the heightening of experience through reflexivity that makes possible the enjoyment of pain as well as self-enjoyment. There is raw pleasure and refined pleasure, sensuous pleasure and moral or spiritual pleasure. On the scale of social values, the concept is subject to variation. What is interpreted in the text as second-order observation was accomplished in those days via a distance from oneself and from the world. See, e.g., anonymous (Marquis de Caraccioli), *La jouissance de soi-même* (rpt. Utrecht-Amsterdam, 1759). (The inference from the incommunicability of the self to the necessity of self-enjoyment is remarkable [ibid., p. 3].)

33. There is no lack of attempts to go beyond the juxtaposition of perspectives. Arthur C. Danto, *The Transfiguration of the Commonplace: A Philosophy of Art* (Cambridge, Mass., 1981), invites us to consider that "the spectator stands to artist as reader to writer in a kind of spontaneous collaboration. In terms of the logic of artistic identification, simply to identify one element imposes a whole set of other identifications which stand or fall with it. *The whole thing moves at once*" (p. 119; author's emphasis). This formulation only requires a better theoretical contextualization of its words and concepts.

34. I deliberately do not say: intention.

35. One can find a similar view in Arthur C. Danto, although he works with the dangerous concept of interpretation: "The Appreciation and Interpretation of Works of Art," in Danto, *The Philosophical Disenfranchisement of Art* (New York, 1986), pp. 23–46. Interpretation, in the sense of the distinction between artworks and other objects, is constitutive for the creation of the work of art. It "transfigures" an ordinary object into a work of art, and the only protection against the arbitrariness of an interpretation resides in its correspondence to the artist's interpretation: "the correct interpretation of object-as-artwork is the one which coincides most closely with the artist's own interpretation" (p. 44).

36. This can be formally described by means of the concept of information. We shall return to this below.

37. This was different in the Middle Ages, because of a passive notion of knowledge that did not construct differences or harmony but simply presupposed and received them.

38. "Is it not," asks Paul de Man, "rather that this unity—which is in fact a semi-circularity—resides not in the poetic text as such, but in the act of interpreting this text?" (*Blindness and Insight: Essays in the Rhetoric of Contemporary Criticism*, 2d. ed. [Minneapolis, 1983], p. 29).

39. This is by no means a novel insight. One can find it in Hogarth, in conjunction with his principle of the flowing ("serpent-like") line. See William Hogarth, *The Analysis of Beauty, written with a view of fixing the fluctuating Ideas of Taste* (London, 1753; Oxford, 1955), p. 28: "But in the common way of taking the view of any opake object, that part of its surface which fronts the eye, is apt to occupy the mind alone, and the opposite, nay even every other part of it, whatever, is left unthought of it at that time: and the least motion we make to reconnoitre any other side of the object, confounds our first idea, for want of the connection of the two ideas, which the complete knowledge of the whole would naturally have given us, if we had considered it in the other way before." One could add that the total impression can be experienced and described as "harmonious" only by way of an unanalyzed (and unanalyzable) abstraction. As Hogarth puts it on p. 82, "this vague answer took in rise from doctrines not belonging to form, or idle schemes built on them."

40. See Gerhard Roth and Helmut Schwegler (who use the terminology of properties and interaction) in "Self-Organization, Emergent Properties, and the Unity of the World," in Wolfgang Krohn et al., eds., *Self-Organization: Portrait of a Scientific Revolution* (Dordrecht, 1990), pp. 35–50.

41. "Arte non dee esser mostrata nell'arte," one reads in Giovanni Paolo Lomazzo, *Idea del Tempio della Pittura* (Milan, 1590), p. 146.

42. On the topic of Enlightenment as the beginning of the development of forms for "modern communication" by means of a substitute paradigm, see Peter Fuchs, *Moderne Kommunikation: Zur Theorie des operativen Displacements* (Frankfurt, 1993), pp. 104ff.

43. See Michel Serres, *Genèse* (Paris, 1982); Serres, *Le cinq sens* (Paris, 1985). On the new sociological institutionalism in France, see Peter Wagner, "Die Soziologie der Genese sozialer Institutionen—Theoretische Perspektiven der 'neuen Sozialwissenschaften' in Frankreich," *Zeitschrift für Soziologie* 22 (1993): 464–76.

44. See Jean-Luc Nancy, *Corpus* (Paris, 1992).

45. For a brief presentation, see Jonathan Culler, *On Deconstruction: Theory and Critique after Structuralism* (Ithaca, N.Y., 1982), pp. 31ff.

46. See William York Tindall, *The Literary Symbol* (Bloomington, Ind., 1955).

47. See Roman Ingarden, *Das literarische Kunstwerk* (1931; 4th ed. Tübingen, 1972), pp. 261ff. See also pp. 270ff. on "fulfilled qualities," "schematized perspectives," "readiness of potential existence," and pp. 353ff. on necessary concretizations. Ingarden's analyses closely follow Husserl's investigations into the referential structure of all meaningful determinations. The referential structure of "blanks" has occasionally been overemphasized, but his decisive analyses of the inevitable difference between phenomena in reality and works of art has not received the attention it deserves. One could, of course, choose totally different "beginnings." See, e.g., William Empson, *Seven Types of Ambiguity* (1930; 2d ed. Edinburgh, 1947).

48. Ibid., p. 269.

49. Umberto Eco, *Opera aperta* (1962; 6th ed. Milan, 1988).

50. Gotthard Günther, "Cognition and Volition: A Contribution to a Cybernetic Theory of Subjectivity," in Günther, *Beiträge zu Grundlegung einer operationsfähigen Dialektik* (Hamburg, 1979), vol. 2, pp. 203–40.

51. In anticipation of what follows, let us note that this distinction between distinctions does not yet concern the problem of coding. On the basis of these differences, coding must make sure that actions and experiences follow the same code, i.e., consider themselves part of the same system.

52. On a concept of communication based on this distinction, see Niklas Luhmann, *Soziale Systeme: Grundriß einer allgemeinen Theorie* (Frankfurt, 1984), pp. 191ff.; trans. as *Social Systems*, trans. John Bednarz, with Dirk Baecker (Stanford, Calif., 1995), pp. 137ff.

53. In the sense explained in Chapter 1, section IX, above.

54. Any other version of the theory would have to claim that the system consisted of marble and bodies, thoughts and communications, paper and printer's ink. And what makes such a system into a system would have to be sought in these mysterious "ands."

55. The fact that precious materials—such as gold and jewels in the Middle Ages—have lost their artistic role affirms this trend.

56. See Yehuda Elkana, "Die Entstehung des Denkens zweiter Ordnung im klassischen Griechenland," in Elkana, *Anthropologie der Erkenntnis: Die Entwicklung des Wissens als episches Theater einer listigen Vernunft* (Frankfurt, 1986), pp. 344–75. See also G. E. R. Lloyd, *Magic, Reason and Experience: Studies in the Origin and Development of Greek Science* (Cambridge, 1979). Lloyd presents a wealth of pertinent material but fails to focus on the—for us—decisive issue.

57. See, programatically, Jonathan Richardson, *A Discourse on the Dignity, Certainty, Pleasure and Advantage of the Science of a Connoisseur* (1719), quoted from *The Works*, (London, 1773; rpt. Hildesheim, 1969), pp. 239–346.

58. See Iain Pears, *The Discovery of Painting: The Growth of Interest in the Arts in England, 1680–1768* (New Haven, Conn., 1988), esp. pp. 181ff.

59. For a typical manifestation of the insecurities around the mid-eighteenth century, see Denis Diderot, *Traité du beau,* quoted from *Œuvres,* Pléiade ed. (Paris, 1951), pp. 1105–42. We disregard Diderot's indecisiveness about the question of the possible benefit of an aesthetic criterion.

60. See Nelson Goodman, *Languages of Art: An Approach to a Theory of Symbols* (London, 1969), pp. 99ff.

61. In the Middle Ages and early modernity discussions of the "mirror" discovered—albeit in different constellations—the possibility of seeing the invisible in the double move of making seeing invisible and of making visible a seeing that cannot see itself. The concern, however, was not ours, i.e., to see what others are unable to see.

62. See Niklas Luhmann, "Wie lassen sich latente Strukturen beobachten?" in Paul Watzlawick and Peter Krieg, eds., *Das Auge des Betrachters—Beiträge zum Konstruktivismus: Festschrift für Heinz von Foerster* (Munich, 1991), pp. 61–74.

63. For an overview, see Volker Meja and Nico Stehr, eds., *Der Streit um die Wissenssoziologie,* 2 vols. (Frankfurt, 1982).

64. See Gisela M. A. Richter, "Perspective, Ancient, Medieval and Renaissance," in *Scritti in onore di Batholomeo Nogara* (Vatican City, 1937), pp. 381–88. According to Richter, this also holds, contrary to a widely held opinion, for theory (Vitruvius).

65. The first comprehensive treatment is perhaps Leon Battista Alberti, *Della Pittura* (1436; Florence, 1950).

66. On variety and sameness, see William Hogarth, *The Analysis of Beauty, written with a view of fixing the fluctuating Ideas of Taste* (London, 1753; Oxford, 1955), pp. 34f.

67. See Jurgis Baltrusavitis, *Anamorphoses ou perspectives curieuses* (Paris, 1955).

68. Ibid., p. 6, or p. 42: "La perspective n'est pas un instrument des représentations exactes, mais un mensonge."

69. See esp. Giulio Troili, *Paradossi per pratticare la prospettiva senza saperla* (1672; Bologna, 1863), e.g., p. 12: "li riuscirà di pratticare la Prospettiva senza saperla, e scoprirà con l'occhi del corpo tutta quello che si considerà con gl'occhi del intelletto."

70. See the counternovel by Henry Fielding, *An Apology for the Life of Mrs. Shamela Andrews* (London, 1741).

71. In Jean Paul's *Die unsichtbare Loge,* § 1, "Verlobungsschach—graduierter Rekrut—Kopulier-Katze," Ernestine (who by and large is certainly virtuous and innocent) must teach tricks to a cat and turn over a chess game in order to land in the desired marriage.

72. Niels Werber, *Literatur als System: Zur Ausdifferenzierung literarischer Kommunikation* (Opladen, 1992), pp. 68ff., provides evidence for this trend.

73. See Chapter 1, n. 42, above.

74. On skepticism about the preference for striking, extraordinary, sudden, and scandalous subjects, see Werber, *Literatur als System*, pp. 75ff. A counternovel that refers to this trend by depicting an unexciting, everyday life is Ludwig Tieck's *Peter Lebrecht*. An appropriate form for this type of literature, along with its own criteria for quality, did not exist until the mystery novel was invented one hundred years later.

75. See René Girard, *Mensonge romantique et vérité romanesque* (Paris, 1961).

76. See the distinction between "flat characters / round characters" in E. M. Forster, *Aspects of the Novel* (1927; rpt. London, 1941). See also Christine Brooke-Rose, "The Dissolution of Character in the Novel," in Thomas C. Heller et al., eds., *Reconstructing Individualism: Autonomy, Individualism, and the Self in Western Thought* (Stanford, Calif., 1968), pp. 184–96. This further development can perhaps be explained by the fact that the theme of latent motives turns into a cultural commonplace that no longer requires literary-fictive treatment. Once again, one can work with characters whose motives no longer matter.

77. The formulation is Jean Paul's, *Hesperus*, quoted from the edition by Norbert Miller, *Works*, vol. 1 (Munich, 1960), p. 712.

78. This comes fatally close to the concept of duty in Kant's ethics.

79. For a representative monograph, see Edmund Burke, *A Philosophical Enquiry into the Origin of Our Ideas of the Sublime and the Beautiful* (1756; New York, 1958). On the contemporary context, see also Samuel H. Monk, *The Sublime: A Study of Critical Theories in XVIIIth-Century England* (1925; 2d ed. Ann Arbor, 1960).

80. Nicolas Boileau-Despréaux, *Traité du Sublime*, preface, quoted from *Œuvres* (Paris, 1713), pp. 595–604 (596). See also Boileau's adamant resistance to applying the old concept of style to this phenomenon (p. 601).

81. Boileau, "Reflexions critique sur quelques passages du Rheteur Longinus," in *Œuvres*, pp. 491–592, 590 (erroneous pagination).

82. Since such constipation is no longer imminent, "das Erhabene, das ja bloß eine Art vornehmer Purganz sein soll [läuft] Gefahr, ebenfalls aus der Mode zu kommen" (August Wilhelm Schlegel, *Die Kunstlehre* [Pt. 1 of the lectures on literature and art], quoted from *Kritische Schriften und Briefe*, vol. 2 [Stuttgart, 1963], p. 58). Leopardi appears to confirm this assessment via a detour through boredom: "La noia è in qualche modo il più sublime dei sentimenti umani" (Giacomo Leopardi, *Pensieri* [Leipzig, n.d.], p. 41). It is difficult to avoid the impression that, along with the dangers of constipation, the laxative of the sublime once again becomes fashionable.

83. In Ludwig Tieck's novella *Die Klausenburg*, quoted from *Schriften*, vol. 12 (Frankfurt, 1986), pp. 143f.

84. The formulation may be new, but the notion that the world requires an observer for its perfection is an old Christian idea.

85. Tieck, *Die Kunstlehre*, p. 49.

86. See Philip G. Herbst, *Alternatives to Hierarchies* (Leiden, 1976), p. 88. Herbst mentions further "primary distinctions" that generate logical relationships and fight for predominance, such as the ontological distinction between being and nonbeing.

87. Karl Philipp Moritz, *Schriften zur Ästhetik und Poetik* (Tübingen, 1962), esp. pp. 92, 115ff.

88. Kristeva, *Semeiotikè*, p. 11.

89. See, e.g., Niklas von Kues, *De visione Dei*, quoted from *Philosophisch-Theologische Schriften*, vol. 3 (Vienna, 1967), pp. 93–219, esp. his remarkable formulation "Et hoc scio solum *quia* scio me nescire" (XIII, p. 146; my emphasis, N. L.).

90. For an elaboration of this point, see Niklas Luhmann, "Kontingenz als Eigenwert der modernen Gesellschaft" ("Contingency as Modern Society's Defining Attribute").

91. For the special case of art, see the quote from Sidney, n. 30 above.

92. Here we think immediately of Friedrich Schiller. The fixation of the self on the distinction between unity and distinction (or "opposition") is especially impressive—and confusing—in Karl Wilhelm Ferdinand Solger, *Vorlesungen über Ästhetik*, ed. Karl Wilhelm Ludwig Heyse (Leipzig, 1829; Darmstadt, 1973). In Solger's belated product, multiplying distinctions while holding on to the notion of the idea as the ultimate unity is driven to the point where the reader loses all orientation and control and no longer knows how to retain a unified concept of the idea (the constitutional monarch in the realm of distinctions) in the face of so many distinctions. Raising this question, however, presupposes the capacity to question the distinction between unity and distinction as a distinction. This question should have propelled German Idealism to recognize itself as being grounded in a paradox. Although this did not happen, one finds paradoxical formulations throughout Solger's work (e.g., p. 53, "Im *Selbstbewußtsein* wird das Allgemeine und Besondere als dasselbe erkannt"). This explains why the concept of the symbol once again refers specifically to the appearance of the general in the particular. See esp. Friedrich Schelling, *Philosophie der Kunst* (Darmstadt, 1960), p. 50: "Darstellung des Absoluten mit absoluter Indifferenz des Allgemeinen und Besonderen *im Besonderen* ist nur symbolisch möglich."

93. See Martin Heidegger, *Sein und Zeit*, 6th ed. (Tübingen, 1949), § 2 and § 27.

94. Huesca, 1649; Madrid, 1969.

95. Solger, *Vorlesungen über Aesthetik*.

96. See Niklas Luhmann, "Deconstruction as Second-Order Observing," *New Literary History* 24 (1993): 763–82.

97. See de Man, *Blindness and Insight*, especially Wlad Godzich's pertinent Introduction.

98. Spencer Brown's formal calculus is constructed in such a manner, al-

though he does not include second-order observation in it—the figure of "reentry" merely opens a perspective on this type of observation. See Elena Esposito, "Ein zweiwertiger nicht-selbstständiger Kalkül," in Dirk Baecker, ed., *Kalkül der Form* (Frankfurt, 1993), pp. 96–111. The incompatibility of forms (observing operations) to be avoided corresponds to what linguists mean by performative contradiction, or what deconstructivists would call the contradiction in language against itself.

99. This tendency manifests itself in authors as diverse as Herbert A. Simon, "From Substantive to Procedural Rationality," in Spiro J. Lastis, ed., *Method and Appraisal in Economics* (Cambridge, 1976), pp. 129–48; or Jürgen Habermas, *Faktizität und Geltung. Beiträge zur Diskurstheorie des Rechts und des demokratischen Rechtsstaates* (Frankfurt, 1992) (who, not accidentally, refers to the technically powerful media of money and law, neither of which requires external justification).

§ 3

1. See further Niklas Luhmann, "Das Medium der Kunst," *Delfin* 4 (1986): 6–15; rpt. in Frederick D. Bunsen, ed., *"ohne Titel": Neue Orientierungen in der Kunst* (Würzburg, 1988), pp. 61–71.

2. See Gabriel Marcel's (forgotten) study *Etre et Avoir* (Paris, 1935).

3. As a metaphor for memory as a condition of learning, see Plato, *Theaetetus,* 191 Cff. See also Aristotle's crucial supplement in *Peri Psyches,* 424 a 18–20, which suggests that the wax receives and preserves the impression but not the material that causes it. (At stake here is precisely not the traditional concept of matter.)

4. We owe this suggestion to Fritz Heider, "Ding und Medium," *Symposion* 1 (1926): 109–57, who elaborates this distinction with reference to the perceptual media of seeing and hearing. The medium/form difference (medium/object in Heider) is built into the classical subject/object difference as a kind of mediating concept that requires no transfer from the outside to the inside. Here lie notable foundations for an epistemology that would be neither transcendental nor dialectical. This has been overlooked heretofore, presumably because the theory is presented as a theory of perception rather than a theory of cognitive processes that can be true or false. But this is worth noting, if one searches for concepts applicable not only in epistemology but also in the theory of art, which are capable of clarifying interconnections in the development of both. We have altered Heider's model considerably, especially by giving up the idea that a medium is externally determined whereas a form (Heider's "object") is determined internally. The external/internal distinction already presupposes form.

5. There is no need to decide whether there really "are" such things as natural constants to begin with. If so, it would be of no consequence to our distinction between medium and form.

6. See Kay Junge, "Medien als Selbstreferenzunterbrecher," in Dirk Baecker, ed., *Kalkül der Form* (Frankfurt, 1993), pp. 112–51.

7. See, e.g., Robert B. Glassman, "Persistence and Loose Coupling in Living Systems," *Behavioral Sciences* 18 (1973): 83–98; Karl E. Weick, *Der Prozess des Organisierens* (Frankfurt, 1985), esp. pp. 163ff., 264ff., and several essays in Jost Halfmann and Klaus Peter Japp, eds., *Riskante Entscheidungen und Katastrophenpotentiale: Elemente einer soziologischen Risikoforschung* (Opladen, 1990).

8. See, e.g., Friedrich Schlegel's Jena lecture *Transzendentalphilosophie*, 1800–1801, quoted from *Kritische Friedrich-Schlegel-Ausgabe*, vol. 12 (Munich, 1964), pp. 37f.: "*Die Materie ist kein Gegenstand des Bewußtseyns.* Nämlich es ist das Merkmahl des Chaos, daß nichts darinnen unterschieden werden kann; und es kann nichts ins Bewußtseyn kommen, was nicht unterschieden ist. Nur die Form kommt ins empirische Bewußtseyn. Was wir für Materie halten, *ist Form.*"

9. A "reentry" in the sense of George Spencer Brown's formal calculus, *Laws of Form* (1969; rpt. New York, 1979), pp. 69ff.

10. We find the same asymmetry in the relation between system and environment, a form that possesses an inside (system) and an outside (environment). This relation, too, entails the possibility of a reentry of the form into the form, i.e., of the distinction between self-reference and hetero-reference within the system.

11. "Von ästhetischer Erfahrung sprechen wir vielmehr erst, wenn unser Verstehen die Ordnung bloßen Wiedererkennens verläßt und das Wiedererkannte zum Material macht, an dem es Bestimmungen auswählt und aufeinander bezieht" (Christoph Menke-Eggers, *Die Souveränität der Kunst: Ästhetische Erfahrung nach Adorno und Derrida* [Frankfurt, 1988], p. 63).

12. The common understanding of memory tends to privilege remembering over forgetting. This is why this aspect deserves further elaboration. What matters is discrimination, the difference or distinction, the form of remembering/forgetting. It goes without saying that forgetting requires other facilities of organization and control than remembering does. One needs no reasons to forget something, although forgetfulness can be embarrassing. Besides, the structure of forgetting depends on the respective medium. Money, for example, routinely forgets all the concrete circumstances that may have motivated a specific payment, and in so doing, it restricts remembering to the level of second-order observation.

13. Regarding the history of theory, it is worth noting that the constant/variable distinction owes its present significance, particularly in attribution theory, to Heider's psychology of perception.

14. Gracián bases his (rhetorical) theory of art on this notion. See, e.g., Baltasar Gracián, *Agudeza y arte de ingenio*, 2 vols. (Huesca, 1649; Madrid, 1969), *Discurso* XX (vol. 1, p. 204): "Son los tropos y figuras retóricas materia y como fundamento para que sobre ellos levante sus primores la agudeza , y lo que la retórica tiene por formalidad, este nuestra arte por materia sobre que echa el es-

malte de su artificio." Or, *Discurso* L (vol. 2, p. 159): "que la agudeza tiene por materia y por fundamento muchas de las figuras retóricas, pero dales la forma y realce del concepto."

15. For an elaboration of this point, see Niklas Luhmann, *Soziale Systeme* (Frankfurt, 1982), pp. 92–147; trans. as *Social Systems,* trans. John Bednarz, with Dirk Baecker (Stanford, Calif., 1995), pp. 59–102.

16. At this point it might be useful to point out that the Husserlian metaphor of the world horizon is just a metaphor. Taking it seriously could lead to the erroneous assumption that the world is something distant, although no one seriously believes that objects in close proximity exist outside of the world.

17. In the terminology of Heinz von Foerster, this means that meaning can be realized only by "non-trivial machines" that use their own output as input and thus become mathematically incalculable. Or, to speak with Spencer Brown, reentry gives rise to a condition that presents itself to the system as an "unresolvable indeterminacy."

18. So far as we know, only religion can accept this question and answer it with reference to God. Or it can reverse the answer and derive an argument for the existence of God from the indistinguishability of the world as a whole.

19. A lengthy quotation from Henri Focillon, *The Life of Forms in Art* (New York, 1992) is in order: "Light not only illuminates the internal mass [of a cathedral, N. L.] but collaborates with the architecture to give it its needed form. Light itself is form, since its rays, streaming forth at predetermined points are compressed, attenuated or stretched in order to pick out the variously unified and accented members of the building for the purpose either of tranquillizing it or of giving it vivacity."

20. See Denis Diderot, *Paradoxe sur le Comédien,* quoted from *Œuvres,* Pléiade ed. (Paris, 1951), pp. 1033–88.

21. On the controversies concerning theater and poetry, see Russell Fraser, *The War Against Poetry* (Princeton, N.J., 1970); Jean-Christophe Agnew, *Worlds Apart: The Market and the Theater in Anglo-American Thought, 1550–1750* (Cambridge, 1968). We shall return to the specifically religious critique of art during the Reformation and Counter Reformation (Chapter 4, section IX, below).

22. For a phenomenological description of the separation of literary spaces/ times from the space and time of the world in which this separation takes place, see Roman Ingarden, *Das literarische Kunstwerk* (1931; 4th ed. Tübingen, 1972), pp. 233ff.

23. On the necessary recourse to the *quantitative* operation of *macromolecular* processes, see Heinz Förster (Heinz von Foerster), *Das Gedächtnis: Eine quantenmechanische Untersuchung* (Vienna, 1948); see further von Foerster, "Molecular Ethology: An Immodest Proposal for Semantic Clarification," in G. Unger, ed., *Molecular Mechanism in Memory and Learning* (New York, 1970), pp. 213–48.

24. Gernot Böhme, "Atmosphere as the Fundamental Concept of a New Aesthetics," *Thesis Eleven* 36 (1993): 113–26, develops a different notion of atmosphere in conjunction with his reflections on an ("ecological") aesthetics of nature. The primary difference here is the subject/object schema rather than the space/place difference; but the problem is, as in our case, that the primary difference cannot do justice to the atmospheric, although it is indispensable for the purpose of presentation.

25. See esp. Agnew, *Worlds Apart.*

26. In this context, it is worth noting that the transitions in Hegel's theory are guaranteed not only by theoretical means (e.g., by the notion of the concept) but also by means of a developmental *narrative* of Spirit.

27. As they do for Lessing, who, in *Laocoön*, § XV–XVIII, relegates painting to space and poetry to time; quoted from *Lessings Werke* (Leipzig-Vienna, n.d.), vol. 3, pp. 100ff. However, Lessing infers the semantic meaning of forms all too quickly from their spatial or temporal anchoring (or their meaning from the medium).

28. Some authors have suggested that "fitness for movement" is the rule for the optimal proportion of bodies in artworks. See William Hogarth, *The Analysis of Beauty, written with a view of fixing the fluctuating Ideas of Taste* (London, 1753; Oxford, 1955), pp. 103f. See also the quote by Lomazzo in Hogarth, *The Analysis of Beauty*, p. 5.

29. This is emphasized by Joan Evans, *Pattern: A Study of Ornament in Western Europe from 1180 to 1900*, 2 vols. (Oxford, 1931; New York, 1975), vol. 1, p. xxxv: "The first essential of decoration is a defined and limited space." To *begin* with such a clearing of space or time makes sense only if there is the intent and possibility of integrating varied redundancies in the form of ornaments.

30. See Herder (in search of a general concept of beauty), *Viertes Kritisches Wäldchen*, II, quoted from Bernhard Suphan, ed., *Herders Sämmtliche Werke*, vol. 4, (Berlin, 1978), pp. 44ff.

31. To clarify this even further: readers know, of course, that the lady does not know. Siebenkäs knows that the one who died is not the Siebenkäs buried here but his wife, who is buried elsewhere, so that he (and the reader) but not the lady knows of the impending marriage. Most likely, the reader will await with excitement how the text dissolves cognitive discrepancies through communication-in-the-text (and this is precisely what happens). Despite this shared knowledge, the intuition—the imagination of what would have to be perceived in such a case—remains separate and incommunicable (one can verify this by considering one's disappointment when watching the scene on film).

32. This is already a phenomenological (Husserlian) interpretation of Spencer Brown's notion of the unmarked space.

33. This formulation takes into consideration the logic of a "transjunctive" application of distinctions as developed by Gotthard Günther. See esp. "Cybernetic

Ontology and Transjunctional Operations," in Günther, *Beiträge zur Grundlegung einer operationsfähigen Dialektik* (Hamburg, 1976), vol. 1, pp. 249–328.

34. This explains the notion of form in Focillon, which at first appears contradictory. On the one hand, "form signifies only *itself*"; on the other hand, "it also suggests the existence of other forms" (Focillon, *The Life of Forms in Art,* p. 34). The meaning of these statements resides in their own form, in what they exclude as their other side, namely, the notion of content or matter and the idea of form as a sign for something else.

35. See Gregory Bateson, *Steps to an Ecology of Mind* (New York, 1972), p. 453.

36. Let us note in passing that this statement no longer holds for attempts to break the symmetry of the two sides with a minimal effort, in order to stage the invitation to unfold the paradox.

37. See Helen Peters, ed., *John Donne, Paradoxes and Problems* (Oxford, 1980). More mature pieces are scattered throughout Donne's poetic work.

38. See A. E. Malloch, "The Technique and Function of the Renaissance Paradox," *Studies in Philology* 53 (1956): 191–203; Michael McCanless, "Paradox in Donne," *Studies in the Renaissance* 13 (1966): 266–87.

39. See Hogarth, *The Analysis of Beauty*, p. 22: "no stress might be laid on the figures to the prejudice of the work itself."

40. The degradation of the merely ornamental, whose effects are still felt today, can be traced to the introduction of the concept of beauty into the artistic doctrines of the early Renaissance. The preceding rhetorical tradition already distinguished between clear and flawless speech, on the one hand, and *ornamentum*, on the other, while the emphasis of rhetorical schooling and artistry remained focused on *ornamentum*. See Quintilian, *Institutionis Oratoriae libri XII*, Book VII, Chap. 3 (Darmstadt, 1975), vol. 2, pp. 150ff. In the Middle Ages, the notion of *ornatus mundus* elucidated the beauty of the creation—the sky with its stars, the air populated by birds, the fish in the water, and humans on earth. See Guillaume de Conches, *In Timeum*, quoted from Rosario Assunto, *Die Theorie des Schönen im Mittelalter* (Cologne, 1963), p. 151. The humanism of the early Renaissance in Italy retained the notion of *ornatum/ornato* in its earlier richness. On the distinction *puro/ornato*, see Michael Baxandall, *Painting and Experience in Fifteenth-Century Italy* (Oxford, 1972). With the introduction of conceptual concerns about the idea of beauty, all of this changed. One no longer distinguished the ornament from the simple, raw, artless production, but from its "composition," which was now the only thing that mattered. No matter how beauty was subsequently defined, the new terminology required a distinction between natural beauty, on the one hand, and ornament, decoration, and supporting supplement, on the other. As a starting point, see Leon Battista Alberti, *De re aedificatoria* (1450–1452; Milan, 1966); and Michael Jäger, *Die Theorie des Schönen in der italienischen Renaissance* (Cologne, 1990), pp. 44ff. In theories of

architecture that follow Alberti, the distinction is firmly established. See, e.g., Luca Pacioli, *De divina proportione* (1497), quoted from the Italian edition by Andrea Masimi in Arnoldo Bruschi et al., eds., *Scritti rinascimentali di architettura* (Milan, 1978), pp. 23–244 (93) and other statements in the same volume. Independently of the fluctuating and repeatedly failing definitions of the beautiful, one continued to insist on the merely subordinate role of ornaments, which was meant to focus attention on the essential but not to distract from it. (Still widely accepted is Karl Philipp Moritz, *Schriften zur Ästhetik und Poetik: Kritische Ausgabe* [Tübingen, 1962], pp. 72, 109ff.) Current discussions still oppose the ornament as adornment or decoration to the true meaning of art, but are more sensitive to the influence of the ornament on the development of artistic styles—an ongoing discussion since the nineteenth century. See Ernst H. Gombrich, *Ornament und Kunst: Schmucktrieb und Ordnungssinn in der Psychologie des dekorativen Schaffens* (Stuttgart, 1982). But the functional difference remains: the artwork deserves more attention than does mere decoration (ibid., p. 74).

41. *Redundancy* is a beautiful, almost ornamental word, and it indicates precisely what is meant here—the return of a wave (*unda*).

42. See, e.g., Antonio Minturno, *L'arte poetica* (1563; Naples, 1725), pp. 435f.

43. Gombrich, *Ornament und Kunst*, pp. 177, 220f.

44. In the developmental history of a painter from Lüneburg, Otto Brix, landscape first withdrew to the lower edge of the painting, only to become superfluous once the painter began to focus on "cosmic" paintings.

45. In the terminology of Moritz, *Schriften zur Ästhetik und Poetik*, pp. 151–57 (with reference to drama). Similarly, Kant considers drawing the essential element in all the visual arts (including architecture and garden art) and distinguishes it from mere adornment. See *Kritik der Urteilskraft*, § 14.

46. A more precise analysis would, of course, have to be more complex and take into account that persons are not only characterized by actions and that some actions (trivial ones) merely serve to transport the plot. See Roland Barthes, *L'aventure sémiologique* (Paris, 1985), pp. 189ff., 207ff., with texts from the 1960s.

47. In the terminology of E. M. Forster, *Aspects of the Novel* (1927; rpt. London, 1949).

48. On this shift, see Klaus Hammacher, "Jacobis Romantheorie," in Walter Jaeschke and Helmut Holzhey, eds., *Früher Idealismus und Frühromantik: Der Streit um die Grundlagen der Ästhetik (1795–1805)* (Hamburg, 1990), pp. 174–89.

49. Again, following Moritz, *Schriften zur Ästhetik und Poetik*, p. 99: "Und so müssen nun auch bei der Beschreibung des Schönen durch Linien, diese Linien selbst, zusammengenommen, das Schöne seyn, welches nie anders als durch sich selbst bezeichnet werden kann; weil es eben da erst seinen Anfang nimmt, wo die Sache mit ihrer Bezeichnung sein wird."

50. On the many variations on this general access to art, see Hans Ulrich

Gumbrecht and K. Ludwig Pfeiffer, eds., *Stil: Geschichten und Funktionen eines kulturwissenschaftlichen Diskurselements* (Frankfurt, 1986).

51. We shall return to this point in section VII of this chapter and in Chapter 5, section IV, below.

52. This is where Moritz, *Schriften zur Ästhetik und Poetik*, pp. 99f., grounds the special status of poetry among the fine arts.

53. This accounts for the much-discussed closeness of poetic language and irony—but also, and for this very reason, for the inverse possibility of a striking naïveté, by which poetry recommends itself and its worldview. We think of E. T. A. Hoffmann and Hölderlin. As a consequence, the "subject" apprehends its distanced relation to the relation between language and world as a possibility for self-reflection.

54. On this use of the distinction between denotation and connotation, see Cleanth Brooks, *The Well Wrought Urn: Studies in the Structure of Poetry* (New York, 1947).

55. We cannot interrupt our analysis here to embark on historical analyses, but it is worth noting that the increasing complexity of social communication about the world makes it all the more necessary to renounce referential mimesis completely (or else use it as material) and to focus poetic meaning exclusively on the connotative level.

56. See Michael Riffaterre, *Semiotics of Poetry* (Bloomington, Ind., 1978); he uses the corresponding distinction between "meaning" (for reference) and signification.

57. Riffaterre (ibid., p. 4), speaks of two levels or stages of reading.

58. The notion of the "symbolic" is justified in this context, since the poem at once operates *and* observes: "The poem is an instance of the doctrine which it asserts; it is both the assertion and the realization of the assertion" (Brooks, *The Well Wrought Urn*, p. 17).

59. As in John Donne's "The Canonization," which contains the lines, analyzed by Brooks (ibid., pp. 3ff.): "We can dye by it, if not live by love / And if unfit for tombes and hearse / our legend be, it will be fit for verse."

60. See William Empson, *The Structure of Complex Words* (1951). See also Empson, *Seven Types of Ambiguity* (1930; 2d ed. Edinburgh, 1947), and Brooks, *The Well Wrought Urn*.

61. For an overview, see Jonathan Culler, *Framing the Sign: Criticism and Its Institutions* (Norman, Okla., 1988). On Empson, see Culler, *Framing*, pp. 85ff.

62. Julia Kristeva, *Semeiotikè: Recherches pour un sémanalyse* (Paris, 1969), p. 53 (author's emphasis). Or more concisely, "having no law but wit" (Sir Philip Sidney, *The Defense of Poetry* [1595; Lincoln, Nebr., 1970], p. 12).

63. Following Tzvetan Todorov, *The Fantastic: A Structural Approach to a Literary Genre* (Cleveland, 1973).

64. Traditionally, difficulty has been considered a precondition for an artwork's

pleasing effect. In order to please, the work must exhibit a sufficient amount of controlled variety. See, e.g., Torquato Tasso, *Discorsi dell'arte poetica e in particolare sopra il poema eroico* (1587), quoted from *Prosa* (Milan, 1969), p. 388: "Questa varietà si fatta tanto sarà più lodevole quanto recarà secco più di difficoltà." See also Hogarth's notion, based on his reflections on drawing a line (which concern the ornament), of a sufficient difficulty ("intricacy") of artworks (Hogarth, *The Analysis of Beauty*, pp. 41ff.). Today, the question is whether works of art may have become too difficult to be accessible to the general public. The reason may be that the works no longer communicate why are the way they are.

65. See Talcott Parsons, *Zur Theorie der sozialen Interaktionsmedien* (Opladen, 1980), esp. pp. 211ff. Talcott Parsons and Gerald M. Platt, *The American University* (Cambridge, Mass., 1973). See further Rainer M. Baum, "On Societal Media Dynamics," in Jan J. Loubser et al., eds., *Explorations in General Theory in Social Science* (New York, 1976), vol. 2, pp. 579–608.

66. Emphasizing the relationship between structuring and praxis, Anthony Giddens describes "structuration" as a "virtual order of differences." See Giddens, *Central Problems in Social Theory: Action, Structure and Contradiction in Social Analysis* (London, 1979), p. 3; and Giddens, *The Constitution of Society: Outline of the Theory of Structuration* (Berkeley, Calif., 1984). By contrast, the older structuralism could integrate the problem of time only through the relativizing concession that even structures may change.

67. For a more detailed account, see Niklas Luhmann, "Das Kunstwerk und die Selbstreproduktion der Kunst," in Gumbrecht and Pfeiffer, *Stil,* pp. 620–71. See also Chapter 5, section IV, below.

68. "Non essendo quella altro che accoppiamento di parole," one reads in Torquato Tasso, *Discorsi dell'arte poetica,* p. 392, which is associated here not with the concept of form but with the concept of the ornament.

69. Tasso (ibid.) follows the common division: "magnifica o sublime, mediocre ed umile."

70. See Hans Ulrich Gumbrecht, "'Phoenix aus der Asche' oder: Vom Kanon zur Klassik," in Aleida and Jan Assmann, eds., *Kanon und Zensur: Archäologie der literarischen Kommunikation* II (Munich, 1987), pp. 284–99; Gumbrecht, "Klassik ist Klassik, eine bewundernswerte Sicherheit des Nichts?" in F. Nies and K. Stierle, eds., *Die Französische Klassik* (Munich, 1989), pp. 441–94.

71. "Das Klassische ist durch den bestimmt, für den es klassisch ist," one reads in Novalis, *Blüthenstaub,* No. 52, quoted from *Werke, Tagebücher und Briefe Friedrich von Hardenbergs,* ed. Hans-Joachim Mähl and Richard Samuel (Darmstadt, 1978), vol. 2, p. 247.

72. See Louis Gabriel Ambroise (Vicomte de Bonald), *Sur les ouvrages classiques* (1810), quoted from *Œuvres complètes,* vol. II (Paris, 1858; rpt. Geneva, 1982), pp. 227–43.

73. Other observers have noticed that here art is no longer displayed as art. "Es ist ein beweinenswerter Anblick," writes Friedrich Schlegel, "einen Schatz der trefflichsten und seltensten Kunstwerke wie eine gemeine Sammlung von Kostbarkeiten zusammen aufgehäuft zu sehen." In "Über die Grenzen des Schönen," quoted from *Dichtungen und Aufsätze*, ed. Wolfdietrich Rasch (Munich, 1984), pp. 268–76 (269). But there is no need to exaggerate. One might as well try not to let one's view of the artwork be spoiled by the museum.

§ 4

1. See Georg Simmel, *Über sociale Differenzierung: Soziologische und psychologische Untersuchungen* (Leipzig, 1890), and Emile Durkheim, *De la division du travail social* (Paris, 1893). On the currency of this assumption, see Jeffrey C. Alexander and Paul Colomy, eds., *Differentiation Theory and Social Change: Comparative and Historical Perspectives* (New York, 1990).

2. See, e.g., Charles Tilly, "Clio and Minerva," in John C. McKinney and Edward A. Tiryakian, eds., *Theoretical Sociology: Perspectives and Developments* (New York, 1970), pp. 433–36; Edward A. Tiryakian, "On the Significance of De-differentiation," in S. N. Eisenstadt and H. J. Helle, eds., *Macro-Sociological Theory: Perspectives on Sociological Theory*, vol. 1 (London, 1985), pp. 118–34.

3. Compare Parsons's fatal answer to this question, which states that subsystems specializing in one of four possible functions must fulfill all of these four functions themselves and can be recognized as such only in this way—a requirement that resulted in an endless repetition of the schema within the schema.

4. In his theory of a general action system, Talcott Parsons proposed a concept of the nonarbitrary nature of the consequences of system differentiation, which resembles our own despite differences in detail. We would suggest that this is the heart of Parsons's theory, which yielded a number of fruitful comparative analyses.

5. To clarify the matter we should note that we are talking about *operations* that separate system and environment. As far as *observations* are concerned, the reentry of the form into the form generates the internal distinction between self-reference and hetero-reference.

6. This argument clearly shows that the system's dependency on other systems for the fulfillment of certain functions is the condition and mark of the autonomy of every functional system. Specific independence depends, in other words, on a considerable degree of specific dependency. This must be kept in mind when encountering the repeated objection that the dependency of art on a monetary market economy could infringe upon the autonomy of the art system.

7. See, e.g., Benedetto Varchi, *Lezzione nella quale si disputa della maggioranza delle arti . . .* (1547), quoted from Paola Barocchi, ed., *Trattati d'arte del cinquecento*, vol. 1 (Bari, 1960), pp. 1–58.

8. One can find a justification for this trend, e.g., in George Puttenham, *The Arte of English Poesie* (1589; Cambridge, 1970), pp. 42ff.

9. See Torquato Tasso on the styles of "magnifica o sublime, mediocre ed umile" in *Discorsi dell'arte e in particolare sopra il poema eroico*, quoted from *Prosa* (Milan, 1969), pp. 349–729 (392ff.).

10. See Henri Testelin, *Sentiments de plus Habiles Peintres sur la Pratique de la Peinture et la Sculpture* (Paris, 1696), quoted from the unpaginated Introduction. See also pp. 12f., 17.

11. See Aldo Schiavone, *Nascita della giurisprudenza: Cultura aristocratica e pensiero giuridico nella Roma tardo-repubblicana* (Bari, 1976), pp. 36ff. Similarly, Samuel Richardson states at the beginning of the eighteenth century that for the typical gentleman, art is "a fine piece of workmanship, and difficult to be performed, but produces only pleasant ornaments, mere superfluidities" (in *Discourse on the Dignity, Certainty, Pleasure and Advantage of the Science of a Connoisseur* [1719], quoted from *The Works* [London, 1773; rpt. Hildesheim, 1969], pp. 241–346 [244]).

12. See the distinction between an internal (mental) and an external *disegno* (one put into practice) in Federico Zuccaro, *L'idea dei Pittori, Scultori ed Architetti* (Turin, 1607), quoted from *Scritti d'Arte Federico Zuccaro* (Florence, 1961), pp. 149–352 (explicitly, p. 152).

13. On situating this idea within the sociological tradition of "functional equivalents," see Niklas Luhmann, "Funktion und Kausalität," in Luhmann, *Soziologische Aufklärung*, vol. 1 (Opladen, 1970), pp. 9–30.

14. This remark is directed against a tradition that believed it sufficed to define meaning from the perspective of consciousness.

15. For more elaborate analyses, see Niklas Luhmann, *Soziale Systeme: Grundriß einer allgemeinen Theorie* (Frankfurt, 1984), pp. 91–147; trans. as *Social Systems*, trans. John Bednarz, with Dirk Baecker (Stanford, Calif., 1995), pp. 59–102.

16. See, e.g., Hans Belting, *Bild und Kult: Eine Geschichte des Bildes vor dem Zeitalter der Kunst* (Munich, 1990).

17. For such a view, see Dirk Baecker, *Die Beobachtung der Kunst in der Gesellschaft*, ms. 1994.

18. See Kant, *Kritik der Urteilskraft*, § 49.

19. See the distinction between narrow and broad coupling in Peter Fuchs, *Moderne Kommunikation: Zur Theorie des operativen Displacements* (Frankfurt, 1993), pp. 139ff.

20. See Chapter 3, section III, above.

21. See the well-known passage in Max Horkheimer and Theodor W. Adorno, *Dialektik der Aufklärung* (1947), quoted from Adorno, *Gesammelte Schriften*, vol. 3 (Frankfurt, 1981), pp. 141ff. See also the initially unpublished chapter "Das Schema der Massenkultur," ibid., pp. 299ff.

22. See George Spencer Brown, *Probability and Scientific Inference* (London, 1957), on corresponding reflections on the worldly meaning of the calculus of probability.

23. Roman Ingarden, in *Das literarische Kunstwerk* (1931; 4th ed. Tübingen, 1972), p. 234, notes with astonishment that this "modification of being" is so unique that it can barely be put into words.

24. See the portrayal of habitual communication in everyday life when others are present, or in television dialogues, in politics, and so forth by Rainald Goetz in such titles as *Angst, Festung, Kronos* (Frankfurt, 1989–1993). I am referring here to a conversation with Rainald Goetz.

25. See Arthur C. Danto, *The Transfiguration of the Commonplace: A Philosophy of Art* (Cambridge, Mass., 1981).

26. The notion of *admiratio* combines astonishment and admiration [*Verwunderung und Bewunderung*]. Moreover, it oscillates between the (positive or negative) *states of the soul* and the *effectuation* of such states via a striking incident that has been rendered plausible. See Baxter Hathaway, *Marvels and Commonplaces: Renaissance Literary Criticism* (New York, 1968). In the theory of art, this prevents—as early as Aristotle—a notion of *mimesis/imitatio* as mere copying. The most compact and concise formulation of this concept can be found in Descartes, *Les passions de l'âme*, quoted from *Œuvres et Lettres*, Pléiade ed. (Paris, 1952), Art. 53, p. 723. *L'admiration* is the prime passion, an astonishment in the face of deviation. It is not yet knowledge—*not yet coded in the binary true/false*. In current terminology, one might speak of an "irritation" or "perturbation." The function of art apparently is to prepare the ground for something that can subsequently be elaborated under conditions of binary coding (of art as well?).

27. See Ulrich Schulz-Buschhaus, "Bandellos Realismus," *Romanisches Jahrbuch* 37 (1986): 107–26.

28. On the necessity of defending poetry in a state of (an allegedly) declining social reputation against the pretentious truth claims of philosophy and historiography, see, e.g., Sir Philip Sidney, *The Defense of Poetry* (1595; Lincoln, Nebr., 1970), pp. 13ff.

29. See Niels Werber, *Literatur als System: Zur Ausdifferenzierung literarischer Kommunikation* (Opladen, 1992), esp. pp. 63ff. Werber maintains that the distinction interesting/boring will be used from now on as a code by the system. See also Gerhard Plumpe, *Ästhetische Kommunikation der Moderne*, vol. 1, *Von Kant bis Hegel* (Opladen, 1993), pp. 22f., 156ff. This view conflicts with a number of noteworthy remarks, especially by the romantics, on the notion of the interesting, and it is at odds with the further development of this notion in the idea of the beautiful. There seems to be a general agreement, however, that the notion that art must be interesting results from its orientation toward the market.

30. Not surprisingly, this holds for other functional systems as well. We find

an emphasis on such code values as lawfulness, truth, affluence in the sense of property, and so forth, though there is not yet a sufficiently formal specification of function to explain why the code displays a positive *and a negative* value.

31. For important analyses of how the world is presupposed and produced as a basis for belief that allows consciousness to shift its awareness, see Edmund Husserl, *Erfahrung und Urteil: Untersuchungen zur Genealogie der Logik* (Hamburg, 1948), esp. § 7–9, pp. 23ff. Husserl's emphasis is on the world as presupposition—on how it typifies connective possibilities and thus serves as a substratum that makes possible the shifting of experiential horizons. Reversing this point, one could argue that recursive operation and the possibility of repetition it implies are constitutive of the emergence of identity and of typifications that are understood to be a substratum of reality and that whatever is actualized as intention and communication passes lightly over its surface.

32. Hegel, *Vorlesungen über die Ästhetik*, Pt. 1, quoted from G. E. W. Hegel, *Werke in zwanzig Bänden*, vol. 13 (Frankfurt, 1970), p. 199. On p. 125, Hegel writes about Dutch painting: "Gegen die vorhandene prosaische Realität ist daher dieser durch Geist produzierte Schein das Wunder der Identität, ein Spott, wenn man will, und eine Ironie über das äußerliche natürliche Dasein."

33. We need to remind ourselves, however, that such a sense of reality requires that there be something else from which it distinguishes itself, whether this might be—possibly misleading—language, or whether it might be religion, statistics, or politics.

34. "In einem wahrhaft schönen Kunstwerk soll der Inhalt nichts, die Form aber alles tun," one reads, e.g., in Friedrich Schiller, *Über die ästhetische Erziehung des Menschen in einer Reihe von Briefen*, 22d letter, quoted from Friedrich Schiller, *Sämtliche Werke*, vol. 5, 4th ed. (Munich, 1967), p. 639. Earlier in the text, Schiller rejects the notion of a "middle ground" between form and matter, maintaining that art can "cancel" [*aufheben*] this distinction—but how? one might ask, if not in the form of a reentry of the form into the form.

35. See Niklas Luhmann, *Soziologie des Risikos* (Berlin, 1991), esp. 168ff.

36. Following Alberti, an early version of this problem concerns the relationship between harmonious proportion and variety. See Paolo Pino, *Dialogo di pittura* (1548) quoted from Paola Barocchi, ed., *Trattati d'arte del cinquecento*, vol. 1 (Bari, 1960), pp. 93–139 (104). See also the warning against an excess of "deliberate" variety in Lodovico Dolce, *Dialogo della pittura* (1557), quoted from the Barocchi edition, ibid., pp. 141–206 (179f.); and Giovanni Paolo Lomazzo, *Trattato dell'arte della pittura et architettura* (Milan, 1585), Chap. 26, pp. 89f. Henri Testelin, *Sentiments de plus Habiles Peintres sur la Pratique de la Peinture et la Sculpture* (Paris, 1696), p. 18, distinguishes the variety of contrast from the economy of contours and warns of "incompatible things" (p. 19). In poetics, one finds the distinction between *verisimile* (for redundancy) and *meraviglioso* or *mirabile*

(for variety) alongside the old distinction between the one and the many (*unità/moltitudine*). See, e.g., Torquato Tasso *Discorsi dell'arte poetica e in particolare sopra il poema eroico* (1587), quoted from *Prosa* (Milan, 1969). On *unità/moltitudine* = *varietà*, see Tasso, pp. 372ff.; he opts for *moltitudine* because it is pleasing. What matters in the distinction *verisimile/meraviglioso* is an "accoppiamento" (p. 367) to be accomplished by a "maggior diletto" "o più del verisimile o più del mirabile" (p. 366). John Dryden, to mention a final example, maintains that English theater is superior to French theater because it exhibits greater variety while paying attention to the demands of redundancy ("variety if well order'd"). See John Dryden, *Of Dramatick Poesie: An Essay*, 2d ed. (1684; London, 1964), pp. 78ff. (quote on p. 79), and also Chap. 6, n. 35.

37. See Umberto Eco's fitting formulation: "L'arte più que *cognoscere* il mondo, *produce* dei complimenti del mondo, delle forme autonome che s'aggiungiano a quelle esistenti esibendo leggi proprie et vita personale" (*Opera aperta* [1962; 6th ed. Milan, 1988], p. 50).

38. Evidence for this view from outside the mainstream (which is therefore symptomatic) can be found, e.g., in Karl Heinrich Heydenreich, *System der Ästhetik* (Leipzig, 1790; rpt. Hildesheim, 1978).

39. See, e.g., Howard Rheingold, *Virtual Reality* (New York, 1991); Martin Kubaczek, "Zur Entwicklung der Imaginationsmaschinen: Der Text als virtuelle Realität," *Faultline* 1 (1992): 93–102; or some of the contributions in Gerhard Johann Lischka, ed., *Der entfesselte Blick: Symposion, Workshops, Ausstellung* (Bern, 1993).

40. See Mark Siemons, "Dämonen im Büro: Die Computer-Messe 'System 93' droht mit virtuellen Welten," *Frankfurter Allgemeine Zeitung*, October 23, 1993, p. 27.

41. See esp. Hans Ulrich Gumbrecht, "Für eine Erfindung des mittelalterlichen Theaters aus der Perspektive der frühen Neuzeit," in *Festschrift für Walter Haug und Burghart Wachinger* (Tübingen, 1992), vol. 2, pp. 827–48.

42. August Wilhelm Schlegel, *Die Kunstlehre* (Pt. 1 of the lectures on literature and art), quoted from *Kritische Schriften und Briefe*, vol. 2 (Stuttgart, 1963), p. 13. Justifications of this view vary according to whatever terminology is accepted at the time. A well-known eighteenth-century version states, e.g., that beauty pleases *necessarily* and *immediately* and therefore has no place for the intervention (= association) of interests. See Francis Hutcheson, *An Inquiry Concerning Beauty, Order, Harmony, Design*, Treatise I of his *Inquiry into the Original of Our Ideas of Beauty and Virtue* (1725; 4th ed., 1738; critical ed. The Hague, 1973), § 1, XIII, pp. 36f. For an elaboration from the viewpoint of associationist psychology, which excludes even art criticism with its interfering reflections, see Archibald Alison, *Essays on the Nature and Principles of Taste* (Edinburgh-London, 1790; rpt. Hildesheim, 1968). On criticism, see pp. 7ff. Others aim directly at self-

reference and infer from it the necessity of disregarding utility (even if there is one), as, e.g., Karl Philipp Moritz in his definition of the beautiful as "that which is completed in itself." See his *Schriften zur Ästhetik und Poetik: Kritische Ausgabe* (Tübingen, 1962), pp. 3ff.

43. In classical and romantic aesthetics, to postulate an "end in itself" was a way of blocking references to further purposes beyond the work and of presenting the work as closed in upon itself.

44. On the history of this originally theological formula, see Werner Strube, "'Interessenlosigkeit': Zur Geschichte eines Grundbegriffs der Ästhetik," *Archiv für Begriffsgeschichte* 23 (1979): 148–74.

45. See Jean-Paul Sartre, *Qu'est-ce que la littérature?* in *Situations,* II (Paris, 1948), pp. 91ff.: unlike the shoemaker, the writer cannot produce for his own demand.

46. Friedrich Schiller, *Über die ästhetische Erziehung des Menschen in einer Reihe von Briefen,* quoted from *Sämtliche Werke,* vol. 5 (Munich, 1967), p. 638. Schiller is no rigorous thinker, and his claim cannot be meant seriously; otherwise one could not speak of an aesthetic education to begin with, nor could one expect a political amelioration of the state by way of such a detour. Indeed, the individual could not be understood as a focus for the integration of diverse domains of life.

47. See Karl Wilhelm Ferdinand Solger, *Vorlesungen über Ästhetik,* ed. Karl Wilhelm Ludwig Heyse (Leipzig, 1829; rpt. Darmstadt, 1973), p. 51.

48. We shall return to this question in Chapter 5, below.

49. See Chapter 3, above.

50. According to Arthur O. Lovejoy, *The Great Chain of Being: A Study of the History of an Idea* (1936; rpt. Cambridge, Mass., 1950).

51. For examples from England, see Russell Fraser, *The War Against Poetry* (Princeton, 1970), pp. 144ff.

52. See Erving Goffman, *Frame Analysis: An Essay on the Organization of Experience* (New York, 1974). Earlier formulations of this sort can be found in Max Weber, Edmund Husserl, and Alfred Schütz, who maintain that interpretive understanding and the transcendence of the momentary nature of experience in time presuppose typified patterns of order. A frame analysis has the advantage that it does not depend on similarity between the frame and a detail accessible from within this frame. *Pace* Alexander Dorner, the museum does not have to be a *Gesamtkunstwerk.*

53. See Francisco Varela, "A Calculus for Self-reference," *International Journal of General Systems* 2 (1975): 5–24.

54. See again Heinz von Foerster's notion of "double closure" in *Observing Systems* (Seaside, Calif., 1981), pp. 304ff.

55. In the wake of the critique of the theory of logical empiricism, see esp.

Kenneth J. Gergen, *Toward Transformation in Social Knowledge* (New York, 1982), pp. 100ff.

56. Consider the abstract nature of this argument: in this context, material and morality are functionally equivalent forms of hetero-reference that constrain the work's room for play so long as they are not—as hetero-references—subject to the internal control by forms.

57. Spencer Brown, *Laws of Form* (1969; rpt. New York, 1979), pp. 10, 12.

58. In the sense of Michael Polanyi, *Personal Knowledge* (Chicago, 1958). For more on the same topic, see issue 1/2 of *Revue internationale de systémique* 6 (1992).

59. We again refer to Derrida, "Signature Event Context," in *Margins of Philosophy*, trans. Alan Bass (Chicago, 1982), pp. 307–30.

60. Ibid.

61. One can certainly reject this conceptual decision, but one would then sacrifice almost everything gained by the concept.

62. Frequently, the point has been made that evolution theory breaks with an "archaeological" explanation in terms of origins. Even causal observation and explanation are evolutionary possibilities and vary according to the complexity of the system.

63. For a corresponding historical account of the European university, see Rudolf Stichweh, *Der frühmoderne Staat und die europäische Universität: Zur Interaktion von Politik und Erziehungssystem im Prozeß ihrer Ausdifferenzierung (16.–18. Jahrhundert)* (Frankfurt, 1991).

64. For examples, see James Hall, *A History of Ideas and Images in Italian Art* (London, 1983), pp. 4ff. and passim.

65. Belting, *Bild und Kult*, p. 538.

66. For a study that draws on an analysis of contemporary treatises, see Michael Baxandall, *Painting and Experience in Fifteenth-Century Italy* (Oxford, 1972).

67. We think of Michelangelo's notorious and often-mentioned appearance in front of the Pope—with his felt cap on his hat. For a justification, see Francisco de Hollanda, *Vier Gespräche über die Malerei, geführt zu Rom 1538* (Vienna, 1899), p. 23. It is important not to mistake this behavior for courtly service.

68. See Caroll W. Westfall, "Painting and the Liberal Arts: Alberti's View," *Journal of the History of Ideas* 30 (1969): 487–506.

69. See esp. Martin Warnke, *Hofkünstler: Zur Vorgeschichte des modernen Künstlers* (Cologne, 1985); further, Klaus Disselbeck, "Die Ausdifferenzierung der Kunst als Problem der Ästhetik," in Henk de Berg and Matthias Prangel, eds., *Kommunikation und Differenz: Systemtheoretische Ansätze in der Literatur- und Kunstwissenschaft* (Opladen, 1993), pp. 137–58.

70. For an overview, and on the ambiguous relationship to birth nobility, see Warnke, *Hofkünstler*, pp. 202ff.

71. "Eadem ratione [= *suo iure*, thanks to exceptional talent, N. L.] dicimus nobilem pictorem, nobilem oratorem, nobilem poetam," says the interlocutor in Cristoforo Landino, *De vera nobilitate* (ca. 1440; Florence, 1970), p. 55. What matters is "la virtù propria," proclaims the painter Paolo Pino, not without pride (*Dialogo di Pittura* [Vinegia, 1548], quoted from Paola Barocchi, ed., *Trattati d'arte del cinquecento*, vol. 1 [Bari, 1960], pp. 132f.). Pino goes on to emphasize the significance of education and of distinguished social intercourse (p. 136).

72. See Benedetto Varchi, *Lezzione nella quale si disputa della maggioranza delle arti e qual sia piu nobile, la scultura o la pittura* (1547), in Barocchi, *Trattati d'arte del cinquecento*, vol. 1, pp. 1–58. See also Pino, in Barocchi, *Trattati d'arte del cinquecento*, vol. 1, pp. 127ff. (Painting is superior to sculpture.)

73. On predecessors from the humanist rhetorical tradition who offered concepts (e.g., *varietas* or *ornamentum*) that became relevant later, see Michael Baxandall, *Giotto and the Orators: Humanist Observers of Painting in Italy and the Discovery of Pictorial Composition 1350–1450* (1971; rpt. Oxford, 1988), and Baxandall, *Painting and Experience in Fifteenth-Century Italy*. The typical motive was already to evaluate artists and artworks, to praise them and distinguish among them.

74. Efforts to assimilate to the norms of an aristocratic lifestyle are evident from very early on—especially in the claim that the artist does not work for money and is rewarded not for a single work but for his *virtù*, as well as in the notion that works of art cannot be paid for with money. Within the context of a biographical report, see Girolamo Frachetta, *Dialogo del Furore Poetico* (Padua, 1581; rpt. Munich, 1969), p. 4. For an overview, see Warnke, *Hofkünstler*, p. 194. Such considerations have nothing to do with criteria of artistic evaluation but concern the relationship between art and the economy.

75. See the references in Chapter 1, n. 93.

76. Early references (from around 1500) to renowned artists who managed to gain a certain independence can be found in Donat De Chapeaurouge, *Die Anfänge der freien Gegenstandswahl durch den Künstler*, in *Schülerfestgabe für Herbert von Einem* (Bonn, 1965), pp. 55–62. On unauthorized deviations from the contract and on tendencies to stray from given models, see H. W. Janson, "The Birth of 'Artistic License': The Dissatisfied Patron in the Early Renaissance," in Guy F. Lytle and Stephen Orgel, eds., *Patronage in the Renaissance* (Princeton, 1981), pp. 344–53. On the (overestimated) influence of learned humanists on artistic commissions, see Charles Hope, "Artists, Patrons, and Advisers in the Italian Renaissance," in Lytle and Orgel, *Patronage in the Renaissance*, pp. 239–343.

77. A caesura as radical as this one can be responsibly posited only in retrospect. It must be further differentiated according to regions or artistic genres. If one aims at a broader concept of specifically cultural accomplishments, one finds that patronage and market orientation overlap each other at all times. See (with-

out specific textual evidence) Raymond Williams, *The Sociology of Culture* (New York, 1982), pp. 38ff.

78. See Francis Haskell, "The Market for Italian Art in the Seventeenth Century," *Past and Present* 15 (1959): 48–59.

79. How difficult it must have been to come to terms with this delicate question can be inferred from the amount of space dedicated to it in de Hollanda's dialogues on painting (1538). See de Hollanda, "Gespräche über die Malerei," pp. 37, 95ff., 141ff.

80. See Iain Pears, *The Discovery of Painting: The Growth of Interest in the Arts in England, 1680–1768* (New Haven, Conn., 1988). On further developments, especially on price increases for paintings, see Gerald Reitlinger, *The Economics of Taste: The Rise and Fall of Picture Prices 1760–1960* (London, 1961). For a comprehensive treatment of the topic that includes literature and politics, see Michael Foss, *The Age of Patronage: The Arts in England 1660–1750* (London, 1974). On the situation in Holland (which was characterized by an underdeveloped patronage system, by estate auctions and lotteries, by a scarcity of specialized art dealers, by localized production, and by the lack of reputations capable of driving up the prices), see John Michael Montias, *Artists and Artisans in Delft: A Socio-Economic Study of the Seventeenth Century* (Princeton, N.J., 1982), esp. pp. 183ff. On the breakdown of the Italian system of patronage, which led to an export-oriented art market and to Italian artists being active abroad, see Francis Haskell's detailed study (which treats the seventeenth *and* the eighteenth centuries), *Patrons and Painters: A Study in the Relations Between Italian Art and Society in the Age of the Baroque* (London, 1963). From an entirely different viewpoint—namely, of *doux commerce* and the thematic of images—see further David H. Solkin, *Painting for Money: The Visual Arts and the Public Sphere in Eighteenth-Century England* (New Haven, Conn., 1993).

81. On nostalgic reminiscences concerning a lost security, see Pears, *The Discovery of Painting*, pp. 133ff.

82. This concerns only the genres of painting and etching, although, for poetry, one finds similar observations about the increasing dominance of publishing houses and the reading public. This holds for the new periodicals and especially for the novel, which aims to present accessible individual destinies and an exciting plot.

83. A remark by Michael Hutter, "Literatur als Quelle wirtschaftlichen Wachstums," *Internationales Archiv für Sozialgeschichte der deutschen Literatur* 16 (1991): 1–50 (11).

84. See Jonathan Richardson, who places great trust in the clarity of distinctions and cognitive competence in *A Discourse on the Dignity, Certainty, Pleasure and Advantage of the Science of a Connoisseur* (1719), quoted from *The Works* (London, 1773; rpt. Hildesheim, 1969), pp. 239–346. On the context and on

Richardson's history of reception, see also Lawrence Lipking, *The Ordering of the Arts in Eighteenth-Century England* (Princeton, N.J., 1970), pp. 109ff.

85. See Foss, *The Age of Patronage*, pp. 33ff.

86. Pears, *The Discovery of Painting*, pp. 32f., formulates the problem: "If absolute standards existed and men were equipped to recognise those standards, then plainly a divergence of opinion indicated that some people functioned better than others."

87. See, e.g., William Hogarth, *The Analysis of Beauty, written with a view of fixing the fluctuating Ideas of Taste* (London, 1753; Oxford, 1955), esp. pp. 23ff. The distinction between competent and incompetent criticism on the basis of objective criteria is, of course, much older. See, e.g., de Hollanda, "Gespräche über die Malerei," pp. 137ff.

88. See Thomas E. Crow, *Painters and Public Life in Eighteenth-Century Paris* (New Haven, Conn., 1985), pp. 1ff.

89. "All this was leading to a growing appreciation of pictures as pictures rather than as exclusively the records of some higher truth; a body of connoisseurs was coming into being prepared to judge pictures on their aesthetic merits, and consequently the subject-matter of painting was losing its old primaeval importance." This is how Haskell, *Patrons and Painters*, p. 130, characterizes this trend.

90. See Foss, *The Age of Patronage*, pp. 162ff.; and further Raymond Williams, *Culture and Society 1780–1950* (Harmondsworth, Middlesex, 1961), pp. 50ff. Williams dates the beginnings of the dependence of literature on the market to the second and third decades of the eighteenth century. But one already finds similar observations somewhat earlier, e.g., in Shaftesbury. On Shaftesbury's vain attempts to distance himself (in printed books!) from the book market, see Jean-Christophe Agnew, *Worlds Apart: The Market and the Theater in Anglo-American Thought, 1550–1750* (Cambridge, 1986), pp. 162ff.

91. The reader, "diese unbekannte Gottheit," one reads (!) in *Peter Leberecht*. See Ludwig Tieck, *Frühe Erzählungen und Romane* (Munich, n.d.), p. 136. One also finds the demand that the reader should forget as quickly as possible, so that new books can be written and sold.

92. Williams, *Culture and Society*, p. 53.

93. See Gerhardt Plumpe, *Ästhetische Kommunikation der Moderne*, vol. 1, *Von Kant bis Hegel* (Opladen, 1993). Plumpe describes aesthetics as a reaction to the social differentiation of the art system.

94. See Klaus Disselbeck, *Geschmack und Kunst: Eine systemtheoretische Untersuchung zu Schillers Briefen "Über die ästhetische Erziehung des Menschen"* (Opladen, 1987).

95. Hegel, *Vorlesungen über die Ästhetik*, vol. 1, in *Werke*, vol. 13 (Frankfurt, 1970), p. 25. See also Plumpe, *Ästhetische Kommunikation*, p. 300, with an eye to the problem of systems differentiation.

96. See Walter Benjamin's well-known study *Der Begriff der Kunstkritik in der deutschen Romantik* (Frankfurt, 1973).

97. Hegelians would respond that pure self-reference is possible nonetheless, namely, as "absolute Spirit"—a spirit that excludes only exclusion—or, as we would put it, as paradox.

98. On the transition from symbol to sign, see also Kristeva, *Semeiotikè: Recherches pour un sémanalyse* (Paris, 1969), pp. 116ff.: "La deuxième moitié du Moyen Age (XIIIe–XVe siècle) est une période de transition pour la culture européenne: la pensée du signe remplace celle du symbole" (116). A comparison with our own use of the concepts of symbol and sign reveals differences, which we do not need to elaborate here. The next turning point, which occurs in the nineteenth and twentieth centuries, remains outside Kristeva's analysis, even though she addresses this shift elsewhere, in conjunction with text-art (e.g., p. 244).

99. See Heinrich Cornelius Agrippa von Nettesheim, *De occulta philosophica libri tres* (1531), quoted from *Opera*, 2 vols. (Hildesheim, 1970), vol. 1, pp. 1–499. On mathematics, see esp. Book II, pp. 153ff.; on religion, see Book III, pp. 310ff.

100. Henri Gouhier has shown that Descartes's dualistic metaphysics excludes symbolization (Henri Gouhier, "Le refus du symbolisme dans le humanisme cartesien," in *Umanesimo e simbolismo, Archivio di filosofia* [1958], pp. 65–74).

101. This holds for other and quite different usages as well. In ancient Greek, *symbōlaion* meant an agreement or contract, especially when fixed in writing; in this sense, the symbol is a characteristic feature, it provides evidence for something.

102. The symbol not only has a religious meaning that refers to the Creator but also corresponds to the family tradition in aristocratic societies. In both contexts, the origin is conceived in terms of a presence of the past whereby, in most cases, it is not explicitly restricted to the dimension of time. In the same sense, the goal (*telos*) is already present, even if the movement is still under way.

103. See Wilhelm Perpeet, *Ästhetik im Mittelalter* (Freiburg, 1977).

104. See M. M. Davy, *Essai sur la symbolique romane* (Paris, 1955). On further connections, see Albert Zimmermann, ed., *Der Begriff der Repraesentatio im Mittelalter: Stellvertretung, Symbol, Zeichen, Bild* (Berlin, 1971).

105. On this issue, and on the gradual transformation of this guiding difference into the code immanent/transcendent, see Niklas Luhmann, "Die Ausdifferenzierung der Religion," in Luhmann, *Gesellschaftsstruktur und Semantik*, vol. 3 (Frankfurt, 1989), pp. 259–357.

106. This example, representative of medieval symbolism, is from Eugenio Battisti, "Simbolo e Classicismo," in *Umanesimo e simbolismo, Archivio di filosofia* (1958), pp. 215–33.

107. In the sense of *medium* introduced in Chapter 3.

108. Kristeva, *Semeiotikè*, p. 116 (author's emphasis).

109. See also Renate Lachmann, *Gedächtnis und Literatur* (Frankfurt, 1990), pp. 27ff.

110. On this point, see Belting's detailed study, *Bild und Kult.*

111. Stimulated by print, emblematics became a fashion in sixteenth-century texts and graphics that encroached on the terrain of the symbol. See Pierre Mesnard, "Symbolisme et Humanisme," in *Umanesimo e simbolismo, Archivio di filosofia* (1958), pp. 123–29.

112. On the much-debated emergence of modern "fictional" theater, see Agnew, *Worlds Apart,* who emphasizes parallel developments in the realms of exchange and of supply markets.

113. Kristeva, *Semeiotikè*, p. 117.

114. See, e.g., the famous *Iconologia* by Cesare Ripa (Rome, 1603), which has since appeared in many enlarged editions. A modern, abbreviated version was published by Piero Buscaroli (Milan, 1992).

115. A wealth of freshly invented allegories and conceits can be found in Baltasar Gracián, *Criticón oder Über die allgemeinen Laster des Menschen* (1651–1657; Hamburg, 1957). The narrative is only a pretext for a sequence of allegories related to the world and to morality.

116. See Kant, *Kritik der Urteilskraft,* § 59: "Beide sind Hypothesen, d.i. Darstellungen (*exhibitiones*); nicht bloße Charakterismen, d.i. Bezeichnungen der Begriffe durch begleitende sinnliche Zeichen, die gar nichts zu der Anschauung des Objekts Gehöriges enthalten." See also Hans Georg Gadamer, "Symbol und Allegorie," in *Umanesimo e simbolismo, Archivio di filosofia* (1958), pp. 23–28; Gadamer, *Wahrheit und Methode: Grundzüge einer philosophischen Hermeneutik,* 3d ed. (Tübingen, 1972), pp. 68ff. See also Moritz's rejection of allegory on the grounds that allegory, as a sign, conflicts with the essence of beauty as self-perfection, in Moritz, "Über die Allegorie," quoted from *Schriften zur Ästhetik und Poetik,* pp. 112–25.

117. Gadamer, *Wahrheit und Methode,* p. 73.

118. See Solger, *Vorlesungen über die Ästhetik,* esp. pp. 126ff.

119. The so-called logic of Port-Royal (1662) constitutes a milestone in this development. Significantly, it rejects all forms of (obscure) symbolism in the interest of both religious reform and the new rationalism. See Antoine Arnauld and Pierre Nicole, *La logique ou l'art de penser . . . ,* critical ed. (Paris, 1965). At the same time, a sensuous theory of cognition emerged in England. Both were dominated by interest in a semantic stability that could circumvent the agenda of religion and the disposition of the nobility; this was therefore retrospectively described as "bourgeois."

120. On this turn, see Hans Ulrich Gumbrecht and K. Ludwig Pfeiffer, eds.,

Materialität der Kommunikation (Frankfurt, 1988); trans. in part as *Materialities of Communication*, trans. William Whobrey (Stanford, Calif., 1994).

121. The use of the theater as a metaphor for this kind of production is a familiar topic of historical investigation. On the deliberate and circular structure of this order, which includes even the political asymmetry of sovereignty, see also Louis Marin, *Le portrait du roi* (Paris, 1981).

122. Last but not least, religious art profited from this expansion, which, in the sixteenth and seventeenth centuries, had at its disposal many means of representing transcendence—e.g., by depicting its reflection in the faces of those who observed it. On the other hand, this presupposed (and required) the freedom to turn inward. The representation itself no longer effectuated the presence of transcendence.

123. See Norman Knox, *The Word "Irony" and Its Context, 1500–1750* (Durham, N.C., 1961). According to Knox, not until the eighteenth century, in the wake of Defoe and Swift, did the use of irony explode the boundaries of a learned, rhetorical doctrine. This point is affirmed by Georg Lukács's contention, in *Die Theorie des Romans* (Berlin, 1920), that irony is the formal principle of the novel.

124. This was a contemporary truism that included language. "Il significato del nome si dica l'essenza della cosa," one reads in Zuccaro, *L'idea dei Pittori*, p. 153.

125. See Warnke, *Hofkünstler*, pp. 241ff., 270ff.

126. The classical monograph on this topic is Edward Young, *Conjectures on Original Composition* (1759), in *The Complete Works* (London, 1854; rpt. Hildesheim, 1968), pp. 547–86.

127. This was still the case in the early eighteenth century. In his essay "Goust," Roger de Piles demands from the painter an "attempt to be more than a copyist," while explicitly excluding the imitation of antique perfection, quoted from *Diverses Conversations sur la Peinture* (Paris, 1727), pp. 44 and 48. Jonathan Richardson elaborates the distinction between imitating nature and copying an artwork, pointing out that copying an artwork leaves the artist less freedom than creating an original work. See Richardson, *An Essay on the Whole Art of Criticism as It Relates to Painting*, quoted from *The Works*, pp. 159–238 (223). See also André Félibien, *L'idée du peintre parfait* (London, 1707), p. 74, as well as the entries on original and copy in Jacques Lacombe, *Dictionnaire portatif des Beaux-Arts* (Paris, 1752), pp. 177, 461, where the distinction acquires the status of a lexically secured essence.

128. See Kant's effort, already mentioned, to rethink the concept in terms of the distinction schematic/symbolic, which aims to posit the beautiful as a symbol of morality (not as a schematic relation), in *Kritik der Urteilskraft*, § 59. What remains of the symbol's rich meaning is only the indirection of the relationship between the faculty that supplies meaning (reason) and the symbol's sensuous presentation.

129. Joseph Simon, *Philosophie des Zeichens* (Berlin, 1989), raises this question against the background of a *lebensphilosophisch*, pragmatic, and existentialist theoretical tradition.

130. See Kant, *Kritik der Urteilskraft*, § 49.

131. "Geist, in ästhetischer Bedeutung, heißt das belebende Prinzip im Gemüthe," writes Kant, ibid.

132. See also Paul de Man, "The Rhetoric of Temporality," in de Man, *Blindness and Insight: Essays in the Rhetoric of Contemporary Criticism* (1979; 2d ed. Minneapolis, 1983), pp. 187–228); he emphasizes the increasingly problematic nature of temporality and the necessity of "nature" as a factor that stabilizes temporality in subjective experience.

133. "Eine höhere Philosophie zeigt uns, daß nie etwas von außen in ihn hineinkommt, daß er nichts als reine Tätigkeit ist," writes August Wilhelm Schlegel (*Die Kunstlehre*, p. 25).

134. Commenting on the literature of the turn of the twentieth century, Kristeva writes, "Il s'agit d'un passage de la dualité (du signe) à la productivité (transsigne)" (*Semeiotikè*, p. 244).

135. We might draw again on Spencer Brown: "Let there be a form distinct from the form. Let the mark of the distinction be copied out of the form into such another form. Call any such copy of the mark a token of the mark" (*Laws of Form*, p. 4). Without following these injunctions, *one cannot go on.*

136. See Hegel, *Vorlesungen über die Philosophie der Religion I*, in *Werke*, vol. 16 (Frankfurt, 1969), esp. pp. 101f.

137. See Paul de Man, *The Rhetoric of Romanticism* (New York, 1984). De Man points out that the answer to the deconstruction of the symbol lies in a return to the self-consciously distanced figures of allegory, following early modernism—if not in art, at least in "literary criticism." See Paul de Man, *Allegories of Reading: Figural Language in Rousseau, Nietzsche, Rilke, and Proust* (New Haven, Conn., 1979).

138. August Wilhelm Schlegel, *Die Kunstlehre*, p. 105, locates the original unity of art in dance, since dance uses both space and time. One might also think of the ornament (see Chapter 3, section IV, above).

139. See Davy, *Essai sur la symbolique romane*, p. 173.

140. "La pittura è proprio poesia, cioè invenzione le qual fa apparere quello, que non è," one reads, e.g., in Pino, *Dialogo di pittura*, p. 115. Typically, Horace's dictum is understood as an *invitation for imitation*—see, e.g., Pomponius Gauricus, *Super arte poetica Horatii* (ca. 510), quoted from a reprint of a 1541 edition (Munich, 1969), folio D II: "Poesis imitari debet picturam." As in Horace, painting is primary. But Gauricus traces the comparison to Simonides, which means it antedates the Platonic/Aristotelian doctrine of mimesis. For a summary, see Rensselaer W. Lee, "Ut pictura poesis: The Humanistic Tradition of Painting,"

Art Bulletin 22 (1940): 197–269. Lee traces the popularity of this formula to the humanist tradition, with its interest in human actions. This explains its displacement, in the eighteenth century, by other interests, especially in nature. Lessing's *Laocoön* will treat the limits of the comparison between painting and poetry in systematic fashion by distinguishing between the corresponding media of word and image, and Herder's critique of Lessing will show that Lessing's inference from succession (in poetry) to actions was premature. See Herder, *Erste Kritische Wäldchen*, quoted from *Herders Sämmtliche Werke*, ed. Bernhard Suphan, vol. 3 (Berlin, 1878), esp. § 16 and § 17, pp. 133ff.

141. Zuccaro *L'idea dei Pittori*, pp. 131ff.

142. A common formula speaks of "the arts and literature."

143. We take this to be symptomatic of a new formulation that today would be described as autopoiesis. It is not just a grammatical mistake of the type "a smoked fish-dealer."

144. On this development, see esp. Paul Oskar Kristeller, "The Modern System of the Arts" (1951), quoted from Kristeller, *Renaissance Thought II: Papers on Humanism and the Arts* (New York, 1965), pp. 163–227. See further Gunther Scholtz, "Der Weg zum Kunstsystem des deutschen Idealismus," in Walter Jaeschke and Helmut Holzhey, eds., *Früher Idealismus und Frühromantik: Der Streit um die Grundlagen der Ästhetik (1795–1805)* (Hamburg, 1990), pp. 12–29; Plumpe, *Ästhetische Kommunikation*, pp. 25ff.

145. Perhaps we should add here that the famous "querelle des anciens et modernes" toward the end of the seventeenth century confronted the difficulty of embracing the sciences and technological developments along with what was later distinguished as art. Under such conditions, comparative historical judgments are obviously difficult and controversial.

146. We shall return to this point in Chapter 7, below.

147. See Kristeller, "The Modern System of the Arts."

148. See Charles Dejob, *De l'influence du Concile de Trente sur la littérature et les beaux-arts chez les peuples catholiques* (Paris, 1884; rpt. Geneva, 1969), who presents these events as a religious success story of Catholicism. One finds a more sophisticated picture in Federico Zeri, *Pittura e Controriforma: L' "arte senza tempo" di Scipione da Gaeta* (Turin, 1957); Emile Mâle, *L'art religieux après le Concile de Trente: Etude sur l'iconographie de la fin du XVIe siècle, du XVIIe siècle, du XVIIIe siècle* (Paris, 1932), offers detailed, thematically coherent analyses of paintings. On the corresponding Protestant measures, which were not directed against innovative artistic audacity but polemicized in an Old Testament manner against idol worship and the distractions that kept churchgoers from their pious duties, see John Phillips, *The Reformation of Images: The Destruction of Art in England, 1535–1660* (Berkeley, Calif., 1973). On the reverberations that were felt until the eighteenth century, see Pears, *The Discovery of Painting*, pp. 41ff. On the corre-

sponding rejection of the theater, see Fraser, *The War Against Poetry*, esp. pp. 29ff.; and Agnew, *Worlds Apart*.

149. In current neurophysiological terminology, one might speak of a repeated "impregnation" of cells that are no longer occupied. See Heinz von Foerster, *Das Gedächtnis: Eine quantenmechanische Untersuchung* (Vienna, 1948).

150. See Baxandall, *Painting and Experience in Fifteenth-Century Italy*.

151. Baxter Hathaway, *Marvels and Commonplaces: Renaissance Literary Criticism* (New York, 1968), provides a detailed account of this dispute.

152. Ibid., p. 117. See also pp. 133ff.

153. Susie I. Tucker, *Enthusiasm: A Study in Semantic Change* (Cambridge, 1972), illustrates this bifurcation with detailed evidence from the seventeenth and eighteenth centuries.

154. See Belting, *Bild und Kult*, pp. 510ff.

155. To mention details: one objected to Michelangelo's *Last Judgment* on the grounds that it depicts devils without horns, angels without wings, Christ without his beard, the kisses of the blessed, and generally too much nudity (although theologians could hardly claim that the focus of Christ's resurrection is clothing). Figures that are unknown in traditional clerical history but are included in the picture for aesthetic reasons (to fill a space or serve as an ornament) have to be eliminated. Sacred figures must not be presented too realistically. Mary at the cross, fainting? No way! She is depicted standing upright: *stabat*.

156. See the treatises of church officials in vol. 2 of Barocchi, ed., *Trattati d'el arte del Cinquecento*, which include, among others, Giovanni Andrea Gilio, *Dialogo nel quale si ragiona degli errori e degli abusi de'pittori circa d'historie* (1564), and Gabriele Paletotti, *Discorso intorno alle imagini sacre et profane* (1582). The mediocre intellectual quality of these treatises suggests that they defend a lost position.

157. See Werner Weisbach, *Der Barock als Kunst der Gegenreformation* (Berlin, 1921).

158. "L'extrême habilité des artistes fait douter de leur sincérité," observes Mâle, *L'art religieux après le Concile de Trente*, p. ix.

§ 5

1. On the system of science, see Niklas Luhmann, *Die Wissenschaft der Gesellschaft* (Frankfurt, 1990), esp. pp. 194ff.; on the legal system, Luhmann, "Die Codierung des Rechtssystems," *Rechtstheorie* 17 (1986): 171–203, and Luhmann, *Das Recht der Gesellschaft* (Frankfurt, 1993), pp. 165ff.; on the educational system, Luhmann, "Codierung und Programmierung: Bildung und Selektion im Erziehungssystem," in Luhmann, *Soziologische Aufklärung*, vol. 4 (Opladen, 1987), pp. 182–201; on the economic system, Luhmann, *Die Wirtschaft der Gesellschaft* (Frankfurt, 1988), pp. 84ff., 187ff. and passim; on the health care system, Luh-

mann, "Der medizinische Code," in Luhmann, *Soziologische Aufklärung*, vol. 5 (Opladen, 1990), pp. 183–95.

2. George Spencer Brown, *Laws of Form* (1969; rpt. New York, 1979), p. 1.

3. See, e.g., Julia Kristeva, "Poésie et négativité," in Kristeva, *Semeiotikè: Recherches pour un sémanalyse* (Paris, 1969), pp. 246–77 (explicitly on p. 265), further pp. 150ff. The function of the "zero" is not a negation of meaning; on the contrary, it is meant to exclude the absence of meaning.

4. Gotthard Günther calls the processing of such acceptance/rejection distinctions with reference to a primarily positive/negative disjunction a "transjunctional operation" and argues that treating such a possibility in logical terms requires a structurally rich, multivalent logic capable of dissolving the paradoxes that arise within a bivalent logic. See Gotthard Günther, "Cybernetic Ontology and Transjunctional Operations," in Günther, *Beiträge zu einer operationsfähigen Dialektik*, vol. 1 (Hamburg, 1976), pp. 249–328.

5. "If conditionality is an essential component in the concept of organization," writes W. Ross Ashby, "Principles of the Self-Organizing System," quoted from Walter Buckley, ed., *Modern Systems Research for the Behavioral Scientist: A Sourcebook* (Chicago, 1968), pp. 108–28 (109).

6. See George Spencer Brown, "Self-Reference, Distinctions and Time," *Teoria Sociologica* 1/2 (1993): 47–53.

7. See Niklas Luhmann, "Das Moderne der modernen Gesellschaft," in Luhmann, *Beobachtungen der Moderne* (Opladen, 1992), pp. 11–49 (29f.); trans. as "Modernity in Contemporary Society," in Luhmann, *Observations on Modernity*, trans. William Whobrey (Stanford, Calif., 1998), pp. 1–21.

8. Sigfried J. Schmidt, *Die Selbstorganisation des Sozialsystems Literatur im 18. Jahrhundert* (Frankfurt, 1989), advances the opposite view concerning the distinction literary/nonliterary, as does Peter Fuchs, *Moderne Kommunikation: Zur Theorie des operativen Displacements* (Frankfurt, 1993), pp. 164ff., concerning the distinction art/nonart as a system code. We concede that literature or, more generally, art, must distinguish itself in this manner (how else?) from other things. There is no doubt that the avant-garde programmatically emphasized this referential distinction. However, it does not sufficiently describe the internal structure of *preferences*, which functions as a code. On the basis of this structure, the art system exposes itself to the paradoxical distinctions between inside and outside or between universalism and specification. In addition, a code would have to generate programs that "operationalize" the system's preferences at the level of its *operations*. Here the art/nonart distinction is as unsatisfactory as beautiful/ugly.

9. For an overview, see Niels Werber, *Literatur als System: Zur Ausdifferenzierung literarischer Kommunikation* (Opladen, 1992).

10. E.g., in the abundance of moral ambiguities in the self-commenting au-

tobiographies of Ludwig Tieck's *William Lovell*, and, of course, in the work's theoretical reflections.

11. The first quotation is from *Lucinde*, the second from the essay "Über Lessing." See Friedrich Schlegel, *Werke in zwei Bänden* (Berlin, 1980), vol. 2, p. 35, and vol. 1, p. 110.

12. "Moralität ohne Sinn für Paradoxie ist gemein," states Friedrich Schlegel, ibid., vol. 1, p. 272.

13. Moreover, one also finds formulations that do not refer to ideals or values and therefore come closer to current notions of balance. See, e.g., Giovanni Paolo Lomazzo, *Idea del Tempio della Pittura* (Milan, 1590), p. 62: "differenze è quella cosa per la quale si discerne, & avverisce l'amicitia & l'inimicitia delle cose." And on p. 83: "Belezza non è altro che una certa gratia vivace & spirituale, la qual per il raggio divino prima s'infonde ne gl'Angeli in cui si vedeno le figure di qualuna sfera che si chiamano in loro essemplari, & l'Idee; poi passa ne gli animi, ove le figure si chiamano ragioni, & notitie; & finalemente nella materia ove si dicono imagini & forme."

14. In his *Erstes Kritisches Wäldchen* with reference to examples from antiquity. See Bernhard Suphan, ed., *Herder Sämmtliche Werke*, vol. 3 (Berlin, 1878), pp. 52ff. (quotation on p. 59).

15. For a historically extensive treatment, see Hans Robert Jauss, ed., *Die nicht mehr schönen Künste: Grenzphänomene des Ästhetischen, Poetik und Hermeneutik*, vol. 3 (Munich, 1968).

16. See, e.g., Henri Testelin, *Sentiments des plus Habiles Peintres sur la Pratique de la Peinture et la Sculpture* (Paris, 1696), pp. 39f.

17. See, e.g., William Hogarth, *The Analysis of Beauty, written with a view of fixing the fluctuating Ideas of Taste* (London, 1753; Oxford, 1955), pp. 32ff., 61ff. Hogarth makes the remarkable assumption that the principles of producing beautiful works (for Hogarth, forms of drawing a line) are not applicable to ugly objects, so that a representation of such objects (although it is admissible) requires a deviation from these principles. The "waving line" of beauty is not suited for this purpose (pp. 67f.). See also the distinction between the drawing (*trait*) of persons (*noble/grossière*) according to their social "condition" in Testelin, *Sentiments des plus Habiles Peintres*, pp. 12, 13, 17, 40.

18. See Gotthold Ephraim Lessing, *Laoköon, oder über die Grenzen der Malerei und Poesie* (1766), quoted from *Lessings Werke*, vol. 3 (Leipzig-Vienna, n.d.), pp. 1–194.

19. See Friedrich Schlegel, "Vom ästhetischen Wert der griechischen Kommödie," quoted from *Werke in zwei Bänden* (Berlin, 1980), vol. 1, pp. 3–14, esp. p. 8, with emphasis on the differentiation and specialization of the code: "Nichts verdient Tadel in einem Kunstwerk als Vergehungen wider die Schönheit und wider die Darstellung: das Häßliche und das Fehlerhafte." Note how

Schlegel already distinguishes between the figural and the operative component of representation.

20. See Niklas Luhmann, "Ist Kunst codierbar?" in Luhmann, *Soziologische Aufklärung*, vol. 3 (Opladen, 1981), pp. 245–66.

21. Claiming that this is possible because of prior aesthetic experiences with artworks does little to salvage the terminology. Especially for people, this claim is dubious. (In fact, the opposite might be so: experience with artworks helps recognize the beauty in ugly people.) Besides, this subterfuge offers no clue as to what exactly enables works of art to serve as a paradigm of beauty.

22. For Kant, this seems to be evident: "Man kann überhaupt Schönheit (Sie mag Natur- oder Kunstschönheit sein) den *Ausdruck* ästhetischer Ideen nennen; nur daß in der schönen Kunst diese Idee durch einen Begriff vom Objekt veranlaßt werden muß" (*Kritik der Urteilskraft*, § 51). Yet soon thereafter, Kant talks about the beauty of the word, of gesture, and of tones (articulation, gesticulation, and modulation).

23. See, e.g., Francis Hutcheson, *An Inquiry Concerning Beauty, Order, Harmony, Design*, Treatise I of his *Inquiry into the Original of Our Ideas of Beauty and Virtue* (1725; 4th ed., 1738; critical ed. The Hague, 1973), § 4, II, p. 55.

24. Schiller, e.g., grounds the *unity* of the idea of beauty in the fact that there can be only *one* equilibrium of reality and form. See *Über die ästhetische Erziehung des Menschen in einer Reihe von Briefen*, quoted from Schiller, *Sämtliche Werke*, vol. 5 (Munich, 1967), p. 619. See also Karl Wilhelm Ferdinand Solger, *Vorlesungen über Ästhetik*, ed. Karl Wilhelm Ludwig Heyse (Leipzig, 1829; rpt. Darmstadt, 1973), esp. pp. 47ff.

25. As when August Wilhelm Schlegel writes in *Die Kunstlehre* (vol. 1 of the *Vorlesungen über schöne Literatur und Kunst*): "Das Schöne ist eine symbolische Darstellung des Unendlichen" (quoted from *Kritische Schriften und Briefe*, vol. 2 [Stuttgart, 1963], p. 81).

26. See Jean Paul, *Vorschule der Ästhetik*, quoted from *Werke*, vol. 5 (Munich, 1963), p. 43: "Schönheit sei, wie es einen Zirkel der Logik gibt, der Zirkel der Phantasie, weil der Kreis die reichste, einfachste, unerschöpflichste, leichtfaßlichste Figur ist; aber der wirkliche Zirkel ist ja selber eine Schönheit, und so würde die Definition (wie leider jede) ein logischer."

27. Parsons employs this formulation in his theory of symbolically generalized media of exchange.

28. See Jacques Derrida, *Of Grammatology*, trans. Gayatri Chakravorty Spivak (Baltimore, 1974).

29. Michel Serres, *Le Parasite* (Paris, 1980).

30. See Mary Douglas, *Purity and Danger: An Analysis of Concepts of Pollution and Taboo* (Harmondsworth, Middlesex, 1970).

31. A remarkable example is the manuscript, available only as a copy, of *The Codex Nuttall: A Picture Manuscript from Ancient Mexico*, ed. Zelia Nuttall (rpt.

New York, 1975). Examples of this sort illustrate the effects of evolution. Even though the representations all focus on the same thing, there is a diversification of species, a wealth of forms that depends on cultural tradition and is not immediately intelligible today.

32. This is expressed explicitly in the above-mentioned *Codex Nuttall* but also more indirectly in the Greek world of heroes and demigods, whose significance rested primarily on the fact that the aristocracy traced its origins to them.

33. See Plato, *Sophistes*, 253 D–E.

34. Ibid., D, the first lines.

35. The first example is *technē tēs grammatikēs*, ibid., 253 A.

36. See Joan Marie Lechner, *Renaissance Concepts of the Commonplace* (New York, 1962; rpt. Westport, Conn., 1974). Even in the seventeenth century, one still found statements such as: "reasons urging [passions, N. L.] proceed from solid amplifications, amplifications are gathered from common places, common places fit for oratorical persuasion concern a part of Rhetorick called Invention." See Thomas Wright, *The Passions of the Minde in Generall* (1604; enlarged ed. London, 1630), p. 185.

37. See Boileau, who takes up the ancient distinction between amplification and proof in his translation of Longinus. For amplification ("ne sert qu'à estendre et à exagerer"), see Nicolas Boileau-Despréaux, *Traité du Sublime*, quoted from *Œuvres* (Paris, 1713), pp. 593–692, 631ff. According to Thomas Sprat, the Royal Society of London for the Improving of Natural Knowledge made a decisive move "to reject all the amplifications, digressions and swellings of style" (Sprat, *The History of the Royal Society of London . . .* [London, 1667; rpt. London, 1966], p. 113).

38. See Kant, *Kritik der Urteilskraft*, Intro. VI. (Not accidentally, this remark occurs in the context of investigations that aspire to an aesthetics.)

39. See Sir Philip Sidney, *The Defense of Poetry* (1595; Lincoln, Nebr., 1970), p. 12. Soon thereafter, this seems to have become the general opinion. See, e.g., Jonathan Richardson, *A Discourse on the Dignity, Certainty, Pleasure, and Advantage of the Science of a Connoisseur* (1719), quoted from *The Works* (London, 1773; rpt. Hildesheim, 1969), pp. 241–346 (247ff.).

40. In the sixteenth and seventeenth centuries, such publications occupied an important place, especially in the realm of painting. For examples, see Christoforo Sorte, *Osservazioni nella pittura* (1580), quoted from Paola Barocchi, ed., *Trattati d'arte del cinquecento*, vol. 1 (Bari, 1960), pp. 271–301; or, more extensively, Giovanni Paolo Lomazzo, *Trattato dell'arte, della Pittura, Scultura ed architettura*, 3 vols. (1584; Rome, 1844).

41. See Gotthard Günther, "Die historische Kategorie des Neuen," in Günther, *Beiträge zur Grundlegung einer operationsfähigen Dialektik* (Hamburg, 1980), vol. 3, pp. 183–210.

42. On "ballads" and mystery stories motivated by executions, see esp. Len-

nard J. Davis, *Factual Fictions: The Origins of the English Novel* (New York, 1983), pp. 42ff.

43. See Sidney, *The Defense of Poetry*, pp. 13ff.

44. Raising this issue assumed that the Aristotelian concept of nature was no longer intelligible and that the text of the *Poetics* was used merely for purposes of quotation and illustration.

45. See Baxter Hathaway, *Marvels and Commonplaces: Renaissance Literary Criticism* (New York, 1968), pp. 158ff. The context is the Italian discussion of classical and contemporary texts, which was later taken up in France and England. Torquato Tasso still emphasizes both intelligibility and astonishing novelty. An artwork that pleases "non sarà più chiara e più distinta, ma molto più portarà di novità e di meraviglia," in *Discorsi dell'arte poetica e in particolare sopra il poema eroico*, quoted from Tasso, *Prosa* (Milan, 1969), p. 388. One can already discern the new tendency to foreground novelty.

46. See (Pseudo) Cicero, *Ad Herennium*, III, XXII, quoted from The Loeb Classical Library edition (Cambridge, Mass., 1968), pp. 218ff. On subsequent developments, see Paolo Rossi, "La costruzione delle immagini nei trattati di memoria artificiale del Rinascimento," in *Umanesimo e simbolismo*, *Archivio di filosofia* (1958), pp. 161–78; Cesare Vasoli, "Umanesimo e Simbologia nei primi scritti Lulliani e mnemotechnici del Bruno," ibid., pp. 251–304. See also Frances A. Yates, *The Art of Memory* (Chicago, 1966).

47. This is indeed noticed and emphasized—even by Jonathan Richardson, *A Discourse on the Dignity*, p. 270: "nor can any man pronounce upon the pleasure of another"—despite the author's concern with the solid principles of a science of expertise as a precondition of pleasure.

48. On the corresponding notion of time, see Chapter 3, section III, above.

49. Another, equally transitory solution might have been a sophisticated technique for covering over the traces of the rules on which an artwork was based and subsequently deflecting the admiration to the successful deception. Rooted in the older rhetorical tradition, this notion of art was especially important for the sixteenth and seventeenth centuries. See Gerhard Schröder, *Logos und List* (Königsstein/Ts., 1985).

50. It is difficult to appreciate Hogarth's opinion that ugly objects defy representation in accordance with the recipe for beauty (curved lines): "The ugliness of the toad, the hug, the bear and the spider are totally void of this waving-line." See Hogarth, *The Analysis of Beauty*, pp. 66f.

51. See Arthur C. Danto, *The Transfiguration of the Commonplace: A Philosophy of Art* (Cambridge, Mass., 1981). Danto must have recourse to contrived examples in order to demonstrate complete indistinguishability. If an artist were to create two identical (indistinguishable) objects without marking one as the copy of the other, such a program could communicate only one thing: that this is the program.

52. See the complex analysis of "without" as a condition for beauty in Jacques Derrida, *The Truth in Painting*, trans. Geoff Bennington and Ian McLeod (Chicago, 1987), pp. 83ff.

53. The twentieth letter of Schiller, *Briefe über die ästhetische Erziehung des Menschen*, p. 634 n.

54. Schiller, "Notwendige Grenzen beim Gebrauch schöner Formen," ibid., p. 688.

55. As we note in passing, this insight dissolves the traditional nexus between freedom and power in the political context and the nexus between freedom and hierarchy in the social context, which does not mean that cognition (in the sense of exploring a space for decisions) cannot be influenced by power or by hierarchical positions.

56. Robert Glanville, *Objekte* (Berlin, 1988), claims that this is true for all objects. This is not easy to see. It is remarkable, however, that this claim is made by an architect.

57. See, e.g., Karl Philipp Moritz, "Die metaphysische Schönheitslinie," in *Schriften zur Ästhetik und Poetik* (Tübingen, 1962), pp. 151–57 (157): "Das Gehörige weglassen [or rather: das gehörige Weglassen, N. L.], ist also eigentlich das wahre Wesen der Kunst, die mehr negativ, als positiv zu Werke gehen muß, wenn sie gefallen soll." One can trace this view into our own century, e.g., to Mondrian.

58. Explicitly, August Wilhelm Schlegel, *Die Kunstlehre* (Pt. 1 of the lectures on literature and art), quoted from *Kritische Schriften und Briefe*, vol. 2 (Stuttgart, 1963), p. 71. See also Chapter 4, section VII, above.

59. On the separation of these distinctions in a sociotheoretical context, see also Niklas Luhmann, "Das Moderne der modernen Gesellschaft," in Luhmann, *Beobachtungen der Moderne* (Opladen, 1992), pp. 11–49 (25ff.); trans. as "Modernity in Contemporary Society," in Luhmann, *Observations on Modernity*, trans. William Whobrey (Stanford, Calif., 1998), pp. 1–21 (9ff.)

60. On his version of the reentry paradox, which duplicates the framing of the artwork within the work itself and thereby shows that this is the work's own program, see David Roberts, "The Paradox of Form: Literature and Self-Reference," *Poetics* 21 (1992): 75–91; "The form within the form frames the enclosing form."

61. Johann Joachim Winckelmann, *Geschichte der Kunst des Altertums* (1763–1768), quoted from *Sämtliche Werke*, vols. 3–6 (1825; rpt. Osnabrück, 1965).

62. For an elaboration of this point, see Niklas Luhmann, "Das Kunstwerk und die Selbstreproduktion der Kunst," in Hans Ulrich Gumbrecht and K. Ludwig Pfeiffer, eds., *Stil: Geschichten und Funktionen eines kulturwissenschaftlichen Diskurselements* (Frankfurt, 1986), pp. 620–72.

63. Henri Focillon, *The Life of Forms in Art* (New York, 1992), p. 47.

64. The Church of the Holy Spirit, located in front of the train station in

Bern, combines in a remarkable manner rococo elements with neoclassical stylistic forms—of course, without following a postmodern manner of construction.

65. See Chapter 3, section VII, above.

66. August Wilhelm Schlegel recognizes this problem and solves it via the notion of the "perfection" of the individual work (see *Die Kunstlehre*, p. 20), but
the problem undergoes a modification that invites consideration of national distinctions. "Sonst aber muß jedes Kunstwerk aus seinem Standpunkte betrachtet
werden; es braucht nicht ein absolut Höchstes zu erreichen, es ist vollendet,
wenn es ein Höchstes in seiner Art, in seiner Sphäre, seiner Welt ist; und so erk-
lärt sich wie es zugleich ein Glied in einer unendlichen Reihe von Fortschritten,
und dennoch an und für sich befriedigend und selbstständig sein kann." However, Schlegel's inference of an infinite progress for the notion of perfection does,
to put it mildly, beg the question.

67. Not accidentally in the realm of architecture and radiating from it. One
thinks of Viollet-le-Duc, of the restoration of cathedrals, and of the rebuilding
of Carcassonne.

68. Exceptions are ironic or strangely rendered stylistic quotations such as
those that can be found in the music of Stravinsky or Schnittke.

§ 6

1. See, e.g., the distinction *beau réal / beau relatif* in Denis Diderot, *Traité du
beau*, quoted from *Œuvres*, Pléiade ed. (Paris, 1951), pp. 1105–42 (1127ff.).

2. See Georg Kauffmann, *Die Entstehung der Kunstgeschichte im 19. Jahrhundert* (Opladen, 1993).

3. Comparing historiography and poetry, Sir Philip Sidney speaks of "old
moth-eaten records," *The Defense of Poetry* (1595; Lincoln, Nebr., 1970), p. 15.

4. Herbert Spencer, "What Is Social Evolution?" *The Nineteenth Century* 44
(1898): 348–58 (353). For a more detailed account, see the chapters on "The Law
of Evolution," in Herbert Spencer, *First Principles*, 5th ed. (London, 1887),
pp. 307ff.

5. See several of the contributions in *Revue internationale de systémique* 7,
no. 5 (1993).

6. See Marion Blute, "Sociocultural Evolutionism: An Untried Theory," *Behavioral Science* 24 (1979): 46–59. There are counterexamples, as well, thanks to
the numerous contributions of Donald T. Campbell.

7. On this version of the problem, see Magoroh Maruyama, "Postscript to the
Second Cybernetics," *American Scientist* 51 (1963): 250–56.

8. See Niklas Luhmann, "The Paradox of System Differentiation and the
Evolution of Society," in Jeffrey C. Alexander and Paul Colomy, eds., *Differentiation Theory and Social Change: Comparative and Historical Perspectives* (New

York, 1990), pp. 409–40; Niklas Luhmann and Raffaele De Giorgi, *Teoria della società* (Milan, 1992), pp. 169ff.

9. On Schelling's significance in developing this line of questioning, see Wilhelm G. Jacobs, "Geschichte und Kunst in Schellings 'System des tranzscendentalen Idealismus,'" in Walter Jaeschke and Helmut Holzhey, eds., *Früher Idealismus und Frühromantik: Der Streit um die Grundlagen der Ästhetik (1795–1805)* (Hamburg, 1990), pp. 201–13. Schelling only arrived at another teleology of history that entailed, apart from a cosmopolitan society of constitutional states (peace), an epiphany of art that unfolds its unique paradox of a both conscious and unconscious life in history.

10. See Chapter 4, sections IVff., above.

11. Friedrich Schlegel ascertains: "und gewiß ist die Arabeske [understood as "diese künstlich geordnete Verwirrung, diese reizende Symmetrie von Widersprüchen, dieser wunderbare ewige Wechsel von Enthusiasmus und Ironie"] die älteste und ursprünglichste Form der menschlichen Fantasie" (*Gespräch über die Poesie*, quoted from *Werke in zwei Bänden* [Berlin, 1980], vol. 2, p. 164). For detailed evidence, see also Franz Boas, *Primitive Art* (Oslo, 1927; New York, 1955).

12. Ernst Gombrich's important monograph *Ornament und Kunst: Schmucktrieb und Ordnungssinn in der Psychologie des dekorativen Schaffens* (Stuttgart, 1982) contains a wealth of material from all ages, but it is ordered in view of factual concerns and does not claim to offer a history of the ornament and its relationship to the evolution of art. For a historical account that illustrates how the European development of the ornament profited from its subordination to architectural and structural innovations, and later to specifically artistic stylistic inventions, see Joan Evans, *Pattern: A Study of Ornament in Western Europe from 1180 to 1900*, 2 vols. (1931; rpt. New York, 1975). For the beginnings of this division in the construction of gothic cathedrals, see also Otto von Simson, *The Gothic Cathedral: The Origins of Gothic Architecture and the Medieval Concept of Order* (New York, 1965), e.g., p. 5: "Here ornamentation is entirely subordinated to the pattern produced by the structural members, the vault ribs and supporting shafts; the aesthetic system is determined by these."

13. See Chapter 3, n. 40, above.

14. See, e.g., Michel Angelo Biondo, *Von der hochedlen Malerei* (1547; German trans. Vienna, 1873; rpt. Osnabrück, 1970), pp. 24f., 28ff.

15. Biondo believes that *beauty appears on the outside* of the painted objects (in the drawing? but Biondo speaks of composition); see ibid., p. 30.

16. See Wolfgang Kemp, "Disegno: Beiträge zur Geschichte des Begriffs zwischen 1547 und 1607," *Marburger Jahrbuch für Kunstwissenschaft* 19 (1974), pp. 219–40.

17. First ed. (Venice, 1587), quoted from Torquato Tasso, *Prosa* (Milan, 1969), p. 349. The formulation "ed vestirla ultimamente con que' più esquisiti orna-

menti" clearly shows ambivalence toward the ornament: on the one hand, it earns rhetorical praise; on the other hand, it is marginalized as a decoration after the fact.

18. Tasso, *Discorso terzo*, pp. 392ff.

19. See Chapter 3, section IV, above.

20. For detailed evidence, see Evans, *Pattern*. The difficulty of distinguishing such external suggestions from stylistic developments within the art system is obvious, and it proves once more how artificial the separation between art and ornament really is.

21. Jacques Derrida has dealt with the "parergon" in relation to the "ergon" with reference to Kant's *Third Critique* in *The Truth in Painting*, trans. Geoff Bennington and Ian McLeod (Chicago, 1987).

22. See Francis Hutcheson, *An Inquiry Concerning Beauty, Order, Harmony, Design*, Treatise I of his *Inquiry into the Original of Our Ideas of Beauty and Virtue* (1725; 4th ed., 1738; critical ed. The Hague, 1973), § 1, III, pp. 38f.

23. See section IV of this chapter.

24. Hutcheson, *Inquiry*, § 2, III, p. 40. In the theory of art, such formulas were already common in the sixteenth century, i.e., long before Leibniz.

25. Ibid., § 4, I–III, pp. 74ff.: "casual conjunctions of ideas." The defense against unwanted associations is a clear indication of differentiation.

26. See William Hogarth, *The Analysis of Beauty, written with a view of fixing the fluctuating Ideas of Taste* (London, 1753; Oxford, 1955). On ornamentation as a principle of intensification from "less to more," see p. 35. On the "waving line" as a "line of beauty" and on the "serpentine line" as a "line of grace," see p. 650. Other authors also emphasize the connection between the visual arts and the ornament. Art is "greatly ornamental" in Jonathan Richardson, *A Discourse on the Dignity, Certainty, Pleasure and Advantage of the Science of A Connoisseur* (1719), quoted from *The Works* (London, 1773; rpt. Hildesheim, 1969), pp. 241–346 (245, see also 268). There has been a long tradition of emphasizing the movement of the line; see, e.g., Federico Zuccaro, *L'idea dei Pittori, Scultori ed Architetti* (Turin, 1607), quoted from *Scritti d'arte Federico Zuccaro* (Florence, 1961), p. 220, on the *disegno eriterno*: "La linea dunque è proprio corpo ex sostanza visiva del disegno esterno." Antoine Coypel, *Discours prononcez dans les conférences de l'Académie Royale de peinture et de sculpture* (Paris, 1721), pp. 46ff.; Karl Philipp Moritz, "Die metaphysische Schönheit," in Mortitz, *Schriften zur Ästhetik und Poetik* (Tübingen, 1962), pp. 151–57. Or, as a lexical entry under "contours," see Jacques Lacombe, *Dictionnaire portatif des Beaux-Arts* (Paris, 1752), p. 174.

27. In his *Vierten Kritischen Wäldchen*, Herder writes, e.g., that poetry could learn from architecture how to handle uniformity and proportion, and from painting—since the latter is "zu ihrem Hauptzwecke zu kalt, zu trocken, zu gleichförmig," poetry should adopt the "eigene Linie der Schönheit," a "schönes

Unebenmaß." Quoted from *Herders Sämmtliche Werke*, ed. Bernhard Suphan (Berlin, 1878), vol. 4, p. 165.

28. Zuccaro, *L'idea dei Pittori*, pp. 237ff.

29. Historically, the legitimization of the fantastic has to do with Plato's universalization of the principle of imitation (*Sophistes*). Imitation becomes intrinsically paradoxical: it can refer both to existing and to nonexisting objects. In *Sophistes* 236 C, Plato distinguishes accordingly between *eidolopoiikē, eikastikē,* and *phanstastikē*, while presupposing that art can never be beautiful if it translates solely natural proportions. But the dialectic of distinguishing turns the problem into a dichotomy. In the late Renaissance, one adopted this distinction in the theory of poetry as well as in painting. See, e.g., the *imitazione icastica/ imitazione fantastica* distinction in Gregorio Comanini, *Il Figino overo del fine della pittura* (1591), quoted from Paola Barocchi, ed., *Trattati d'arte del cinquecento*, vol. 3 (Bari, 1962), pp. 237–379 (265ff.). Remarkable theological difficulties arise when this distinction is applied to the representation of the divine. One can only opt for *icastica*—the ontologically stronger side of the distinction—even though God has no visible form. And the manner in which God must be represented is prescribed. After all, we are in the period of the Counter-Reformation after the Council of Trent.

30. See esp. Karl Philipp Moritz, *Vorbegriffe zu einer Theorie der Ornamente* (Berlin, 1793; rpt. Nördlingen, 1986); and on this text, Günter Oesterle, "'Vorbegriffe zu einer Theorie der Ornamente': Kontroverse Formprobleme zwischen Aufklärung, Klassizismus und Romantik am Beispiel der Arabeske," in Herbert Beck, Peter C. Bol, and Eva Mack-Gérard, eds., *Ideal und Wirklichkeit in der bildenden Kunst im späten 18. Jahrhundert* (Berlin, 1984), pp. 119–39.

31. See Karl Konrad Polheim's monograph *Die Arabeske: Ansichten und Ideen aus Friedrich Schlegels Poetik* (Paderborn, 1966); further, with a view toward the novel, Dietrich Mathy, *Poesie und Chaos: Zur anarchistischen Komponente der frühromantischen Ästhetik* (Munich, 1984), esp. pp. 99ff.

32. See Gustav René Hocke, *Die Welt als Labyrinth, Manier und Manie in der europäischen Kunst: Von 1520 bis 1650* (Hamburg, 1959); Hocke, *Manierismus in der Literatur* (Hamburg, 1959); Hocke, *Malerei der Gegenwart: Der Neo-Manierismus vom Surrealismus zur Meditation* (Munich, 1975).

33. This trend may correspond to a commercial need, that is, to a structural coupling of literature and the economy. The reader has to read ever new books in order to experience suspense.

34. *Fortuna* or, by choice, *perturbazione*. See Torquato Tasso, *Discorsi dell'arte*, p. 389. By way of a variety guaranteed by the episodes of a *favola*, Tasso already distances himself from the schema good luck / misfortune, "perché la varietà de gli episodi in tanto è lodevole in quanto non corrompe l'unità della favola, nè genera in lei confusione" (p. 391).

35. The full quotation reads as follows: "T''is evident that the more the persons are, the greater will be the variety of the Plot. If then the parts are manag'd so regularly that the beauty of the whole be kept intire, and that the variety become not a perplex'd and confus'd mass of accidents, you will find it infinitely pleasing to be led in a labyrinth of design, where you see some of your way before you, yet discern not the end till you arrive at it" (John Dryden, *Of Dramatick Poesie: An Essay*, 2d ed. [1684; London, 1964], pp. 8off.).

36. For some suggestions, see Hutcheson, *An Inquiry Concerning Beauty*, § 6, XI, p. 78.

37. Hogarth, *The Analysis of Beauty*, p. 61.

38. See the fitting formulation "factual fictions" in Lennard J. Davis, *Factual Fictions: The Origins of the English Novel* (New York, 1983).

39. Moritz, *Vorbegriffe zu einer Theorie der Ornamente.*

40. Schlegel, *Gespräch über die Poesie*, pp. 173ff.

41. See Georg Lukács, *Die Theorie des Romans: Ein geschichtsphilosophischer Versuch über die großen Formen der Epik* (Berlin, 1920; Neuwied, 1971).

42. As an aside: the eighteenth century's claim that poetry is older than prose may have been motivated by the fact that, in poetry, the ornamentation that holds the work together is recognized more easily than in prose, namely, as rhythm.

43. For an overview, see Gombrich, *Ornament und Kunst*, pp. 45ff.

44. See Kant, *Kritik der Urteilskraft*, § 48: "Zur *Beurteilung* schöner Gegenstände, als solcher, wird *Geschmack*, zur schönen Kunst selbst aber, d.i. zur *Hervorbringung* solcher Gegenstände wird Genie erfordert." An evolutionary theoretical interpretation of this passage has been suggested by Niels Werber, *Literatur als System: Zur Ausdifferenzierung literarischer Kommunikation* (Opladen, 1992), p. 45. One could also think of a systems-theoretical interpretation, which might concur even more closely with Kant's intention: gathering variety is the business of genius; taking care of redundancy is the business of taste. Romanticism later rejected "taste" because of its strong market orientation and insisted that genius by no means acts arbitrarily, but is capable of self-discipline. Jean Paul, *Vorschule der Ästhetik*, quoted from *Werke*, vol. 5 (Munich, 1963), pp. 56ff., speaks of the *Besonnenheit* of genius. See also Raymond Williams, *Culture and Society 1780–1950* (Harmondsworth, Middlesex, 1961), pp. 61f., with reference to Coleridge and Keats. Variation and selection, or operation and observation, might be distinguished in this way as well. At any rate, the theory of art cannot be reduced to one of these elements. Upon second sight, the "schöne Objektivität der Unbesonnenheit" (Jean Paul, *Vorschule der Ästhetik*, p. 72) requires correction by the difference-generating operation of the distinguishing observation.

45. On this late-nineteenth-century habit, see William James, "Great Man, Great Thought and the Environment," *The Atlantic Monthly* 46 (1880): 441–59, (against Spencer). Against this view (albeit with a different adversary in mind),

see Herbert Spencer, "What Is Social Evolution?" *The Nineteenth Century* 44 (1898): 348–59 (356f.). See also, from the circle of the Prague Structuralists, Jan Mukarowski, "Das Individuum und die literarische Funktion," in Mukarowski, *Kunst, Poetik, Semiotik* (Frankfurt, 1989), pp. 213–37.

46. Consider, e.g., computer-generated forms (in music or in painting).

47. On this and on the following, see Niklas Luhmann and Raffaele De Giorgi, *Teoria della società*, pp. 187ff.

48. Günter Ellscheid speaks of the hermeneutic significance of the displaced interest in Günter Ellscheid and Winfried Hassemer, eds., *Interessenjurisprudenz* (Darmstadt, 1971), Introduction, p. 5.

49. We deliberately bracket the question of whether this might yield a better or worse adaptation of the system to its environment, for this question is far less relevant than the older Darwinist theory assumed. All that is important is continuing the system's autopoiesis—no matter what its structures may be.

50. This holds especially for living organisms. See Robert B. Glassman, "Persistence and Loose Coupling in Living Systems," *Behavioral Science* 18 (1973): 83–98. From the domain of living organisms, the concept of loose coupling has entered the social sciences as a formula for the necessity of interrupted interdependencies.

51. See Chapter 5, above.

52. See Chapter 3, section IV, above, and section II of this chapter.

53. Jan Assmann, *Das kulturelle Gedächtnis: Schrift, Erinnerung und politische Identität in frühen Hochkulturen* (Munich, 1992), p. 90.

54. See, e.g., Gotthold Ephraim Lessing, *Laoköon, oder über die Grenzen der Malerei und Poesie,* quoted from *Lessings Werke* (Leipzig-Vienna, n.d.), vol. 3, pp. 1–194 (48ff.).

55. We do not deny that there had been art even *before* one began to distinguish in this manner. Without recourse to previous states, there can be no evolution. But distinctions that trigger evolution presuppose more than that.

56. For evidence of this diversity, see the contributions in Hans Ulrich Gumbrecht and K. Ludwig Pfeiffer, eds., *Stil: Geschichten und Funktionen eines kulturwissenschaftlichen Diskurselements* (Frankfurt, 1986).

57. "Frames" in the sense of Erving Goffmann, *Frame Analysis: An Essay on the Organization of Experience* (New York, 1974).

58. Famous in this regard is Claude Lévi-Strauss, *Totemism* (Boston, 1963).

59. We shall return to this point in Chapter 7, below.

60. We are thinking here, of course, of Alexander Gottlieb Baumgarten, *Aesthetica*, vol. 1 (Frankfurt/Oder, 1750), but also of a more general discussion, as, e.g., in Diderot's *Traité du beau*.

61. See section II of this chapter.

62. On sources from late antiquity, see Wilhelm Perpeet, *Ästhetik im Mittelalter* (Freiburg, 1977), esp. pp. 38ff. (on Augustine).

63. The formulation is from Otloh von St. Emeran (emphasis by N. L.), quoted from Rosario Assunto, *Die Theorie des Schönen im Mittelalter* (Cologne, 1963), p. 149. Again and again, we must point out, this goes together with a passive notion of cognition that does not *make* but only *receives* distinctions.

64. On the development of this insight from Alberti to Palladio and beyond, see Robert Klein, "La forme de l'intelligible," in *Umanesimo e simbolismo, Archivio de filosofia* (1958), pp. 103–21; Rudolf Wittkower, *Architectural Principles in the Age of Humanism* (London, 1949).

65. This is Sir Philip Sidney's formulation in *The Defense of Poetry*, p. 9.

66. This happens long before the notorious *querelle* toward the end of the seventeenth century. See August Buck, "Aus der Vorgeschichte der Querelle des Anciens et des Modernes in Mittelalter und Renaissance," *Bibliothèque de l'Humanisme et de la Renaissance* 20 (1958): 127–41; Buck, *Die "querelle des anciens et des modernes" im italienischen Selbstverständnis der Renaissance und des Barocks* (Wiesbaden, 1973); Elisabeth Gösmann, *Antiqui und Moderni im Mittelalter: Eine geschichtliche Standortbestimmung* (Munich, 1974); Albert Zimmermann, ed., *Antiqui und Moderni: Traditionsbewußtsein und Fortschrittsbewußtsein im späten Mittelalter, Miscellanea Mediaevalia*, vol. 9 (Berlin, 1974); Robert Black, "Ancients and Moderns in the Renaissance: Rhetoric and History in Accolti's 'Dialogue on the Preeminence of Men of His Own Time,'" *Journal of the History of Ideas* 43 (1982): 3–32.

67. See Francis Hutcheson, *An Inquiry into the Original of Our Ideas of Beauty and Virtue*. Hutcheson begins by stating, "The importance of any truth is nothing else than its moment, or efficacy, to make men happy, or to give them the greatest and most lasting pleasure."

68. These are Parsons's insights!—which occur, not accidentally, in the context of his notion of evolution theory. See, e.g., Talcott Parsons, *The System of Modern Societies* (Englewood Cliffs, N.J., 1971), p. 27; and in more detail, Parsons, "Comparative Studies and Evolutionary Change," quoted from Talcott Parsons, *Social System and the Evolution of Action Theory* (New York, 1977), pp. 279–320 (307ff.).

69. On the situation in England, see Joan Pittock, *The Ascendancy of Taste: The Achievement of Joseph and Thomas Warton* (London, 1973); on the situation in France, see, e.g., Siegfried Jüttner, "Die Kunstkritik Diderots (1759–1781)," in Helmut Koopmann and J. Adolf Schmoll, called Eisenwerth, eds., *Beiträge zur Theorie der Künste im 19. Jahrhundert* (Frankfurt, 1971), vol. 1, pp. 13–29.

70. Karl Heydenreich, "Was ist der Zweck selbst werth," in Heydenreich, *System der Ästhetik* (Leipzig, 1790; rpt. Hildesheim, 1978), p. 181.

71. In the context of elaborate reflections (which, however, fail to clarify the relationship between objecthood and the "adequate objectivity of the will"), see Arthur Schopenhauer, *Die Welt als Wille und Vorstellung*, vol. 1, § 41, quoted from *Werke*, vol. 1 (Darmstadt, 1961), p. 296.

72. The efficacy of natural selection has always been disputed in the realm of sociocultural evolution, but without sufficient backing—e.g., by arguing for a teleologically oriented selection, or simply because one was unwilling to accept "the fight for survival" and success as the arbiter of social evolution. Against these dubious arguments, others have attempted to establish the theory of sociocultural evolution on the basis of environmental selection. See, e.g., Michael Schmid, *Theorie sozialen Wandels* (Opladen, 1982), esp. pp. 189ff. Systems-theoretical reasons prevent us from following this trend, which runs into difficulties that we will have to address: namely, the problem of how autopoiesis can be combined with evolution.

73. Despite the provocative formulation, this insight is familiar. See, e.g., G. Ledyard Stebbins, *The Basis of Progressive Evolution* (Chapel Hill, N.C., 1969), p. 117; Erich Jantsch, *The Self-Organizing Universe: Scientific and Human Implications of the Emerging Paradigm of Evolution* (Oxford, 1980).

74. This holds for modern thought in general. Not intentions, but the unconscious is the origin; or, not the unconscious, but the repression that makes an unconscious necessary; or, not the repression, but the sociostructural realities that trigger repression. In other words: their evolution is the origin.

75. See Gunther Teubner, "Hyperzyklus in Recht und Organisation: Zum Verhältnis von Selbstbeobachtung, Selbstkonstitution und Autopoiese," in Hans Haferkamp and Michael Schmid, eds., *Sinn, Kommunikation und soziale Differenzierung: Beiträge zu Luhmanns Theorie sozialer Systeme* (Frankfurt, 1987), pp. 89–128; Teubner, "Episodenverknüpfung: Zur Steigerung von Selbstreferenz im Recht," in Dirk Baecker et al., eds., *Theorie als Passion* (Frankfurt, 1987), pp. 423–46; Teubner, *Recht als autopoietisches System* (Frankfurt, 1989), esp. pp. 36ff. See also Werner Kirsch and Dodo zu Knyphausen, who build upon this idea in "Unternehmungen als 'autopoietische' Systeme?" in Wolfgang H. Staehle and Jörg Sydow, eds., *Managementforschung* 1 (1991): 75–101.

76. Clearly in Chinese writing and its emergence from the practice of divination. See Léon Vandermeersch, "De la tortue à l'achillée: China," in Jean Pierre Vernant et al., *Divination et rationalité* (Paris, 1974), pp. 29–51.

77. See Michael Hutter, "Die frühe Form der Münze," in Dirk Baecker, ed., *Probleme der Form* (Frankfurt, 1993), pp. 159–80; trans. as "The Early Form of Money," in Dirk Baecker, ed., *Problems of Form,* trans. Michael Irmscher, with Leah Edwards (Stanford, Calif., 1999), pp. 107–20; see also Hutter, "The Case of Money," in Richard W. England, ed., *Evolutionary Concepts in Contemporary Economics* (Ann Arbor, Mich., 1994), pp. 111–36.

78. Of course, we are not questioning the high artistic achievements, e.g., of Chinese painting or Indian music. Nor do we intend to look down on these accomplishments from a European perspective. We merely point out that one cannot speak of evolution in these cases, nor of structural changes heading toward

an ever-increasing improbability. On the contrary, what impresses us in art forms of this kind is the constancy of the perfection accomplished. To be sure, there are developments in Chinese painting that could be interpreted as evolution—especially the shift from a linear and distinctly ornamental style of contours to a spontaneous style that expresses the unity of the brush stroke and the painterly result. But one can hardly claim that such changes lead to the differentiation of a self-evolving art system. Rather, Chinese painting is an indication of what kinds of evolutionary opportunities reside in ornamental art forms. Apart from that, the exact dating of the "take off" of European developments is debatable, but only if the conceptual basis for such a discussion is sufficiently secured. I personally consider the fifteenth century the decisive period. One must concede differences between individual European territories, which increasingly begin to consider themselves to be nations and distinguish themselves from one another. The mannerist style and Dutch painting are worlds apart—however, from the perspective we are advancing here, we are dealing with phenomenally different variants of one and the same process.

79. Particularly famous are the paradoxes of John Donne, which point toward Italian influences (Berni, Lando, and so forth). See Helen Peters, ed., *John Donne, Paradoxes and Problems* (Oxford, 1980); A. E. Malloch, "The Techniques and Function of the Renaissance Paradox," *Studies in Philology* 53 (1956): 191–203; and Michael McCanless, "Paradox in Donne," *Studies in the Renaissance* 13 (1966): 266–87.

80. According to Gotthard Günther, "Cybernetic Ontology and Transjunctional Operations," in *Beiträge zur Grundlegung einer operationsfähigen Dialektik* (Hamburg, 1976), vol. 1, pp. 249–328.

81. One of the best analyses of this development is still the interlude in Max Weber, *Gesammelten Aufsätze zur Religionssoziologie*, vol. 1, quoted from the 5th ed. (Tübingen, 1963), pp. 536–73. On the dissociation of art (poetry) from science in the sixteenth century, see further Gerhart Schröder, *Logos und List: Zur Entwicklung der Ästhetik in der frühen Neuzeit* (Königsstein, Ts., 1985).

82. On the situation in the seventeenth century, see Niklas Luhmann, *Liebe als Passion: Zur Codierung von Intimität* (Frankfurt, 1982); trans. as *Love as Passion: The Codification of Intimacy*, trans. Jeremy Gaines and Doris L. Jones (Cambridge, Mass., 1986; rpt. Stanford, Calif., 1998).

83. See, e.g., Ellery Schalk, *From Valor to Pedigree: Ideas of Nobility in France in the Sixteenth and Seventeenth Centuries* (Princeton, N.J., 1986); Claudio Donati, *L'idea di nobilità in Italia: Secoli XIV–XVIII* (Bari, 1988).

84. On the efforts to cultivate a specific certainty of judgment, see Richardson, *A Discourse on the Dignity, Certainty, Pleasure and Advantage of the Science of a Connoisseur*, pp. 241–346. Some decades later, Hogarth rejects the concept of "connoisseur," which he finds arrogant and irritating. See Hogarth, *The Analysis*

of Beauty, esp. pp. 26ff., and his subsequent attempt to ground a theory of the visual arts *objectively.*

85. See Baltasar Gracián, *El discreto* (1646; Buenos Aires, 1960).

86. Insistence on difference is apparently more important than an exact knowledge of criteria. The admission of the difficulty of judgment is often qualified by assurances of the following kind: "il est cependant tres assurés qu'il y a un bon et un movais goust." See (Jean Baptiste Morvan), Abbé de Bellegarde, *Reflexions sur le ridicule et sur les moyens de l'éviter,* 4th ed. (Paris, 1699), pp. 160ff. Similarly Roger de Piles, *Diverses Conversations sur la Peinture* (Paris, 1727), p. 37, after rejecting the imposition of having to provide a definition of taste: "La manière dont l'esprit est capable d'envisager les choses selon qu'il est bien ou mal tourné." Apparently, the notion of taste aims at the necessity of an (evolutionary) selection without being able to provide a criterion.

87. See the entry "goût" in the *Encyclopédie* (Voltaire).

88. This is why it is possible to bemoan evolutionary changes as a decay of good taste. A notorious example is Madame Dacier (Anne Lefebre), *Des causes de la corruption du Goust* (Paris, 1714).

89. Quoted from Jüttner, "Die Kunstkritik Diderots (1759–1781)," p. 18.

90. On the nexus between "taste" and "good breeding," see, e.g., Anthony, Earl of Shaftesbury, *Characteristicks of Men, Manners, Opinions, Times,* 2d ed. (n.p., 1714; rpt. Farnborough, Hants., 1968), e.g., vol. 3, pp. 162ff.; but for Shaftesbury, "good breeding" is no longer inborn but acquired (p. 164). See also Jean-Baptiste Dubos, *Reflexions critiques sur la poésie et la peinture* (rpt. Paris, 1733), vol. 2, pp. 334ff., who further dissolves the concept ("le public se restreint suivant l'ouvrage dont il est question de juger" [p. 336]).

91. For evidence, see Ernst H. Gombrich, *Norm and Form: Studies in the Art of the Renaissance* (1966; 3d ed. London, 1978).

§ 7

1. See Morris Weitz, "The Role of Theory in Aesthetics," *Journal of Aesthetics and Art Criticism* 15 (1956): 27–35; Maurice Mandelbaum, "Family Resemblances and Generalizations Concerning the Arts," *American Philosophical Quarterly* 2 (1965): 219–28.

2. This is a tendency (albeit not an elaborated one) in the "institutional" theory of art, which investigates the practices and conventions of the art system (like the institutional theories of law proposed, e.g., by Hart or MacCormick). See George Dickie, *Art and the Aesthetic: An Institutional Analysis* (Ithaca, N.Y., 1974).

3. With reference to social systems in general, see Niklas Luhmann, *Soziale Systeme: Grundriß einer allgemeinen Theorie* (Frankfurt, 1984), pp. 182f. and else-

where; trans. as *Social Systems*, trans. John Bednarz, with Dirk Baecker (Stanford, Calif., 1995), pp. 129f.

4. See Renate Lachmann, *Gedächtnis und Literatur: Intertextualität in der russischen Moderne* (Frankfurt, 1990).

5. "Redescriptions" in the sense of Mary Hesse, *Models and Analogies in Science* (Notre Dame, 1966), pp. 157ff. See also p. 54, n. 65.

6. By contrast, Friedrich Schlegel points out that poetry is art as well (*Werke in zwei Bänden* [Berlin, 1980], vol. 2, p. 155). The need to defend this notion shows that it is no longer taken for granted.

7. For a conscientious study that emphasizes the "philosophical" context, see Gerhard Plumpe, *Ästhetische Kommunikation der Moderne*, vol. 1, *Von Kant bis Hegel* (Opladen, 1993).

8. For the period after Adorno, see David Roberts, *Art and Enlightenment: Aesthetic Theory after Adorno* (Lincoln, Nebr., 1991), p. 21: "Aesthetic theory can no longer claim a vantage point *beyond art.*"

9. Paul Valéry raises this question in *Variété*, quoted from *Œuvres*, Pléiade ed., vol. 1 (Paris, 1957), p. 1240: "Si l'Esthétique pouvait être, les arts s'évanouiraient nécessairement devant elle, c'est-à-dire devant leur essence." On the disappointing fruitlessness of a philosophical aesthetics for the self-reflection of art, see also Eckard Heftrich, "Das ästhetische Bewußtsein und die Philosophie der Kunst," in Helmut Koopmann and J. Adolf Schmoll, called Eisenwerth, eds., *Beiträge zur Theorie der Kunst im 19. Jahrhundert* (Frankfurt, 1971), vol. 1, pp. 30–43. Apart from being aimed at the romantics, this critique is primarily addressed to Goethe and Schiller.

10. We need not only think of Hegel. For illustrations see, e.g., Friedrich Schlegel's *Lucinde*, quoted from *Werke in zwei Bänden* (Berlin, 1980), vol. 2, pp. 5–99, esp. p. 88.

11. Rosario Assunto elaborates this point in *Die Theorie des Schönen im Mittelalter* (Cologne, 1963). See also Wilhelm Perpeet, *Ästhetik im Mittelalter* (Freiburg, 1977).

12. For bibliographical references, see Chapter 6, n. 66.

13. After the proliferation of print, one finds an extensive body of literature devoted to this issue, especially in Italy. See Bernard Weinberg, *A History of Literary Criticism in the Italian Renaissance*, 2 vols. (Chicago, 1961); Baxter Hathaway, *The Age of Criticism: The Late Renaissance in Italy* (Ithaca, N.Y., 1962).

14. This is evident in eighteenth-century depictions of life in the cities (London, Paris) and in the aestheticization of country life.

15. With reference to the educational system, see Niklas Luhmann and Karl Eberhard Schorr, *Reflexionsprobleme im Erziehungssystem*, 2d ed. (Frankfurt, 1988); on the system of science, see Niklas Luhmann, *Die Wissenschaft der Gesellschaft* (Frankfurt, 1990), pp. 469ff.; on the legal system, see Luhmann, *Das Recht der*

Gesellschaft (Frankfurt, 1993), pp. 469ff.; on intimate relationships, see Luhmann, *Liebe als Passion: Zur Codierung von Intimität* (Frankfurt, 1982); trans. as *Love as Passion: The Codification of Intimacy*, trans. Jeremy Gaines and Doris L. Jones (Cambridge, Mass., 1986; rpt. Stanford, Calif., 1998).

16. Niklas Luhmann and Raffaele De Giorgi, *Teoria della società* (Milan, 1992), pp. 360ff.

17. See Federico Zuccaro, *L'idea dei Pittori, Scultori ed Architetti* (Turin, 1607), quoted from *Scritti d'arte Federico Zuccaro* (Florence, 1961), pp. 149–312 (149ff.).

18. On the already-stale discussion occasioned by the construction of the cathedral of Milan, see James S. Ackermann, "'Ars sine scientia nihil est': Gothic Theory of Architecture at the Cathedral of Milan," *Ars Bulletin* 31 (1949): 84–111. Today we would say that a conflict between theory and practice was at stake; but this opposition did not exist at the time.

19. For an investigation of the striking stylistic changes in Guercino, see Dennis Mahon, *Studies in Seicento Art and Theory* (London, 1947; rpt. Westport, Conn., 1971).

20. Rudolf Stichweh, *Der frühmoderne Staat und die europäische Universität: Zur Interaktion von Politik und Erziehungssystem im Prozeß ihrer Ausdifferenzierung (16.–18. Jahrhundert)* (Frankfurt, 1991).

21. See also Rudolf Stichweh, "System/Umwelt-Beziehungen europäischer Universitäten in historischer Perspektive," in Christoph Oehler and Wolff-Dietrich Webler, eds., *Forschungspotentiale sozialwissenschaftlicher Hochschulforschung: Bundesrepublik Deutschland-Österreich-Schweiz* (Weinheim, 1988), pp. 377–94.

22. Support of art by the church could now assume the form of support by territorial states governed by the church.

23. See Chapter 4, section VI, above.

24. On such zones of overlapping, e.g., in the educational system, see also Luhmann and Schorr, *Reflexionsprobleme im Erziehungssystem*, pp. 53ff. We are thinking in particular of the family, but also of the economy (the education of apprentices and so on).

25. Leon Battista Alberti characterizes these artists in the introduction to his treatise *Della Pittura* (1436) as "nobilissimi et meravigliosi intellecti" (Florence, 1950), p. 53.

26. For the inversion of this proposition, which suggests itself today, see Michael Serres, *La genèse* (Paris, 1982).

27. On this context of *pulchrum*, see, e.g., Hieronymous Cardanus, *De Uno Liber*, quoted from *Opera Omnia* (Lyon, 1663), vol. 1, pp. 277–83 (278).

28. For the sake of our argument, there is no need to clarify the question whether the common presentation of this transformation in terms of the conceptual pair animistic/mechanistic is sufficient. For an investigation of this problem with reference to Pomponazzi, Cardano, and Telesio, see Eckhard Keßler,

"Selbstorganisation in der Naturphilosophie der Renaissance," *Selbstorganisation* 3 (1992): 15–29. The conflict between animism and mechanism results from the attempt to go beyond the determination of the one as a number and, hence, as a *fictio mentis*.

29. On the development of science toward a state severed from a religiously defined cosmos and without aesthetic obligations, see Wolfgang Krohn, "Die 'Neue Wissenschaft' der Renaissance," in Gernot Böhme et al., *Experimentelle Philosophie: Ursprünge autonomer Wissenschaftsentwicklung* (Frankfurt, 1977), pp. 13–128.

30. A different set of distinctions indicates this rupture in the evolution of art. *Before* this rupture, the beauty of mathematical proportion (understood in Platonic terms) was positioned against sensuous pleasure. See Robert Klein, "La forme et l'intelligible," in *Umanesimo e simbolismo, Archivio di filosofia* (1958), pp. 103–21; on the construction of the gothic cathedral, see Otto von Simson, "Wirkungen des christlichen Platonismus auf die Entstehung der Gothik," in Joseph Koch, ed., *Humanismus, Mystik und Kunst in der Welt des Mittelalters*, 2d ed. (Leiden, 1959), pp. 159–79; von Simson, *The Gothic Cathedral: The Origins of Gothic Architecture and the Medieval Concept of Order* (New York, 1965); on Renaissance architecture (Alberti, Bramante, Palladio), see Rudolf Wittkower, *Architectural Principles in the Age of Humanism* (London, 1949). The visibility of the principles of construction was therefore not an issue (or only a secondary issue). *After* this rupture, the situation was the opposite: art became a matter of deceiving the senses, hence a way of enriching experience.

31. See, e.g., Chap. 17, "De artibus artificiosisque rebus" of Hieronymus Cardanus, *De subtilitate libri XXI* (Nürnberg, 1550), pp. 316f., which rejects the unnecessarily subtle method of Raymundus Lullus (p. 295).

32. See Alastair Fowler, *Spenser and the Numbers of Time* (London, 1964); Fowler, ed., *Silent Poetry: Essays in Numerological Analysis* (London, 1970).

33. See the painter Paolo Pino, *Dialogo di Pittura* (1548), quoted from Paola Barocchi, ed., *Trattati d'arte del cinquecento*, vol. 1 (Bari, 1960), pp. 93–139.

34. Ibid., p. 115.

35. Quoted from the edition by Andrea Masini in Arnaldo Baruschi et al., eds., *Scritti rinascimentali di architettura* (Milan, 1978), pp. 23–144. See also Wittkower, *Architectural Principles*.

36. See Carlo Borromeo, *Instructiones fabricae et supellectilis ecclesiasticae*, quoted from Barocchi, *Trattati d'arte del cinquecento*, vol. 3 (Bari, 1960), pp. 1–113.

37. On the religious aspect of this debate, see Heinz Schlaffer, *Poesie und Wissen: Die Entstehung des ästhetischen Bewußtseins und der philologischen Erkenntnis* (Frankfurt, 1990).

38. For an overview, see Robert J. Clements, "Condemnation of the Poetic Profession in Renaissance Emblem Literature," *Studies in Philology* 43 (1946): 213–32.

39. See Plato, *Republic*, II, XVIIff. and X.

40. See Russell Fraser, *The War Against Poetry* (Princeton, N.J., 1970).

41. For contemporary evidence, see Sir Philip Sidney, *The Defense of Poetry* (1595; rpt. Lincoln, Nebr., 1970). For an overview, see further the texts in G. Gregory Smith, ed., *Elizabethan Critical Essays*, 2 vols. (London, 1904).

42. Sidney complains that historians, "captivated to the truth of a foolish world," provide poor examples (ibid., p. 22).

43. Representative of many others is Antonio Minturno, *L'arte poetica* (1563; Naples, 1725), p. 39. See further Bernardino Daniello, *La poetica* (Vinegia, 1536), pp. 5 and 44ff.; Torquato Tasso, *Discorsi dell'arte poetica e in particolare sopra il poema eroico* (1587), quoted from *Prosa* (Milan, 1969), esp. the first two *discorsi*.

44. See Agnolo Segni, *Raggionamento sopra le cose pertinenti alla poetica* (Florence, 1581), pp. 17–19, quoted from Baxter Hathaway, *Marvels and Commonplaces: Renaissance Literary Criticism* (New York, 1968), p. 51.

45. On the allusions to the planned French marriage of Queen Elizabeth, see David Norbrook, *Poetry and Politics in the English Renaissance* (London, 1984), pp. 88f.

46. "Soll die Kunst täuschen oder bloß scheinen?" Schlegel will ask with reference to Shakespeare; the answer to this question requires, according to Schlegel, "die tiefste Spekulation und die gelehrteste Kunstgeschichte." See critical fragment no. 121, quoted from Schlegel, *Werke*, vol. 1, p. 184. In his *Gespräch über die Poesie* (vol. 2, p. 177), Schlegel questions this very question—that is, its underlying distinction: "Es ist darin (in der romantischen Poesie) gar keine Rücksicht genommen auf den Unterschied von Schein und Wahrheit, von Spiel und Ernst."

47. This issue was debated extensively in the seventeenth century on the occasion of the letters of a Portuguese nun, published by Guilleragues, which were composed in such an emotional state that they fly in the face of the rules of writing classical love letters. See the new edition of the *Lettres portugaises*, by F. Deloffre and J. Rougeot (Paris, 1962). Are these letters authentic or not? This question is difficult to decide. And holding the book in one's hands doesn't help. On the strategies of confusing facts and fiction in the beginning of the modern novel, see also Lennard J. Davis, *Factual Fictions: The Origin of the English Novel* (New York, 1983). A modern version of this play with framing frames is found in Pasolini's novelistic fragment *Petrolio*. A group, which remains anonymous, decides to subject the text's protagonist, Carlo, to surveillance. The spy who has been selected for this task fabricates detailed reports of his observations. One night the suitcase containing these reports is stolen, which makes it impossible, even for Pasolini, the author of the novel, to provide an accurate account of the facts. ("This, of course, is reflected in my narrative.") He is forced to replace the now "unreadable" texts by the imagination, by *his* imagination, and in so doing, he renders *himself* visible as someone who has plenty of obscenities to report and,

as the reader might suspect, is not entirely without interest in the matter. "The reader shall forgive me for presenting him with such boring matters; but I simply *live* the genesis of my book." See Pier Paolo Pasolini, *Petrolio* (Berlin, 1994), quotations on pp. 63f. Even the boredom imputed to the reader is part of the frame boredom/interest, which the author obviously uses to speculate on an interest by the reader that supports his own inclinations.

48. Especially in conjunction with the foundation of the Academia del Disegno in Florence (1563). The word itself is documented much earlier. See Francesco Doni, *Il Disegno* (Venice, 1549), which I did not have a chance to consult directly.

49. For a successful implementation of beauty, see esp. Baltasar Gracián, *Agudeza y arte de ingenio*, 2 vols. (Huesca, 1649; Madrid, 1969). See also the important Introduction by Benito Pelegrín to the French translation of this work, *Art et figures de l'esprit* (Paris, 1983). According to Gracián's *Criticón oder Über die allgemeinen Laster des Menschen,* "everything in life happens as if in an image, indeed in the imagination" ([1651–1657; Hamburg, 1957], p. 108). This is why philosophical wisdom comes about only by way of a disillusionment (*desengaño*). But this move annuls whatever beauty and happiness contribute to the success of truth as a merely communicative requirement.

50. "Verdad amiga, dijo la Agudeza, non hay manjar más desabrido en estos estragados tiempos que un desengaño a secas, que digo desabrido! no hay bocado más amargo que una verdad desnuda" (Gracián, *Discurso* LV, *Agudeza y arte de ingenio*, vol. 2, pp. 191–92). Similarly, Federico Zuccaro, *L'idea dei Pittori*, p. 271: *disegno* is necessary in order to instill vitality and practical use into intelligence and the sciences.

51. Gracián, *Discurso* XV, *Agudeza y arte de ingenio*, vol. 1, p. 163.

52. See Hans Ulrich Gumbrecht, *Eine Geschichte der Spanischen Literatur*, 2 vols. (Frankfurt, 1990), esp. vol. 1, pp. 80ff. Fitting out individuality with ontological and religious ambivalence is characteristic of Spanish literature. It can be traced back to the *Libro de buen amor,* by an author who calls himself Juan Ruiz, Arcipreste de Hita (ca. 1300), especially if one compares this text to its model, the *Confessions of St. Augustine.* On the *Libro,* see Gumbrecht, *Eine Gechichte der Spanischen Literatur,* vol. 1, pp. 97ff.

53. See Gerhart Schröder, *Logos und List: Zur Entwicklung der Ästhetik in der frühen Neuzeit* (Königstein, Ts., 1985), esp. pp. 36f., 88, 253ff.

54. See, e.g., George Puttenham, *The Arte of English Poesie* (London, 1589; rpt. Cambridge, 1970), passim.

55. In Plato's *Sophistes,* 253 D, the hiding place assumes the form of a law against paradox.

56. For example, the belief that the mixture of blood in a flea that had bitten the lovers would be the same as the result of a love affair. See "The Flea," John

Donne, *The Complete English Poems* (Harmondsworth, Middlesex, 1971). On references to Ramism and the abstraction according to species and genres, see also Michael McCanless, "Paradox in Donne," *Studies in the Renaissance* 13 (1966): 266–87. Characteristic of presentations of paradox is that they warn the reader—*outside of the text*—not to believe in them, for example, in dedicatory prefaces. See, e.g., Anthony Mundy, *The Defence of Contraries* (London, 1593; rpt. Amsterdam, 1969), folio A 3: "Let no manne thinke then, that I or any other would be so sencelesse, as to holde directly any of these vaine reasons," or the counterpublication by Ortensio Lando, *Confutatione del libro de paradossi nuovamente composta in tre orationi distinta* (n.p, n.d.).

57. We have already pointed out the new orientation toward a complementarity of roles in the wake of the differentiation of the art system. See Chapter 6, section V, above.

58. See, e.g., Pomponius Gauricus, *De sculptura* (ca. 1501; Leipzig, 1886), pp. 110ff. The author thinks of this work as the first scientific treatise on sculpture.

59. See John Dryden, *Of Dramatick Poesie: An Essay*, 2d ed. (London, 1684), p. 50.

60. See Charles Hope, "Artists, Patrons, and Advisors in the Italian Renaissance," in Guy Fitch Lytle and Stephen Orgel, eds., *Patronage in the Renaissance* (Princeton, N.J., 1981), pp. 293–343.

61. Matteo Pellegrini, *I Fonti Dell Ingenio, ridotti ad arte* (Bologna, 1650), p. 61.

62. Gracián, *Criticón*, p. 61.

63. For an overview of seventeenth- and eighteenth-century materials, see Arthur O. Lovejoy, "Nature as Aesthetic Norm," *Modern Language Notes* 42 (1927): 444–50.

64. On the ambiguities in Plato, see Gunter Gebauer and Christoph Wulf, *Mimesis: Kultur—Kunst—Gesellschaft* (Reinbek, 1992), pp. 50ff. These ambiguities are reflected in the secondary literature on Plato.

65. The eighteenth century still holds onto the notion of an imitation that includes music, even though it can do so only on the basis of associationist psychology. See, e.g., Francis Hutcheson, *An Inquiry Concerning Beauty, Order, Harmony, Design*, Treatise I of his *Inquiry into the Original of Our Ideas of Beauty and Virtue* (1725; 4th ed., 1738; critical ed. The Hague, 1973), p. 81; Abbé Batteux, *Les beaux arts réduits à un même principe*, 2d ed. (Paris, 1747), pp. 39ff., 259ff. To the extent that music is attributed to internal emotional states, it becomes impossible to distinguish between imitation and the effectuation of such states. Once one sacrifices the guiding idea of imitation, music can take on a leadership role in art—e.g., in romanticism, where music takes its place next to poetry.

66. Sidney, *The Defense of Poetry*, p. 12. Gracián radicalizes this notion—dissimulation is *imitatio Christi*, the imitation of a God concealed behind a human form.

67. For details, see Hathaway, *Marvels and Commonplaces*.

68. See, e.g., Benedetto Varchi, *Lezzione nella quale se disputa della maggioranza delle arti . . .* (1547), quoted from Barocchi, ed., *Trattati d'arte del cinquecento*, vol. I, pp. 141–206; Pino, *Dialogo di Pittura*, p. 115. See also Chapter 4, n. 140, above.

69. See, e.g., Lodovico Dolce, *Dialogo della pittura* (1557), quoted from Barocchi, *Trattati d'arte del cinquecento*, vol. I, pp. 141–206: "la pittura . . . non essere altro che imitazione della natura" (p. 152), and "Deve adunque il pittore procacciar non solo d'imitar, ma di superar la natura" (p. 172).

70. "Suele faltarle de eminencia a la imitación, lo que alcanza de facilidad": so Gracián describes this reserved attitude, this shift of emphasis from adequacy to artistic skill (Gracián, *Discorso* LXIII, *Agudeza y arte de ingenio*, vol. 2, p. 257).

71. "Fácil es adelantar lo commenzado; arduo el inventar, y despúes de tanto, cerca de insuperable"—this is how Gracián begins his treatise (*Agudeza y arte de ingenio*, vol. I, p. 47). In Zuccaro, *L'idea dei Pittori*, pp. 225ff., one finds a similar view in the form of the distinction between *disegno naturale* and *disegno artificiale*. The former operates intuitively; only the latter reaches perfection.

72. See Paolo Pino, quoted above, n. 33. As an example of the highly developed literature on artistic technique, which in itself offers occasions for reflection, see, e.g., Giovanni Paolo Lomazzo, *Trattato dell'arte, della Pittura, Scultura et architettura*, 3 vols. (Milan, 1584; Rome, 1844).

73. See Roger de Piles, *Cours de peinture par principes* (Paris, 1708), pp. 1ff. The "sociological" observation (pp. 12f.) that the artist's reputation (Raphael in the Vatican museum) suffices to attract spectators, who then walk by other beauties, is remarkable. See also Chapter 1, n. 42, above.

74. See, e.g., Giovanni Paolo Lomazzo, *Idea del Tempio della Pittura* (Milan, 1590), p. 146: "Arte non dee esser mostrata nell'arte."

75. On painting, see de Piles, *Cours de peinture par principes*, p. 3; or Antoine Coypel, *Discours prononcez dans les conférences de l'Académie Royale de Peinture et Sculpture* (Paris, 1721), pp. 35, 96, 161ff.; on poetry, see Lodovico Antonio Muratori, *Della perfetta Poesia Italiana* (Modena, 1706), pp. 71f.; on the fine arts in general, see Batteux, *Les beaux arts réduits à un même principe*.

76. On this opposition, which was introduced in the seventeenth century and dominated the eighteenth century, see esp. Chap. 3 ("The Creative Imagination: Imitation and Originality") in Joan Pittock, *The Ascendancy of Taste: The Achievement of Joseph and Thomas Warton* (London, 1973), pp. 75ff.

77. See Michelangelo Biondo, *Von der hochedlen Malerei* (1547; German trans. Vienna, 1873; rpt. Osnabrück, 1970), pp. 1ff.

78. Even of nature, one says: "La natura imita sé stessa," Pino, *Dialogo di Pittura*, p. 113.

79. Jacques Derrida still detects imitation here. See his "Economimesis," in Sylviane Agacinski et al., *Mimesis des articulations* (Paris, 1975), pp. 55–93.

80. See, e.g., without transcendental-theoretical foundations but with reference to sensibility, Karl Heinrich Heydenreich, *System der Ästhetik* (Leipzig, 1790). The rejection of imitation still must be mentioned and justified (pp. 187ff., against Batteux and Moritz). The problem still presents itself within a theory oriented toward subjective experience.

81. This might even be true for Jean Paul, whose insistence on imitation is motivated by his polemic against transcendental philosophy and insists on the respect due to the real world but not on the validity of its phenomenal appearance. See Jean Paul, *Vorschule der Ästhetik*, quoted from *Werke*, vol. 5 (Munich, 1963), pp. 7–456; and *Clavis Fichtiana seu Leibgeberiana, Werke*, vol. 3 (Munich, 1961), pp. 1011–56.

82. Jean Paul's example, *Vorschule der Ästhetik*, p. 43, is to represent pain as pleasure.

83. In the form, e.g., of a narration within the narration, which is subsequently discussed in the primary narration and which is justified despite its obvious deviation from the story. See Ludwig Tieck's novella *Das Fest zu Kenelworth* (which is about the young Shakespeare and therefore is beyond doubt), quoted from Ludwig Tieck, *Shakespeare-Novellen* (Berlin, 1981), pp. 7–45 (pp. 21ff.).

84. See esp. Zuccaro, *L'idea dei Pittori*, pp. 152f.

85. Leonardo da Vinci, *Notebooks* (New York, n.d.), pp. 61, 73f.

86. "In the presence of nature nothingness is not found," states da Vinci (ibid.).

87. See Zuccaro, *L'idea dei Pittori*, p. 151: "Disegno in quanto che si trova in tutte le cose, increate, & create, invisibili, & visibili; spirituali, & corporali. ..." On an alleged pronouncement by Michelangelo, see Francisco de Hollanda, *Vier Gespräche über die Malerei, geführt zu Rom 1538* (Vienna, 1899), p. 117.

88. Zuccaro, *L'idea dei Pittori*, pp. 271ff.

89. Ibid., p. 151.

90. See Erich Köhler, "'Je ne sais quoi': Ein Kapitel aus der Begriffsgeschichte des Unbegreiflichen," in Köhler, *Esprit und arkadische Freiheit: Aufsätze aus der Welt der Romania* (Frankfurt, 1966), pp. 230–86.

91. See Marvin T. Herrick, "Some Neglected Sources of Admiratio," *Modern Language Notes* 62 (1947): 222–26.

92. René Descartes, *Les passions de l'âme*, Art. 53, quoted from *Œuvres et Lettres*, Pléiade ed. (Paris, 1952), pp. 723f. Descartes emphasizes that admiration occurs *before* one knows what it is about and that it is therefore experienced without distinction ("point de contraire"), that is, prior to an observation that can be fixed.

93. The word *gusto* was, of course, known much earlier—see, e.g., in Lodovico Dolce, *Dialogo della Pittura*, p. 165. But here *gusto* as natural taste ("senza lettere") is opposed to learned judgment without a specification of rank. The *semantic success* of the concept will require a *social revalorization*.

94. For more details, see Rosalie L. Colie, *Paradoxia Epidemica: The Renais-*

sance Tradition of Paradox (Princeton, N.J., 1966). On the continuation of this tradition into the twentieth century, see Hugh Kenner, *Paradox in Chesterton* (London, 1948).

95. Not just as an "exercise of wit," as Mundy writes in *The Defence of Contraries*, A 3. See also n. 56, above.

96. According to Schröder, "die prärationale Betroffenheit und Faszination des anderen wird von Corneille als Mittel eingesetzt und zugleich als (theatralisches) Mittel aufgedeckt," *Logos und List*, p. 281.

97. Concerning Kafka and Derrida, see David Roberts, "The Law of the Text of the Law: Derrida before the Law," ms. 1992, p. 18.

98. See J. H. Hexter, *The Vision of Politics on the Eve of the Reformation: More, Machiavelli, and Seyssel* (London, 1973); Christopher Hill, "Protestantismus, Pamphlete, Patriotismus und öffentliche Meinung im England des 16. und 17. Jahrhunderts," in Bernhard Giesen, ed., *Nationale und kulturelle Identität: Studien zur Entwicklung des kollektiven Bewußtseins in der Neuzeit* (Frankfurt, 1991), pp. 100–20.

99. See Hans Ulrich Gumbrecht for an alternative view of the problems that arise in the attempt to make sense of the medieval practice of performance on the basis of innovations introduced in the sixteenth century. Gumbrecht, "Für eine Erfindung des mittelalterlichen Theaters aus der Perspektive der frühen Neuzeit," *Festschrift für Walter Haug und Burghart Wachinger* (Tübingen, 1992), pp. 827–48.

100. See, e.g., Varchi, *Lezzione*, pp. 25f.

101. The significance of the senses for communicating the motives of obedience is emphasized explicitly. See, e.g., Johann Christian Lünig, *Theatrum Ceremoniale Historico-Politicum*, 2 vols. (Leipzig, 1719–1720), vol. 1, p. 5. It is tempting to speak of latent functions that resist transformation into motives.

102. On the clash between ceremony and a media-dependent public sphere, see Jörg Jochen Berns, "Der nackte Monarch und die nackte Wahrheit: Auskünfte der deutschen Zeitungs- und Zeremonialschriften des späten 17. und frühen 18. Jahrhunderts zum Verhältnis von Hof und Öffentlichkeit," *Daphnis* 11 (1982): 315–49 (340ff.).

103. See, e.g., Julius Bernhard von Rohr, *Einleitung zur Ceremoniel-Wissenschaft der Privat-Personen* (Berlin, 1728), pp. 2f.

104. We have mentioned Lünig and von Rohr. See also Friedrich Wilhelm von Winterfeld, *Teutsche und Ceremonial-Politica* (Frankfurt-Leipzig, 1700), pp. 257ff. (part 2 of a general treatise on civil society); Julius Bernhard von Rohr, *Einleitung zur Ceremoniel-Wissenschaft der großen Herren* (Berlin, 1729).

105. Kant, *Kritik der Urteilskraft*, § 49.

106. See Chapter 5, section II, above.

107. For an elaboration of this point, see Chapter 4, section IV, above.

108. See some of the shorter treatises by Richardson, reprinted in *The Works* (London, 1773; rpt. Hildesheim, 1969).

109. Concerning the context of the Académie Royale de Peinture et de Sculpture, see, e.g., Henri Testelin, *Sentiments des plus Habiles Peintres sur le Pratique de la Peinture et la Sculpture* (Paris, 1696), lectures, 1670ff.; or Coypel, *Discours prononcez*. Studies of this sort create the impression of fulfilling a dutiful ritual.

110. Coypel, *Discours prononcez*, p. 6.

111. See Thomas E. Crow, *Painters and Public Life in Eighteenth-Century Paris* (New Haven, Conn., 1985).

112. This kind of complexity—a sign of age—and exaggeration of distinctions in the theory of taste is exemplified in Archibald Alison, *Essays on the Nature and Principles of Taste* (Edinburgh-London, 1790; rpt. Hildesheim, 1968).

113. Derrida demonstrates a hierarchization of already hierarchical distinctions within this text in "Economimesis." Perhaps this covert hierarchization failed to satisfy the striving of romantic reflection toward indeterminacy.

114. See the references in Chapter 4, n. 144, above.

115. See, e.g., the "Proemio" in Varchi, *Lezzione*.

116. See a broad, historically oriented dissertation by Anke Wiegand, *Die Schönheit und das Böse* (Munich, 1967); further Niels Werber, *Literatur als System: Zur Ausdifferenzierung literarischer Kommunikation* (Opladen, 1992).

117. See Alexander Gottlieb Baumgarten, *Aesthetica*, vol. 1 (Frankfurt/Oder, 1750; rpt. Hildesheim, 1970). The links to the tradition are well marked in Baumgarten's introduction of the concept of aesthetics: "Aesthetica (theoria liberalium artium, gnoseologia inferior, ars pulchre cogitandi, ars analogia rationis) est scientia cognitionis sensitivae" (§ 1). But precisely this grounding in tradition makes it difficult for contemporaries such as Kant to trust the name.

118. For the quality of such testimony, it might have been significant that in Greek cities, regionally far-reaching diplomatic contacts or sports contacts were concentrated in the hands of the nobility, even in places (such as Athens) where the nobility no longer applied for city offices.

119. See Plumpe, *Ästhetische Kommunikation der Moderne*; further Gernot Böhme's critical review of this development, which refers aesthetics back to the original meaning of *aisthesis*, in *Für eine ökologische Naturästhetik* (Frankfurt, 1989); Böhme, "Atmosphere as a Fundamental Concept of a New Aesthetics," *Thesis Eleven* 36 (1993): 113–26.

120. Explicitly in Heydenreich, *System der Ästhetik* (1790).

121. See Götz Müller, "Jean Pauls Ästhetik im Kontext der Frühromantik und des Deutschen Idealismus," in Walter Jaeschke and Helmut Holzhey, eds., *Früher Idealismus und Frühromantik: Der Streit um die Grundlagen der Ästhetik (1795–1805)* (Hamburg, 1990), pp. 150–73.

122. For an exemplary study, see John Bender, *Imagining the Penitentiary:*

Fiction and the Architecture of Mind in Eighteenth-Century England (Chicago, 1987).

123. See Hegel's *Vorlesungen über die Ästhetik I,* in *Werke,* vol. 13 (Frankfurt, 1970), p. 13.

124. See Bender, *Imagining the Penitentiary,* pp. 35ff.

125. See, e.g., Johann Christoph Gottsched, *Versuch einer Critischen Dichtkunst vor die Deutschen* (Leipzig, 1730).

126. In Lomazzo, *Trattato dell'arte,* and *Idea del Tempio,* one still finds *intelletto* rather than *gusto,* and the same holds for Zuccaro, *L'idea dei Pittori.* There is no doubt that the words *gusto* and *gustoso* are used occasionally. In the eighteenth century, one will explicitly distinguish between taste and the intellect and assign these faculties to different systems: "Le Goût est dans les Arts ce que l'Intelligence est dans les Sciences," writes the Abbé Batteux (*Les beaux arts réduits à un même principe,* p. 58). He continues in the vein of the inside/outside schema by stating that taste refers to ourselves, whereas intelligence refers to the object.

127. We find formulations of this sort in Lamindo Pritanio (= Lodovico Antonio Muratori), *Riflessioni sopra il buon gusto Intorno le Scienze e le Arti* (Venice, 1708). See further Muratori, *Della perfetta Poesia Italiana,* pp. 57ff.

128. "Noi per buon gusto intendiamo il cognoscere ed il giudicare ciò che sia difettoso, o imperfetto, o mediocre nelle Scienze o nell'Arti per guardarsen; e ciò che sia il meglio, e il perfetto" (Muratori, *Riflessioni sopra il buon gusto,* p. 13).

129. See, explicitly, Jean Baptiste Morvan, Abbé de Bellegarde, *Réflexions sur le ridicule et sur les moyens de l'eviter,* 4th ed. (Paris, 1699), pp. 160ff.

130. See, e.g., John Gilbert Cooper, *Letters concerning Taste and Essays on Similar and Other Subjects,* 3d ed. (London, 1757), pp. 6f.; Jean Le Rond d'Alembert, *Réflexions sur l'usage et sur l'abus de la philosophie dans les matières de goût,* quoted from *Œuvres complètes,* vol. 4 (rpt. Geneva, 1967), pp. 326–33 (332), accepts this proposition only in ordinary cases ("pour l'ordinaire"), because many pleasant illusions become transparent in retrospective analyses. But he nonetheless believes that "les vraies beautés gagnent toujours à l'examen" (332), only that it is unclear what those "vraies beautés" are and how one distinguishes retrospectively between a short-lived illusion and genuine beauty.

131. On the basis of an older tradition, d'Alembert, *Réflexions,* p. 327, distinguishes between *grand* for everybody and *fin* for sensitive people. Similarly, Denis Diderot, *Traité du beau,* quoted from *Œuvres,* Pléiade ed. (Paris, 1951), pp. 1105–42 (1134), distinguishes between *homme sauvage* and *homme policé* on the basis of distinct concepts of beauty. Apart from that, one finds that the competent judgment of a selected public is again differentiated into the judgment of experts (who have interests and are able to deceive the public for a while, if not permanently) and public judgment. See Jean-Baptiste Dubos, *Reflexions critiques sur la poésie et sur la peinture* (rpt. Paris, 1733), vol. 2, pp. 320ff. These distinctions

indicate the emphasis on an ultimately irrational expertise in artistic matters that is uncorrupted by interests.

132. See William Hogarth, *The Analysis of Beauty, written with a view of fixing the fluctuating Ideas of Taste* (London, 1773; Oxford, 1955).

133. According to Herder's formulation in his *Ersten Kritischen Wäldchen*, in *Herders Sämtliche Werke*, ed. Bernhard Suphan, vol. 3 (Berlin, 1878), p. 7.

134. See, e.g., Gonthier-Louis Fink, "Das Bild des Nachbarvolkes im Spiegel der deutschen und französischen Hochaufklärung (1750–1789)," in Giesen, ed., *Nationale und kulturelle Identität*, pp. 453–92; see further Bernhard Giesen and Kay Junge, "Vom Patriotismus zum Nationalismus: Zur Evolution der 'Deutschen Kulturnation,'" in ibid., pp. 255–303. Apart from that, let us recall our remarks on the emergence of a new concept of "culture" (Chapter 3, section VII, and Chapter 6, section I, above).

135. Hogarth, *The Analysis of Beauty*, pp. 4f., 24.

136. Ibid., esp. pp. 23ff. We find a similar critique from the perspective of another painter in Coypel, *Discours prononcez*, pp. 30ff.

137. According to Kant, the judgment of taste is "ein Urteil in Beziehung auf die Geselligkeit, sofern sie auf empirischen Regeln beruht" (*Kritik der Urteilskraft*, § 7). See also Kant's "Reflexionen zur Anthropologie," no. 743, from his posthumous writings (*Akademie-Ausgabe*, vol. 15.1 [Berlin, 1923], p. 327), where Kant clearly distinguishes between sociability and objectivity.

138. See *Peter Leberecht*, Pt. 2, Chap. 4, quoted from Ludwig Tieck, *Frühe Erzählungen und Romane* (Munich, n.d.).

139. See Karl Wilhelm Solger, *Vorlesungen über Ästhetik*, ed. Karl Wilhelm Ludwig Heyse (Leipzig, 1829; rpt. Darmstadt, 1973).

140. See Alfred Baeumler's classic monograph *Das Irrationalitätsproblem in der Ästhetik und Logik des 18. Jahrhunderts bis zur Kritik der Urteilskraft* (Darmstadt, 1967).

141. See Baumgarten, *Aesthetica*. It has frequently been pointed out that the *name* "aesthetics," while it makes sense in view of this transitional period, is in truth inappropriate for a theory of art; however, once the terminology was introduced, it remained. See, e.g., Friedrich Schlegel, *Kritische Fragmente*, no. 40, quoted from *Werke*, vol. 1, p. 170, or the beginning of Hegel, *Vorlesungen über die Ästhetik*, quoted from *Werke*, vol. 13 (Frankfurt, 1970), p. 13.

142. In his introductory remarks to the *Aesthetica*, Baumgarten repeatedly insists on cognition—"Aesthetica (theoria liberalium artium, gnoseologia inferior, ars pulchre cogitandi, ars analogia rationis) est scientia cognitionis sensitivae" (§ 1)—which creates the impression of an exclusion. What is to be excluded is the inquiry into the unity of the distinction that underlies all "aesthetic" observations. What must be excluded is paradox.

143. Hans Freier, "Ästhetik und Autonomie: Ein Beitrag zur idealistischen

Entfremdungskritik," in Bernd Lutz, ed., *Deutsches Bürgertum und literarische Intelligenz 1750–1800* (Stuttgart, 1974), pp. 329–83 (339).

144. Karl Philipp Moritz, "Über die bildende Nachahmung des Schönen," in *Schriften zur Ästhetik und Poetik*, in *Kritische Ausgabe* (Tübingen, 1962), pp. 63–93 (78).

145. We take the precaution of pointing out that in this theoretical context, "Idea" no longer corresponds to the Platonic idea. The function of the concept within the current theoretical design is a different one. One seeks to recapture the old eidetic of nature in the medium of subjectivity.

146. See esp. letters no. 15, 26, and 27 in Friedrich Schiller, *Über die ästhetische Erziehung des Menschen in einer Reihe von Briefen*, quoted from Friedrich Schiller, *Sämtliche Werke*, vol. 5, 4th ed. (Munich, 1967), pp. 614ff., 655ff.

147. Jacques Derrida, *The Truth in Painting*, trans. Geoff Bennington and Ian McLeod (Chicago, 1987), p. 116.

148. Freier, "Ästhetik und Autonomie," p. 330, distinguishes between the autonomy of art, of the artwork, and of the aesthetic, which roughly corresponds to the distinction between the art system, operative programs, and system reflection that we employed above.

149. See Jean Paul, *Vorschule der Ästhetik*, p. 464.

150. On the shift from "imitation" to "autonomy" in Kant, see also Werber, *Literatur als System*, pp. 39ff. Before Kant, the word *autonomy* had an exclusively political, or, starting in the Middle Ages, a juridical meaning. Kant displaces the concept onto the subject. This is why Schelling and Schiller can apply the concept of autonomy to art, not systematically at first, but with reference to the genius who generates his autonomy and his creativity out of his own nature. Our own use of "autonomy" is *not* in accordance with the semantics of that time.

151. Jean Paul takes every measure to resist philosophy: for example, parody, or even a return to the principle of imitation (see, e.g., *Clavis Fichtiana seu Leibgeberiana* and *Vorschule der Ästhetik*).

152. See August Wilhelm Schlegel, *Die Kunstlehre*, Pt. 1 of the lectures on literature and art, quoted from *Kritische Schriften und Briefe*, vol. 2 (Stuttgart, 1963), p. 9.

153. The problem poses itself in all functional systems, and it often remains debatable—e.g., for the pedagogical value of pedagogical theory or with reference to the status of legal dogma or legal theory as a (self-acknowledged) source of positive law. Controversies of this sort ultimately depend on institutional and organizational conditions, e.g., on the role of pedagogy in the education of teachers or on the openness of the legal system to a "law of judical precedence" that is justified by current legal opinion because it cannot be justified innovatively as a kind of legislation. From theology, one expects a positive, committed relationship to belief, even though the effects of theology do not always corre-

spond to this assumption. From the theory of science, one expects a more non-scientific (nonhypothetical, dogmatic) self-relation, and so forth.

154. "Ist das Reale außer uns: so sind wir ewig geschieden davon; ist es in uns: so sind wirs selber" (Jean Paul, *Vorschule der Ästhetik*, p. 445).

155. This is how Earl R. Wasserman, *The Subtler Language: Critical Readings of Neoclassic and Romantic Poems* (Baltimore, 1959), interprets the changing demands that are placed on the language of lyric poetry from Dryden to Shelley.

156. The question of what reality is in itself is still a matter of dispute. See, e.g., N. Katherine Hayles, "Constrained Constructivism: Locating Scientific Inquiry in the Theater of Representation," in George Levine, ed., *Realism and Representation: Essays on the Problem of Realism in Relation to Science, Literature, and Culture* (Madison, Wis., 1993), pp. 27–43.

157. This notion, which implies a distance from all variants of postmodern constructivism, can be demonstrated by a somewhat extensive quotation: "Der Idealismus in jeder Form muß auf die eine oder die andre Art aus sich herausgehen, um in sich zurückkehren zu können und zu bleiben, was er ist. Deswegen muß und wird sich aus seinem Schoß ein neuer, ebenso grenzenloser Realismus erheben" (Friedrich Schlegel, *Gespräch über die Poesie*, pp. 161ff.).

158. As we know from Mikhail M. Bakhtin, *Rabelais and His World* (Cambridge, Mass., 1968).

159. In the sense of Spencer Brown's "law of crossing" (*Laws of Form* [1969; rpt. New York, 1979], p. 2): "The value of the crossing made again [that is, back across the *same* boundary, N. L.] is not the value of the crossing." The movement back and forth asserts the distinction only *on condition that it remains the same*.

160. On the history of this distinction as a frame of narrative, see Davis, *Factual Fictions*.

161. Jean Paul, *Vorschule der Ästhetik*, p. 88.

162. Ibid., p. 87.

163. A similar strategy underlies E. T. A. Hoffmann's *Elixiere des Teufels*—elements of the story do not really come from the Devil, but the narration gains plausibility by making the reader believe they do.

164. Walter Schulz adopts this guiding metaphor to present the historical situation of the philosophy of art in his *Metaphysik des Schwebens: Untersuchungen zur Geschichte der Ästhetik* (Pfullingen, 1985).

165. This is the point of Peter Fuchs's interpretation of romanticism in *Moderne Kommunikation: Zur Theorie des operativen Displacements* (Frankfurt, 1993), pp. 79ff.

166. See also Ludwig Tieck, *William Lovell*, quoted from *Frühe Erzählungen und Romane* (Munich, n.d.), p. 603: "Es ist ein Fluch der auf der Sprache des Menschen liegt, daß keiner den anderen verstehen kann."

167. Friedrich Schlegel, *Lucinde,* in *Werke,* vol. 2, p. 74.

168. The reflection on writing is foregrounded when not only the author writes and the reader reads but the protagonists in the novel write as well, or when the protagonist, as in Tieck's *William Lovell,* is accessible only through written testimony (letters). The author can then exploit and ironize, at both levels, the typical accessories of the horror novel, while withholding from the reader which one of the protagonist's heterogeneous written testimonies constitutes the true "meaning of the story." In the final analysis, the "miraculous" and the "sublime" appear trivial in that they can be explained biographically. Uncertainty explodes every dimension of a possible hermeneutic search for a deeper meaning. As textual content, writing affirms what one is supposed to think of the fact that even the author is only a writer—a typical effect of a reentry that throws the observer into an "unresolvable indeterminacy" (Spencer Brown, *Laws of Form,* p. 57) and makes him realize *that nothing else is intended.*

169. See, e.g., Friedrich Schlegel, "Über die Philosophie," quoted from *Werke,* vol. 2, pp. 101–29 (118).

170. "Die Schrift hat für mich ich weiß nicht welchen geheimen Zauber, vielleicht durch die Dämmerung von Ewigkeit, welche sie umschwebt," writes Schlegel (ibid., p. 104). As an author, Schlegel imagines that life is writing—to paraphrase it in somewhat metaphysical terms. For another example, see the text, discovered by Jochen Hörisch, of the romantic naturalist Johann Wilhelm Ritter: "Die erste und zwar absolute Gleichzeitigkeit (von Wort und Schrift) lag darin, daß das Sprachorgan selbst schreibt, um zu sprechen. Nur der Buchstabe spricht, oder besser: Wort und Schrift sind gleich an ihrem Ursprung eines, und keines ohne das andere möglich" (Ritter, *Fragmente aus dem Nachlaß eines jungen Physikers—Ein Taschenbuch für Freunde der Natur, Zweites Bändchen* [Heidelberg, 1810], p. 229, quoted from Jochen Hörisch, "Das Sein der Zeichen und die Zeichen des Seins: Marginalien zu Derrida's Ontosemiologie," in Jacques Derrida, *Die Stimme und das Phänomen: Ein Essay über das Problem des Zeichens in der Philosophie Husserls* [Frankfurt, 1979], p. 14). On romanticism as a culture of writing, see also Walter J. Ong, *Interfaces of the Word: Studies in the Evolution of Consciousness and Culture* (Ithaca, N.Y., 1977), pp. 272ff.; and Peter Fuchs, *Moderne Kommunikation,* vol. 1, pp. 97ff.

171. E.g., by August Wilhelm Schlegel.

172. Paul de Man, *Blindness and Insight: Essays in the Rhetoric of Contemporary Criticism* (1979; 2d ed. Minneapolis, 1983), p. 196. Even before romanticism, however, one occasionally finds the notion that nature is experienced in an observation trained in art. See, e.g., Denis Diderot's "Essai sur la Peinture," quoted from *Œuvres,* Pléiade ed. (Paris, 1951), pp. 1143–1200 (1156): "Il semble que nous considérions la nature comme le résultat de l'art." Decisive here is the shift of the nature/art distinction toward action and experience. This shift avoids the collision between God as creator and the artist as the producer of a single work.

173. Especially in early romanticism. See Philippe Lacoue-Labarthe and Jean-Luc Nancy, *L'absolu littéraire: Théorie de la Littérature du romantisme allemand* (Paris, 1978), Introduction.

174. In "Über Goethes 'Meister,'" Friedrich Schlegel writes of "criticism as a high form of poetry": "daß sie über die Grenzen des sichtbaren Werkes mit Vermutungen und Behauptungen hinausgeht. Das muß alle Kritik, weil jedes vortreffliche Werk, von welcher Art es auch sei, mehr weiß als es sagt, und mehr will als es weiß," quoted from Schlegel, *Werke*, vol. 1, p. 154.

175. In contrast to the current discussion in legal theory provoked by Ronald Dworkin. What the romantics called "criticism" becomes now, with the same intention, "constructive interpretation," which is supposed to generate the best possible version of the text. See Ronald Dworkin, *Law's Empire* (Cambridge, Mass., 1986), pp. 52f. and throughout; on the same topic, see further David Couzens Hoy, "Dworkin's Constructive Optimism v. Deconstructive Legal Nihilism," *Law and Philosophy* 6 (1987): 321–56. In this way, one arrives despite all scruples at the notion that there must be a single correct decision in current law.

176. "Monotheismus der Vernunft und des Herzens, Polytheismus der Einbildungskraft und der Kunst, dies ist's was wir bedürfen," states the "Älteste Systemprogramm des deutschen Idealismus" (quoted from Hegel, *Werke*, vol. 1 [Frankfurt, 1971], pp. 234–36).

177. See August Wilhelm Schlegel, *Die Kunstlehre*, pp. 23ff. (29).

178. This is the topic of Walter Benjamin's dissertation, *Der Begriff der Kunstkritik in der deutschen Romantik* (Frankfurt, 1973). However, Benjamin interprets the relationship between medium and form (pp. 82f.) as a continuum, as a transition or intensification rather than as a difference. To be sure, Benjamin cites Friedrich Schlegel's formulation of the "boundaries of the visible work" (pp. 81, 84), beyond which resides the idea of art, but he does not elaborate Schlegel's terminology on his own (p. 52, n. 141).

179. Jean Paul, *Vorschule der Ästhetik*, § 27: "und das Begrenzte ist erhaben, nicht das Begrenzende" (108).

180. E.g., in Solger, *Vorlesungen über Ästhetik*, pp. 125, 199f. See also Jean Paul, *Vorschule der Ästhetik*, § 48, pp. 148ff., where he argues that one must study the semblance of seriousness in order to get at the seriousness of appearance. Hence the incompatibility of irony and the comic.

181. See Hans J. Haferkorn, "Zur Enstehung der bürgerlich-literarischen Intelligenz und des Schriftstellers in Deutschland zwischen 1750 und 1800," in Bernd Lutz, ed., *Literaturwissenschaft und Sozialwissenschaften 3: Deutsches Bürgertum und Literarische Intelligenz 1750–1800* (Stuttgart, 1974), pp. 113–275; Giesen and Junge, "Vom Patriotismus zum Nationalismus."

182. August Wilhelm Schlegel suggests that and how one can dispense with the Idea: "Das Schöne ist eine symbolische Darstellung des Unendlichen" (*Die Kunstlehre*, p. 81).

183. The theme of a *change* of identity, e.g., in the sexual relationship between brother and sister, was common before romanticism, and it becomes evident that this is a *literary* topic that presupposes *writing*. For evidence from the Italian Renaissance, see Graziella Pagliano, "Sociologia e letteratura, ovvero storie di fratelli e sorelle," *Rassegna Italiana di Sociologia* 35 (1994): 151–62.

184. See, e.g., Hoffmann, *Ritter Gluck*, quoted from E. T. A. Hoffmann, *Musikalische Novellen und Schriften*, ed. Richard Münnich (Weimar, 1961), pp. 35–55.

185. Friedrich Schlegel, "Über Lessing," quoted from *Werke*, vol. 1, pp. 103–35 (123).

186. Novalis, *Fragmente II*, no. 2167, quoted from *Werke/Briefe Dokumente*, ed. Ewald Wasmuth, vol. 3 (Heidelberg, 1957) (numbers follow this edition).

187. A formulation pertaining to postmodern architecture can already be applied to romanticism: "Whereas a mythology was given to the artist in the past by tradition and by patron, in the postmodern world it is chosen and invented" (Charles Jencks, "Postmodern vs. Late-Modern," in Ingeborg Hoesterey, ed., *Zeitgeist in Babel: The Postmodernist Controversy* [Bloomington, Ind., 1991], pp. 4–21 [9]).

188. On the misrecognition of the functional differentiation of the social system, which is already widely established, see Klaus Disselbeck, *Geschmack und Kunst: Eine systemtheoretische Untersuchung zu Schillers Briefen "Über die ästhetische Erziehung des Menschen"* (Opladen, 1987).

189. See, e.g., Ludwig Tieck's novella *Das Zauberschloß* (1830).

190. For an overview, see David Roberts, *Art and Enlightenment: Aesthetic Theory after Adorno* (Lincoln, Nebr., 1991). See also Christoph Menke-Eggers, *Die Souveränität der Kunst: Ästhetische Erfahrung nach Adorno und Derrida* (Frankfurt, 1988).

191. Max Horkheimer and Theodor W. Adorno, *Dialektik der Aufklärung* (1947), quoted from Theodor W. Adorno, *Gesammelte Schriften*, vol. 3 (Frankfurt, 1981).

192. This could be demonstrated by a more detailed analysis of new forms of "fantastic" art. A wealth of materials can be found in Christian W. Thomsen and Jens Malte Fischer, eds., *Phantastik in Literatur und Kunst*, 2d ed. (Darmstadt, 1985). See also Tzvetan Todorov, *The Fantastic* (Ithaca, N.Y., 1973). Todorov's answer is that the fantastic renders the issue of supernatural influences undecidable (!).

193. See Stéphane Mallarmé's famous "Un coup de dés jamais n'abolira le hazard," Preface, quoted from *Œuvres complètes*, Pléiade ed. (Paris, 1945), pp. 453–77: "Les 'blancs,' en effet, assument l'importance, frappent d'abord; la versification en exigea" (453).

194. These are Heidegger's words. See "Der Ursrprung des Kunstwerks," in Martin Heidegger, *Holzwege* (Frankfurt, 1950), pp. 7–68 (51f.).

195. We might speculate whether negating every tie to the past amounts to negating any decidable future; after all, the future presupposes something *from which* it distinguishes itself.

196. See Theodor W. Adorno, *Ästhetische Theorie*, in Adorno, *Gesammelte Schriften*, vol. 7 (Frankfurt, 1970).

197. See Chapter 2, section I, above.

198. Umberto Eco, *Opera aperta* (1962; 6th ed. Milan, 1988), p. 177, maintains that even an open work must be recognizable as a work. But other factors must limit the continuation of a work. A piano piece by Stockhausen can be re-arranged in various ways, but one cannot continue it by singing "Lilli Marleen."

199. On the notion of an "outside of the calculus of forms," see Elena Esposito, "Ein zweiwertiger nicht-selbstständiger Kalkül," in Dirk Baecker, ed., *Kalkül der Form* (Frankfurt, 1993), pp. 96–111.

200. Spencer Brown, *Laws of Form*, p. 57.

201. For further considerations of this matter, see Arthur C. Danto, *The Transfiguration of the Commonplace: A Philosophy of Art* (Cambridge, Mass., 1983).

202. This can be accomplished from above or from below, by offering a massive amount of erudition that has become unintelligible or by speaking the slang of the lower classes (Burroughs, Pasolini), which makes sense only to those who are not addressed as readers.

203. That this case can be subsumed under the concept of autonomy has been disputed, e.g., by Wolfgang Welsch, "Übergänge," *Selbstorganisation* 4 (1993): 11–15. But Welsch seems to restrict autonomy to the resistance against external regimentation and infringement, and today this is certainly no longer a problem. However, it is unclear how the search for transitions, for contact with "life" or, finally, the assault on the distinction between art and nonart could be made intelligible, if not in terms of an autonomous action.

204. See Werner Hofmann, *Die Kunst, die Kunst zu verlernen* (Vienna, 1993).

205. Ibid., p. 47.

206. Here, the differentiation of the art system is especially blatant if one considers the potential reaction were one to attempt to make such works accessible to people who live in the dumps and are forced to build dwellings from trash.

207. See Karl-Heinrich Bette, *Theorie als Herausforderung: Beiträge zur systemtheoretischen Reflexion der Sportwissenschaft* (Aachen, 1992), pp. 60ff.

208. See Michael Baldwin, Charles Harrison, and Mel Ramsden (with reference to T. J. Clark), "On Conceptual Art and Painting, and Speaking, and Seeing," *Art-Language* n.s. 1 (1994): 30–69 (45).

209. On such "signal systems," see Raymond Williams, *The Sociology of Culture* (New York, 1982), pp. 130f.

210. One of the formulas for this technique is "a painting which is not to be seen" (Baldwin et al., "On Conceptual Art," pp. 44ff., 63ff.).

211. Of course, buildings must be excluded from this claim. But an aria, for example, is not tested as to whether it can be performed by someone who has a cold, and at what degree of infection.

212. See David Roberts, "The Law of the Text of the Law: Derrida before Kafka," ms., 1992.

213. On this and the following, see Rosalind E. Krauss, "The Originality of the Avant-Garde: A Postmodern Repetition," in Ingeborg Hoesterey, ed., *Zeitgeist in Babel,* pp. 66–79.

214. Ibid., p. 68.

215. On this division, considered from the perspective of self-reference/hetero-reference, see further Gerhard Plumpe, "Systemtheorie und Literaturgeschichte: Mit Anmerkungen zum deutschen Realismus im 19. Jahrhundert," in Hans Ulrich Gumbrecht and Ursula Link-Heer, eds., *Epochenschwellen und Epochenstrukturen im Diskurs der Literatur- und Sprachhistorie* (Frankfurt, 1985), pp. 251–64.

216. See Fuchs, *Moderne Kommunikation,* pp. 163ff. Fuchs proposes the difference *Bezeichnung/Nichtbezeichnung* as the "Midas-code" of modern art. It is well known that this leads to a dead end.

217. On "concept art," see, e.g., Victor Burgin, "The Absence of Presence: Conceptualism and Postmodernism," in Burgin, *The End of Art Theory: Criticism and Postmodernity* (London, 1986), pp. 29–50 (29): "Today the excitement has died down. Recollected in tranquillity conceptual art is now being woven into the seamless tapestry of 'art history.' This assimilation, however, is being achieved only at the cost of amnesia in respect of all that was most radical in conceptual art."

218. The relevant literature on this topic has grown out of proportion. (This would be reason enough for a communication system to end the discussion.) For a compilation of heterogeneous contributions, see Hoesterey, *Zeitgeist in Babel.*

219. For a short presentation, which includes his own leading early work, see Jencks, "Postmodern vs. Late-Modern," pp. 4–21.

220. Christo's response to this question is particularly striking: if objects can no longer legitimize their boundaries and distinctions, they must be wrapped.

221. Jencks, "Postmodern vs. Late-Modern," p. 9.

222. A parallel trend is evident in the rapidly alternating fashions in the consulting business for organizations, which leads to ever new self-designations.

223. The form of "quotation" indicates that the works' diversity is emphasized rather than melded together and that their diversity is remembered rather than forgotten. The difference is marked in a manner that can be recognized by an informed audience. For a wealth of material on this topic, see Lachmann, *Gedächtnis und Literatur.*

224. Jacques Derrida, *Margins of Philosophy,* trans. Alan Bass (Chicago, 1982), p. 66.

225. See Talcott Parsons, "Pattern Variables Revisited: A Response to Robert Dubin," *American Sociological Review* 25 (1960): 467–83; rpt. in Parsons, *Sociological Theory and Modern Society* (New York, 1967), pp. 192–219. In Parsons, this combination refers specifically to the adaptive subsystem of the social system, but it occurs in this form only when the differentiation of the general action system has progressed far enough.

226. See already Novalis, *Blüthenstaub* 109: "Die gewöhnliche Gegenwart verknüpft Vergangenheit und Zukunft durch Beschränkung. Es entsteht Kontiguität, durch Erstarrung, Krystallisation. Es gibt aber eine geistige Gegenwart, die beyde durch Auflösung identifiziert." Quoted from *Werke, Tagebücher und Briefe Friedrich von Hardenbergs* (Darmstadt, 1978), vol. 2, p. 283.

227. See Lomazzo, *Idea del Tempio,* pp. 8ff.

228. This might be a reason why one speaks again of "conceptual art."

229. See Boris Groys, "Die Erzeugung der Sichtbarkeit: Innovation im Museum: Nicht das Kunstwerk ändert sich, sondern sein Kontext," *Frankfurter Allgemeine Zeitung,* January 28, 1995, n.p.

230. Incidentally, the same holds for the latest esoteric interests and for all versions of religious fundamentalism. The parallels between these social contexts and aesthetics are noticeable in the tendency, typical of recent religious or quasi-religious movements, to insist on "experience" as an argument: like an experience mediated by perception, inner experience supplies certainty in situations that, considered in themselves, could be different. A similar tendency is evident in the passion of the mass media for "true stories" that draw on "personal experience" and expose highly individual perceptions and opinions. This kind of communication supplies reality *without the obligation of consensus.*

231. See n. 224, above.

232. Nelson Goodman, *Ways of Worldmaking* (Indianapolis, 1978), and Goodman, *Languages of Art* (Indianapolis, 1968).

233. The notion is from Michel Serres, *Le parasite* (Paris, 1980).

234. The most familiar critique of an "object"-oriented "aesthetics" is probably Martin Heidegger's "Der Ursprung des Kunstwerks."

235. See Paul de Man, *The Resistance to Theory* (Minneapolis, 1986), pp. 67f. and throughout.

236. See Danto, *The Transfiguration of the Commonplace,* and Danto, *The Philosophical Disenfranchisement of Art* (New York, 1986).

237. See the exhibition "Das Bild der Außtellung" in the *Heiligenkreuzhof,* Vienna (May 27–July 17, 1993). The catalogue, published by Markus Brüderlin (Academy for Applied Art, Vienna), contains texts that reflect upon this framing of the framing of the frame.

238. As structuralists or poststructuralists, for example, or as "new literary criticism," neo-Marxists, and so on. On these "institutional" states of affairs, which

become more and more chaotic (thus corresponding to the growth of the universities), see Jonathan Culler, *On Deconstruction: Theory and Criticism after Structuralism* (Ithaca, N.Y., 1982); Culler, *Framing the Sign: Criticism and Its Institutions* (Norman, Okla., 1988).

239. Danto, *The Philosophical Disenfranchisement of Art.*

240. Roberts, *Art and Enlightenment*, pp. 150, 158.

241. On this question, see Arthur C. Danto, "Deep Interpretation," *The Philosophical Disenfranchisement of Art*, pp. 47–67.

242. For the opposite view, see Gebauer and Wulf, *Mimesis: Kultur-Kunst-Gesellschaft*; the authors return to a pre-Aristotelian notion of *mimesis* and shift the emphasis from world acceptance to world creation.

243. It is crucial to identify the controlling function of this terminology, which permitted both Hegel and Marx to think of the end of opposition as a desirable end. One could hardly make this claim with regard to the end of all distinctions (entropy).

244. See Arthur C. Danto, "The End of Art," in *The Philosophical Disenfranchisement of Art*, pp. 81–115.

245. Roberts, *Art and the Enlightenment.*

246. See Julia Kristeva's observations on a "paragrammatic" perspective in "Pour un sémiologie des paragrammes," in Kristeva, *Semeiotikè: Recherches pour un sémanalyse* (Paris, 1969), pp. 174ff. The position of the nothing (not being able to see) (= 0) is replaced by the distinction (= 2), which is an effect of an operation that is only what it is (= 1). The paragrammatic description prefers the 2 (the double) instead of the 1 and "le zéro comme non-sens n'existe pas dans le réseau paragrammatique. Le zéro est deux qui sont un" (p. 193).

247. For sometime, group psychology has demonstrated the opposite claim, if only under extremely contrived conditions. Any reader can convince himself of this if he imagines someone who claims that the book he is about to finish does not exist.

248. See section VI of this chapter.

249. One must read this carefully. What is at stake here is not the psychic construction of reality, which is simply the result of perceiving an artwork or of listening to it without conflicting with other operations of the same system in ways that lead to failure.

250. Virgil, *Aeneid*, Book VI, 129 (Oxford, 1972), p. 4.

Index

In this index an "f" after a number indicates a separate reference on the next page, and an "ff" indicates separate references on the next two pages. A continuous discussion over two or more pages is indicated by a span of page numbers, e.g., "pp. 57–58." *Passim* is used for a cluster of references in close but not consecutive sequence.

narrative, 221f; and science, 254; and
romanticism, 289
Universality, 34, 197, 211, 291, 303
Unmarked space. *See* Marked/
unmarked space
Utility, 150, 152–53, 155, 217f, 255, 308
Utterance, 11, 18, 40, 67, 96, 106;
distinguished from information,
23–25, 39–40, 79, 284, 288, 298,
300

Valéry, Paul, 382n9
Value, 235, 250, 280, 300
Variation, evolutionary, 223–25f, 229,
234, 236, 238, 240f
Variety, 105, 114f, 120, 125, 141, 148, 221f,
255, 297, 299, 315, 376n44
Vasari, Giorgio, 258
Verbal communication, 10, 16, 18, 21,
25, 93, 141
Veronese, Paolo, 162, 212
Vico, Giambattista, 198
Virtual reality, 151
Visibility/invisibility: and form, 33f; of
world, 33, 42, 54, 57, 61, 67, 74, 91–
92f, 96, 119, 294, 305; and paradox,
42, 149; and first-order observation,
91; and second-order observation, 91,
205; and unity, 91; and space/time,

112; and symbol, 169ff, 177; and
hetero-reference, 205; and style, 210;
and distinction, 250; and boundary,
264; and art criticism, 286
Visual art, 14, 17, 21, 69, 77, 130, 159,
182, 247, 289–90, 310. *See also*
Drawing; Painting; Sculpture
Voltaire, 189

Warhol, Andy, 293
Wasserman, Earl R., 326n54
Whitehead, Alfred North, 46
Whole/part, 120, 136
Williams, Raymond, 359n90
Willms, Bernard, 33
Winckelmann, Johann, 130, 208, 230
Wittgenstein, Ludwig, 90, 244
World: perception of, 5–7, 14, 16; as
medium, 11; art's relation to, 28f, 33,
36, 42, 57, 92, 118, 142f, 146, 149–50;
unity of, 28f, 57, 169, 206, 254,
328n77; invisibility of, 33, 42, 54, 57,
61, 67, 74, 91–92f, 96, 108, 119, 294,
305; creation of, 304
Writing, 15, 17, 21, 32, 38, 106, 130, 157,
167, 196, 232n29, 250, 284–85, 291,
319n2

Zuccaro, Federico, 220, 386n50, 389n87

MERIDIAN

Crossing Aesthetics

Giorgio Agamben, *Homo Sacer: Sovereign Power and Bare Life*

Emmanuel Levinas, *Of God Who Comes to Mind*

Bernard Stiegler, *Technics and Time, 1: The Fault of Epimetheus*

Werner Hamacher, *pleroma—Reading in Hegel*

Serge Leclaire, *Psychoanalyzing*

Serge Leclaire, *A Child Is Being Killed*

Sigmund Freud, *Writings on Art and Literature*

Cornelius Castoriadis, *World in Fragments: Writings on Politics, Society, Psychoanalysis, and the Imagination*

Thomas Keenan, *Fables of Responsibility: Aberrations and Predicaments in Ethics and Politics*

Emmanuel Levinas, *Proper Names*

Alexander García Düttmann, *At Odds with AIDS: Thinking and Talking About a Virus*

Maurice Blanchot, *Friendship*

Jean-Luc Nancy, *The Muses*

Massimo Cacciari, *Posthumous People: Vienna at the Turning Point*

David E. Wellbery, *The Specular Moment: Goethe's Early Lyric and the Beginnings of Romanticism*

Edmond Jabès, *The Little Book of Unsuspected Subversion*

Hans-Jost Frey, *Studies in Poetic Discourse: Mallarmé, Baudelaire, Rimbaud, Hölderlin*

Pierre Bourdieu, *The Rules of Art: Genesis and Structure of the Literary Field*

Nicolas Abraham, *Rhythms: On the Work, Translation, and Psychoanalysis*

Jacques Derrida, *On the Name*